D0092159

KOVELS'
DEPRESSION
GLASS &
DINNERWARE
PRICE LIST

BOOKS BY
RALPH AND TERRY KOVEL

American Country Furniture 1780–1875

A Directory of American Silver, Pewter, and Silver Plate

Kovels' Advertising Collectibles Price List

Kovels' American Art Pottery

Kovels' American Silver Marks

Kovels' Antiques & Collectibles Fix-It Source Book

Kovels' Antiques & Collectibles Price List

Kovels' Book of Antique Labels

Kovels' Bottles Price List

Kovels' Collector's Guide to American Art Pottery

Kovels' Collectors' Source Book

Kovels' Depression Glass & American Dinnerware Price List

Kovels' Depression Glass & Dinnerware Price List

Kovels' Dictionary of Marks—Pottery and Porcelain

Kovels' Guide to Selling, Buying, and Fixing Your Antiques and Collectibles

Kovels' Guide to Selling Your Antiques & Collectibles

Kovels' Illustrated Price Guide to Royal Doulton

Kovels' Know Your Antiques

Kovels' Know Your Collectibles

Kovels' New Dictionary of Marks—Pottery & Porcelain

Kovels' Organizer for Collectors

Kovels' Price Guide for Collector Plates, Figurines,
Paperweights, and Other Limited Editions

Kovels' Quick Tips: 799 Helpful Hints on How to Care for Your Collectibles

SIXTH EDITION

KOVELS'
DEPRESSION GLASS & DINNERWARE PRICE LIST

Ralph and Terry Kovel

THREE RIVERS PRESS
NEW YORK

Copyright © 1998 by Ralph and Terry Kovel

All rights reserved. No part of this book may be reproduced or transmitted in any form or by any means, electronic or mechanical, including photocopying, recording, or by any information storage and retrieval system, without permission in writing from the publisher.

Published by Three Rivers Press, a division of Crown Publishers, Inc., 201 East 50th Street, New York, New York 10022. Member of the Crown Publishing Group.

Random House, Inc., New York, Toronto, London, Sydney, Auckland www.randomhouse.com

THREE RIVERS PRESS and colophon are trademarks of Crown Publishers, Inc.

Printed in the United States of America

Library of Congress Cataloging-in-Publication Data
Kovel, Ralph M.
Kovels' depression glass & dinnerware price list / Ralph and Terry Kovel. — 6th ed.
p.   cm.
Rev. ed. of: Kovel's depression glass & American dinnerware price list. 5th ed. 1995.
Includes bibliographical references.
1. Depression glass—Catalogs.   2. Ceramic dinnerware—United States—History—20th century—Catalogs.   I. Kovel, Terry H.
II. Kovel, Ralph M.   Kovel's depression glass & American dinnerware price list.
III. Title.
NK5439.D44K67 1998
738'.0973'075—dc21   97-49034

ISBN 0-517-80310-7

Sixth Edition

10 9 8 7 6 5 4 3 2 1

Contents

Acknowledgments

Many dealers, collectors, and companies helped with prices and information. Thank you to Antiques World, Backward Glances, Barbara Balin, Diane Brouhle, The Collector's Corner, Depression Delights, Marilyn Emans, Fenner's Antiques, Fiesta Plus, Mary Finegan (Marfine Antiques), First Glass Glass, Ida Fuchs, The Glass Cupboard, Glass Connection, Goldmine Farm Antiques, Grandma's China Closet, Grandma's Cupboard, Grier & Sowden Antiques & Collectibles, Fred Haggert, Helen Hartwick, Alex James, Larry W. Jones, Barry M. Klein, Little Church Ant, Lucky Penny, Stacey Lundy, McLieb's Home Page, Jim Medeiros & Ken Paruti, Moore's Antiques, Christine Nagy, Betty Newbound, Old Things, Olde Loved Things, Nadine Pankow, Past Times Collectibles, Michael E. Pratt, Laird D. Shively, Something Old, Lindy Spinks, T & J's Yesteryear Collectibles, Tickled Pink Antiques, Twentieth Century Designs, Watch World, Larry D. Wells, Ron Whitcomb, Joel Wilson (China Specialties Inc.), Wits' End Antiques, Allen Wutke, Delmer H. Youngen.

Thanks also to Benjamin Margalit who took many of the pictures in this book and to Leo Walter, Jr., and his staff, Jon and Chris, of Stagecoach Antiques who helped us locate dozens of pattern examples for the pictures.

And thank you to the staff at Crown, PJ Dempsey, our editor, Pam Stinson-Bell, and Merri Ann and Dave Morrell. Putting a book like this together takes extra attention to details. Thanks to our staff, Edie and Cherrie Smrekar, Kitty Busher, Grace DeFrancisco, Marcia Goldberg, Karen Kneisley, Eleanore Melzak, Gloria Pearlman, Nancy Saada, Virginia Warner, Anne Wochner, but most of all to Gay Hunter, who reads every word of copy, checks every picture, and then explains all the problems to the rest of us.

DEPRESSION GLASS

Introduction

This book is a price report. Prices are actual offerings in the marketplace last year. They are not an average. The high and low prices represent different sales. Prices reported are not those from garage or house sales or flea markets. They are only from dealers who understand the Depression glass market and who sell at shops, at shows, or through national advertising.

This is a book for beginners as well as for serious collectors of Depression glass. We have included those patterns, both Depression and "elegant" patterns of glass, most often offered for sale at glass shows. The pattern names used are from original catalogs. Most of the patterns included in earlier books are still to be found here because collectors still buy these patterns. Many newly popular patterns are also included. We have made no effort to give an exact definition of the term "Depression glass." If a pattern of American glassware was made between 1925 and 1970 and if it is known to some collectors or dealers as Depression glass, we have included it here.

Opaque glass was popular in the 1930s. Each of the colors was given a special name by the company that produced it. Monax or Ivrene are opaque white glasswares. Opaque green glass was known by a variety of names. Jade green is a generic name used by many companies. Jade-ite was the green used by Anchor Hocking; Jadite was a color of glass and a pattern of green kitchenware made by Jeannette Glass Company. To avoid unnecessary confusion, we have chosen to always spell the word *Jadite* when referring to the color in this book. Delphite, an opaque blue glass, is sometimes spelled "delfite" in the ads, but we have chosen to always use the "Delphite" spelling.

A few rules were followed in the wording of entries. It is always a sugar & creamer, not a creamer & sugar. A pickle dish is listed as a pickle. A relish dish is called a relish. A refrigerator jar is a leftover. An open salt dish is listed as a salt, but a salt shaker has its full name. Some pieces were made for dual use. A champagne (glass) may also be called a high sherbet by some factories. Any glass with a stem is called a goblet in this book. A tumbler can have a flat or footed bottom but not a high stem. A shot glass is listed here as a whiskey. This year we list not only the size of a plate but also what it is commonly called, so it would be a "plate, dinner, 10 in." The size of a dinner plate varies slightly with each pattern and we have used the actual size. If there is a pair of candlesticks or salts or compotes, the word *pair* is included as the last word in the listing.

A bibliography of Depression glass books is included in a new form. It is not a traditional bibliography. Instead we have made it more "user friendly." Look up the factory that made your pattern of glass. (If you don't know the factory name, you will find it in the paragraph listing prices in the main section of the book.) Under the factory name is a list of the most collectible patterns made by that factory. Some factories changed their names. Anchor Hocking changed from Hocking Glass Company to Anchor Hocking Glass Corporation to Anchor Hocking Corporation. We have used the name most in use during the years the glass was made. Some patterns that are listed are priced in this book; some are not. The listing also includes the books that picture or discuss your pattern. General books about Depression glass are listed separately.

This book is not an in-depth study of Depression glass. The beginner who needs more information about patterns, manufacturers, color groups, or how and where to buy should use the improved bibliography-pattern list and the club lists we have included.

This year there is a warning if a reproduction of a pattern is known. It has been added to the paragraphs found in the main listing. There is also a list of known reproductions at the end of the Depression glass section. All of these lists follow the last glass price entries. Hundreds of patterns, many not listed in other price books, are included here. The best way to learn about Depression glass is to attend the regional and national shows devoted to glass. Your local newspaper or the collectors' publications listed in this book will print the dates and locations.

When a dealer says a piece is "Book One," it is a pattern of glassware in the book *Colored Glassware of the Depression Era 1* by Hazel Marie Weatherman, a revision of *A Guidebook to Colored Glassware of the 1920's and 1930's*. "Book Two" refers to patterns in the book *Colored Glassware of the Depression Era 2* by Weatherman. These books are out of print.

Ceramic dinnerware and the prices for these pieces can be found in the second half of this book.

Particular patterns can be found by using either the Depression Glass or Dinnerware main listings, both of which are arranged alphabetically. Depression Glass begins on page 11 and Dinnerware on page 121.

Ralph and Terry Kovel,
Accredited Senior Appraisers,
American Society of Appraisers
March 1998

Clubs and Publications

CLUBS

Akro Agate Collectors Club, *Clarksburg Crow* (newsletter), 10 Bailey St., Clarksburg, WV 26301-2524.

Fenton Art Glass Collectors of America, Inc., *Butterfly Net* (newsletter), P.O. Box 384, Williamstown, WV 26187.

Fostoria Glass Collectors, Inc., *Glass Works* (newsletter), P.O. Box 1625, Orange, CA 92856.

Fostoria Glass Society of America, Inc., *Facets of Fostoria* (newsletter), P.O. Box 826, Moundsville, WV 26041.

Heisey Collectors of America, *Heisey News* (newsletter), 169 W. Church St., Newark, OH 43055.

Michiana Association of Candlewick Collectors, *MACC Spyglass* (newsletter), 17370 Battles Rd., South Bend, IN 46614.

National Cambridge Collectors, Inc., *Cambridge Crystal Ball* (newsletter), P.O. Box 416, Cambridge, OH 43725-0416.

National Candlewick Collectors Club, *Candlewick Collector* (newsletter), 6534 South Ave., Holland, OH 43528.

National Depression Glass Association, *News & Views* (newsletter), P.O. Box 8264, Wichita, KS 67208-0264.

National Fenton Glass Society, *Fenton Flyer* (newsletter), P.O. Box 4008, Marietta, OH 45750.

National Imperial Glass Collectors Society, *Glasszette* (newsletter), P.O. Box 534, Bellaire, OH 43906.

National Milk Glass Collectors Society, *Opaque News* (newsletter), 500 Union Cemetary Rd., Greensburg, P.A 15601.

Tiffin Glass Collectors Club, *Tiffin Glassmasters* (newsletter), P.O. Box 554, Tiffin, OH 44883.

Westmoreland Glass Society, Inc., *Westmoreland Glass Society, Inc.* (newsletter), P.O. Box 2883, Iowa City, IA 52240-2883.

PUBLICATIONS

Antique Trader Weekly (newspaper), P.O. Box 1050, Dubuque, IA 52004-1050.

Daze (newspaper), 10271 State Rd., Box 57, Otisville, MI 48463.

Fire-King News (newsletter), PO Box 473, Addison, AL 35540.

Glass Collector's Digest (magazine), P.O. Box 553, Marietta, OH 45750-9979.

Kovels on Antiques and Collectibles (newsletter), P.O. Box 22200, Beachwood, OH 44122.

***Matching Services: China, Silver, Crystal* (leaflet), Ralph and Terry Kovel, P.O. Box 22900, Beachwood, OH 44122.**

The Original Westmoreland Glass Collector's Newsletter (newsletter), P.O. Box 143, North Liberty, IA 52317.

Color Names

This is a list of some of the most confusing color names:

AMBER	Apricot, Golden Glow, Topaz
BLUE-GREEN	Ultramarine
CLEAR	Crystal
DEEP BLUE	Cobalt, Dark Blue, Deep Blue, Ritz Blue
GREEN	Emerald, Forest Green, Imperial Green, Nu-Green, Springtime Green
MEDIUM BLUE	Azure, Madonna
LIGHT BLUE	Moonlight
OPAQUE BLACK	Black
OPAQUE BLUE	Delphite
OPAQUE GREEN	Jadite
OPAQUE OFF-WHITE	Azurite, Chinex, Clambroth, Cremax, Ivrene
OPAQUE WHITE	Milk White, Monax
PINK	Azalea, Cheri-Glo, Flamingo, Heatherbloom, Nu-Rose, Rose, Rose Glow, Rose Marie, Rose Pink, Rose Tint, Wild Rose
PURPLE	Amethyst, Black Amethyst, Burgundy
RED	Carmen, Royal Ruby, Ruby Red
YELLOW & RED	Lemonade & Oxblood (marbleized colors in Akro Agate)

·A·

ACCORDION PLEATS, see Round Robin

ADAM

Adam, sometimes called Chain Daisy or Fan & Feather, is a glass pattern made from 1932 to 1934 by the Jeannette Glass Company, Jeannette, Pennsylvania. Sets can be found most often in Pink, but Crystal, Delphite, and Green pieces were also made. A few pieces are known in Yellow, but this does not seem to have been a standard production color. Reproductions have been made in Green and Pink. They are listed at the end of the Depression Glass section.

CRYSTAL

Tumbler, 4 1/2 In. 27.50
Tumbler, 5 1/2 In. 52.00

GREEN

Ashtray,
 4 1/2 In. . . . . . .22.50 to 28.00
Berry Bowl,
 4 3/4 In. . . . . . .15.00 to 18.00
Bowl, 5 3/4 In. . .37.50 to 46.00
Bowl, 7 3/4 In. . .24.00 to 32.00
Bowl, Vegetable, Oval,
 10 In. 35.00
Butter, Cover . .315.00 to 325.00
Cake Plate, Footed,
 10 In. . . . . . . .23.00 to 30.00
Coaster, 3 1/4 In. .19.00 to 20.00
Creamer . . . . . . .17.50 to 22.00
Cup 22.00
Cup & Saucer . .28.00 to 36.00
Grill Plate,
 9 In. . . . . .18.00 to 20.00
Pitcher, Square, 32 Oz.,
 8 In. 45.00
Plate, Dinner,
 9 In. . . . . .26.00 to 30.00
Plate, Salad, Square,
 7 3/4 In. . . . . . .13.50 to 17.50
Plate, Sherbet,
 6 In. . . . . .8.00 to 9.50
Platter, 11 3/4 In. 32.00
Punch Bowl, Base 90.00
Relish, 2 Sections, 8 In. . . .27.00
Saucer . . . . .4.50 to 7.00
Sherbet, 3 In. . . . .35.00 to 37.50
Sugar 18.00
Sugar &
 Creamer . . . . .37.00 to 39.00
Tumbler,
 4 1/2 In. . . . . . .27.50 to 29.00
Tumbler, Iced Tea,
 5 1/2 In. . . . . . .45.00 to 60.00

PINK

Ashtray,
 4 1/2 In. . . . . . .28.00 to 30.00
Berry Bowl, 4 3/4 In.
 . . . . .15.00 to 19.00
Bowl, Cereal,
 5 3/4 In. . . . . . .40.00 to 46.00
Bowl, Cover, 9 In. 65.00
Bowl, Dessert,
 4 3/4 In. . . . . . .12.00 to 17.00
Bowl, Square, 9 1/2 In. . . .30.00
Bowl, Vegetable, Oval,
 10 In. . . . . . . .28.00 to 50.00
Butter, Cover 85.00

◆❖◆

If you live in an earthquake area, a few precautions may help limit damage. Be sure there is a lip on the edge of a shelf that holds dishes and glassware. Use dental wax to stick the objects to the shelf. Keep cabinet doors locked so pieces will not fall out. Magnetic "childproof" locks also help.

◆❖◆

Cake Plate, Footed,
 10 In. . . . . . . .22.00 to 28.00
Candlestick, 4 In.,
 Pair . . . . .90.00 to 100.00
Candy Jar,
 Cover . . . . . .85.00 to 105.00
Coaster, 3 1/4 In. 22.00
Creamer 20.00
Cup & Saucer . .25.00 to 35.00
Grill Plate,
 9 In. . . . . .20.00 to 24.00
Pitcher, 32 Oz., 8 In. 40.00
Plate, Breakfast, Square,
 9 In. . . . . .29.00 to 39.00
Plate, Luncheon, 8 In. 65.00
Plate, Salad, Square,
 7 3/4 In. . . . . . .12.50 to 14.00
Plate, Sherbet,
 6 In. . . . . .7.00 to 12.50
Platter,
 11 3/4 In. . . . . .23.00 to 30.00
Relish, 2 Sections, 8 In. . .30.00
Salt & Pepper, Footed,
 4 In. . . . . .73.00 to 80.00
Saucer 7.00
Sherbet, 3 In. . . . .26.50 to 35.00
Sugar, Cover 33.00
Tumbler,
 4 1/2 In. . . . . . .26.50 to 30.00
Tumbler, Iced Tea, Footed,
 5 1/2 In. . . . . . .52.00 to 70.00
Vase, 7 1/2 In. 350.00

AKRO AGATE

Picture a marble cake with the irregular mixture of colors running through the batter. This is what Akro Agate is usually like—a marbleized mixture of clear and opaque colored glass. The Akro Agate Company, Clarksburg, West Virginia, originally made children's marbles. The marbleized dinnerware and other glass children's sets were made in many colors from 1932 to 1951. Lemonade & Oxblood is a marbleized yellow and red glass.

AMBER

Bowl, Child's, Interior Panel,
3 3/8 In. . . . . . .17.50 to 18.00
Creamer, Child's, Interior
Panel, 1 3/8 In. 28.00
Creamer, Child's, Stippled
Band 75.00
Cup, Child's, Stippled
Band 12.00
Cup & Saucer, Child's,
Interior Panel 18.50
Plate, Child's, Interior Panel,
4 1/4 In. . . . . .8.00 to 8.50
Plate, Child's, Stippled Band,
3 3/4 In. . . . . .6.00 to 7.00
Saucer, Child's, Interior
Panel, 3 1/4 In. . . .5.00 to 7.00
Saucer, Child's, Stippled
Band 5.00
Sugar & Creamer, Child's,
Interior Panel 35.00
Teapot, Child's, Interior
Panel, 2 5/8 In. 35.00
Tumbler, Child's, Stippled
Band 10.00

BLUE

Ashtray, 3 3/4 In. 9.00
Ashtray, Leaf, 4 1/8 In. 5.00
Ashtray, Shell 6.00
Bowl, Child's, Concentric
Ring, 3 1/4 In. 25.00

Bowl, Child's, Interior
Panel, 3 3/8 In. 65.00
Bowl, Graduated Dart,
3-Footed,
5 1/4 In. . . . . . .10.00 to 22.50
Bowl, Stacked Disc,
Footed, 5 In. 20.00
Creamer, Child's, Chiquita,
1 1/2 In. . . . . . .10.00 to 18.00
Creamer, Child's, Chiquita,
Opaque, 1 1/2 In. 15.00
Creamer, Child's, Interior Panel,
1 3/8 In. . . . . . .38.00 to 50.00
Creamer, Child's, Stacked
Disc & Interior Panel . . .50.00
Cup, Child's, Chiquita,
1 1/2 In. . . . . . . .7.00 to 12.00
Cup, Child's, Concentric
Ring 16.00
Cup, Child's, Interior
Panel, 1 1/4 In. 28.00
Cup, Child's, Stacked
Disc & Interior Panel,
1 3/8 In. 60.00
Cup & Saucer, Child's,
Stacked Disc & Interior
Panel, 1 1/4 In. 75.00
Jar, Hat, Cover,
Mexicali 20.00
Pitcher, Child's, Stacked
Disc, 2 7/8 In. .12.00 to 25.00
Planter, Rectangular,
8 In. 10.00
Plate, Child's, Chiquita,
3 3/4 In. . . . . . . .7.00 to 10.00
Plate, Child's, Closed
Handles, Octagonal 16.00
Plate, Child's, Interior
Panel, 3 1/4 In. 28.00
Plate, Child's, Octagonal,
4 1/4 In. . . . . . .4.00 to 10.00
Plate, Child's, Raised Daisy,
3 1/4 In. . . . . . .16.00 to 21.00
Saucer, Child's, Chiquita,
3 1/8 In. . . . . .4.00 to 5.00
Saucer, Child's, Interior Panel,
3 1/8 In. . . . . . .12.00 to 23.00
Sugar, Child's, Chiquita,
Opaque, 1 1/2 In. 15.00
Sugar, Child's, Interior
Panel 90.00
Sugar, Cover, Child's,
Stacked Disc & Interior
Panel, Large 100.00
Sugar & Creamer, Child's,
Chiquita 20.00

Sugar & Creamer, Child's,
Stacked Disc, 1 1/4 In. . .12.00
Sugar & Creamer, Interior
Panel 50.00
Teapot, Child's, Interior
Panel, 2 5/8 In. 45.00
Teapot, Child's,
Octagonal 15.00
Teapot, Child's, Stacked
Disc . . . . .6.00 to 14.00
Tumbler, Child's, Stacked
Disc & Interior Panel . . .11.00

BROWN

Ashtray, Square, 5 In. 6.00

CHARTREUSE

Cup, Child's, Concentric
Ring 35.00

GRAY

Cigarette Holder 15.00
Vase, Handles 9.00

GREEN

Ashtray, Leaf 5.00
Ashtray, Shell 6.00
Ashtray, Square, 2 7/8 In. . .6.00
Bowl, Child's, Interior Panel,
3 3/8 In. . . . . . .15.00 to 35.00
Bowl, Graduated Dart,
3-Footed,
5 1/4 In. . . . . . .12.00 to 15.00
Bowl, Utility, Tab Handle,
9 In. 50.00
Creamer, Child's, Chiquita,
Opaque, 1 1/2 In. 7.00
Creamer, Child's, Interior Panel,
1 1/2 In. . . . . . .25.00 to 30.00
Creamer, Child's, Stacked
Disc . . . . .6.00 to 11.00
Cup, Child's,
Chiquita . . . . .3.00 to 6.00
Cup, Child's, Concentric
Ring 4.00
Cup, Child's, Interior
Panel . . . . . . .16.00 to 18.00
Cup, Child's, Octagonal,
Large 10.00
Cup, Child's, Raised
Daisy 25.00
Cup, Child's, Stippled
Band 15.00
Cup & Saucer, Child's,
Chiquita 5.00
Cup & Saucer, Child's,
Interior Panel 35.00
Cup & Saucer, Child's,
Stippled Band 19.50

Flowerpot, Stacked
Disc, Footed,
2 1/4 In. . . . . . . .6.00 to 8.00

Pitcher, Child's, Interior
Panel 30.00

Pitcher, Child's, Stacked
Disc . . . . .8.00 to 10.00

Pitcher, Child's, Stippled
Band 28.00

Planter, Lily, 5 1/4 In. 8.00

Planter, Oval, 6 In. 7.00

Planter, Rectangular,
6 In. 8.00

Planter, Rectangular,
8 In. 8.00

Plate, Child's, Chiquita,
Opaque 5.00

Plate, Child's, Closed
Handles, Octagonal 5.00

Plate, Child's, Concentric
Rib . . . . .2.00 to 3.00

Plate, Child's, Concentric
Ring, 3 1/4 In. 10.00

Plate, Child's, Interior
Panel . . . . .9.00 to 20.00

Plate, Child's,
Otagonal . . . . . .2.50 to 5.00

Plate, Child's, Stippled
Band 7.50

Saucer, Child's, Chiquita,
Opaque 3.00

Saucer, Child's, Concentric
Ring . . . . .2.00 to 3.00

Saucer, Child's, Interior
Panel . . . . .7.00 to 8.00

Saucer, Child's, Stippled
Band 5.00

Soap Dish 25.00

Sugar, Child's, Chiquita . . .5.00

Sugar & Creamer, Child's,
Stacked Disc 12.00

Tea Set, Child's,
Octagonal 170.00

Teapot, Child's, Interior
Panel 40.00

Teapot, Child's, Stippled
Band 37.50

Tumbler, Child's, Raised
Daisy 25.00

Tumbler, Child's, Stippled
Band 11.00

Urn, Grecian, Beaded Top,
3 1/4 In. 5.50

Urn, White Floral,
3 1/4 In. 10.00

LEMONADE

Cigarette Jar 10.00

Creamer 50.00

Cup . . . . .36.00 to 38.00

Plate 30.00

Saucer . . . . . . .24.00 to 25.00

Smoker Set, Jar, Square
Ashtray, 5 Piece 25.00

Urn, Grecian, 3 1/4 In. . . .12.00

ORANGE

Ashtray, Leaf 5.00

Ashtray, Shell 6.00

Basket, 2 Handles 22.50

Bowl, Utility,
Tab Handle 50.00

Flowerpot, Footed,
2 1/2 In. 8.00

Jar, Hat,
Mexicali . . . . .30.00 to 40.00

Urn, Floral 10.00

Urn, Grecian, 3 1/4 In. 7.00

PINK

Cup, Child's, Interior
Panel, 1 1/4 In. 29.00

Plate, Child's, Interior
Panel, 4 1/4 In. 16.00

Saucer, Child's, Concentric
Ring, 2 3/4 In. 2.50

Saucer, Child's, Interior
Panel, 2 3/4 In. 12.00

Saucer, Child's, Octagonal,
2 3/4 In. 8.00

PUMPKIN

Bowl, Utility, Tab Handle,
9 In. 65.00

Cup, Child's, Concentric
Ring, 1 3/8 In. 22.00

Cup, Child's, Interior
Panel, 1 3/8 In. 35.00

Cup, Child's, Octagonal . .25.00

PURPLE

Cup, Child's, Chiquita,
1 1/2 In. 30.00

WHITE

Bowl, Utility, Tab Handle,
9 In. 50.00

Creamer, Stacked Disc,
1 1/4 In. 11.00

Mortar & Pestle 10.00

Powder Jar, Colonial
Lady 90.00

Saucer, Concentric
Ring, 2 3/4 In. 1.50

❖

**The best time to buy
an antique is when
you see it.**

❖

Saucer,
Octagonal . . . . .3.00 to 10.00

Tumbler, Child's, Stacked
Disc, 2 In. . . . . . .4.00 to 6.00

YELLOW

Butter, Child's, Cover 75.00

Creamer, Child's, Stacked
Disc, 1 1/4 In. 11.00

Plate, Child's, Concentric
Rib, 3 1/4 In. 3.00

Plate, Child's, Interior
Panel, 4 1/4 In. 17.00

Saucer, Child's, Concentric
Rib, 2 3/4 In. 2.50

Saucer, Child's, Concentric
Ring, 3 1/8 In. 12.00

Saucer, Child's, Interior
Panel, 2 3/4 In. 13.00

Saucer, Child's, Raised
Daisy, 2 1/2 In. 13.00

Saucer, Octagonal,
2 3/4 In. . . . . .5.00 to 6.00

ALICE

An 8 1/2-inch plate, cup, and
saucer were apparently the only
pieces made in the Alice pat-
tern. This 1940s pattern was
made by the Anchor Hocking
Glass Corporation, Lancaster,
Ohio, in Opaque White with a
pink or blue border and in
Jadite. Other related sections in
this book are Charm, Fire-
King, Gray Laurel, Jadite,
Jane-Ray, Peach Lustre, Philbe,
Swirl Fire-King, Turquoise
Blue, and Wheat.

JADITE

Cup & Saucer 6.00

WHITE

Cup, Blue Trim 15.00

Cup & Saucer,
Blue Trim 15.00

Plate, Dinner, Blue Rim,
8 1/2 In. . . . . . .20.00 to 25.00

ALPINE CAPRICE

Caprice and Alpine Caprice were made from the same molds. Alpine Caprice has a satin finish, Caprice is transparent. Alpine Caprice, made by the Cambridge Glass Company, Cambridge, Ohio, about 1936, was made in Blue, Crystal, and Pink satin-finished glass.

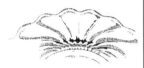

BLUE

Bowl, Crimped, Footed,
13 In. . . . . . .150.00 to 175.00
Candlestick, 5 In. 62.50
Candlestick, Prisms, 7 In.,
Pair 160.00
Relish, 3 Sections 95.00

ALPINE CAPRICE, see also
Caprice

AMERICAN

American is a pattern made to resemble the pressed glass of an earlier time. It was introduced by Fostoria Glass Company, Moundsville, West Virginia, in 1915 and remained in production until the factory closed in 1986. Most pieces were made

❖

Rubber cement solvent, available at art and office supply stores, has many uses. Put a few drops on a paper towel and use it to rub off ink smudges, adhesive tape glue, and label glue from glass or porcelain.

❖

of clear, colorless glass known as Crystal. A few pieces are known in Amber, Blue, Green, Yellow, and Milk Glass. It is similar to Cube pattern, but after looking carefully, you will soon learn to tell the two patterns apart. Many pieces of American pattern were reproduced after 1987. They are listed at the end of the Depression Glass section.

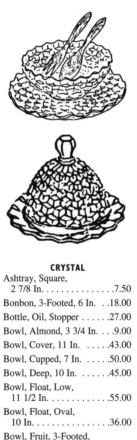

CRYSTAL

Ashtray, Square,
2 7/8 In. 7.50
Bonbon, 3-Footed, 6 In. . .18.00
Bottle, Oil, Stopper 27.00
Bowl, Almond, 3 3/4 In. . . .9.00
Bowl, Cover, 11 In. 43.00
Bowl, Cupped, 7 In. 50.00
Bowl, Deep, 10 In. 45.00
Bowl, Float, Low,
11 1/2 In. 55.00
Bowl, Float, Oval,
10 In. 36.00
Bowl, Fruit, 3-Footed,
10 1/2 In. 35.00
Bowl, Fruit, Shallow,
13 In. 80.00
Bowl, Handles, 8 1/2 In. . .60.00
Bowl, Lemon, Cover,
5 1/2 In. 43.00

Bowl, Lily Pond, 12 In. . .65.00
Bowl, Oval, Deep,
11 3/4 In. 45.00
Bowl, Rolled Edge,
11 In. 43.00
Bowl, Tricornered, Handle,
5 In. 15.00
Bowl, Vegetable, 2 Sections,
Oval, 10 In. 32.00
Bowl, Wedding, Cover,
6 1/2 In. 90.00
Butter, Cover, 1 Lb. 90.00
Butter, Round, Cover 45.00
Cake Plate, Handles,
10 In. 24.00
Cake Plate, Round
Pedestal, 10 In. 90.00
Cake Stand, Square,
10 In. . . . . . . .85.00 to 95.00
Candlestick, 2-Light, 6 1/2 In.,
Pair . . . . . . .95.00 to 105.00
Candlestick, 3 In.,
Pair . . . . .22.00 to 30.00
Candlestick, Octagon Base,
6 In., Pair . . . .50.00 to 55.00
Candlestick, Round Base,
4 3/8 In., Pair 60.00
Candlestick, Square,
Column, 7 In., Pair . . .190.00
Candy Box, 3 Sections,
Triangular . . . .65.00 to 75.00
Candy Dish, Cover,
Footed 38.00
Cheese & Cracker, With
Bowl, 12 In. . . .45.00 to 55.00
Coaster, 3 3/4 In 12.00
Condiment Bottle,
Stopper 125.00
Cream & Sugar, Tray,
3 Piece 23.00
Creamer, 2 3/8 In. 9.00
Cup & Saucer . . .8.00 to 10.00
Cup & Saucer,
Footed . . . . . . .8.00 to 14.00
Decanter, Stopper, 24 Oz.,
9 1/4 In. . . . . . .80.00 to 85.00
Decanter Set, Cordial,
Scotch, Gin, Rye, With
Rack, 5 Piece 395.00
Goblet, Cocktail, Cone, Footed,
3 Oz., 2 7/8 In. 10.00
Goblet, Cocktail, Oyster,
3 1/2 In. . . . . . .10.00 to 16.00
Goblet, Hexagonal Foot, 10 Oz.,
4 3/4 In. . . . . . . .7.00 to 10.00

Goblet, Low, 9 Oz.,
4 3/8 In. 8.00

Goblet, Water, Hexagonal Foot,
6 7/8 In. . . . . . .11.00 to 14.00

Hat, 3 In. . . . . . . .18.00 to 24.00

Hat, 4 In. . . . . . . .40.00 to 45.00

Ice Bucket, Metal Handle,
6 In. 55.00

Ice Tub, Large, 6 1/2 In. . .60.00

Jam Jar, Cover . .55.00 to 60.00

Mayonnaise, Divided,
5 In. 18.00

Mayonnaise, Footed,
Underplate, Ladle,
3 Piece 55.00

Mustard, Footed, Cover . .30.00

Nappy, Cover, 5 In. 25.00

Picture Frame, Oval 15.00

Pitcher, 1 Pt., 5 3/8 In. . . .33.00

Pitcher, 1/2 Gal., 8 In. . . .60.00

Pitcher, 2 Pt., 7 1/4 In. . . .60.00

Pitcher, 3 Pt. . . . .45.00 to 70.00

Pitcher, No Ice Lip,
1/2 Gal. 200.00

Plate, Bread & Butter,
6 In. 10.00

Plate, Dinner,
9 1/2 In. . . . . . .18.00 to 25.00

Plate, Lemon, Handles,
6 1/2 In. 12.00

Plate, Salad,
7 In. . . . . .8.00 to 10.00

Plate, Salad,
8 1/2 In. . . . . . .11.00 to 15.00

Platter, Oval, 10 1/2 In. . .40.00

Platter, Oval, 12 In. 60.00

Punch Bowl, Base,
18 In. 325.00

Punch Bowl, Low Base,
14 In. . . . . . .175.00 to 275.00

Punch Bowl,
Tom & Jerry 240.00

Punch Cup, Flared Rim . .12.00

Punch Cup, Straight
Edge . . . . .9.00 to 12.50

Relish, 4 Sections, 9 In. . .45.00

Salt, Individual, 2 In.,
Set Of 12 . . . . .90.00

Salt & Pepper,
3 In. . . . . .18.00 to 20.00

Salt & Pepper, Individual,
2 In. 24.00

Salt & Pepper, Tray,
3 Piece . . . . . .25.00 to 35.00

Sauceboat, Liner,
2 Piece 47.00

Snack Set, 2 Piece 24.00

Soup, Cream, 5 In. 50.00

Sugar, Tea, 2 1/4 In. 14.00

Sugar & Creamer, Tea . . .18.00

Sundae, 6 Oz.,
3 1/8 In. . . . . .7.00 to 9.00

Syrup, Dripcut,
6 1/2 Oz. 55.00

Syrup, Glass Lid,
10 Oz. 145.00

Tidbit, Crook Handle 30.00

Tom & Jerry Set, Bowl,
8 Mugs 340.00

Toothpick . . . . . .19.00 to 25.00

Torte Plate, 14 In. 30.00

Torte Plate, 18 In. 125.00

Torte Plate, Oval,
13 1/2 In. . . . . .40.00 to 45.00

Tray, 4 Sections,
6 1/2 In. 35.00

Tray, 4 Sections,
10 3/4 In. 135.00

Tray, Center Handle,
12 In. 40.00

Tray, For Sugar &
Creamer, 6 3/4 In. 12.00

Tray, Muffin, 10 In. 35.00

Tray, Oval, 6 In. 40.00

Tray, Square, 10 In. 110.00

Tumbler, 5 Oz.,
4 3/4 In. . . . . . .10.00 to 13.00

Tumbler, Flared, 8 Oz.,
4 1/4 In. 13.00

Tumbler, Flared, Footed,
12 Oz., 6 In. 14.00

Tumbler, Iced Tea,
12 Oz. . . . . . . .16.00 to 20.00

Tumbler, Juice, Hexagonal
Foot, 5 Oz. 15.00

Tumbler, Luncheon,
Footed 11.00

Tumbler, Old Fashioned,
6 Oz. 10.00

Vase, Flared, 6 In. 23.00

Vase, Flared, 9 1/2 In. . .115.00

Vase, Flared, Footed,
10 In. 90.00

Vase, Square, Footed,
9 In. 38.00

Vase, Straight Sides,
6 In. 30.00

Vase, Straight Sides,
10 In. 90.00

Vase, Straight Sides,
12 In. 135.00

Vase, Sweet Pea,
4 1/2 In. . . . . . .75.00 to 85.00

GREEN
Pitcher 450.00

MILK GLASS
Bowl, Wedding, Cover . . .95.00

AMERICAN BEAUTY, see English
Hobnail

AMERICAN PIONEER

Panels of hobnail-like protrusions and plain panels were used in the design of American Pioneer. It was made by Liberty Works, Egg Harbor, New Jersey, from 1931 to 1934. Crystal, Green, and Pink dishes are easily found. Amber is rare.

CRYSTAL
Cup & Saucer 14.00

Plate, Luncheon, 8 In. 10.00

Sugar & Creamer 37.50

GREEN
Console, 10 3/8 In. 69.00

Cup . . . . .12.00 to 15.00

Cup & Saucer 17.00

Dish, Mayonnaise,
4 1/4 In. 90.00

Ice Bucket, 6 In. 79.00

Pitcher, 5 In. 100.00

Plate, Luncheon,
8 In. . . . . .6.00 to 16.00

Sugar, 3 1/2 In. 22.00

PINK
Bowl, Handle, 9 In. 22.00

Candy Jar, Footed, 1 Lb. . .95.00

Coaster, 3 1/2 In. 30.00

Creamer 25.00

Cup & Saucer 14.00

Plate, 8 In. 14.00

AMERICAN SWEETHEART

In 1930 Macbeth-Evans Glass Company introduced American Sweetheart. At first it was made of pink glass, but soon other colors were added. The pattern continued in production until 1936. Blue, Cremax, Monax, Pink, and Red pieces were made. Sometimes a gold, green, pink, platinum, red, or smoky black trim was used on Monax pieces. There is a center design on most plates, but some Monax plates are found with plain centers. One of the rarest items in this pattern is the Monax sugar bowl lid. The bowls are easy to find but the lids seem to have broken.

BLUE
Console, 18 In. 1500.00
Sandwich Server,
    15 1/2 In. . . .375.00 to 625.00

CREMAX
Berry Bowl, Master,
    9 In. 35.00

MONAX
Berry Bowl, Master,
    9 In. . . . . .65.00 to 70.00
Bowl, Cereal,
    6 In. . . . . .12.00 to 20.00

Bowl, Vegetable, Oval,
    11 In. 85.00
Chop Plate,
    11 In. . . . . . .15.00 to 22.00
Console, 18 In. 425.00
Creamer, Footed . .8.50 to 10.00
Cup 10.00
Cup & Saucer . .10.50 to 16.00
Pie Plate, 9 In. 12.00
Plate, Bread & Butter,
    6 In. . . . . .4.00 to 6.50
Plate, Dinner,
    9 3/4 In. . . . . .22.00 to 28.00
Plate, Dinner,
    10 1/4 In. . . . .25.00 to 27.50
Plate, Luncheon,
    9 In. . . . . .11.00 to 13.00
Plate, Salad,
    8 In. . . . . .7.00 to 10.00
Platter, Oval,
    13 In. . . . . . . .60.00 to 75.00
Salt & Pepper, Footed . . .375.00
Saltshaker 195.00
Salver, 12 In. . . . .15.00 to 25.00
Saucer . . . . .3.00 to 4.00
Sherbet, Footed,
    4 1/4 In. . . . . .16.00 to 19.00
Soup, Cream, 4 1/2 In. . .120.00
Sugar, Footed . . . . .7.00 to 9.00
Sugar & Creamer,
    Footed . . . . . . .12.00 to 22.00
Tidbit, 2 Tiers,
    12 In. 100.00

PINK
Berry Bowl,
    3 3/4 In. . . . . .70.00 to 80.00
Berry Bowl, Master,
    9 In. . . . . .45.00 to 65.00
Bowl, Cereal,
    6 In. . . . . .12.00 to 20.00
Bowl, Vegetable,
    Oval, 11 In. . . .60.00 to 80.00
Creamer,
    Footed . . . . . . .13.00 to 15.00
Cup . . . . .15.00 to 18.00
Cup & Saucer . .16.00 to 22.00
Pitcher, 60 Oz.,
    7 1/2 In. 850.00
Pitcher, 80 Oz.,
    8 In. . . . . . .675.00 to 825.00
Plate, Bread & Butter,
    6 1/2 In. . . . . . . .5.00 to 7.00
Plate, Dinner,
    10 In. . . . . . . .34.00 to 40.00

Plate, Salad,
    8 In. . . . . .10.00 to 16.00
Platter, Oval,
    13 In. . . . . . . .50.00 to 57.00
Salt & Pepper,
    Footed . . . . .475.00 to 525.00
Saltshaker,
    Footed . . . . .225.00 to 250.00
Salver, 12 In. . . . ,19.00 to 30.00
Saucer . . . . .4.00 to 4.50
Sherbet, Footed,
    3 3/4 In. . . . . .20.00 to 25.00
Sherbet, Footed,
    4 1/4 In. . . . . .17.00 to 22.00
Soup, Cream,
    4 1/2 In. . . . . .60.00 to 95.00
Soup, Dish,
    9 1/2 In. . . . . .60.00 to 65.00
Sugar 15.00
Tumbler, 4 3/4 In. 150.00
Tumbler, 5 Oz.,
    3 1/2 In. . . . .85.00 to 110.00
Tumbler, Water, 9 Oz.,
    4 1/4 In. . . . .75.00 to 100.00

RED
Cup 110.00
Plate, Salad,
    8 In. . . . . . . .65.00 to 115.00
Salver, 12 In. 230.00
Tidbit, 3 Tiers 1150.00

ANNIVERSARY

Pink Anniversary pattern was made from 1947 to 1949, but it is still considered Depression glass by collectors. Crystal pieces are shown in a 1949 catalog. In the 1970s, Crystal and Iridescent, a carnival-glass-like amber color, were used. The pattern was the product of the Jeannette Glass Company, Jeannette, Pennsylvania.

CRYSTAL

Bowl, Fruit, 9 In.	. . . . . . .10.00
Butter, Cover	. . .24.00 to 29.00
Candy Jar, Cover	. . . . . .22.00
Creamer	. . . . .4.00
Cup & Saucer	. . . .3.00 to 5.00
Goblet, Wine, 2 1/2 Oz.	. . . . .8.00
Plate, Dinner, 9 In.	. . . . . . .5.00
Plate, Sandwich, 12 1/2 In.	. . . . .13.00
Plate, Sherbet, 6 1/4 In.	. . . . .2.00 to 3.50
Sherbet	. . . . .5.00 to 6.00
Sugar & Creamer	. . . . .8.00 to 17.50
Vase, 6 1/2 In.	. . . . .13.00

PINK

Berry Bowl, 4 7/8 In.	. . . .11.00
Bowl, Fruit, 9 In.	. . . . . .47.00
Creamer, Footed	. . . . . . .16.00
Cup & Saucer	. . . . .15.00
Goblet, Wine, 2 1/2 In.	. . .18.00
Plate, Dinner, 9 In.	. . . . . .17.00
Sandwich Server, 12 1/2 In.	. . . . .25.00
Sherbet, Footed	. . . . .16.00
Vase, Ruffled Edge, 6 1/2 In.	. . . . .39.00

APPLE BLOSSOM, see Dogwood

AUNT POLLY

U.S. Glass Company, a firm with factories in Indiana, Ohio, Pennsylvania, and West Virginia, made Aunt Polly glass. Luncheon sets can be found in Blue, Green, and Iridescent. Pink pieces have been reported. The pattern was made in the late 1920s until c.1935.

BLUE

Berry Bowl, 4 3/4 In.	. . . .15.00
Bowl, Pickle, Handle, 7 1/4 In.	. . . . .28.00
Butter, Cover	. .190.00 to 200.00
Candy Dish, 2 Handles, Footed	. . . . . .30.00 to 39.00
Plate, Sherbet, 6 In.	. . . . .7.00 to 15.00
Sherbet	. . . . . . .10.00 to 14.00
Sherbet, Footed	. . .8.00 to 15.00
Sugar	. . . . .25.00
Tumbler, 3 5/8 In.	. . . . . .29.00 to 35.00

GREEN

Butter, Cover	. . . . .220.00
Candy Dish, Handle, Footed	. . . . .26.00
Sherbet	. . . . . . .8.00 to 11.00
Vase, Footed, 6 1/2 In.	. . .25.00

IRIDESCENT

Butter	. . . . .90.00
Sherbet	. . . . .5.00

AURORA

The Hazel Atlas Glass Company made Aurora pattern glass in the late 1930s. Fewer than ten different pieces were made in Cobalt Blue and Pink; an even smaller quantity in Crystal and Green.

BLUE

Bowl, Cereal, 5 3/8 In.	. . . . . .15.00 to 18.00
Bowl, Deep, 4 1/2 In.	. . . . . .47.00 to 52.00
Creamer	. . . . . .18.00 to 23.00
Cup	. . . . .11.00 to 19.50
Cup & Saucer	. .18.00 to 22.00
Plate, Sherbet, 6 1/2 In.	. . . . . . .8.00 to 14.00

Saucer	. . . . .5.00
Tumbler, 4 3/4 In.	. . . . . .18.00 to 24.00

CRYSTAL

Bowl, Cereal, 5 3/8 In.	. . .20.00
Bowl, Deep, 4 1/2 In.	. . . .60.00
Creamer	. . . . .24.00
Cup & Saucer	. . . . .22.00

AVOCADO

Although the center fruit looks more like a pear, the pattern has been named Avocado. It was made originally from 1923 to 1933 by the Indiana Glass Company, Dunkirk, Indiana, primarily in Green and Pink. Some Crystal pieces were also produced. In 1974, a reproduction line of pitchers and tumblers appeared in Amethyst, Blue, Frosted Pink, Green, Pink, and Red. By 1982, pieces were made in Amber. The pattern is sometimes called Sweet Pear or No. 601.

CRYSTAL

Bowl, 2 Handles, Oval	. . .17.00
Bowl, Deep, 9 1/2 In.	. . . . . .22.00 to 35.00
Bowl, Salad, 7 1/2 In.	. . . .12.00

To ship small pieces of glass, try this trick: Put the glass in a Styrofoam cup, then wrap in bubble wrap or several layers of paper. Stuff sides and bottom of a large box filled with breakable antiques with Styrofoam trays. You can usually get extras from your grocery store.

GREEN

Bowl, 2 Handles,
5 1/4 In. . . . . . .32.00 to 37.00
Bowl, 2 Handles, 8 In. . . .30.00
Bowl,
9 1/2 In. . . . .120.00 to 135.00
Bowl, Preserve, Handle,
7 In. . . . . .15.00 to 20.00
Bowl, Salad,
7 1/2 In. . . . . . .50.00 to 55.00
Cake Plate, Handles,
10 1/2 In. 50.00
Cup 24.00
Plate, 6 3/8 In. . . .14.00 to 17.00
Plate, Luncheon,
8 1/4 In. . . . . . .15.00 to 16.00
Saucer 25.00
Sherbet, Footed . .53.00 to 58.00
Sugar & Creamer,
Footed . . . . . . .75.00 to 80.00

PINK

Bowl, Deep, 9 1/2 In. . . .125.00
Bowl, Handles, 8 In. 25.00
Cake Plate, Handle,
10 In. 39.00
Cup 30.00
Cup & Saucer 45.00
Plate, Luncheon,
8 1/4 In. 18.00
Plate, Sherbet, 6 3/4 In. . .13.00
Sugar & Creamer 85.00

B PATTERN, see Dogwood

BALLERINA, see Cameo

·B·

BAMBOO OPTIC

Bamboo Optic pattern was made by Liberty Works of Egg Harbor, New Jersey, about 1929. Pink and Green luncheon sets and other pieces were made. The pattern resembles Octagon.

GREEN

Candlestick, 5 1/2 In. 12.00
Octagon, Cup 5.00

BANDED CHERRY, see Cherry Blossom

BANDED FINE RIB, see Coronation

BANDED PETALWARE, see Petalware

BANDED RAINBOW, see Ring

BANDED RIBBON, see New Century

BANDED RINGS, see Ring

BAROQUE

Fostoria Glass Company of Moundsville, West Virginia, made Baroque, or No. 2496, from 1936 to 1966. The pattern was made in Crystal, Azure (blue), Gold Tint, Topaz (yellow), and Green. The same molds were used to make other glass patterns decorated with etched designs.

AZURE

Bowl, 3-Footed, 7 In. 28.00
Bowl, 6 1/2 In. 25.00
Bowl, Salad, Deep 95.00
Candlestick, 2-Light,
4 1/2 In. 40.00
Candlestick,
4 In. . . . . .25.00 to 35.00
Celery Dish, 11 In. 54.00
Cup & Saucer . .24.00 to 35.00
Nappy, Handle 34.00
Plate, Bread & Butter,
6 In. 12.00
Plate, Salad, 7 1/2 In. 15.00
Salt & Pepper 120.00
Sugar & Creamer, Tray,
Individual 90.00
Torte Plate, 13 In. 85.00
Tumbler, Water, Footed,
9 Oz., 5 1/2 In. .36.00 to 38.00
Vase, 7 In. 125.00

CRYSTAL

Bowl, Handle, 4 In. 10.00
Candlestick, 7 3/4 In. 50.00
Goblet, Water, 9 Oz.,
6 3/4 In. 12.00
Sugar, Individual, 3 In. 4.00
Vase, 7 In. 40.00

TOPAZ

Bowl, 4-Footed,
10 1/2 In. 32.00
Bowl, Flared, 12 In. 42.00
Bowl, Handle, 10 1/2 In. . .42.00
Bowl, Rolled Edge,
11 In. 80.00
Candy Dish, Cover,
3 Sections 125.00

Compote, 5 1/2 In. 39.50

Compote, 6 1/2 In. 45.00

Goblet, Water, 9 Oz.,
6 3/4 In. 30.00

Ice Bucket, 4 3/8 In. 125.00

Jam Jar, Cover 85.00

Mayonnaise, Liner,
5 1/2 In. 40.00

Mustard, Cover 110.00

Plate, Bread & Butter,
7 In. 10.00

Plate, Luncheon,
8 1/2 In. 20.00

Relish, 3 Sections,
10 1/2 In. . . . . .25.00 to 40.00

Rose Bowl, 3 3/4 In. 95.00

Sugar, Individual, 3 In. . . .16.50

Sugar & Creamer, Footed,
3 1/2 In. 20.00

Tidbit, 3-Footed, 8 In. 22.00

Torte Plate,
14 In. . . . . .30.00 to 38.00

BASKET, see No. 615

BERWICK, see Boopie

BEVERAGE WITH SAILBOATS, see
White Ship

BIG RIB, see Manhattan

BLOCK, see Block Optic

BLOCK OPTIC

Block Optic, sometimes called
Block, was made from 1929 to
1933 by the Hocking Glass
Company, Lancaster, Ohio.
Slight variations in the design
of some pieces, like creamers
and sugars, show that the pattern was redesigned at times.
Green is the most common
color, followed by Crystal,
Pink, and Yellow. Amber and
Blue examples are harder to
find. Some pieces were made
with a black stem or a black flat
foot.

CRYSTAL

Candy Jar, 6 1/4 In. 49.50

Goblet, Wine, 4 1/2 In. . . .22.00

Pitcher, Bulbous,
7 5/8 In. 26.00

Pitcher, Water, 8 1/4 In. . .28.00

Plate, Breakfast, 9 In. 20.00

Sandwich Tray,
10 1/4 In. . . . . .11.00 to 17.00

Saucer, 6 1/8 In. 6.00

Whiskey 15.00

GREEN

Berry Bowl, Master,
8 1/2 In. . . . . . .22.00 to 32.00

Bowl, 4 1/2 In. . .27.50 to 30.00

Bowl, 4 1/4 In. . . . .7.00 to 8.00

Bowl, Cereal,
5 1/4 In. . . . . . .13.00 to 16.00

Bowl, Console, Rolled Edge,
11 3/4 In. . . . .75.00 to 125.00

Bowl, Salad, 7 In. 125.00

Butter, Cover 19.00

Candlestick, Single 50.00

Candy Jar, Cover,
2 1/4 In. . . . . . .25.00 to 50.00

Candy Jar, Cover,
6 1/4 In. . . . . . .65.00 to 77.50

Cup . . . . .5.50 to 9.00

Cup & Saucer . .12.00 to 17.00

Goblet, Wine, 4 1/2 In. . . .35.00

Ice Bucket 53.00

Ice Tub . . . . . .40.00 to 66.50

Mug 39.50

Pitcher, Bulbous, 54 Oz.,
7 5/8 In. 70.00

Pitcher, Water, 54 Oz., 8
1/2 In. 38.00

Plate, Dessert, 6 In. 2.50

Plate, Dinner,
9 In. . . . . .22.00 to 27.50

Plate, Luncheon,
8 In. . . . . .3.75 to 7.00

Plate, Sherbet, 6 In. 2.00

Salt & Pepper,
Footed . . . . . . .30.00 to 40.00

Saltshaker,
Footed . . . . . . .15.00 to 18.00

Saltshaker, Squatty 42.00

Saucer, 5 1/2 In. 10.00

Sherbet, 3 1/4 In. . .4.50 to 6.00

Sherbet, Thin, 4 3/4 In. . . .17.00

Sugar & Creamer,
Dark Base 45.00

Sugar & Creamer, Footed,
3 1/8 In. . . . . . .25.00 to 30.00

Sugar & Creamer,
Squatty 30.00

Sugar & Creamer,
Tall . . . . .25.00 to 26.00

Tumbler, 5 Oz.,
4 5/8 In. . . . . . .20.00 to 24.00

Tumbler, Old Fashioned,
3 7/8 In. 20.00

Tumbler, Water, Footed,
9 Oz. 22.00

PINK

Candleholder, Pair,
1 3/4 In. 75.00

Candy Jar, Cover,
2 1/4 In. 50.00

Candy Jar, Pedestal 125.00

Console, Rolled
Edge . . . . . .85.00 to 155.00

Cup . . . . .5.00 to 7.00

Cup & Saucer 15.00

Goblet, 5 3/4 In. 25.00

Ice Tub . . . . . .89.00 to 97.00

Pitcher, Water, 54 Oz.,
1/2 In. 40.00

Plate, Dinner, 9 In. 30.00

Plate, Luncheon,
8 In. . . . . .5.00 to 6.00

Plate, Sherbet,
6 In. . . . . .2.75 to 5.00

Saltshaker, Footed 38.00

Saucer 8.00

Saucer, Cup Ring,
6 1/8 In. 7.00

Sherbet,
4 3/4 In. . . . . . .12.50 to 15.00

Sherbet, Stem, 3 1/4 In. . . .9.00

Sugar, Cone 12.50

Sugar & Creamer, Cone . .20.00

Sugar & Creamer, Tall . . .23.00

Tumbler, Juice, 5 Oz. 20.00

Tumbler, Water, Footed,
9 Oz., 5 3/4 In. 15.00
Tumbler, Water, Footed,
10 Oz., 6 In. 30.00

YELLOW

Candy Jar, Cover,
2 1/2 In. . . . . . .60.00 to 64.00
Goblet, 7 In. . . . .34.00 to 35.00
Plate, Dinner,
9 In. . . . . .38.00 to 42.00
Plate, Luncheon, 8 In. 5.00
Plate, Sherbet, Square,
3 1/4 In. 9.00
Sugar & Creamer 22.50
Sugar & Creamer,
Handle 29.50

BOOPIE

With a name like Boopie, it must have some other attraction. This Anchor Hocking Glass Corporation pattern was made in the late 1940s and 1950s. Only glasses of various sizes are known, including the 3 1/2-ounce, 4-ounce, 6-ounce, and 9-ounce. The pattern came in Crystal, Forest Green, and Royal Ruby.

CRYSTAL

Sherbet, Footed, 6 Oz. 4.00

FOREST GREEN

Goblet, Water, 9 Oz. 10.00
Sherbet, Footed, 6 Oz. 6.50

ROYAL RUBY

Goblet, Cocktail, 4 Oz. . . .10.00
Goblet, Water, 9 Oz. 12.00
Sherbet, Footed, 6 Oz. 7.50
Tumbler, Footed, 6 Oz. . . .10.00

BOUQUET & LATTICE, see
Normandie

BRIDAL BOUQUET, see No. 615

BUBBLE

Names of Depression glass patterns can be depressingly confusing. Bubble is also known as Bullseye, the original name given by Anchor Hocking Glass Corporation, or as Provincial, the 1960s name. Bubble was made in many colors, originally in Crystal, Pale Blue, and Pink. Dark Green was issued in 1954. Milk White and Ruby Red were made in the 1960s. Recently, Yellow pieces have been seen, possibly made in the 1950s. Reproductions appeared in the 1980s in Green, Jadite, Pink, and Royal Ruby. They usually have an anchor mark on the bottom. They are listed at the end of the Depression Glass section.

BLUE

Berry Bowl, 4 In. 9.00
Berry Bowl, Master,
8 3/8 In. . . . . .16.00 to 18.00
Bowl, Cereal,
5 1/4 In. . . . . .10.00 to 12.50
Bowl, Fruit,
4 1/2 In. . . . . . .9.00 to 16.00
Creamer 35.00
Cup 5.00
Cup & Saucer . . . .3.50 to 9.00
Grill Plate,
9 3/8 In. . . . . .20.00 to 22.00

◆

Glassware, old or new, requires careful handling. Stand each piece upright, not touching one another. Never nest pieces. Wash in moderately hot water and mild detergent. Avoid wiping gold or platinum banded pieces while glasses are hot. Never use scouring pads or silver polish on glass. With an automatic dishwasher, be sure the water temperature is under 180 degrees.

◆

Plate, Bread & Butter,
6 3/4 In. . . . . . . .1.75 to 5.00
Plate, Dinner,
9 3/8 In. . . . . . .5.00 to 12.00
Platter, Oval,
12 In. . . . . . . .14.00 to 17.50
Saucer . . . . .1.00 to 3.00
Soup, Dish,
7 3/4 In. . . . . .13.00 to 18.00
Sugar 18.00
Sugar &
Creamer . . . .40.00 to 55.00

CRYSTAL

Berry Bowl, 4 In. . .2.50 to 4.00
Berry Bowl, Master,
8 3/8 In. . . . . . . .6.00 to 9.00
Berry Set, 11 Piece 25.00
Bowl, Fruit,
4 1/2 In. . . . . . . .2.00 to 5.00
Candlestick, Pair 18.00
Creamer 4.00
Cup & Saucer . . . .4.00 to 5.50
Goblet, Wine 7.00
Nappy, 5 1/2 In. 7.00
Plate, Bread & Butter,
6 3/4 In. . . . . . . .2.00 to 3.00
Plate, Dinner,
9 3/8 In. . . . . . . .3.00 to 7.00

Salt & Pepper 10.00
Sherbet, 5 Oz. 10.00
Sugar . . . . .4.00 to 6.00
Tumbler, Water, 9 Oz. 6.00

GREEN
Bowl, Cereal,
   5 1/4 In. . . . . . .11.00 to 16.00
Bowl, Fruit, 4 1/2 In. 7.00
Creamer . . . . . . .10.00 to 13.00
Creamer, Footed 13.50
Cup . . . . .5.00 to 11.00
Cup & Saucer . .10.00 to 14.00
Goblet, Water, 9 Oz. 13.50
Grill Plate, 9 3/8 In. 25.00
Plate, Bread & Butter,
   6 3/4 In. 5.00
Plate, Dinner,
   9 3/8 In. . . . . . .18.00 to 24.00
Saucer 5.00
Sherbet 9.00
Sugar . . . . .9.00 to 12.00
Sugar & Creamer 24.00
Tumbler, Juice, Footed,
   4 1/2 In. 11.50

MILK WHITE
Berry Bowl, 4 In. 4.00
Berry Bowl, Master,
   8 3/8 In. 6.50
Bowl, Fruit, 4 1/2 In. 4.50
Creamer 4.00
Sugar & Creamer 12.00

RUBY RED
Berry Bowl, Master,
   8 3/8 In. . . . . . .18.00 to 35.00
Bowl, Fruit,
   4 1/2 In. . . . . . . .9.00 to 11.00
Cup . . . . .4.50 to 11.00
Cup & Saucer . . .9.50 to 12.50
Goblet, Cocktail 17.00
Plate, Dinner,
   9 3/8 In. . . . . . .19.00 to 20.00
Tumbler, Iced Tea,
   12 Oz. . . . . . . .10.00 to 19.50
Tumbler, Juice,
   6 Oz. . . . . .8.00 to 10.00
Tumbler, Lemonade,
   16 Oz. . . . . . . .15.00 to 18.00
Tumbler, Old Fashioned,
   8 Oz., 3 1/4 In. 15.00
Tumbler, Water, 9 Oz.,
   4 1/4 In. . . . . . .9.00 to 12.00
Water Set, 7 Piece 50.00

YELLOW
Goblet, Water, 9 Oz. 7.00

BULLSEYE, see Bubble

BURPLE

Burple is not a mistype but a real name used by the factory. Anchor Hocking Glass Corporation, Lancaster, Ohio, made Crystal, Forest Green, and Ruby Red dessert sets in this pattern in the 1940s. There are also two sizes of bowls.

GREEN
Batter Bowl, Spout 25.00
Berry Bowl, 8 1/2 In. 12.00

BUTTERFLIES & ROSES, see
   Flower Garden with
   Butterflies

BUTTONS & BOWS, see Holiday

CABBAGE ROSE, see Sharon

**CABBAGE ROSE WITH SINGLE
ARCH,** see Rosemary

• C •

CAMEO

Cameo is understandably called Ballerina or Dancing Girl because the most identifiable feature of the etched pattern is the silhouette of the dancer. This pattern must have sold well when made by Hocking Glass Company from 1930 to 1934 because many different pieces were made, from dinner sets and servers, to cookie jars and lamps. The pattern was made in Crystal, sometimes with a platinum trim, and in Green, Pink, and Yellow. In 1981 reproductions were made of both Pink and Green Cameo salt and pep-

per shakers. Children's dishes have recently been made in Green, Pink, and Yellow; but there were never any old Cameo children's dishes.

CRYSTAL
Candy Jar, Cover, 4 In. . . .80.00
Grill Plate, Closed Handles,
   10 1/2 In. 12.00
Plate, Dinner, 9 1/2 In. . . .18.00
Plate, Luncheon, 8 In. 10.00
Plate, Sherbet,
   6 In. . . . . .4.00 to 5.00
Relish, 3 Sections 30.00
Sugar 20.00
Tumbler, Footed, 9 Oz.,
   5 In. 20.00

GREEN
Berry Bowl, Master,
   8 1/4 In. 35.00
Bowl, Cereal, 5 1/2 In. . . .35.00
Bowl, Console, 3-Footed,
   11 In. . . . . .65.00 to 74.00
Bowl, Salad,
   7 1/2 In. . . . . . .52.00 to 55.00

Bowl, Soup, Rim, 9 In. . . .68.00
Bowl, Vegetable, Oval,
   10 In. . . . . . . .30.00 to 35.00
Butter 200.00
Cake Plate,
   10 In. . . . . . . .22.00 to 25.00
Cake Plate, 3-Footed,
   10 In. . . . . . . .12.00 to 22.00
Candlestick, 4 In.,
   Pair . . . . . .105.00 to 135.00
Candy Jar, Cover,
   4 In. . . . . .50.00 to 70.00
Coaster 13.00
Compote, 5 In. . .32.00 to 34.00
Cookie Jar,
   Cover . . . . . . .50.00 to 52.50
Creamer,
   3 1/4 In. . . . . .20.00 to 25.00
Cup 17.00
Cup, Handle, 6 In. 20.00
Cup & Saucer . .16.90 to 20.00
Decanter,
   Stopper . . . . .150.00 to 175.00
Dish, Mayonnaise,
   5 In. . . . . .27.50 to 47.50
Goblet, Water, 6 In. 55.00
Goblet, Wine,
   4 In. . . . . .62.00 to 77.50
Grill Plate,
   10 1/2 In. . . . . .8.00 to 15.00
Grill Plate, Closed Handles,
   10 1/2 In. . . . .15.00 to 20.00
Jam Jar, 2 In. 195.00
Pitcher, Juice, 36 Oz.,
   6 In. 60.00
Pitcher, Milk, 20 Oz.,
   5 3/4 In. 200.00
Pitcher, Water, 56 Oz.,
   8 1/2 In. . . . . .52.00 to 60.00
Plate, Dinner,
   9 1/2 In. . . . . .15.00 to 24.00
Plate, Luncheon,
   8 In. . . . . .10.00 to 14.00
Plate, Sherbet,
   6 In. . . . . .4.50 to 5.00
Plate, Square, 8 1/2 In. . . .40.00
Platter, Oval,
   12 In. . . . . . . .20.00 to 27.00
Relish, 3 Sections, Footed,
   7 1/2 In. . . . . .27.00 to 30.00
Salt & Pepper . . .67.50 to 73.00
Sandwich Server, 10 In. . .15.00
Sherbet,
   3 1/8 In. . . . . .13.00 to 15.00

Sherbet, 4 7/8 In. 35.00
Soup, Cream 165.00
Soup, Dish,
   9 In. . . . . .35.00 to 75.00
Sugar, 3 1/4 In. 22.00
Sugar, 4 1/4 In. 25.00
Sugar & Creamer,
   Low . . . . .43.00 to 47.00
Syrup, 20 Oz.,
   5 3/4 In. 250.00
Tray, Domino 190.00
Tumbler, 15 Oz.,
   5 1/4 In. 75.00
Tumbler, Footed, 11 Oz.,
   5 3/4 In. . . . . .65.00 to 72.50
Tumbler, Juice, 5 Oz.,
   3 3/4 In. . . . . .22.00 to 29.00
Tumbler, Water, 9 Oz.,
   4 In. . . . . .20.00 to 29.00
Tumbler, Water, 10 Oz.,
   4 3/4 In. 30.00
Tumbler, Water, Footed,
   9 Oz., 5 In. . . . .25.00 to 27.00
Vase, 5 3/4 In. 150.00
Vase, 8 In. 40.00

YELLOW
Bowl, Cereal,
   5 1/2 In. 30.00
Bowl, Vegetable, Oval,
   10 In. 40.00
Cup . . . . .6.00 to 8.00
Cup & Saucer . . .7.00 to 11.00
Grill Plate,
   10 1/2 In. . . . . .10.00 to 17.00
Grill Plate, Closed Handles,
   10 1/2 In. . . . . . .4.50 to 6.00
Plate, Bread & Butter,
   6 In. 4.50
Plate, Dinner, 9 1/2 In. . .8.50 to 12.00
Plate, Luncheon, 8 In. 11.00

❖

**Never allow water to
evaporate in a glass
vase. It will leave a
white residue that may
be impossible to
remove.**

❖

Plate, Sherbet, 6 In. 2.50
Platter, 12 In. 43.00
Sherbet,
   3 1/8 In. . . . . .35.00 to 40.00
Sugar, Round 18.00
Tumbler, Footed, 9 Oz.,
   5 In. 18.00

CANDLEWICK

Candlewick was made by Imperial Glass Company, Bellaire, Ohio, from 1936 to 1982. A few pieces are still being made. Many similar patterns have been made by other companies. The beaded edge is the only design. Although the glass was first made in Crystal, it has also been produced in Black, Nut Brown, Sunshine Yellow, Ultra Blue, and Verde (green). Some pieces of Crystal are decorated with gold. Pieces have been found in Red, Pink, Lavender, and Amber, and with fired-on gold, red, blue, or green beading. Some sets were made with etchings and hand-painted designs. Reproductions have been made. They are listed at the end of the Depression Glass section.

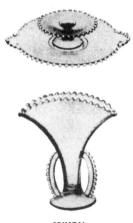

CRYSTAL
Ashtray, Bridge 6.00
Ashtray, Eagle 65.00

Ashtray, Nesting, Square,
    3 Piece 120.00
Basket, 6 1/2 In. 40.00
Bowl, 10 1/2 In. 20.00
Bowl, 2 Handles,
    4 1/2 In. 16.00
Bowl, 3-Footed, 6 In. 70.00
Bowl, 5 1/2 In. 22.00
Bowl, 5 In. 12.50
Bowl, Belled, 10 1/2 In. . .50.00
Bowl, Belled, 12 In. 60.00
Bowl, Divided, 6 In. 22.00
Bowl, Divided, Oblong,
    7 In. 22.00
Bowl, Footed, Low,
    9 In. 120.00
Bowl, Heart, 5 1/2 In. 20.00
Bowl, Heart, 9 In. 145.00
Bowl, Relish, 12 In. 125.00
Bowl, Square, 5 In. 125.00
Bowl, Vegetable, Cover,
    8 In. 250.00
Butter, 5 1/2 In. 32.50
Cake Stand,
    11 In. . . . . . . .70.00 to 75.00
Canape, Set, 2 Piece 20.00
Candleholder, 4 In.,
    Pair 20.00
Candleholder, Handle,
    5 In., Pair 100.00
Coaster 6.00
Cocktail, 4 Oz. . .16.00 to 22.00
Compote, Cheese 20.00
Cordial, 1 Oz. 70.00
Creamer, Demitasse 10.00
Creamer, Pedestal 15.00
Cruet, Oil, Beaded Base,
    4 Oz. 60.00
Cruet, Oil, Beaded Base,
    6 Oz. 70.00
Cup & Saucer . . .8.00 to 15.00
Cup & Saucer, Tea 8.00
Dish, Mayonnaise,
    Sections, 3 Piece 55.00
Float Bowl, 12 In. 40.00
Goblet, 10 Oz. 18.00
Goblet, Water,
    9 Oz. . . . . . . .16.00 to 24.00
Goblet, Wine, 4 Oz. 25.00
Goblet, Wine, 5 Oz. 28.00
Gravy Boat,
    Underplate 180.00

Mustard 35.00
Pitcher, 80 Oz. 170.00
Plate, 7 In. 7.00
Plate, Canape, 6 In. 9.00
Plate, Crimped, Handles,
    6 3/4 In. 30.00
Plate, Deviled Egg,
    12 In. . . . . . .155.00 to 165.00
Plate, Dinner,
    10 1/2 In. 37.50
Plate, Luncheon, Gold
    Floral, 8 1/2 In. 150.00
Platter, Oval, 16 In. 210.00
Punch Bowl Set,
    19 Piece 600.00
Punch Bowl Set, Liner,
    15 Piece 325.00
Relish, 4 Sections,
    Round 16.50
Relish, Oblong, 10 In. . . .100.00
Relish, Rectangular,
    12 In. 85.00
Salt & Pepper,
    Individual 12.50
Salt Dip 12.00
Saltshaker, 2 1/4 In. 9.00
Sherbet, 5 Oz. 12.00
Strawberry Set, 2 Piece . . .95.00
Sugar & Creamer,
    Tray 28.00
Tray, Oval, 9 In. 40.00
Tumbler, 12 Oz. 12.00
Tumbler, Footed, 5 Oz. . . .24.00
Tumbler, Footed, 9 Oz. . . .20.00
Vase, Miniature 55.00
Wafer Tray 25.00

RED
Bowl 250.00
Candleholder 450.00
Tumbler, 9 Oz. 105.00

VERDE
Ashtray, Heart 35.00

CAPE COD

Cape Cod was a pattern made
by the Imperial Glass Company,
Bellaire, Ohio, from 1932. It is
usually found in Crystal but
was also made in Amber,
Azalea (pink), Black, Cobalt
Blue, Green, Light Blue, Milk

Glass, and Ruby. In 1978 the
dinner set was reproduced. The
cruet was reproduced in 1986
without the rayed bottom.

AMBER
Salt & Pepper 35.00
CRYSTAL
Bowl, 11 In. 40.00
Bowl, 15 In. 75.00
Bowl, Oval, 11 In. 100.00
Cake Plate,
    Birthday . . . .110.00 to 275.00
Cake Plate, Square,
    4-Footed, 10 In. 90.00
Cake Stand, Footed,
    10 1/2 In. 40.00
Cake Stand, Footed,
    11 In. 100.00
Candy Dish, Cover 65.00
Mug, Handle, 12 Oz. 42.50
Pepper Mill, Large 87.50
Pepper Mill & Salt 45.00
Plate, 14 In. 35.00
Plate, Cupped, 16 In. 50.00
Plate, Dinner,
    10 In. . . . . . . .20.00 to 36.00
Plate, Salad, 7 1/2 In. 5.00
Punch Set, 15 Piece 230.00
Relish, 3 Sections 22.00
Relish, Plain Edge,
    3 Sections 28.00

Tray, Square, 7 In. 48.00
Tumbler, Water, Footed,
  10 Oz. ......10.00 to 11.00
Whiskey, 2 1/2 Oz. 15.00

RUBY
Salt & Pepper, Pair 15.00

CAPRICE

Caprice was advertised in 1936 as the most popular crystal pattern in America. It was made until 1953. Over 200 pieces were made in the line. Frosted pieces were called Alpine Caprice, the name given by the maker, Cambridge Glass Company, Cambridge, Ohio. The sets were made in Amber, Amethyst, Blue, Cobalt Blue, Moonlight Blue, Crystal, Emerald Green, Light Green, Pink, and Milk Glass. Reproductions are being made in Cobalt Blue and Moonlight Blue. They are listed at the end of the Depression Glass section.

AMETHYST
Pitcher, Ball, 80 Oz. 225.00

BLUE
Ashtray, Footed, With
  Place Card 15.00
Ashtray, Round, 4 In. 3.50
Ashtray, Round, 5 In. 24.00

Lock your doors and windows. In 65 to 82 percent of all home burglaries, the burglar enters through a door. Most often the doors were unlocked.

Ashtray, Triangular,
  2 1/2 In. 15.00
Bonbon, Footed, Square,
  6 In. 50.00
Bonbon, Handles,
  4 1/2 In. 39.00
Bonbon, Handles, Square,
  6 In. 48.00
Bowl, 4-Footed,
  10 In. ......60.00 to 100.00
Bowl, 4-Footed,
  11 1/2 In. 95.00
Bowl, 7 3/4 In. 11.50
Bowl, Belled, 3-Footed,
  11 In. 100.00
Bowl, Crimped, 4-Footed,
  9 1/2 In. 95.00
Bowl, Crimped, 4-Footed,
  10 1/2 In. 95.00
Bowl, Crimped, 4-Footed,
  11 In. 115.00
Bowl, Deep, Square,
  5 3/4 In. 10.00
Bowl, Fruit, Crimped,
  5 In. 125.00
Bowl, Square Bottom,
  6 In. 7.00
Bowl, Swirl, 4 3/4 In. 7.00
Candlestick, 2 1/2 In.,
  Pair ....60.00 to 64.00
Candlestick, 2-Light,
  Pair 165.00
Candlestick, 3-Light,
  6 In. 100.00
Candlestick, Prisms,
  Pair 150.00
Candy Dish, Cover, 3-Footed,
  6 In. ....100.00 to 125.00
Celery Dish 85.00

Cigarette Box, With
  4 Shell Ashtrays, Box,
  5 Piece 125.00
Compote, 7 In. 50.00
Cruet, 5 Oz. 350.00
Cup & Saucer 45.00
Decanter, 35 Oz. 495.00
Goblet, Champagne 35.00
Jam Jar, 7 In. 65.00
Nut Dish, Individual,
  2 1/2 In. 60.00
Pitcher, Ball, 80 Oz. 310.00
Plate, 4-Footed,
  14 In. 65.00
Plate, 4-Footed,
  15 In. 100.00
Plate, Lemon, Handle,
  6 In. 35.00
Plate, Luncheon,
  8 1/2 In. ....32.00 to 35.00
Plate, Salad, 7 1/2 In. 32.00
Relish, 3 Sections 55.00
Salt & Pepper,
  Individual 190.00
Saucer ....6.00 to 15.00
Sugar, 3 3/4 In. ..22.00 to 28.00
Sugar, 3 In. 10.00
Sugar & Creamer 75.00
Sugar & Creamer,
  Individual .....50.00 to 52.50
Tumbler, 5 Oz. 135.00
Tumbler, 12 Oz. 58.00
Tumbler, 3 1/2 In. 5.00
Tumbler, 4 1/4 In. 5.50
Tumbler, Blown,
  12 Oz. 125.00
Tumbler, Footed, 5 Oz. ...60.00
Vase, 4 1/2 In. 275.00
Vase, Sweet Pea, 7 In. ...75.00

CRYSTAL
Bowl, Oval, 7 1/2 In. 14.00
Bowl, Silver Overlay,
  Floral, 10 In. 35.00
Candlestick, 2 1/2 In.,
  Pair 35.00
Candlestick, 2-Light,
  Pair 90.00
Candlestick, Prism, 7 In.,
  Pair 150.00
Cigarette Holder 75.00
Cruet, Handle, 4 Oz.,
  5 In. 95.00

Cruet, Oil,
3 Oz. . . . . . . .25.00 to 35.00

Cruet, Oil, Stopper,
5 Oz. 65.00

Cup & Saucer . .15.00 to 16.50

Decanter, Sherry 395.00

Goblet, Water,
9 Oz. . . . . . . .20.00 to 30.00

Goblet, Wine,
2 1/2 Oz. . . . . .27.50 to 47.50

Jug, Ball, 80 Oz. 150.00

Mayonnaise,
2 Sections 57.50

Plate, Anniversary 40.00

Plate, Dinner, 9 1/2 In. . . .40.00

Plate, Luncheon,
8 1/2 In. . . . . . .13.00 to 15.00

Plate, Salad,
7 1/2 In. . . . . . .12.50 to 16.00

Punch Bowl, Footed . . .2995.00

Salt & Pepper 35.00

Saltshaker, Handle 27.50

Sherbet, Tall 16.00

Tray 17.50

Tumbler, 12 Oz.,
5 1/4 In. 30.00

Tumbler, Footed,
10 Oz. . . . . . . .18.00 to 20.00

Tumbler, Iced Tea, Footed,
12 Oz. . . . . . . .30.00 to 37.50

LIGHT GREEN
Whiskey, 2 Oz. 50.00

PINK
Bowl, Salad, Cupped,
13 In. 495.00

Candy Dish, 3-Footed,
Cover 295.00

Mayonnaise, Footed,
Handle 95.00

Plate, Lemon, 6 In. 50.00

CAPRICE, see also Alpine
Caprice

CARIBBEAN

The rippled design of Caribbean is slick and modern in appearance and has attracted many collectors. It was made by Duncan & Miller Glass Company, Washington, Pennsylvania, from 1936 to 1955.

Sets were made of Crystal, Crystal with ruby trim, Amber, Blue, and Red glass. The Duncan & Miller catalogs identify the line as No. 112.

AMBER
Punch Cup 10.00

BLUE
Bowl, 9 In. 65.00

Bowl, Liner, 12 1/2 In. . . .58.00

Candy Dish, Cover 90.00

Celery Dish 35.00

Cigarette Box, Tray 75.00

Cocktail Shaker 170.00

Compote, Cheese 40.00

Cruet, Stopper 80.00

Cruet, Tray 195.00

Finger Bowl,
4 1/2 In. 32.00

Ice Bucket, 6 1/2 In. 125.00

Nappy, Handles, 6 In. 12.00

Pitcher, Water,
8 1/4 In. 895.00

Plate, Bread & Butter,
6 In. 10.50

Plate, Dinner,
10 1/2 In. 100.00

Punch Cup 12.00

Relish, 5 Sections 85.00

Sugar & Creamer 45.00

Tumbler, Water, Footed,
9 Oz. 41.00

Vase, Flared, 6 In. 48.00

Vase, Straight Sides,
8 In. 68.00

CRYSTAL
Bowl, Tab Handles,
9 1/2 In. 35.00

Goblet, 3 Oz.,
4 1/4 In. 25.00

Relish, 5 Sections 40.00

RED
Punch Cup 12.00

CENTURY

Century pattern was made by Fostoria Glass Company from 1926 until 1986. It is a plain pattern with a slightly rippled rim. Full dinner sets were made of clear Crystal.

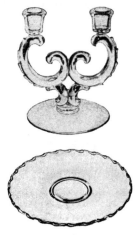

CRYSTAL
Bonbon 15.00

Bowl, 8 In. 20.00

Bowl, 12 In. 35.00

Bowl, Handle,
4 1/2 In. . . . . . . .9.00 to 15.00

Bowl, Serving, 2 Handles,
9 1/2 In. . . . . . .28.00 to 35.00

Butter, Red Stripes
On Base, 1/2 Lb. 65.00

Cake Plate, Low Pedestal,
12 In. 35.00

Candlestick, 4 1/2 In.,
Pair 28.00

Cruet 45.00

Cup 15.00

Cup & Saucer 15.00

Pitcher, 16 Oz., 6 1/8 In. . .50.00

Relish, 2 Sections,
7 3/8 In. 12.00

Relish, 3 Sections 20.00

Sugar & Creamer,
Footed 14.00

Sugar & Creamer,
Large 18.00

Tidbit, 2 Tiers,
10 1/4 In. 45.00

Tidbit, 3-Footed,
8 1/8 In. 14.00

Tray, Muffin, Handles,
9 1/2 In. 25.00

Vase, Bud,
6 In. . . . . .14.00 to 15.00

CHAIN DAISY, see Adam

CHANTILLY

As late as the 1960s the Jeannette Glass Company, Jeannette, Pennsylvania, made a pattern called Chantilly that is collected by Depression glass buffs. It was made in Crystal and Pink.

CRYSTAL
Bowl, Flared, 4-Footed,
12 In. 50.00

Candy Dish, 3 Sections,
Sterling Knob Cover . . .75.00

Cocktail Shaker, Sterling
Knob, 32 Oz. 150.00

Mayonnaise Set, 3 Piece . .40.00

Relish, 5 Sections 50.00

Salt & Pepper, Silver
Top, Handles 35.00

PINK
Decanter, Sherry 395.00

Goblet, Iced Tea, Footed,
12 Oz. 30.00

Goblet, Water, 10 Oz. 30.00

Shaker, Handle 27.50

CHARM

Charm is a pattern of Fire-King dinnerware made from 1950 to 1954. The square-shaped dishes were made by Anchor Hocking Glass Corporation of Lancaster, Ohio. The dinnerware was made of Forest Green, Royal Ruby, Jadite (opaque green), and Azurite (opaque blue-white). Collectors often refer to

the color name rather than the pattern name when describing these pieces. It is sometimes called Square. Other related sections in this book are Alice, Fire-King, Gray Laurel, Jadite, Peach Lustre, Philbe, Swirl Fire-King, Turquoise Blue, and Wheat.

AZURITE
Cup & Saucer 3.00

Plate, Dinner,
9 1/4 In. . . . . . .15.00 to 20.00

Plate, Luncheon,
8 3/8 In. 5.00

Saucer . . . . .1.00 to 2.50

Sugar . . . . .4.00 to 6.00

FOREST GREEN
Berry Bowl,
4 3/4 In. . . . . . . .4.00 to 5.50

Bowl, Salad, 7 3/8 In. 10.00

Bowl, Vegetable, Oval,
8 1/2 In. 22.00

Cup & Saucer . . . .5.00 to 6.50

Mixing Bowl, No. 3,
6 In. 7.00

Plate, Dinner, 9 1/4 In. . . .35.00

Plate, Luncheon,
8 3/8 In. . . . . .5.00 to 7.00

Plate, Salad,
6 5/8 In. . . . . .5.00 to 7.00

Platter, 11 In. 25.00

Saucer . . . . .1.00 to 2.00

Soup, Dish,
6 In. . . . . . . .15.00 to 23.00

Sugar & Creamer 11.00

❖

Antique glass should be handled as if it has been repaired and might fall apart. Hold a pitcher by the body, not the handle. Pick up stemware by holding both the stem and the bowl. Hold plates in two hands, not by the rim.

❖

JADITE
Cup 9.00

Cup & Saucer 12.00

Plate, Luncheon, 8 3/8 In. . .9.00

ROYAL RUBY
Cup & Saucer 9.00

Plate, Luncheon,
8 3/8 In. 11.00

Saucer 3.00

CHEROKEE ROSE

The Tiffin glass factory can be traced back to the 1840s, when Joseph Beatty made glass in Steubenville, Ohio. The factory failed and was purchased by Alexander Beatty in 1851. He was joined by his sons and moved to Tiffin, Ohio, in 1888. The company became part of U.S. Glass Company in 1892 and was still operating in 1963 when U.S. Glass went bankrupt. Employees bought the plant and it went through several changes of ownership until it closed in 1980. Cherokee Rose was one of the popular glass patterns made by Tiffin in the 1940s and 1950s. The glass was made only in Crystal.

CRYSTAL
Cordial, 1 Oz. 47.50

Goblet, Cocktail,
3 1/2 Oz. . . . . .12.00 to 22.50

Goblet, Water, 8 Oz. 17.50

Plate, Luncheon, 8 In. 16.00

Plate, Sherbet, 6 In. 2.00

Sherbet, Stemmed 20.00

Tumbler,
Iced Tea . . . . .29.00 to 35.00

Vase, Bud, 8 In. 30.00

CHERRY, see Cherry Blossom

CHERRY BLOSSOM

Cherry Blossom is one of the most popular Depression glass patterns. It has been called Banded Cherry, Cherry, or Paneled Cherry Blossom by some collectors. The pattern was made by the Jeannette Glass Company, Jeannette, Pennsylvania, from 1930 to 1939. Full dinner sets, serving pieces, and a child's set were made in a wide range of colors. Pieces were made in Crystal, Delphite (opaque blue), Green, Jadite (opaque green), Pink, and Red. During the course of production, molds were changed, resulting in several shapes and styles for some pieces. Many reproductions of Cherry Blossom pieces have been made and sold in recent years. They are listed at the end of the Depression Glass section.

CRYSTAL
Plate, Dinner, 9 In. 20.00

DELPHITE
Berry Bowl,
    4 3/4 In. . . . . . .14.00 to 15.00

Berry Bowl, Master,
    8 1/2 In. 50.00
Bowl, Vegetable, 2 Handles,
    9 In. . . . . .22.00 to 30.00
Child's Set,
    14 Piece . . . .310.00 to 325.00
Creamer 22.00
Cup & Saucer . .22.00 to 24.00
Cup & Saucer, Child's . . .42.00
Plate, Child's, 6 In. 13.00
Plate, Dinner,
    9 In. . . . . .17.00 to 22.50
Sandwich Server, 2 Handles,
    Round, 10 1/2 In. 20.00
Saucer, Child's 7.00
Sugar, Child's 45.00
Sugar & Creamer 29.00
Tumbler, Water, Footed,
    9 Oz. . . . . .16.00 to 25.00

GREEN
Berry Bowl,
    4 3/4 In. . . . . . .17.50 to 19.00
Berry Bowl, Master,
    8 1/2 In. . . . . .56.00 to 58.00
Bowl, 2 Handles,
    9 In. . . . . .55.00 to 65.00
Bowl, Cereal, 5 3/4 In. . . .46.00
Bowl, Fruit, 3-Footed,
    10 1/2 In. 90.00
Bowl, Oval, 9 In. 37.00
Bowl, Round, 8 1/2 In. . . .48.00
Butter, Cover . . .85.00 to 98.00
Cake Plate . . . . .35.00 to 39.00
Coaster, 6 In. . . . .12.00 to 14.00
Creamer . . . . . .20.00 to 22.00
Cup 23.50
Grill Plate, 9 In. .22.00 to 26.00
Mug, 7 Oz. 185.00
Pitcher, Footed, 36 Oz.,
    8 In. . . . . .55.00 to 65.00
Pitcher, Juice, Scalloped Base,
    6 3/4 In. . . . . .62.00 to 65.00
Pitcher, Water, Flat,
    42 Oz., 8 In. 57.00
Plate, Dinner,
    9 In. . . . . .23.00 to 26.00
Plate, Salad,
    7 In. . . . . .15.00 to 22.00
Plate, Sherbet, 6 In. 8.00
Platter, 11 In. 47.00
Platter, 2 Sections,
    13 In. . . . . . . .30.00 to 65.00

Sandwich Server, 2 Handles,
    10 1/2 In. . . . .25.00 to 30.00
Saucer . . . . .5.00 to 6.00
Sherbet, Footed . .17.00 to 18.00
Soup, Dish 86.00
Sugar, Cover 34.00
Sugar & Creamer,
    Cover 52.00
Tumbler, 9 Oz.,
    4 1/2 In. . . . . .18.00 to 22.00
Tumbler, Footed,
    3 3/4 In. . . . . .20.00 to 22.00
Tumbler, Juice, 3 1/2 In. . .30.00
Tumbler, Juice, Footed,
    4 1/2 In. 18.00
Tumbler, Juice,
    Scalloped, Footed,
    4 1/2 In. . . . . .35.00 to 44.00

PINK
Berry Bowl,
    4 3/4 In. . . . . . .10.00 to 22.00
Berry Bowl, Master,
    8 1/2 In. . . . . .45.00 to 50.00
Bowl, 2 Handles, 9 In. . . .48.00
Bowl, Cereal,
    5 3/4 In. . . . . .30.00 to 40.00
Bowl, Fruit, 3-Footed,
    10 1/2 In. . . . . .85.00 to 90.00
Bowl, Vegetable, Oval,
    9 In. 50.00
Butter, Cover . . .85.00 to 95.00
Cake Plate, Footed,
    10 1/4 In. . . . . .26.00 to 31.00
Child's Set, 14 Piece 300.00
Coaster . . . . .15.00 to 19.50
Creamer . . . . . . .17.00 to 22.50
Cup . . . . .19.50 to 20.00
Cup & Saucer . .21.00 to 27.00
Grill Plate,
    9 In. . . . . .25.00 to 29.50
Pitcher, 36 Oz.,
    6 3/4 In. . . . . .55.00 to 65.00
Pitcher, Cone, Footed,
    8 In. 85.00
Plate, Dinner,
    9 In. . . . . .22.00 to 28.00
Plate, Salad,
    7 In. . . . . .18.00 to 27.00
Plate, Sherbet,
    6 In. . . . . .8.00 to 10.00
Platter, Oval,
    11 In. . . . . . . .40.00 to 45.00
Sandwich Server,
    10 1/2 In. . . . .25.00 to 30.00

Saucer 5.50
Sherbet . . . . .14.00 to 20.00
Soup, Dish,
   7 3/4 In. . . . . . .85.00 to 90.00
Sugar, Cover . . . .28.00 to 43.00
Sugar & Creamer 32.00
Sugar & Creamer,
   Cover . . . . . . .49.00 to 55.00
Tumbler, Juice, Footed, 4 Oz.,
   3 3/4 In. . . . . .20.00 to 27.50
Tumbler, Scalloped Foot,
   8 Oz., 4 1/2 In. 32.50

CHERRY-BERRY

Two similar patterns, Cherry-Berry and Strawberry, can be confusing. If the fruit pictured is a cherry, then the pattern is called Cherry-Berry. If the strawberry is used, then the pattern has that name. The dishes were made by the U.S. Glass Company in the early 1930s in Crystal, Green, Iridescent Amber, and Pink.

GREEN
Berry Bowl, Deep,
   7 1/2 In. . . . . . .18.00 to 19.00
Bowl, 6 1/4 In. 55.00
Butter, Cover 75.00
Plate, Sherbet, 6 In. 11.00
Sugar 25.00
Sugar, Cover 55.00

**Shallow nicks and
rough edges on glass
can sometimes be
smoothed off with
fine emery paper.**

PINK
Creamer, Small 25.00
Plate, Salad, 7 1/2 In. 15.00
Sherbet . . . . . . .9.00 to 13.50

CHERRY-BERRY, see also
   Strawberry

CHINEX CLASSIC

Chinex Classic and Cremax are very similar patterns made by Macbeth-Evans Division of Corning Glass Works from about 1938 to 1942. *Chinex* and *Cremax* are both words with two meanings. Each is the name of a pattern and the name of a color used for other patterns. Chinex is ivory-colored, Cremax is a bit whiter. Chinex Classic, the dinnerware pattern, has a piecrust edge, and just inside the edge is an elongated feathered scroll. It may or may not have a decal-decorated center and colored edging. The Cremax pattern has just the piecrust edge. The decals used on Chinex Classic are either floral designs or brown-toned scenics.

IVORY
Plate, Bread & Butter 4.00
Plate, Dinner,
   9 3/4 In. . . . . . . .4.00 to 6.00
Saucer . . . . .1.50 to 4.00
Sherbet, Footed, Low 6.00
Soup, Dish 8.00
Sugar & Creamer 16.00

IVORY WITH DECAL
Bowl, Cereal, Scenic,
   5 3/4 In. 17.00

Bowl, Vegetable, Scenic,
   9 In. 35.00
Cup & Saucer,
   Scenic 21.50
Plate, Dinner, Scenic,
   9 3/4 In. 20.00
Plate, Sherbet, Scenic,
   6 1/4 In. 7.50
Sandwich Server, Scenic,
   11 1/2 In. 25.00
Sherbet, Scenic 25.00
Soup, Dish, Scenic,
   7 3/4 In. 35.00

CHINEX CLASSIC, see also
   Cremax

CHINTZ

Several companies made a glass named Chintz. To identify Chintz pattern pieces, remember the design is named for the etched pattern, not the shape, of the glass. Fostoria Glass Company made Baroque, a glass shape that included molded fleur-de-lis–shaped handles and ridges. This glass blank was then etched with design No. 338 and then sold as Chintz pattern. The etched design pictures branches of leaves and flowers. It was also used on some vases and other pieces that were not Baroque blanks. Only Crystal pieces were made. Pieces were made from 1940 to 1972. To confuse this even more, the company made other etched designs (Navarre) on the Baroque blanks. Other Chintz patterns were made by A. H. Heisey & Company from 1931 to 1938. They both had etched designs of butterflies and encircled flowers. These Chintz patterns were made in Crystal, Flamingo (pink), Moongleam (green), Sahara (yellow), and Alexandrite (orchid), a glass that turned from blue to purple depending on the lighting source. Pieces listed in this book are for Fostoria Chintz.

CRYSTAL

Bowl, Vegetable, Oval,
9 1/2 In. 195.00

Candlestick, 2-Light,
Pair 60.00

Compote 40.00

Cup & Saucer 25.00

Goblet,
Champagne . . .10.00 to 20.00

Goblet, Sherbet, Low, 6 Oz.,
4 3/8 In. 145.00

Tumbler, Juice, Footed,
5 Oz. 200.00

CHRISTMAS CANDY

Christmas Candy, sometimes called Christmas Candy Ribbon or No. 624, was made by the Indiana Glass Company, Dunkirk, Indiana, in 1937. The pattern, apparently only made in luncheon sets, was made in Crystal, a light green called Seafoam Green, a bright blue called Teal Blue, and dark Emerald Green.

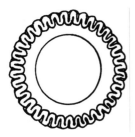

CRYSTAL

Creamer 9.00
Plate, Luncheon, 8 In. 7.00
Sugar 9.00

TEAL BLUE

Plate, Luncheon, 8 In. 12.50

Sandwich Server,
11 1/4 In. 40.00
Saucer 7.00
Sugar, Footed 20.00

CHRISTMAS CANDY RIBBON,
see Christmas Candy

CIRCLE

Circles ring the Circle pattern made by Hocking Glass Company, Lancaster, Ohio, in the 1930s. It is found in Green, Crystal, and Pink. It can be distinguished from the similar Hocking pattern called Ring by the number of groupings of rings—Circle has only one set, Ring has several sets with four rings in each group.

GREEN

Bowl, 4 1/2 In. 15.00
Cup 5.00
Cup & Saucer Set 7.50
Goblet, Water, 8 Oz. 11.00
Goblet, Wine,
4 1/2 In. . . . . . .12.50 to 15.00
Goblet, Wine, Gold Trim,
4 1/2 In. 12.00
Pitcher, 60 Oz. . .32.00 to 35.00
Plate, Luncheon,
8 1/4 In. 11.00
Plate, Sherbet,
6 In. . . . . .2.00 to 3.00
Plate, Sherbet, Gold Trim,
6 In. 1.50
Saucer 2.50
Sherbet, 3 1/8 In. 4.00

Sherbet, 4 3/4 In. 11.00
Sherbet, Gold Trim,
4 3/4 In. 6.00
Tumbler, Iced Tea, 10 Oz.,
5 In. . . . . .16.00 to 17.00
Tumbler, Water, 8 Oz. 9.00

PINK

Plate, Luncheon, 8 In. 8.00
Sherbet, 3 1/8 In. 6.00

CIRCULAR RIBS, see Circle

CLASSIC, see Chinex Classic

CLEO

In 1930 the Cambridge Glass Company, Cambridge, Ohio, introduced an etched pattern called Cleo. Many pieces are marked with the Cambridge C in a triangle. Sets were made in Amber, Blue, Crystal, Green, Pink, and Yellow.

AMBER

Candy Dish, Cover,
3 Sections 105.00
Ice Tub 40.00

BLUE

Cup & Saucer, Decagon . .33.00
Mayonnaise, Liner 13.00
Plate, Decagon, 6 In. 14.00
Plate, Decagon, 8 In. 32.00

GREEN
Cocktail, Insert & Liner . .95.00

PINK
Berry Bowl, Belled,
  5 In. 55.00
Bowl, Vegetable, Oval,
  10 3/4 In. 125.00
Candlestick, 4 In., Pair . . .95.00
Cup & Saucer 18.00
Gravy Boat, Double 220.00
Ice Tub 95.00
Tumbler, Flat, 11 Oz. 48.00
Tumbler, Footed, 6 Oz. . . .25.00

CLOVERLEAF

Three-leaf clovers form part
of the border of Cloverleaf pattern made by Hazel Atlas
Glass Company from 1930 to
1936. It was made in Black,
Crystal, Green, Pink, and Topaz (yellow).

BLACK
Creamer . . . . . . .18.00 to 18.50
Cup 16.00
Cup & Saucer . . .22.50 to 25.00
Plate, Luncheon,
  8 In. . . . . .14.50 to 17.00
Plate, Sherbet,
  6 In. . . . . .37.00 to 38.00
Salt & Pepper . . .80.00 to 85.00
Saltshaker 40.00

**New security idea: Have
one of the neighbors
park a second car in
your driveway. Your
house will look occupied
and the car will be seen
coming and going.**

Saucer . . . . .6.50 to 7.00
Sherbet, Footed . .18.00 to 20.00
Sugar . . . . .15.00 to 20.00
Sugar &
  Creamer . . . . .35.00 to 36.00

GREEN
Bowl, Dessert,
  4 In. . . . . .24.00 to 25.00
Bowl, Salad,
  7 In. . . . . .38.00 to 45.00
Candy Dish, Cover 72.00
Cup 8.00
Cup & Saucer . . .9.00 to 14.00
Grill Plate, 10 1/4 In. 25.00
Plate, Luncheon,
  8 In. . . . . .8.00 to 12.00
Salt & Pepper 35.00
Saucer . . . . .3.00 to 4.50
Sherbet, Footed . . .7.00 to 12.00
Sugar 10.00
Tumbler, 10 Oz.,
  5 3/4 In. . . . . . .25.00 to 39.00

PINK
Cup . . . . .7.00 to 9.00
Plate, Luncheon,
  8 In. . . . . .7.00 to 11.00
Saucer 4.00
Sherbet, Footed 10.00

TOPAZ
Bowl, Dessert, 4 In. 32.00
Candy Dish, Cover 145.00
Cup 10.00
Plate, Luncheon, 8 In. 14.00
Plate, Sherbet,
  6 In. . . . . .7.00 to 8.00
Saucer 5.00
Sherbet . . . . . . .10.00 to 11.00
Sugar . . . . .17.50 to 20.00

COLONIAL

Sometimes this pattern is called
Knife & Fork, although Colonial is the more common
name. It was made by Hocking
Glass Company, Lancaster,
Ohio, from 1934 to 1938. Crystal, Green, and Pink pieces are
more common than Opaque
White.

CRYSTAL
Butter 30.00
Cup 6.00
Goblet, Cocktail, 3 Oz.,
  4 In. 12.00
Goblet, Wine, 2 1/2 Oz.,
  4 1/2 In. 12.00
Pitcher, 68 Oz., 7 3/4 In. . .35.00
Plate, Bread & Butter,
  6 In. 3.00
Plate, Dinner, 10 In. 20.00
Spooner 60.00
Sugar, Cover . . . .9.00 to 20.00
Tumbler, Juice, 5 Oz.,
  3 In. 8.00
Tumbler, Juice, Footed,
  5 Oz. 15.00
Tumbler, Water, 9 Oz.,
  4 In. 10.00

GREEN
Berry Bowl,
  4 1/2 In. . . . . . . .6.00 to 20.00
Berry Bowl, Master,
  9 In. 28.00

Bowl, Vegetable, Oval,
10 In. 10.00

Butter, Cover . . .55.00 to 85.00

Cheese Dish, Cover 500.00

Cup & Saucer 15.00

Goblet, Claret, 4 Oz.,
5 1/4 In. . . . . . .25.00 to 29.00

Goblet, Cocktail, 3 Oz.,
3 1/4 In. . . . . . .19.00 to 29.00

Goblet, Cordial, 1 Oz.,
3 3/4 In. . . . . . .25.00 to 27.00

Goblet, Water, 8 Oz.,
5 3/4 In. . . . . . .25.00 to 32.00

Goblet, Wine, 2 1/2 Oz.,
4 1/2 In. . . . . . .22.00 to 28.00

Grill Plate,
10 In. . . . . .25.00 to 30.00

Pitcher, 54 Oz.,
7 In. . . . . .62.00 to 75.00

Plate, Dinner, 10 In. 45.00

Plate, Sherbet,
6 In. . . . . .6.00 to 8.00

Platter, Oval, 12 In. 30.00

Salt & Pepper 145.00

Sherbet . . . . .16.00 to 17.00

Soup, Cream,
4 1/2 In. . . . . . .65.00 to 71.00

Spooner . . . . .125.00 to 135.00

Sugar . . . . .18.00 to 19.00

Sugar, Cover 35.00

Sugar & Creamer,
Footed 56.00

Whiskey, 1 1/2 Oz.,
2 1/2 In. 15.00

OPAQUE WHITE

Plate, 8 In. 10.00

Saucer 3.00

PINK

Berry Bowl,
4 1/2 In. . . . . . .15.00 to 16.00

Cup 12.00

Cup & Saucer 17.00

Goblet, Claret, 4 Oz.,
5 1/4 In. 38.00

Grill Plate, 10 In. 25.00

Pitcher, 68 Oz., 7 3/4 In. . .75.00

Plate, Dinner, 10 In. 50.00

Sherbet 12.00

Soup, Dish . . . . .75.00 to 90.00

Soup Cream, 4 1/2 In. 65.00

Spooner . . . . .133.00 to 135.00

Tumbler, Footed, 10 Oz.,
5 1/4 In. . . . . . .46.00 to 48.00

Tumbler, Juice, 5 Oz.,
3 In. . . . . .19.00 to 20.00

Tumbler, Juice, Footed, 3 Oz.,
3 1/4 In. . . . . . .17.00 to 21.00

Tumbler, Water, 9 Oz.,
4 In. . . . . .18.00 to 21.00

Tumbler, Water, Footed,
5 Oz., 4 In. 32.00

Whiskey, 1 1/2 Oz.,
2 1/2 In. 11.00

COLONIAL BLOCK

A small set of dishes, mostly serving pieces, was made in Colonial Block pattern by Hazel Atlas Glass Company, a firm with factories in Ohio, Pennsylvania, and West Virginia. The dishes were made in the 1930s in Black, Crystal, Green, and Pink and in the 1950s in White.

CRYSTAL

Bowl, 4 In. 6.00

Bowl, 7 In. 16.00

Butter, Cover 30.00

Creamer 7.00

Goblet, Water, 8 1/2 Oz.,
6 In. 9.00

Sherbet 6.00

Sugar 6.00

GREEN

Bowl, 7 In. 15.00

Butter, Cover . . .29.00 to 60.00

Candy Jar,
Cover . . . . . . .35.00 to 40.00

Goblet . . . . . . .10.00 to 13.00

Sherbet 9.00

Sugar 10.00

Sugar & Creamer 20.00

PINK

Sherbet 9.00

COLONIAL FLUTED

Federal Glass Company made Colonial Fluted or Rope pattern from 1928 to 1933. Luncheon sets were made primarily in Green, although Crystal pieces were also produced.

CRYSTAL

Cup 5.00

Plate, Luncheon, 8 In. 4.00

Plate, Sherbet, 6 In. 2.50

Sugar 5.00

GREEN

Berry Bowl, 4 In. 6.50

Creamer 7.00

Grill Plate 14.00

Plate, Luncheon, 8 In. 5.00

Plate, Sherbet, 6 In. 2.50

Sherbet 6.00

Sugar, Cover 24.00

Sugar & Creamer,
Cover . . . . .28.00 to 30.00

COLONY

Colony was made by Fostoria Glass Company from the 1920s to the 1970s. Red candlesticks and bowls were sold after 1982 under the Maypole name, and matching vases and other pieces were made by Viking. Colony was originally made in Amber, Blue, Crystal, Green, and Yellow. Red was made in the 1980s. Another pattern, also named Colony, was made by Hazel Atlas Glass Company in the 1930s in Crystal, Green, and Pink. Colony is a pattern that has also been called Elongated Honeycomb or Hexagon Triple Band because of the features in the molding. Colony made by Fostoria is listed here. Reproductions have been made. They are listed at the end of the Depression Glass section.

CRYSTAL
Ashtray, Round, 3 In. 10.00
Ashtray, Round, 6 In. 19.00
Bowl, 11 In. 25.00
Bowl, Ice Cream, Square,
  5 1/2 In. 25.00
Bowl, Oval, Footed,
  11 In. 65.00
Cake Plate, Footed,
  12 In. 75.00

❖

Tired of scrubbing and scrubbing glass to remove marks from masking tape and labels? Pat some commercial hand cleaner on the stain; wait 30 minutes. Then rub off the stain with a cloth and wash the glass.

❖

Candlestick, 2-Light,
  6 1/2 In., Pair 55.00
Candlestick, 3 1/2 In.,
  Pair 15.00
Candlestick, Prisms,
  7 1/2 In., Pair 120.00
Candy Dish, Cover 95.00
Compote, Cover,
  6 1/2 In. . . . . . .42.00 to 45.00
Creamer, Footed, 7 Oz. 9.00
Cup & Saucer 8.00
Goblet, Water, 9 Oz.,
  5 1/8 In. . . . . . .10.00 to 14.50
Jelly Dish, Cover, 6 In. . . .42.00
Nappy, Round, 4 1/2 In. . .10.00
Pickle 16.00
Pitcher, Ice Lip,
  8 1/2 In. 100.00
Plate, Luncheon, 8 In. 10.00
Platter,
  12 1/2 In. . . . . .27.00 to 50.00
Punch Cup 20.00
Relish, 2 Sections, Oval . .20.00
Salt & Pepper 16.00
Sherbet, 5 Oz. . . . . .7.00 to 9.00
Sugar, Footed, Open 9.00
Sugar & Creamer,
  Footed 13.00
Sugar & Creamer, Individual,
  2 3/4 In. . . . . . .13.00 to 16.00
Tray, Center Handle,
  11 1/2 In. 30.00
Tray, Muffin, 8 3/8 In. . . .30.00
Wine, 3 1/4 In. . .20.00 to 22.00

PINK
Candy Jar, Cover,
  6 1/2 In. 45.00

COLUMBIA

Columbia pattern can be found in Crystal but is rare in Pink. It was made by Federal Glass Company, Columbus, Ohio, from 1938 to 1942.

CRYSTAL
Bowl, Cereal,
  5 In. . . . . .16.00 to 19.00
Bowl, Ruffled,
  10 1/2 In. . . . . .18.00 to 20.00
Bowl, Salad,
  8 1/2 In. . . . . . .14.00 to 20.00
Butter, Cover . . .16.00 to 25.00
Chop Plate,
  11 In. . . . . .10.00 to 12.00
Cup 8.00
Cup & Saucer . .10.00 to 15.00
Plate, Bread & Butter,
  6 In. . . . . .4.00 to 12.00
Plate, Luncheon,
  9 1/2 In. . . . . . . .9.00 to 10.00
Plate, Snack . . . .30.00 to 42.00
Soup, Dish, 8 In. 20.00
Sugar & Creamer,
  Cover 20.00

PINK
Cup & Saucer 30.00
Plate, Bread & Butter,
  6 In. 13.00
Plate, Luncheon,
  9 1/2 In. 30.00

CORONATION

Coronation was made, primarily in berry sets, by Anchor Hocking Glass Corporation, Lancaster, Ohio, from 1936 to 1940. Most pieces are Crystal or Pink, but there are also Dark Green and Ruby Red sets. The pattern is sometimes called Banded Fine Rib or Saxon. Some of the pieces are confused with those in Lace Edge pattern.

PINK
Berry Bowl, 4 1/4 In. 8.00
Cup 6.00
Plate, Sherbet,
 6 In. . . . . .2.00 to 4.00
Sherbet, Footed 10.00
Tumbler, Footed, 10 Oz.,
 5 In. . . . . .22.00 to 34.00

ROYAL RUBY
Berry Bowl,
 4 1/4 In. . . . . . . .4.50 to 6.75
Berry Bowl, Master,
 8 In. . . . . .14.00 to 15.00
Bowl, Nappy,
 6 1/2 In. . . . . . .10.00 to 15.00

❖

Don't use ammonia on glasses with gold or silver decorations.

❖

CRACKED ICE

Cracked Ice is an Art Deco-looking geometric pattern made by Indiana Glass Company in the 1930s. It was made in Green and Pink.

GREEN
Salt & Pepper, Pair 38.00
Sugar & Creamer 59.00
PINK
Plate, Bread & Butter,
 6 1/2 In. 20.00
Sherbet, 3 In. 20.00

CREMAX

Cremax and Chinex Classic are confusing patterns. There is an added piece of molded design next to the fluted rim trim on Chinex Classic. Also the names Cremax and Chinex refer to colors as well as patterns. Cremax, made by Macbeth-Evans Division of Corning Glass Works, was made from 1938 to 1942. It is a cream-colored opaque glass, sometimes decorated with floral or brown-tinted decals or with a colored rim.

Plate, Dinner, 9 3/4 In 5.00
Plate, Sandwich, Pink
 Border, 11 1/2 In. 13.00

CREMAX, see also Chinex Classic

CUBE, see Cubist

CUBIST

Cubist, or Cube, molded with the expected rectangular and diamond pattern, was made by Jeannette Glass Company from 1929 to 1933. It was made first in Pink and Crystal. Later, Green replaced Crystal, and Amber, Blue, Canary Yellow, Pink, Ultramarine, and White were added. Various shades of some of the colors were made. It has been made recently in Amber, Opaque White, and Avocado.

CRYSTAL
Creamer 3.00
Tumbler, Juice, 9 Oz.,
 4 In. 67.00
GREEN
Bowl, Dessert,
 4 1/2 In. . . . . . .6.00 to 10.00
Bowl, Salad, 6 1/2 In. 18.00
Butter, Cover 60.00
Candy Jar, Cover,
 6 1/2 In. . . . . . .20.00 to 32.00
Coaster, 3 1/4 In. . .8.00 to 9.00
Creamer, Large . . .8.00 to 13.00
Cup 9.00
Cup & Saucer 11.00

Pitcher, Water, Applied
Handle, 9 In. 25.00
Plate, Luncheon,
8 In. . . . . .8.00 to 11.00
Plate, Sherbet, 6 In. 4.00
Powder Jar, Cover 28.00
Salt & Pepper . . .30.00 to 35.00
Saucer 3.00
Sherbet . . . . .7.00 to 8.00
Sherbet, Footed 8.00
Sugar, 3 In. 6.00
Sugar & Creamer Set,
3 In. . . . . .9.00 to 33.00
Tumbler, Water, 9 Oz.,
4 In. 70.00

PINK
Bowl, Dessert,
4 1/2 In. . . . . . . .5.00 to 8.00
Bowl, Salad, 6 1/2 In. 12.00
Butter, Cover . . .57.00 to 70.00
Candy Jar,
Cover . . . . . . .22.00 to 27.00
Coaster, 3 1/4 In. 7.00
Creamer, Large,
3 9/16 In. 6.00
Cup 8.00
Cup & Saucer 10.00
Pitcher, 45 Oz.,
8 1/4 In. 245.00
Plate, Luncheon, 8 In. 6.00
Powder Jar, Cover 25.00
Salt & Pepper,
Pair . . . . .25.00 to 30.00
Saucer 3.00
Sherbet, Footed . . . .7.00 to 8.00
Sugar, 3 In. 5.00
Sugar & Creamer,
Cover . . . . . . .23.00 to 25.00

If you are going to dis-
play a large bowl on a
wooden table, apply self-
adhesive green felt pads
to the bottom of the
bowl. This will keep the
table from being
scratched and the bowl
from chipping.

Tumbler, Water, 9 Oz.,
4 In. 70.00
DAISY, see No. 620
DAISY PETALS, see Petalware
DANCING GIRL, see Cameo

· D ·

DECAGON
Decagon, named for its 10-
sided outline, was made by the
Cambridge Glass Company of
Cambridge, Ohio. The pattern,
dating from the 1930s, was
made in Amber, Black, Cobalt
Blue, Green, Moonlight Blue
(light blue), Pink, and Red.

AMBER
Bottle, Salad Dressing . .110.00
Cruet 32.50
BLACK
Bowl, Flared, 12 In. 65.00
Goblet, Wine 30.00
Tray, For Sugar &
Creamer 45.00
COBALT BLUE
Goblet, 8 Oz. 24.00
Sherbet 20.00
GREEN
Bowl, Cupped, Deep,
5 1/2 In. 55.00
Bowl, Footed, 6 In. 24.00
Bowl, Fruit, Belled,
5 1/2 In. 16.00
Celery Dish 37.00
Creamer . . . . . .15.00 to 25.00
Cruet, 3-Spout 165.00

Cup & Saucer . .10.00 to 11.00
Goblet, Cocktail,
3 1/2 Oz. 24.00
Goblet, Water, 9 Oz. 20.00
Mug, Lemonade,
Handle 55.00
Nut Dish, Footed,
2 1/2 In. 30.00
Pickle, 8 1/2 In. 35.00
Plate, Bread & Butter,
7 1/2 In. 10.00
Plate, Salad,
8 1/4 In. . . . . . .10.00 to 18.50
Relish, 2 Sections,
8 1/2 In. 35.00
Salt & Pepper, 3 In. 50.00
Sandwich Server, Center
Handle 22.00
Sherbet 10.00
Soup, Cream, With Liner .35.00
Soup, Dish, 6 3/4 In. 24.00
Sugar & Creamer 20.00
Tumbler, Juice, 5 Oz. 11.00
Whiskey, Footed,
2 1/2 Oz. 12.00

MOONLIGHT BLUE
Basket, 6 1/4 In. 45.00
Bouillon, Footed 20.00
Candlestick, 5 In. 42.00
Creamer & Sugar 40.00
Cruet, 6 Oz. 195.00
Cup & Saucer 15.00
Goblet, Champagne,
6 Oz. 24.00
Goblet, Water, 9 Oz. 33.00
Goblet, Wine, 2 1/2 Oz. . .35.00
Plate, 2 Handles, 7 In. . . .24.00
Plate, Salad, 7 1/2 In. 15.00
Sandwich Server, Center
Handle 35.00
Sherbet, Low . . . .19.00 to 20.00
Soup, Cream, Liner 45.00
Tray, For Sugar &
Creamer 45.00
Tray, Oval, 9 In. 35.00
Tumbler, Iced Tea, Footed,
12 Oz. . . . . . . .35.00 to 45.00
Tumbler, Water, Footed,
10 Oz. 28.00

PINK
Ice Bucket 85.00
Sherbet, Low 16.00

DELLA ROBBIA

Della Robbia is a heavy glass with raised pears and apples as part of the design. It was made by the Westmoreland Glass Company, Grapeville, Pennsylvania, from 1926 to the 1960s. The pattern was made in Crystal, Roselin, Green, and Amber. Crystal pieces often have fruit stained in natural colors.

CRYSTAL
Bowl, Heart Shape,
   8 In. 125.00
Box, Chocolate, Cover . . .75.00
Candlestick, 4 In.,
   Pair . . . . .45.00 to 55.00
Plate, Luncheon,
   9 In. . . . . .30.00 to 35.00
Plate, Salad, 7 1/4 In. 22.00
Punch Bowl Set,
   13 Piece 700.00
Salver, Footed, 14 In. . . .120.00
Sherbet, Low Foot, 5 Oz.,
   4 3/4 In. . . . . . .19.00 to 26.00
Torte Plate, Crystal,
   14 In. . . . . . . .85.00 to 125.00
Tumbler, Iced Tea,
   12 Oz. 35.00

❖❖

**Never run an ad that
says to call after
6:00 p.m. It is an
announcement that
you are away from
the house during
the day.**

❖❖

Tumbler, Water,
   8 Oz. . . . . .28.00 to 30.00

DIAMOND, see Windsor

DIAMOND PATTERN, see Miss
   America

DIAMOND QUILTED

Imperial Glass Company, Bellaire, Ohio, made Diamond Quilted, sometimes called Flat Diamond, in the 1920s and early 1930s. It was made in Amber, Black, Blue, Crystal, Green, Pink, and Red. Dinner sets, luncheon sets, and serving pieces, including a large punch bowl, were made, but not all items were made in all colors.

BLACK
Cup 20.00
Soup, Cream, 4 3/4 In. . . .20.00

BLUE
Candlestick, Pair 48.00
Plate, Luncheon, 8 In. 16.00
Plate, Sherbet, 6 In. 9.00
Sherbet 13.00
Soup, Cream 19.00
Sugar 20.00
Sugar & Creamer 45.00

GREEN
Candlestick,
   Pair . . . . .24.00 to 25.00
Plate, Luncheon, 8 In. 6.00
Plate, Sherbet, 6 In. 4.00

PINK
Basket, Cookie 150.00
Bowl, Handle, 5 1/2 In. . .15.00
Candlestick 12.00
Candy Jar, Cover 150.00
Cup . . . . .8.00 to 10.00
Plate, Luncheon,
   8 In. 11.00
Sherbet 5.00
Sugar . . . . .8.00 to 13.00

DIANA

Diana is one of the many Depression glass patterns with swirls in the glass, which often cause confusion. Federal Glass Company, Columbus, Ohio, made this pattern, sometimes called Swirled Sharp Rib, from 1937 to 1941. It was made in Amber, Crystal, Green, and Pink and can be distinguished from other swirled patterns by the two sets of swirls used—one in the center of the piece, another on the rim. A Pink bowl was reproduced in 1987.

AMBER
Bowl, Cereal,
   5 In. . . . . .10.00 to 12.00
Bowl, Console, Fruit,
   11 In. . . . . .10.00 to 18.00
Bowl, Salad, 9 In. 20.00
Coaster, 3 1/2 In. 16.00
Creamer 9.00
Cup & Saucer 8.00
Plate, Luncheon,
   9 1/2 In. 8.00
Platter, Oval, 12 In. 13.00
Salt & Pepper 100.00
Saucer 2.00
Shaker 49.00
Sherbet . . . . .7.00 to 9.00
Soup, Cream,
   5 1/2 In. 16.00
Sugar & Creamer 15.00

Tumbler, 9 Oz.,
4 1/2 In. 26.00

CRYSTAL
Bowl, Cereal, 5 In. 4.00
Cup & Saucer 12.00
Cup & Saucer, After
Dinner . . . . . . .10.00 to 13.00
Goblet, Cordial,
1 1/2 Oz. 65.00
Salt & Pepper 20.00
Saucer 1.50
Soup, Cream, 8 1/2 In. 6.00
Tea Set, Child's, Metal
Holder 90.00
Tumbler, 9 Oz. 32.00

PINK
Bowl, Cereal,
5 In. . . . . .3.00 to 11.00
Bowl, Console, Fruit,
11 In. 40.00
Bowl, Salad,
9 In. . . . . .20.00 to 22.00
Candy Jar,
Cover . . . . . . .30.00 to 45.00
Creamer . . . . . .12.00 to 20.00
Cup . . . . .9.00 to 14.00
Cup, After
Dinner . . . . . .10.00 to 30.00
Cup & Saucer . .13.00 to 19.00
Plate, Bread & Butter,
6 In. 3.00
Plate, Dinner, 9 1/2 In. . . .16.00
Platter, Oval, 12 In. 30.00
Salt & Pepper 75.00
Soup, Cream,
5 1/2 In. . . . . . .25.00 to 30.00
Tumbler, 9 Oz. 30.00

DOGWOOD

Dogwood is decorated with a strange flower that has been given many names. Collectors have called this pattern Apple Blossom, B pattern, Magnolia, or Wildrose. It was made from 1930 to 1934 by Macbeth-Evans Glass Company. It is found in Cremax, Crystal, Green, Monax, Pink, and Yellow. Sometimes the Pink pieces were trimmed with gold.

Some pieces were made with such thin walls the factory redesigned the molds to make the pieces thicker.

GREEN
Cake Plate, 13 In. 110.00
Cup . . . . .35.00 to 40.00
Cup & Saucer, Thin 40.00
Plate, Luncheon, 8 In. 8.00
Saucer 7.00

MONAX
Cup 36.00

PINK
Ashtray, Square 5.00
Berry Bowl, Master,
8 1/2 In. . . . . . .58.00 to 60.00
Bowl, Cereal,
5 1/2 In. . . . . . .25.00 to 32.50
Bowl, Cereal, Rolled Edge,
5 1/2 In. . . . . . .55.00 to 80.00
Cake Plate,
13 In. . . . . . .125.00 to 150.00
Creamer, Thick . .19.00 to 27.50
Creamer, Thin . . .15.00 to 19.50
Cup, Thick 15.00
Cup & Saucer,
Thick . . . . . . .20.00 to 25.00
Cup & Saucer,
Thin . . . . .18.00 to 25.00
Grill Plate . . . . .20.00 to 22.00
Pitcher . . . . .220.00 to 230.00
Plate, Bread & Butter,
6 In. . . . . .6.50 to 10.00

Plate, Dinner,
9 1/4 In. . . . . .22.50 to 40.00
Plate, Luncheon,
8 In. . . . . .5.50 to 9.00
Platter, 12 In. 500.00
Salver, 12 In. . . . .28.00 to 40.00
Saucer 7.00
Sherbet, Footed . .30.00 to 40.00
Sugar, Thick,
3 1/4 In. . . . . .16.00 to 21.00
Sugar, Thin,
2 1/2 In. . . . . .15.00 to 18.00
Sugar & Creamer, Thick,
Footed . . . . . .35.00 to 38.00
Sugar & Creamer,
Thin . . . . .30.00 to 36.00
Tumbler, 12 Oz.,
5 In. . . . . .43.00 to 77.50
Tumbler, Decorated, 12 Oz.,
Box, 6 Piece 425.00
Tumbler, Iced Tea, Decorated,
12 Oz. . . . . . .58.00 to 60.00

DORIC

Doric was made by Jeannette Glass Company, Jeannette, Pennsylvania, from 1935 to 1938. The molded pattern has also inspired another name for the pattern, Snowflake. It was made in Delphite (opaque blue), Green, Pink, and Yellow. A few White pieces may have been made.

DELPHITE
Candy Dish, 3 Sections 8.00
Candy Dish, Cover 5.00
Sherbet, Footed . . .6.00 to 10.00

GREEN
Berry Bowl,
4 1/2 In. . . . . . .7.00 to 11.00
Berry Bowl, Master,
8 1/4 In. 26.00
Bowl, Handles, 9 In. 24.00
Creamer . . . . . . .13.00 to 17.00
Pitcher, 36 Oz., 6 In. 45.00
Plate, Salad,
7 In. . . . . .22.00 to 28.00
Plate, Sherbet, 6 In. 5.00
Relish, 4 x 4 In. 16.50
Sherbet 14.00
Sugar & Creamer,
Cover 50.00

PINK
Berry Bowl,
4 1/2 In. . . . . . .8.00 to 12.00
Berry Bowl, Master,
8 1/4 In. . . . . .14.00 to 35.00
Bowl, 2 Handles, 9 In. . . .20.00
Bowl, Vegetable, Oval,
9 In. . . . . .35.00 to 36.00
Cake Plate,
3-Footed . . . . .22.00 to 30.00
Candy Dish, 3 Sections . . .12.50
Candy Dish,
Cover . . . . . . .35.00 to 39.00
Creamer . . . . . .10.00 to 12.00
Cup & Saucer . .11.00 to 14.50
Grill Plate 20.00
Pitcher, 32 Oz.,
5 1/2 In. . . . . .41.00 to 45.00
Pitcher, 48 Oz.,
7 1/2 In. 695.00
Plate, Dinner,
9 In. . . . . .12.00 to 17.50
Plate, Salad,
7 In. 10.00
Plate, Sherbet,
6 In. . . . . .3.50 to 6.50
Platter, Oval,
12 In. . . . . . . .22.00 to 35.00
Salt & Pepper 40.00
Saltshaker 16.00
Sherbet 11.00
Sugar, Cover 13.00
Sugar & Creamer,
Cover . . . . . . .25.00 to 38.00

❖

Moving is a collector's nightmare. Best for wrapping are the rolls of paper used in schools to cover lunch tables. Cut the paper to different sizes before starting to pack. Put paper plates between plates. Wrap saucers in stacks of 10 to 16.

❖

Tray, 8 x 8 In. 36.00
Tray, Handle,
10 In. . . . . . . .12.50 to 17.00
Tumbler, 9 Oz.,
4 1/2 In. 66.00
Tumbler, Footed, 10 Oz.,
4 In. . . . . .60.00 to 69.00

DORIC & PANSY
The snowflake design of Doric alternates with squares holding pansies, so, of course, the pattern is named Doric & Pansy. It, too, was made by Jeannette Glass Company, but only in 1937 and 1938. It was made in Crystal, Pink, and Ultramarine. The Ultramarine varied in color from green to blue. Collectors pay more for the blue shades. A set of child's dishes called Pretty Polly Party Dishes was made in this pattern.

CRYSTAL
Cup & Saucer 13.00
Tray, 2 Handles, 10 In. . . .45.00

PINK
Creamer, Child's 37.00
Saucer, Child's 7.00

ULTRAMARINE
Butter, Cover . .450.00 to 525.00
Creamer, Child's 46.00
Cup, Child's 45.00
Cup & Saucer . .21.00 to 22.00
Cup & Saucer, Child's . . .50.00
Plate, Child's 13.00
Plate, Salad, 7 In. 40.00
Saucer 5.00
Tumbler,
4 1/2 In. . . . . . .85.00 to 90.00

DORIC WITH PANSY, see Doric & Pansy

DOUBLE SHIELD, see Mt. Pleasant

DOUBLE SWIRL, see Swirl

DRAPE & TASSEL, see Princess

DUTCH, see Windmill

DUTCH ROSE, see Rosemary

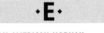

EARLY AMERICAN HOBNAIL, see Hobnail

EARLY AMERICAN ROCK CRYSTAL, see Rock Crystal

EARLY AMERICAN SANDWICH GLASS, see Sandwich Duncan & Miller

ELONGATED HONEYCOMB, see Colony

ENGLISH HOBNAIL

Westmoreland Glass Company, Grapeville, Pennsylvania, made English Hobnail pattern from the 1920s through 1983. It is similar to Miss America except for more rounded hobs and the absence of the typical Hocking sunburst ray on the base. English Hobnail was made in Amber, Cobalt Blue, Crystal, Green, Ice Blue, Opaque White, Pink, Red, and Turquoise. There is much variation in the shading, and a darker amber was made in the 1960s. Red and Pink reproduction pieces were made in the 1980s.

AMBER
Candlestick, 3 1/2 In., Pair	18.00
Candy Dish, Cone	20.00
Cologne Bottle	47.00
Creamer, Footed	24.00
Nappy, 4 1/2 In.	8.00
Plate, Dinner, 10 In.	18.00
Salt & Pepper	75.00
Sherbet, Footed	15.00
Vase, 7 1/4 In.	85.00

COBALT BLUE
Bottle, Toilet, Stopper, 5 Oz.	69.00
Candlestick, 3 1/2 In., Pair	15.00
Goblet, Claret, 5 Oz.	18.00 to 27.00

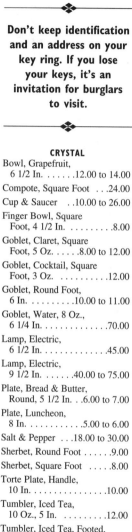

Don't keep identification and an address on your key ring. If you lose your keys, it's an invitation for burglars to visit.

CRYSTAL
Bowl, Grapefruit, 6 1/2 In.	12.00 to 14.00
Compote, Square Foot	24.00
Cup & Saucer	10.00 to 26.00
Finger Bowl, Square Foot, 4 1/2 In.	8.00
Goblet, Claret, Square Foot, 5 Oz.	8.00 to 12.00
Goblet, Cocktail, Square Foot, 3 Oz.	12.00
Goblet, Round Foot, 6 In.	10.00 to 11.00
Goblet, Water, 8 Oz., 6 1/4 In.	70.00
Lamp, Electric, 6 1/2 In.	45.00
Lamp, Electric, 9 1/2 In.	40.00 to 75.00
Plate, Bread & Butter, Round, 5 1/2 In.	6.00 to 7.00
Plate, Luncheon, 8 In.	5.00 to 6.00
Salt & Pepper	18.00 to 30.00
Sherbet, Round Foot	9.00
Sherbet, Square Foot	8.00
Torte Plate, Handle, 10 In.	10.00
Tumbler, Iced Tea, 10 Oz., 5 In.	12.00
Tumbler, Iced Tea, Footed, 12 Oz.	11.00 to 16.00
Tumbler, Juice, 5 Oz., 3 3/4 In.	10.00

GREEN
Ashtray	22.00
Bowl, Hexagonal, Footed, 8 In.	29.00
Candlestick, 3 1/2 In., Pair	28.00
Cup & Saucer	35.00
Goblet, Water, Square Foot, 8 Oz.	25.00
Jam Jar, Cover	35.00
Nappy, 4 1/2 In.	12.00
Plate, Luncheon, Round, 8 In.	11.00
Plate, Sherbet, 6 1/2 In.	4.00
Powder Box, Cover	35.00
Relish, Oval, 8 In.	25.00
Salt & Pepper, Round Foot	75.00 to 85.00
Sherbet, Footed	18.00
Soup, Cream, 4 3/4 In.	20.00
Tumbler, Iced Tea, 12 Oz., 6 In.	18.00
Vase, 7 1/4 In.	55.00

ICE BLUE
Goblet, Water, Square Foot, 8 Oz., 6 1/4 In.	50.00
Plate, Luncheon, Round, 8 In.	25.00
Sherbet, Footed	25.00
Tumbler, Iced Tea, 10 Oz., 4 1/2 In.	50.00

PINK
Basket, 6 In.	80.00
Bowl, 6 In.	23.00
Cup & Saucer	20.00
Finger Bowl, 4 1/2 In.	15.00
Goblet, Champagne, 6 Oz., 6 1/4 In.	18.00 to 26.00
Goblet, Water, 8 Oz.	36.00
Goblet, Wine, 2 Oz.	36.00
Nappy, 4 1/2 In.	9.00 to 15.00
Plate, Luncheon, Round, 8 In.	9.00
Sherbet, Low Footed	18.00
Sugar, Footed	22.00
Sugar & Creamer	25.00
Tumbler, Iced Tea, 12 Oz., 5 In.	13.00
Tumbler, Juice, 5 Oz.	15.00
Vase, 7 1/4 In.	100.00

RED
Basket, 6 In.	125.00

TURQUOISE
Candlestick, 3 1/2 In., Pair	67.00
Goblet, Champagne, 6 Oz., 6 1/4 In.	44.00

Nappy, 4 1/2 In. 18.00

Salt &
  Pepper . . . . .112.00 to 195.00

FAIRFAX

Fairfax was made by Fostoria
Glass Company, Fostoria, Ohio,
from 1927 to 1960. The name
Fairfax refers to a glass blank
and to an etching pattern. The
same glass blanks were used
for other etched designs including June, Trojan, and Versailles. The undecorated blank,
also known as No. 2375, is
popular with collectors. The
same shapes were used to make
other patterns with etched designs. The glass was made in
Amber, Azure (blue), Crystal,
Gold Tint, Green, Orchid, Red,
Rose (pink), and Topaz.

AMBER
Ice Bucket 12.00
Nut Cup,
  Footed . . . . . .14.00 to 15.00
Plate, Mayonnaise 25.00

AZURE
Ashtray 15.00
Bowl, Whipped Cream . . .75.00
Cheese & Cracker 42.00
Goblet, Water, 10 Oz. 25.00
Goblet, Wine 45.00
Ice Bucket 50.00
Nut Cup 25.00
Pitcher, Water, 48 Oz.,
  9 1/2 In. 250.00
Plate, Dinner, 10 In. 58.00
Plate, Luncheon,
  9 1/2 In. 15.00
Saucer 9.00
Shaker, Footed 40.00
Sherbet, Footed 22.00
Sugar Pail 95.00

Tray, Service 150.00

CRYSTAL
Cup & Saucer 7.00
Saucer, After Dinner 5.00

GREEN
Bouillon, Liner 17.50
Bowl, Fruit,
  5 In. . . . . .15.00 to 20.00
Candlestick, 3 In., Pair . . .42.00
Compote, 7 In. 95.00
Compote, Footed,
  5 1/2 In. . . . . . .42.00 to 60.00
Cup 16.00
Cup, After Dinner 10.00
Cup & Saucer 11.50
Cup & Saucer, After
  Dinner 22.00
Finger Bowl . . . .15.00 to 25.00
Gravy Boat 55.00
Pitcher, Water, 48 Oz.,
  9 1/2 In. 175.00
Plate, Dinner,
  10 1/4 In. . . . . .35.00 to 48.00
Plate, Luncheon,
  9 1/2 In. 20.00
Plate, Salad, 7 In. 4.00
Platter, Oval, 10 1/2 In. . .58.00
Platter, Oval,
  12 In. . . . . . . .45.00 to 68.00
Platter, Oval, 15 In. 145.00
Relish, 2 Sections,
  8 1/2 In. 9.00
Relish, 3 Sections,
  11 1/2 In. . . . . .15.00 to 28.00
Salt & Pepper 55.00
Sauceboat, Liner 110.00
Soup, Cream 19.00
Sugar, Cover 33.00

❖

**When the weather is
bad, the auction will
probably be good. Brave
the storm and cold to
attend an auction in
bad weather, when the
crowd will be small and
the prices low.**

❖

Torte Plate 30.00
Vase, Footed,
  7 In. . . . . .46.00 to 75.00

ORCHID
Compote, Footed 48.00
Cup & Saucer 17.00
Cup & Saucer, Footed . . .24.00
Pitcher, Water, 48 Oz.,
  9 1/2 In. 350.00
Plate, Bread & Butter,
  6 In. 7.00
Plate, Luncheon,
  8 1/2 In. 14.00
Plate, Salad, 7 1/2 In. 12.00
Saucer, After Dinner 8.00

ROSE
Bowl, Fruit, 5 In. 12.00
Cheese & Cracker 40.00
Creamer, Footed 18.00
Creamer, Tea 35.00
Cup & Saucer 12.50
Pitcher, Water, 48 Oz.,
  9 1/2 In. 210.00
Plate, 7 In. 5.00
Sugar, Footed 17.00

TOPAZ
Bowl, Fruit,
  5 In. . . . . .7.00 to 15.00
Compote, 7 In. 24.00
Compote, Round, 5 In. . . .65.00
Creamer, Footed 10.00
Cup & Saucer 10.00
Cup & Saucer,
  After Dinner 17.50
Dish, Sweetmeat,
  2 Handles . . . . .11.00 to 18.50
Goblet, Cordial 32.00
Pitcher, Water, 48 Oz.,
  9 1/2 In. . . . .100.00 to 135.00
Plate, Bread & Butter,
  6 In. 2.50
Plate, Dinner, 10 In. 38.00
Plate, Luncheon,
  9 1/2 In. 12.50
Plate, Salad, 7 1/2 In. 5.50
Plate, Salad, 8 3/4 In. 8.00
Relish, 2 Sections 17.00
Salt & Pepper,
  Individual 24.00
Sugar & Creamer 28.00
Whiskey, Footed 25.00

•F•

FAN & FEATHER, see Adam

FINE RIB, see Homespun

FIRE-KING

Fire-King or Fire-King Oven Glass, Fire-King Oven Ware, and Fire-King Dinnerware were all made by Anchor Hocking Glass Corporation, Lancaster, Ohio, from 1941 through 1976. Fire-King Oven Glass is a transparent, pale blue glassware with a lacy decoration. A matching dinnerware set is called Philbe. It was made in Crystal and Pale Blue. Philbe is listed under its own name in this book. Fire-King Oven Ware is an opaque glass made by Anchor Hocking in the 1950s. It was made in Blue, Crystal, Ivory, Jadite, and Pink, or Ivory with gold or colored trim. Some mixing bowls and kitchen sets were made with tulips or red kitchen objects pictured on the sides. Fire-King Dinnerware sets were made in patterns named Alice, Charm, Fleurette, Game Bird, Gray Laurel, Jadite, Jane-Ray, Peach Lustre, Philbe, Primrose, Square, Swirl Fire-King, Turquoise Blue, and Wheat. These are listed in this book in their own sections.

BLUE
Bowl, Cereal,
   5 3/8 In. . . . . . .12.00 to 22.00
Bowl, Measuring,
   16 Oz. 25.00

Bowl, Utility, 8 3/8 In. 16.00
Bowl, Utility, 10 1/8 In. . . .20.00
Casserole, Cover, Individual,
   10 Oz. . . . . . . .9.50 to 12.00
Casserole, Individual,
   10 Oz. . . . . .6.50 to 9.00
Casserole, Knob Cover,
   1 Pt. . . . . .10.00 to 15.00
Casserole, Knob Cover,
   1 Qt. . . . . .11.25 to 15.00
Casserole, Knob Cover,
   2 Qt. 15.00
Custard Cup,
   5 Oz. . . . . .3.00 to 5.00
Custard Cup,
   6 Oz. . . . . .3.00 to 4.50
Hot Plate,
   Tab Handles . . .10.00 to 20.00
Loaf Pan,
   9 x 5 In. . . . . . .18.00 to 22.00
Measuring Cup, 8 Oz. 40.00
Measuring Cup, 16 Oz. . . .25.00
Mug, 7 Oz. 30.00
Nurser, 8 Oz. 30.00
Percolator Top, 2 1/8 In. . . .5.00
Pie Plate, 8 3/8 In. . .6.00 to 9.00
Pie Plate,
   9 5/8 In. . . . . . .8.00 to 11.00
Pie Plate, 9 In. . . . .8.00 to 20.00
Pie Plate, Juice Saver,
   10 3/8 In. 170.00
Roaster,
   8 3/4 In. . . . . . .25.00 to 90.00
Roaster, 10 3/8 In. 45.00
Utility Pan,
   10 1/2 x 2 In. 14.00

CRYSTAL
Baker, Individual, 6 Oz. . . .5.50
Custard Cup, 6 Oz. 2.00
Grease Jar, Cover, Black
   Dot 35.00
Hot Plate, Tab Handles . . .16.00

IVORY
Batter Bowl, Handle,
   1-In. Band 18.00
Bowl, 5 3/8 In. 8.00
Casserole, Knob Cover,
   1 1/2 Qt. . . . . .8.00 to 15.00
Casserole, Knob Cover,
   2 Qt. 15.00
Cup & Saucer, St. Dennis . .7.00
Custard Cup, 6 Oz. 2.50

❖

Glasses decorated with colorful comic or sports figures are often given away as promotions. But be careful— they may fade in sunlight or when washed in the dishwasher.

❖

Grease Jar,
   Tulip . . . . . . .20.00 to 25.00
Hot Plate, Tab Handles . . .18.00
Mixing Bowl, 8 In. 12.00
Mixing Bowl, Blue
   Gazelle, Large 35.00
Mixing Bowl Set, Apple,
   4 Piece 100.00
Mixing Bowl Set, Brown
   Dots, 7, 6 & 4 1/2 In.,
   3 Piece 35.00
Mixing Bowl Set, Red
   Dot, 4 Piece 100.00
Pie Plate, Individual,
   4 3/8 In. 16.00
Refrigerator Jar, Cover,
   4 1/8 x 4 1/8 In. 9.00

JADITE
Batter Bowl . . . .20.00 to 35.00
Mixing Bowl, 8 3/8 In. 9.00
Refrigerator Jar, Crystal
   Cover, 4 x 4 In. 12.00
Skillet 20.00

FLAT DIAMOND, see Diamond Quilted

FLEURETTE

Fleurette is a white Fire-King pattern with decal decoration.
Bowl, Dessert, 4 3/8 In. . . .3.00
Creamer 2.00
Plate, Bread & Butter,
   6 1/4 In. 2.00
Plate, Dinner, 9 1/8 In. 5.00
Plate, Salad, 7 3/8 In. 3.00
Saucer 75
Serva-Snack Set, 2 Piece . .2.50

FLORAGOLD

The iridescent marigold color of carnival glass was copied in this 1950s pattern made by Jeannette Glass Company, Jeannette, Pennsylvania. The pattern is called Floragold or Louisa, the name of the original carnival glass pattern that was copied. Pieces were made in Crystal, Iridescent, Ice Blue, Shell Pink, and Reddish Yellow.

CRYSTAL
Berry Bowl, Square,
  4 1/2 In. . . . . .3.50 to 8.00
Bowl, Cereal, 5 1/2 In. 6.00
Bowl, Deep,
  9 1/2 In. . . . . . .38.00 to 42.50
Bowl, Fruit, Ruffled,
  5 1/2 In. . . . . .7.00 to 8.00
Bowl, Fruit, Ruffled,
  12 In. . . . . .8.00 to 10.00
Bowl, Salad, Ruffled,
  9 1/2 In. . . . . . .8.00 to 10.00
Butter, Cover,
  1/4 Lb. . . . . . . .22.00 to 38.00
Butter, Cover,
  Round . . . . . .40.00 to 42.50
Candlestick, 2-Light,
  Pair 47.50
Candy Dish, Cover,
  5 1/4 In. . . . . . .45.00 to 50.00
Candy Dish, Cover,
  6 3/4 In. 50.00
Coaster, 4 In. . . . .4.75 to 10.00

Creamer . . . . .7.00 to 22.00
Cup . . . . .4.75 to 6.00
Cup & Saucer . .15.00 to 18.00
Pitcher, Water,
  64 Oz. . . . . . . .33.00 to 40.00
Plate, Bread & Butter,
  5 3/4 In. . . . . . .10.00 to 12.00
Plate, Dinner,
  8 1/2 In. . . . . . .22.00 to 40.00
Plate, Sherbet, 5 1/2 In. . .11.00
Platter,
  11 1/4 In. . . . . .22.00 to 28.00
Salt & Pepper, White
  Plastic Cover . .45.00 to 52.00
Saucer . . . . .11.00 to 12.00
Sherbet, Footed . .13.00 to 14.00
Sugar, Cover . . . .17.00 to 22.00
Sugar & Creamer,
  Cover . . . . .23.00 to 25.00
Tray, 13 1/2 In. . .20.00 to 22.00
Tray, With Indentation,
  13 1/2 In. 55.00
Tumbler, Iced Tea, Footed,
  15 Oz. . . . . . .90.00 to 100.00
Tumbler, Water, Footed,
  10 Oz. . . . . . .15.00 to 18.00
Tumbler, Water, Footed,
  11 Oz. 16.00
Water Set, 7 Piece,
  Box 135.00

IRIDESCENT
Bowl, Fruit, Ruffled,
  5 1/2 In. 7.00
Bowl, Ruffled, 9 1/2 In. . .35.00
Bowl, Square, 4 1/2 In. . . .4.00
Butter, Cover,
  1/4 In. . . . . . .16.50 to 22.00
Candlestick, 2-Light,
  Pair . . . . .43.00 to 45.00
Candy Dish, Cover,
  6 3/4 In. 65.00
Candy Dish, Footed,
  5 1/4 In. 8.50
Cup . . . . .5.00 to 8.00
Cup & Saucer 13.00
Platter,
  11 1/4 In. . . . . .19.00 to 22.00
Saucer, 5 1/4 In. 10.00
Sherbet, Footed 15.00
Sugar, Cover 14.00
Tray, 13 1/2 In. . .50.00 to 60.00
Tumbler, Water, Footed,
  10 Oz. 14.00

PINK
Tumbler, Water, Footed,
  10 Oz. 15.00

FLORAL

Poinsettia blossoms are the decorations on Floral patterns made by Jeannette Glass Company from 1931 to 1935. Green is the most common color, although the pattern was also made in Amber, Crystal, Delphite, Green, Jadite, Pink, Red, and Yellow. Reproductions have been made. They are listed at the end of the Depression Glass section.

CRYSTAL
Candy Dish, Cover 22.00
Lemonade Set, 48 Oz.
  Pitcher, 6 Piece 425.00
Sugar, Cover 13.00
Tumbler, Juice, Footed,
  5 In. 19.00

GREEN
Bowl, 7 1/2 In. . .16.00 to 32.50
Bowl, Cover,
  8 In. . . . . .42.00 to 50.00
Bowl, Ruffled,
  4 In. . . . . .18.00 to 25.00
Bowl, Salad, Ruffled,
  7 1/2 In. 20.00
Bowl, Vegetable, Cover,
  8 In. 50.00
Butter, Cover 90.00
Candy Dish,
  Cover . . . . . . .35.00 to 45.00
Candy Jar, Cover 40.00
Coaster, 3 1/4 In. .7.00 to 10.00
Creamer 15.00
Cup . . . . .13.00 to 16.00
Cup & Saucer . .22.00 to 28.00
Ice Tub, 3 1/2 In. 1300.00
Pitcher, Juice, Cone,
  32 Oz., 8 In. . . .33.00 to 39.00

Pitcher, Lemonade,
10 1/4 In. 275.00

Pitcher, Milk, 24 Oz.,
5 1/2 In. 585.00

Plate, Dinner, 9 In. 12.00

Plate, Salad, 8
In. . . . . .10.00 to 15.00

Plate, Sherbet,
6 In. . . . . .7.50 to 9.00

Platter,
10 3/4 In. . . . . .18.00 to 25.00

Relish,
2 Sections . . . .19.00 to 20.00

Salt & Pepper, 6 In. 50.00

Salt & Pepper, Footed,
4 In. 52.00

Saucer . . . . .7.00 to 12.00

Sherbet . . . . .18.00 to 22.00

Sugar, Cover . . . .29.00 to 34.00

Sugar & Creamer,
Cover . . . . .37.00 to 43.00

Tumbler, Juice, Footed,
5 Oz., 4 1/4 In. 21.00

Tumbler, Juice, Footed, 7 Oz.,
4 3/4 In. . . . . .21.00 to 23.00

Tumbler, Water, 9 Oz.,
4 1/2 In. 260.00

Tumbler, Water, Footed, 9 Oz.,
5 1/4 In. . . . . .47.50 to 55.00

Tumbler, Whiskey, Footed,
3 Oz., 3 1/2 In. 400.00

Vase, 8 Sides, 6 7/8 In. . .500.00

PINK

Berry Bowl,
4 In. . . . . .16.00 to 22.50

Bowl, Vegetable, Cover,
8 In. . . . . .43.00 to 60.00

Butter, Cover 95.00

Candy Jar,
Cover . . . . . . .40.00 to 43.00

Coaster 16.50

Creamer . . . . . .10.00 to 20.00

Cup 12.50

Cup & Saucer . .23.00 to 33.00

Pitcher, Juice, Cone, 32 Oz.,
8 In. . . . . .32.50 to 39.00

Plate, Salad,
8 In. . . . . .11.00 to 17.00

Plate, Sherbet,
6 In. . . . . .6.00 to 10.00

Platter, Inner Rim,
9 In. 195.00

Platter, Oval,
10 3/4 In. . . . . .12.00 to 24.00

Relish,
2 Sections . . . .12.00 to 17.00

Salt & Pepper,
4 In. . . . . .45.00 to 50.00

Salt & Pepper,
6 In. . . . . .45.00 to 59.00

Sherbet . . . . . . .15.00 to 20.00

Sugar, Cover . . . .15.00 to 26.00

Sugar & Creamer,
Cover . . . . . . .40.00 to 50.00

Tray, Square, Closed
Handles, 6 In. 75.00

Tumbler, Juice, Footed, 7 Oz.,
4 3/4 In. . . . . .18.00 to 45.00

Tumbler, Water, Footed, 9 Oz.,
5 1/4 In. . . . . .42.00 to 45.00

FLORAL & DIAMOND BAND

Floral & Diamond Band was made by the U.S. Glass Company from the late 1920s until c.1937. It features a large center flower and pressed diamond bands of edging. Luncheon sets were made in varying shades of Pink and Green, but Black, Crystal, and Yellow colors were also used. Some pieces are Iridescent Marigold and are considered carnival glass, called Mayflower by the collectors.

CRYSTAL

Tumbler, Iced Tea, 5 In. . .35.00

GREEN

Berry Bowl,
4 1/2 In. . . . . . . .7.00 to 11.00

Bowl, 8 In. . . . . .13.00 to 17.00

Butter, Cover . .120.00 to 125.00

Creamer, 4 3/4 In. 26.00

Creamer, Small 12.00

Pitcher, Water, 42 Oz.,
8 In. 115.00

Plate, Sherbet, 6 In. 4.00

Sherbet 7.00

Sugar, Small 12.00

Tumbler, Water,
4 In. . . . . .25.00 to 28.00

PINK

Plate, Luncheon, 8 In. 35.00

Sherbet 9.00

FLORAL RIM, see Vitrock

FLORENTINE NO. I

Florentine No. 1, also called Poppy No. 1, is neither Florentine in appearance nor decorated with recognizable poppies. The plates are hexagonal and have scalloped edges, differentiating them from Florentine No. 2 which has round pieces. The pattern was made by the Hazel Atlas Glass Company from 1932 to 1935 in Cobalt Blue, Crystal, Green, Pink, and Yellow. Reproductions have been made. They are listed at the end of the Depression Glass section.

COBALT BLUE

Sugar & Creamer,
Ruffled 125.00

CRYSTAL

Bowl, Cover, Vegetable, Oval,
9 1/2 In. . . . . . .20.00 to 25.00

Creamer . . . . . . .6.50 to 10.00

Cup 6.50

Pitcher, Juice, Footed,
36 Oz., 6 1/2 In. 40.00

Pitcher, Water, 48 Oz.,
7 1/2 In. 70.00

Plate, Dinner,
10 In. . . . . .10.00 to 15.00

Plate, Salad, 8 1/2 In. 7.00

Plate, Sherbet, Footed,
3 Oz. 4.00

Salt & Pepper . . .30.00 to 40.00

Soup, Cream 15.00

Sugar 10.00

Sugar & Creamer 50.00

GREEN

Ashtray,
5 1/2 In. . . . . . .21.00 to 22.00

Berry Bowl,
5 In. . . . . .5.00 to 11.00

Berry Bowl, Master,
8 1/2 In. . . . . . .22.00 to 35.00

Bowl, Cereal, 6 In. 33.00

Bowl, Vegetable, Cover,
Oval, 8 1/2 In. 36.00

Cup . . . . .6.00 to 10.00

Cup & Saucer 12.00

Grill Plate, 10 In. 12.00

Pitcher, 48 Oz., 7 1/2 In. . .63.00

Pitcher, Footed, 36 Oz.,
6 1/2 In. . . . . . .45.00 to 59.00

Plate, Dinner,
10 In. . . . . .16.00 to 18.00

Plate, Salad,
8 1/2 In. . . . . . .6.00 to 12.00

Platter, Oval, 11 1/2 In. . .18.00

Punch Bowl, Base 75.00

Salt & Pepper,
Footed . . . . . . .35.00 to 40.00

Saltshaker, Footed 17.00

Saucer 3.00

Sherbet, Footed, 3 Oz. 9.00

Sugar, Cover 35.00

Sugar & Creamer,
Cover . . . . . . .12.00 to 36.00

Tumbler, Juice, Footed, 5 Oz.,
3 1/4 In. . . . . . .15.00 to 18.00

PINK

Berry Bowl, Master,
8 1/2 In. 36.00

Butter, Cover . .160.00 to 225.00

Grill Plate,
10 In. . . . . .16.00 to 18.00

Nut Cup, Ruffled 20.00

Pitcher, Footed, 36 Oz.,
6 1/2 In. 44.00

Plate, Dinner, 10 In. 27.00

Platter, Oval, 11 1/2 In. . .21.00

Salt & Pepper, Footed 65.00

Sherbet 9.50

Sugar, Cover 42.00

Sugar & Creamer 20.00

Tumbler, Water, Footed,
9 Oz., 5 1/4 In. 25.00

YELLOW

Berry Bowl, Master,
8 1/2 In. 14.00

Bowl, Cereal, 6 In. 35.00

Butter, Cover . .140.00 to 170.00

Creamer 18.00

Gravy Boat,
Underplate 119.00

Grill Plate,
10 In. . . . . .10.00 to 13.00

Pitcher, Juice, Footed, 36 Oz.,
6 1/2 In. . . . . . .40.00 to 45.00

Pitcher, Water, 48 Oz.,
7 1/2 In. 154.00

Pitcher, Water, Footed,
48 Oz., 7 1/2 In. 49.00

Plate, Dinner, 10 In. 13.00

Plate, Salad,
8 1/2 In. . . . . . . .9.00 to 13.00

Platter, Oval, 11 1/2 In. . .28.00

Sherbet 16.00

Sugar, Cover 32.00

Tray, Condiment 95.00

Tumbler, Juice, Footed,
5 Oz., 3 3/4 In. 19.00

Tumbler, Water, Footed,
9 Oz., 5 1/2 In. 35.00

❖

Never put hot glass in cold water, or cold glass in hot water. The temperature change can crack the glass.

❖

FLORENTINE NO. 2

Florentine No. 2, sometimes called Poppy No. 2 or Oriental Poppy, was also made by Hazel Atlas Glass Company from 1934 to 1937. It has round plates instead of the hexagonal pieces of Florentine No. 1, and larger and more prominent flowers. It was made in Amber, Cobalt Blue, Crystal, Green, Ice Blue, and Pink. Reproductions have been made. They are listed at the end of the Depression Glass section.

AMBER

Berry Bowl, 4 1/2 In. 20.00

Berry Bowl, Master,
8 In. . . . . .29.00 to 32.00

Bowl, 5 1/2 In. 52.00

Bowl, Cereal,
6 In. . . . . .36.00 to 49.00

Bowl, Vegetable, Cover,
Oval, 9 In. . . . .70.00 to 78.00

Butter, Cover .129.00 to 160.00

Candlestick, 2 3/4 In. 30.00

Candlestick, 2 3/4 In.,
Pair . . . . .60.00 to 72.00

Coaster,
3 1/4 In. . . . . . .21.00 to 27.50

Coaster, 5 1/2 In. 35.00

Creamer . . . . . . .10.00 to 20.00

Cup 10.00

Cup & Saucer . .12.00 to 15.00

Custard Cup 108.00

Grill Plate,
10 1/4 In. . . . . .13.00 to 16.00

Parfait, 6 In. . . . .60.00 to 66.00

Pitcher, Juice, Cone, 28 Oz.,
7 1/2 In. . . . . . .25.00 to 36.00

Pitcher, Milk, Cone, 24 Oz.,
6 1/4 In. 185.00

Pitcher, Water, 48 Oz.,
7 1/2 In. . . . .150.00 to 206.00

Plate, Dinner,
10 In. . . . . .10.00 to 17.00

Plate, Salad,
8 1/2 In. . . . . . . .7.00 to 10.00

Plate, Sherbet,
6 In. . . . . .3.00 to 8.00

Platter, For Gravy Boat,
12 In. . . . . . . .95.00 to 100.00

Platter, Oval,
11 In. . . . . . . .16.00 to 22.00

Relish, 3 Sections,
10 In. . . . . .28.00 to 30.00

Salt & Pepper . . .48.00 to 55.00

Saucer 5.00

Sherbet, Footed . .10.00 to 13.00

❖

Soup, Cream,
5 In. . . . . .20.00 to 24.00

Sugar 11.00

Sugar, Cover . . . .34.00 to 43.00

Sugar &
Creamer . . . . .20.00 to 21.00

Sugar & Creamer,
Cover 40.00

Tray, Condiment 95.00

Tumbler, Iced Tea, 12 Oz.,
5 In. . . . . .47.00 to 52.00

Tumbler, Juice, 5 Oz.,
3 1/4 In. . . . . . .13.00 to 18.00

Tumbler, Juice, Footed, 5 Oz.,
4 In. . . . . . . .17.00 to 18.00

Tumbler, Water, 9 Oz.,
4 In. . . . . .20.00 to 21.00

Tumbler, Water, Footed, 9 Oz.,
4 1/2 In. . . . . . .30.00 to 38.00

Vase, 6 In. 60.00

CRYSTAL

Berry Bowl,
4 1/2 In. . . . . . .10.00 to 16.00

Bowl, 6 In. 23.00

Candlestick, 2 3/4 In. 25.00

Coaster,
3 1/4 In. . . . . . .12.00 to 13.00

Compote, Ruffled,
3 1/2 In. 20.00

Creamer . . . . .6.00 to 8.00

Cup & Saucer . . .7.00 to 11.00

Nut Cup, Ruffled, 5 In. . . .18.00

Pitcher, Juice, Footed,
28 Oz., 7 1/2 In. 25.00

Pitcher, Milk, Cone,
24 Oz., 6 1/4 In. 30.00

Pitcher, Water, 48 Oz.,
7 1/2 In. . . . . . .50.00 to 55.00

Plate, Dinner, 10 In. 10.00

Plate, Salad, 8 In. . .4.00 to 8.00

Plate, Sherbet,
6 In. . . . . .4.00 to 5.00

Platter, Oval, 11 In. 11.00

Salt & Pepper . . .40.00 to 42.50

Saucer 3.00

Sherbet, Footed 10.00

Soup, Cream . . . . .8.00 to 14.00

Sugar . . . . .7.00 to 8.00

Sugar, Cover 24.00

Tumbler, Iced Tea,
12 Oz., 5 In. 25.00

Tumbler, Water, Footed, 9 Oz.,
4 1/2 In. . . . . . .13.00 to 26.00

Vase, 6 In. 25.00

GREEN

Berry Bowl,
4 1/2 In. . . . . . .13.00 to 15.00

Berry Bowl, Master,
8 In. . . . . .23.00 to 26.00

Bowl, 5 1/2 In. 15.00

Butter, Cover 100.00

Candlestick, Pair 50.00

Candy Dish,
Cover 95.00

Coaster,
3 1/4 In. . . . . . .15.00 to 20.00

Coaster,
5 1/2 In. . . . . . .14.00 to 17.50

Cup . . . . .7.50 to 9.00

Cup & Saucer . .11.00 to 12.00

Grill Plate 12.00

Pitcher, Juice, Cone,
Footed, 28 Oz.,
7 1/2 In. . . . . . .32.00 to 35.00

Plate, Dinner,
10 In. . . . . .15.00 to 17.00

Plate, Salad,
8 1/2 In. . . . . . . .8.50 to 10.00

Plate, Sherbet, 6 In. 4.00

Platter, Oval, 11 In. 16.00

Salt & Pepper,
Footed . . . . . .40.00 to 55.00

Saucer . . . . .3.00 to 5.00

Sherbet, Footed . . .9.00 to 10.00

Soup, Cream,
4 3/4 In. . . . . . .14.00 to 16.00

Sugar & Creamer 18.00

Tumbler, Iced Tea,
12 Oz., 5 In. 45.00

Tumbler, Juice, Footed, 5 Oz.,
3 1/4 In. . . . . . .14.00 to 16.00

Tumbler, Juice, Footed,
6 Oz., 3 1/2 In. 50.00

Tumbler, Water, 9 Oz.,
4 In. . . . . .12.00 to 15.00

Tumbler, Water, Footed, 9 Oz.,
4 1/2 In. . . . . . .26.00 to 32.00

PINK

Berry Bowl, 4 1/2 In. 17.00

Candy Dish,
Cover . . . . . .110.00 to 152.00

Compote, Ruffled,
3 1/2 In. 25.00

Tumbler, Water, Footed, 9 Oz.,
4 1/2 In. . . . . . .13.00 to 26.00

Vase, 6 In. 25.00

Having trouble with a stain in a glass bottle or vase? Fill the bottle with water, drop in an Alka-Seltzer, and let it soak for about 24 hours. Then rub the ring with a brush or a cloth. If the deposit is chemical, this treatment should remove it. If the ring is actually caused by etching of the glass, it cannot be removed unless the bottle is polished.

❖

Nut Cup, Ruffled,
  5 In. . . . . .18.00 to 22.00
Pitcher, Water, 48 Oz.,
  7 1/2 In. 140.00
Tumbler, Juice, Footed, 5 Oz.,
  3 1/4 In. . . . . . .14.00 to 20.00
Tumbler, Water, 9 Oz.,
  4 In. 19.00

FLOWER & LEAF BAND, see
  Indiana Custard

FLOWER BASKET, see No. 615

FLOWER GARDEN WITH BUTTERFLIES

There really is a butterfly hiding in the flower on this U.S. Glass Company pattern called Flower Garden with Butterflies, Butterflies and Roses, Flower Garden, or Wildrose with Apple Blossom. It was made in the late 1920s in a variety of colors, including Amber, Black, Blue, Canary Yellow, Crystal, Green, and Pink.

BLUE
Powder Jar, Cover,
  6 1/4 In. 220.00

CANARY YELLOW
Plate, Salad, Sterling
  Trim, 8 In. 30.00

CRYSTAL
Powder Jar, 7 1/2 In. 80.00

GREEN
Compote 25.00
Plate, Dinner, 10 In. 46.00

PINK
Bottle, Cologne,
  No Stopper 100.00
Powder Jar, Cover, Footed,
  7 1/2 In. 155.00

FLOWER RIM, see Vitrock

FOREST GREEN

There is no need to picture Forest Green in a black-and-white drawing because it is the color that identifies the pattern. Anchor Hocking Glass Corporation, Lancaster, Ohio, made this very plain pattern from 1950 to 1957. Other patterns were also made in this same deep green color, but these are known by the pattern name.

Batter Bowl,
  Spout . . . . .18.00 to 25.00
Bowl, 7 3/8 In. . .13.00 to 20.00
Bowl, Deep,
  5 1/4 In. . . . . . . .8.00 to 9.00
Bowl, Popcorn 9.00
Bowl, Popcorn, 7 Piece . . .75.00
Bowl, Square,
  4 5/8 In. . . . . . . .4.50 to 5.50
Bowl, Vegetable, Square,
  7 3/8 In. . . . . . .15.00 to 22.00
Creamer 6.00
Cup 5.00
Cup, For Snack Plate 9.00
Cup & Saucer,
  Square . . . . .6.00 to 7.00
Mixing Bowl,
  6 In. . . . . .6.00 to 17.00
Pitcher, Milk, 22 Oz.,
  5 3/4 In. . . . . .22.00 to 22.50
Pitcher, Water, Round,
  86 Oz. 45.00
Plate, Bread & Butter, Square,
  6 5/8 In. . . . . . . .6.50 to 7.00
Plate, Dinner, Square,
  9 1/2 In. 12.00
Plate, Luncheon, Square,
  8 3/8 In. 8.00
Platter, Rectangular,
  11 In. . . . . . . .20.00 to 24.00

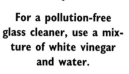

For a pollution-free glass cleaner, use a mixture of white vinegar and water.

Punch Bowl Set,
  14 Piece . . . . .74.00 to 95.00
Punch Cup . . . . . .1.50 to 2.50
Saucer 1.50
Soup, Dish, Square,
  6 In. 16.00
Sugar 6.00
Sugar & Creamer 10.00
Tumbler, Iced Tea,
  13 Oz. 6.00
Tumbler, Iced Tea, 15 Oz.,
  6 1/2 In. . . . . . .6.00 to 10.00
Tumbler, Juice, 5 Oz.,
  3 1/2 In. . . . . . . .3.00 to 4.00
Tumbler, Long Boy,
  15 Oz. 6.00
Tumbler, Water, 9 Oz.,
  4 3/4 In. 4.00
Tumbler, Water, 11 Oz. . . .4.00
Vase, 6 3/8 In. . . . .3.50 to 9.00
Vase, 9 In. 8.00

FORTUNE

Anchor Hocking Glass Corporation made Fortune pattern in 1937 and 1938. The simple design was made in Crystal or Pink.

CRYSTAL
Candy Dish, Cover 22.00

PINK
Berry Bowl, 4 In. . .4.00 to 6.00
Bowl, Handle, 4 1/2 In. . . .4.00
Candy Dish, Cover 25.00

Tumbler, Juice, 5 Oz.,
3 1/2 In. 11.00
Tumbler, Water, 9 Oz.,
4 In. . . . . .10.00 to 14.00

FOSTORIA, see American

FRUITS

Pears, grapes, apples, and other
fruits are displayed in small
bunches on the pieces of Fruits
pattern. Hazel Atlas Glass
Company and several other
companies made this pattern
about 1931 to 1933. Pieces are
known in Crystal, Green, Pink,
and Iridiscent finish.

CRYSTAL
Berry Bowl, 5 In. 12.50
Cup 7.50
Cup & Saucer 13.50
Plate, Luncheon, 8 In. 7.00
Saucer 4.50

GREEN
Cup 8.00
Cup & Saucer . .10.00 to 13.50
Pitcher, Water, 7 In. 70.00
Plate, Luncheon, 8 In. 6.50
Saucer 5.00
Tumbler, Water, Cherry,
4 In. 25.00

**Spray the inside
of a glass flower vase
with a nonstick cooking
spray. This will keep
the vase from staining
if water is left in it
too long.**

GAME BIRD

Game Bird, sometimes called
Wild Bird, was made by
Anchor Hocking Glass Corporation from about 1959 to
1962. The opaque white glass
was decorated with a decal of a
bird.

CANADA GOOSE
Mug, 8 Oz. . . . . .5.50 to 10.00
Tumbler 12.50

MALLARD DUCK
Mug, 8 Oz. . . . . .5.50 to 10.00
Tumbler 12.50

RING-NECKED PHEASANT
Tumbler 12.50

RUFFLED GROUSE
Mug, 8 Oz. . . . . .5.50 to 10.00
Mug Set, 4 Piece 25.00
Tumbler 12.50

GEORGIAN

Georgian, also known as
Lovebirds, was made by the
Federal Glass Company, Columbus, Ohio, from 1931 to
1936. The pattern shows alter-
nating sections with birds in
one and a basket of flowers in
the next, or may have no lovebirds. Dinner sets were made
mostly in Crystal, although
Green pieces were also manufactured. Notice that it is mold-
etched and in no way resembles
the Fenton glass pattern called
Georgian, listed in this book as
Georgian Fenton. Reproduc-

tions have been made. They are
listed at the end of the Depression Glass section.

CRYSTAL
Berry Bowl, Master,
7 1/2 In. 60.00
Bowl, Cereal, 5 3/4 In. . . .22.50
Bowl, Vegetable, Oval,
9 In. 60.00
Butter, Cover 70.00
Platter, Closed Handles,
11 1/2 In. 65.00
Sherbet, Footed 12.00
Sugar & Creamer, Footed,
4 In. 25.00

GREEN
Berry Bowl,
4 1/2 In. . . . . . . .5.00 to 10.00
Bowl, Cereal,
5 3/4 In. . . . . . .16.00 to 26.00
Bowl, Deep,
6 1/2 In. . . . . . .60.00 to 75.00
Bowl, Oval, Salad,
9 In. . . . . .60.00 to 75.00
Butter, Cover . . .70.00 to 85.00
Coaster, Hot Plate, 5 In. . .30.00
Creamer, Footed,
3 In. . . . . .4.00 to 11.00
Creamer, Footed, 4 In. . . .15.00
Cup 10.00
Cup & Saucer . .12.00 to 14.00
Plate, Dinner, 9 1/4 In. . . .32.00
Plate, Luncheon,
8 In. . . . . .8.00 to 11.00
Plate, Sherbet,
6 In. . . . . .5.00 to 8.00
Platter, Closed Handles,
11 1/2 In. . . . . .49.00 to 75.00
Saucer 3.00
Sherbet . . . . . . .9.00 to 15.00
Sugar, Cover, Footed,
3 In. . . . . .35.00 to 53.00

Sugar, Footed,
4 In. . . . . .10.00 to 22.00
Sugar & Creamer, Cover,
Footed, 4 In. . . .25.00 to 63.00
Tumbler, Iced Tea,
12 Oz. . . . . .135.00 to 165.00
Tumbler, Juice, 4 In. 57.00
Tumbler, Water, 9 Oz.,
4 In. . . . . .55.00 to 70.00

GLADIOLA, see Royal Lace

GLORIA

Gloria is an etched glass pattern made by Cambridge Glass Company about 1930. It is similar to the Tiffin pattern called Flanders. Gloria was made in Amber, Crystal, Emerald Green, Green, Heatherbloom (pink-purple), Pink, and Yellow. Full dinner sets were made as well as serving pieces, vases, and candlesticks.

CRYSTAL
Bowl, Salad, Tab Handle,
9 In. 25.00
Cup, Square, Footed 25.00
Plate, Bread & Butter,
6 In. 5.00

Dental wax (ask your dentist about it) is a good adhesive to keep figurines on shelves or lids on teapots.

GREEN
Bowl, Salad, Square,
6 In. 12.00
Plate, Dinner,
9 1/2 In. . . . . . .70.00 to 75.00
YELLOW
Bowl, 2 Handles, 10 In. . .70.00
Bowl, Gold Trim, 13 In. . .75.00
Plate, Dinner, 9 1/2 In. . . .75.00
Plate, Salad, 7 1/2 In. 20.00
Platter, 11 1/2 In. 120.00

GRAPE, see also Woolworth

GRAY LAUREL

Gray Laurel is a Fire-King dinnerware made by Anchor Hocking Glass Corporation in 1953. The pattern has a laurel leaf design around the edge of the plates and bowls and the side of the cups. The pieces are Gray. The same pattern of laurel leaves was made in a lustrous orange-yellow color from 1952 to 1963 and was known as Peach Lustre. Bubble and Boopie pattern crystal stemware was made with a similar design to go with the dinnerware.

Bowl, Dessert, 4 7/8 In. . . .3.00
Creamer, Footed 4.00
Cup 3.00

Custard Cup, 6 Oz. 3.00
Plate, Dinner, 9 1/8 In. 5.00
Saucer 2.00
Sugar, Footed 4.00
Sugar & Creamer, Footed . .4.00

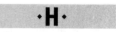

HAIRPIN, see Newport
HANGING BASKET, see No. 615

HARP

The pattern name Harp describes the small lyre-shaped instruments that are included on the borders of these pieces of glass. This Jeannette Glass Company pattern was made from 1954 to 1957. Pieces are found in Crystal, Crystal with gold trim, Light Blue, and Pink.

CRYSTAL
Cake Stand,
9 In. . . . . .18.00 to 25.00
Cake Stand, Gold Trim,
9 In. 15.00
Coaster, Gold
Trim . . . . .3.00 to 4.00
Cup 25.00
Cup & Saucer 35.00
Cup & Saucer,
Gold Trim . . . .18.00 to 35.00
Plate, Bread & Butter,
7 In. 10.50
Plate, Bread & Butter, Gold
Trim, 7 In. . . . .10.00 to 14.00
Tray, Rectangular 30.00
Vase, 6 In. . . . . . .18.00 to 30.00
Vase, Gold Trim,
6 In. . . . . .17.00 to 18.00
PINK
Cake Stand, 9 In. 35.00
Cake Stand, Gold Trim,
9 In. 22.00

HERITAGE

Federal Glass Company, Columbus, Ohio, made Heritage in the 1930s through the 1960s. Evidently the serving pieces were made in Blue, Light Green, and Pink, but the plates and dinnerware pieces were made only in Crystal. Amber and Crystal reproduction bowls were made in 1987.

CRYSTAL
Berry Bowl, 5 In. . .5.00 to 8.00
Berry Bowl, Master,
   8 1/2 In. . . . . . .35.00 to 40.00
Bowl,
   10 1/2 In. . . . . .10.00 to 17.00
Cup . . . . .4.00 to 8.00
Cup & Saucer . . .7.00 to 13.00
Plate, Dinner, 9 1/4 In. . . .12.00
Plate, Luncheon,
   8 In. . . . . .8.00 to 9.00
Sandwich Server,
   12 In. 13.00
Saucer 3.00
Sugar . . . . .20.00 to 22.50
Sugar & Creamer,
   Cover 33.00

HEX OPTIC, see Hexagon Optic

HEXAGON OPTIC

Hexagon Optic, also called Honeycomb or Hex Optic, really does have an accurate, descriptive name. Pink or Green sets of kitchenware were made in this pattern by Jeannette Glass Company, Jeannette, Pennsylvania, from 1928 to 1932. In the years near 1960 some Iridescent sets and some Ultramarine (blue-green) pieces were made.

GREEN
Cup 4.00
Cup & Saucer 6.00
Pitcher, Water, Footed,
   48 Oz., 9 In. 44.00
Plate, Breakfast,
   8 In. . . . . .5.00 to 6.00
Tumbler, Water, 9 Oz.,
   3 3/4 In. 2.00

PINK
Tumbler, Iced Tea, Footed,
   7 In. 5.50

HEXAGON TRIPLE BAND, see Colony

HINGE, see Patrician

HOBNAIL

Hobnail is the name of this pattern, although many similar patterns have been made with the hobbed decorations. Hocking Glass Company, Lancaster, Ohio, made this pattern from 1934 to 1936, and it can be distinguished from other hobbed patterns by a honeycomb design with long sides and pointed ends. Mostly Crystal or Pink beverage sets were made. Some pieces were made with red rims or black feet.

CRYSTAL
Bowl, Cereal,
   5 1/2 In. . . . . .4.00 to 7.00
Cup 4.00

Pitcher, Water, 67 Oz. . . .22.00
Plate, Luncheon, 8 In. 4.00
Plate, Sherbet, 6 In. 2.50
Salt & Pepper 55.00
Sherbet 3.00
Tumbler, Juice, 5 Oz. 4.00
Tumbler, Water, 9 Oz. 5.50
Tumbler, Wine, Footed,
   3 Oz. 8.00
Tumbler, Wine, Red
   Trim, 3 Oz. 5.00
Whiskey,
   1 1/2 Oz. . . . . . .3.50 to 6.00

PINK
Basket 85.00
Cup 8.00
Goblet, Cocktail,
   3 Oz. 45.00
Goblet, Water, 9 Oz. 45.00
Plate, Luncheon,
   8 1/2 In. 30.00
Plate, Sherbet, 6 In. 3.50
Saucer 2.50
Sherbet 7.00
Tumbler, Water,
   10 Oz. 40.00

HOBNAIL, see also Moonstone

HOLIDAY

Holiday is one of the later Depression glass patterns. It was made from 1947 through 1949 by Jeannette Glass Company. The pattern is found in dinnerware sets of Crystal, Iridescent, and Shell Pink (opaque). A few pieces of Opaque Shell Pink were made. The pattern is sometimes also called Buttons & Bows or Russian.

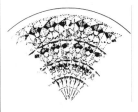

CRYSTAL
Berry Bowl, 5 1/8 In. 12.00
Bowl, Vegetable, Oval,
  9 1/2 In. 28.00
Butter 38.00
Creamer 8.00
Cup 7.00
Pitcher, Milk, 16 Oz.,
  4 3/4 In. 65.00
Plate, Dinner, 9 In. 16.00
Plate, Sherbet, 6 In. 5.00
Platter, Oval, 11 3/8 In. . .22.00
Saucer 4.00
Sherbet 6.00
Soup, Dish, 7 3/4 In. 60.00
Sugar, Cover 25.00
Tumbler, Juice, Footed,
  4 In. 50.00
Tumbler, Water, 10 Oz.,
  4 In. 20.00

IRIDESCENT
Berry Bowl, 5 1/8 In. 9.00
Platter, Oval, 11 3/8 In. . . .9.00
Tumbler, Juice, Footed,
  4 In. 8.00

PINK
Berry Bowl,
  5 1/8 In. . . . . . .5.00 to 14.00
Bowl, Vegetable, Oval,
  9 1/2 In. . . . . . .25.00 to 27.50
Butter, Cover . . .38.00 to 40.00
Cake Plate, Footed,
  10 1/2 In. . . .100.00 to 125.00
Candlestick,
  3 In. . . . . .42.00 to 55.00
Candlestick, 3 In.,
  Pair . . . . . . .110.00 to 115.00
Creamer, Footed . .6.00 to 12.50
Cup . . . . .4.00 to 12.00
Cup & Saucer . .12.00 to 13.00
Pitcher, Milk, 16 Oz.,
  4 3/4 In. . . . . .48.00 to 65.00
Pitcher, Water, 52 Oz.,
  6 3/4 In. . . . . .35.00 to 38.00
Plate, Bread & Butter,
  6 In. 6.00

Plate, Dinner,
  9 In. . . . . .12.00 to 22.00
Plate, Sherbet,
  6 In. . . . . .5.00 to 6.50
Platter, Oval,
  11 3/8 In. . . . .16.00 to 22.50
Sandwich Tray,
  10 1/2 In. 25.00
Saucer . . . . .4.00 to 5.00
Saucer, Ring 4.50
Sherbet . . . . .6.00 to 7.00
Soup, Dish,
  7 3/4 In. . . . . .40.00 to 59.00
Sugar &
  Creamer . . . . .18.00 to 19.00
Sugar & Creamer,
  Cover . . . . . . .33.00 to 35.00
Tumbler, Iced Tea, Footed,
  6 In. . . . . . .150.00 to 195.00
Tumbler, Juice, Footed,
  4 In. . . . . .40.00 to 55.00
Tumbler, Water, 10 Oz.,
  4 In. . . . . .20.00 to 25.00

HOMESPUN
Homespun, often called Fine Rib, is a cause of confusion. Jeannette Glass Company made Crystal, Light Blue, and Pink pieces in this pattern in 1939 and 1940. Hazel Atlas Glass Company made other pieces in Crystal and Cobalt Blue. Homespun made by Jeannette Glass Company is listed here.

BLUE
Pitcher, Juice, 96 Oz. 65.00
Tumbler, Iced Tea, Footed,
  13 Oz., 5 1/4 In. 27.00
Tumbler, Juice, Footed,
  5 Oz., 4 In. . . . .12.00 to 14.50

PINK
Berry Bowl, Master,
  8 1/4 In. 80.00
Bowl, Closed Handles,
  4 1/2 In. . . . . . .10.00 to 12.00
Butter 15.00
Cup . . . . .10.00 to 12.00
Cup & Saucer . .14.00 to 18.00
Plate, Dinner,
  9 1/4 In. . . . . . .15.00 to 17.00
Plate, Sherbet,
  6 In. . . . . .6.00 to 7.00
Platter, Closed Handles,
  Oval, 13 In. 25.00
Saucer 5.50
Sherbet 16.00
Sugar 12.00
Sugar & Creamer 32.00
Tumbler, Iced Tea, Footed,
  15 Oz., 6 1/2 In. 30.00
Tumbler, Juice, Footed,
  5 Oz., 4 In. . . . . .6.00 to 11.00
Tumbler, Water, 9 Oz.,
  4 In. 20.00
Tumbler, Water, Footed,
  9 Oz., 6 1/4 In. 30.00

HONEYCOMB, see Hexagon Optic

HORIZONTAL ROUNDED BIG RIB, see Manhattan

HORIZONTAL FINE RIB, see Manhattan

HORIZONTAL RIBBED, see Manhattan

HORIZONTAL SHARP BIG RIB, see Manhattan

HORSESHOE, see No. 612

❖

Don't turn on the porch light if you will be gone for a long time. It tells everyone that you are away. Install a photo-electric cell light that automatically turns on at dusk and off at daylight, or install a gaslight.

INDIANA CUSTARD

The design makes the old name Flower & Leaf Band clear, but collectors prefer to call this pattern Indiana Custard. It is an opaque glassware of Custard color and Ivory made by the Indiana Glass Company. Primarily luncheon sets were made from the 1930s to the 1950s. Some pieces have bands that are decorated with pastel colors or decal designs. The same pattern was made of Milk Glass in 1957. It was called Orange Blossom.

IVORY
Berry Bowl,
  5 1/2 In. . . . . . .10.00 to 14.00
Berry Bowl, Master,
  9 In. 32.00
Bowl, Vegetable, Oval,
  9 1/2 In. . . . . . .32.50 to 35.00
Butter, Cover . . .45.00 to 72.00
Creamer 6.00
Cup & Saucer 7.00
Plate, Dinner, 9 3/4 In. . . .28.00
Platter, Oval, 11 1/2 In. . .36.00

Don't put glass with an iridescent finish in the dishwasher. The hot water and soap will remove the finish.

Saucer . . . . .8.00 to 12.00
Sugar 15.00
Sugar, Cover . . . .25.00 to 34.00

IRIS

The design of Iris is unusually bold for Depression glass. Molded representations of stalks of iris fill the center of a ribbed plate. Other pieces in the pattern show fewer irises, but the flower is predominant. Edges of pieces may be ruffled or beaded. It was made by Jeannette Glass Company, Jeannette, Pennsylvania, from 1928 to 1932 and then again in the 1950s and 1970s. Early pieces were made in Crystal, Green, Iridescent, and Pink; later pieces were made in Blue-Green, Green, Red-Yellow, or White. The pattern is also called Iris & Herringbone. Reproduction candy vases have been made in a variety of colors since 1977.

CRYSTAL
Berry Bowl, Beaded Edge,
  4 1/2 In. . . . . . .38.00 to 42.00
Berry Bowl, Beaded Edge,
  Master, 8 In. . .80.00 to 125.00
Bowl, Cereal,
  5 In. . . . . . . .115.00 to 125.00

Bowl, Fruit, Ruffled,
  11 In. . . . . . . .20.00 to 58.00
Bowl, Fruit, Straight Edge,
  11 In. . . . . . . .57.50 to 60.00
Bowl, Salad, Ruffled,
  9 1/2 In. 13.00
Butter, Cover . . .47.50 to 55.00
Candlestick,
  Pair . . . . .38.00 to 40.00
Candy Jar,
  Cover . . . . .145.00 to 165.00
Coaster . . . . . .110.00 to 112.00
Creamer 12.00
Cup . . . . .15.00 to 18.00
Cup, After
  Dinner . . . . . .28.00 to 50.00
Cup & Saucer . .25.00 to 30.00
Cup & Saucer, After
  Dinner 225.00
Goblet, Cocktail, 3 Oz.,
  4 1/4 In. . . . . .14.00 to 24.50
Goblet, Cocktail, 4 Oz.,
  5 3/4 In. . . . . .22.00 to 25.00
Goblet, Water, 8 Oz.,
  5 3/4 In. . . . . .23.00 to 29.50
Goblet, Wine,
  4 In. . . . . .15.00 to 16.00
Nut Set 98.00
Pitcher, Water, Footed,
  9 1/2 In. . . . . .35.00 to 40.00
Plate, Dinner,
  9 In. . . . . .50.00 to 58.00
Plate, Luncheon,
  8 In. 125.00
Plate, Sherbet,
  5 1/2 In. . . . . .14.00 to 15.00
Sandwich Server,
  11 3/4 In. . . . .25.00 to 32.00
Sauce Bowl, Ruffled,
  5 In. . . . . .6.00 to 9.00
Saucer . . . . . . .12.00 to 18.00
Saucer, After Dinner 160.00
Sherbet, Footed,
  2 1/2 In. . . . . .25.00 to 32.00
Sherbet, Footed,
  4 In. . . . . .21.00 to 23.00
Soup, Dish,
  7 1/2 In. . . . .155.00 to 175.00
Sugar &
  Creamer . . . . .25.00 to 35.00
Sugar & Creamer,
  Cover . . . . . . .35.00 to 45.00

Tumbler, 4 In. 130.00

Tumbler, 4 Oz.,
5 1/2 In. 25.00

Tumbler, Iced Tea, Footed,
6 In. . . . . .16.00 to 32.00

Vase, 9 In. . . . .28.00 to 32.50

IRIDESCENT

Berry Bowl, Beaded Edge,
4 1/2 In. . . . . . .9.00 to 12.00

Berry Bowl, Master,
Beaded Edge, 8 In. 22.50

Bowl, Fruit, Ruffled,
11 In. . . . . .11.00 to 24.00

Bowl, Salad, Ruffled,
9 1/2 In. . . . . . .13.00 to 18.00

Butter, Cover . . .40.00 to 42.00

Candlestick 20.00

Candlestick, Pair 42.50

Creamer, Footed . .8.00 to 13.00

Cup 14.00

Cup & Saucer . .20.00 to 25.00

Goblet, Wine,
4 In. . . . . .22.00 to 35.00

Pitcher, Water, Footed,
9 1/2 In. . . . . . .36.00 to 40.00

Plate, Dinner,
9 In. . . . . .33.00 to 42.00

Plate, Sherbet,
5 1/2 In. . . . . . .7.50 to 13.00

Plate, Sherbet, Footed,
4 In. . . . . .13.00 to 15.00

Sandwich Server,
11 3/4 In. . . . . .27.00 to 30.00

Sauce Bowl, Ruffled,
5 In. . . . . .21.00 to 25.00

Sauce Bowl Set, Ruffled,
6 Piece 115.00

Sherbet, Footed,
2 1/2 In. . . . . . .11.00 to 14.00

Soup, Dish,
7 1/2 In. . . . . .58.00 to 60.00

Sugar, Cover 20.00

Sugar & Creamer,
Cover 35.00

Tumbler, Iced Tea, Footed,
6 In. . . . . .14.00 to 22.00

Vase, Footed,
9 In. . . . . .20.00 to 27.00

IRIS & HERRINGBONE, see Iris

IVEX, see Chinex Classic;
Cremax

JADITE

Jadite is a color as well as a pattern. Kitchenware was made in Jadite from 1936 to 1938 by Jeannette Glass Company. A matching set of dinnerware in the same green glass was called Jane-Ray. These pieces are listed in their own section. All of the pieces of kitchenware made of Jadite were also made of a blue glass called Delphite, but it is incorrect to call any but the green dishes by the name Jadite. For more information about related patterns and colors, see Alice, Charm, Fire-King, Gray Laurel, Jane-Ray, Peach Lustre, Philbe, Swirl Fire-King, Turquoise Blue, and Wheat in this book.

Ashtray 20.00

Batter Bowl, Handle,
7 1/2 In. 24.00

Batter Jug, Cover 395.00

Berry Bowl, 4 3/4 In. 4.00

Bowl, Cereal, 5 7/8 In. . . .16.00

Bowl, Dessert, 4 3/4 In. . . .6.00

Bowl, Leaf, Handle 8.00

Bowl, Rolled Lip, Deep,
15 Oz. 9.00

Canister, Coffee, Square,
5 1/2 In. 55.00

Canister, Spice, No Cover,
2 x 3 In. 25.00

Cup 5.00

Cup & Saucer . . . .3.00 to 6.00

Cup & Saucer, After
Dinner 88.00

Eggcup 18.00

Jar, Grease, Round 32.00

Jug, Ball, Tilt 175.00

Leftover, Cover,
8 1/2 x 4 1/2 In. 32.00

Leftover, Embossed Cover,
5 x 9 In. 40.00

Leftover, No Cover,
4 1/2 x 5 1/2 In. 16.00

Measuring Cup,
1/3 Cup Size 32.00

Measuring Cup,
1/4 Cup Size 40.00

Mug, Chocolate,
Flared Top 5.00

Mug, Coffee,
7 Oz. . . . . .5.00 to 8.00

Plate, Bread & Butter,
5 1/2 In. 4.25

Plate, Dinner,
9 In. . . . . .6.00 to 11.00

Plate, Salad,
6 3/4 In. . . . . . . .4.00 to 5.00

Plate, Salad, 6 In. . .4.50 to 9.00

Platter, 12 In. 15.00

Reamer, Lemon 35.00

Salt & Pepper 45.00

Salt & Pepper, Square 27.00

Saucer 4.00

Saucer, After Dinner 40.00

Shaving Mug 8.00

Soup, Dish, Flanged,
9 In. 50.00

Tom & Jerry Set,
11 Piece 295.00

Water Dispenser,
Refrigerator 325.00

JAMESTOWN

Jamestown was made by the Fostoria Glass Company from 1958 to 1982. It was made in Amber, Amethyst, Blue, Crystal, Green, Pink, and Red.

AMBER

Bowl, Dessert, 6 In. 15.00

Goblet, 10 Oz. . . . .8.00 to 12.00

Nappy, 6 In. 8.00

Pitcher, Water, 48 Oz.,
7 In. . . . . .50.00 to 90.00

Plate, Luncheon, 7 In. 5.00

Tumbler, Iced Tea,
12 Oz. . . . . . . .10.00 to 15.00

Tumbler, Juice, 5 Oz. 9.00

AMETHYST

Creamer 22.00

Goblet, 10 Oz.,
5 7/8 In. . . . . . .15.00 to 18.00

Tumbler, Iced Tea,
12 Oz., 6 In. 18.00

BLUE

Creamer 27.00

Goblet, 10 Oz.,
5 7/8 In. . . . . . .15.00 to 24.00

Sherbet 18.00

Tumbler, Ice Tea,
12 Oz., 6 In. 22.00

Tumbler, Juice, 5 Oz.,
4 In. 15.00

CRYSTAL

Plate, Salad, 8 In. 15.00

Platter, 14 In. 31.00

GREEN

Goblet, Water, 10 Oz.,
5 7/8 In. 9.50

Sherbet 12.00

Tumbler, Juice, 5 Oz.,
4 In. 20.00

PINK

Plate, Luncheon, 7 In. 24.00

Sherbet 22.00

RED

Goblet, Water, 10 Oz.,
5 7/8 In. 20.00

Sherbet 16.00

Tumbler, Iced Tea,
12 Oz., 6 In. 27.00

JANE-RAY

Jane-Ray is a plain dinnerware with ribbed edge made of Jadite from 1945 to 1963 by Anchor Hocking Glass Corporation, Lancaster, Ohio. The matching kitchenware sets of the same green glass are called Jadite. Other related sections in this book are Alice, Charm, Fire-King, Gray Laurel, Jadite, Peach Lustre, Philbe, Swirl Fire-King, Turquoise Blue, and Wheat.

JADITE

Bowl, Cereal,
5 7/8 In. . . . . . .8.00 to 12.00

Bowl, Dessert,
4 7/8 In. . . . . . . .5.00 to 6.00

Creamer . . . . .5.00 to 6.00

Cup 3.00

Cup & Saucer . . . .3.00 to 6.00

Plate, Dinner,
9 1/8 In. . . . . . .5.00 to 11.00

Plate, Salad,
7 3/4 In. . . . . . . .5.00 to 9.00

Platter . . . . .9.00 to 22.00

Saucer . . . . .1.50 to 4.00

Soup, Dish,
7 5/8 In. . . . . . .8.00 to 17.00

Sugar & Creamer, Cover .14.00

JUBILEE

In the early 1930s the Lancaster Glass Company, Lancaster, Ohio, made this luncheon set decorated with etched flowers. It was made in a yellow shade, called Topaz, and in Pink. Collectors will find many similar patterns. The original Lancaster Jubilee had twelve petals and an open center on each flower.

PINK

Bowl, Fruit, 9 In. 50.00

Candlestick, Pair 50.00

TOPAZ

Bowl, 3-Footed, Curved,
11 1/2 In. 185.00

Creamer 20.00

Cup 14.00

Cup & Saucer . .20.00 to 25.00

Goblet, Water, 10 Oz.,
6 In. . . . . .33.00 to 42.00

Mayonnaise, 16 Petals . .140.00

Pitcher, Water 100.00

Plate, Luncheon,
8 3/4 In. . . . . . .12.00 to 17.00

Plate, Salad,
7 In. . . . . .10.00 to 14.00

Saucer . . . . .5.00 to 6.00

Sugar 20.00

Sugar &
Creamer . . . . .35.00 to 40.00

Tray, 2 Handles,
11 In. . . . . .40.00 to 85.00

Tray, Center Handle,
11 In. 225.00

JUNE

June is one of very few patterns that can be dated with some accuracy from the color. Fostoria Glass Company, Fostoria, Ohio, made full dinnerware sets but changed the color. From 1928 to 1944 the glass was Azure, Green, or Rose. Crystal was made from 1928 to 1952. If your set is Topaz, it dates from 1929 to 1938. Gold-tinted glass was made from 1938 to 1944. Pieces made of color with Crystal stems or bases were made only from 1931 to 1944. Reproductions have been made in Azure (blue), Crystal, Rose (pink), and Topaz (yellow). A liner is a plate that goes under a bowl or gravy boat.

AZURE

Ashtray 75.00
Bouillon, Footed 75.00
Bowl, 5 In. 55.00
Candy, 3 Sections 185.00
Compote 145.00
Cup & Saucer 42.50
Finger Bowl 95.00
Finger Bowl Liner, 6 In. . .25.00
Goblet, Champagne, 6 Oz.,
  6 In. . . . . .50.00 to 55.00
Goblet, Water, 8 1/4 In. . .80.00
Ice Bucket 225.00
Nut Dish 95.00
Plate, Lemon 45.00
Plate, Luncheon,
  8 1/4 In. 24.00
Plate, Salad, 7 1/2 In. 18.50
Salt &
  Pepper . . . . .175.00 to 250.00
Sherbet, High 50.00
Sherbet, Low, 6 Oz.,
  4 1/4 In. 37.50
Tumbler, Iced Tea, Footed,
  6 In. 72.50

CRYSTAL

Berry Bowl, 5 In. 20.00
Compote, 4 In. 45.00
Cup & Saucer . .20.00 to 45.00
Finger Bowl, Liner,
  6 In. 35.00
Grapefruit, Liner 125.00
Ice Bucket, Tongs 85.00
Pitcher 495.00
Plate, Salad, 7 1/2 In. 7.00
Platter, 12 In. 75.00
Sherbet, Low, 6 Oz.,
  4 1/4 In. 20.00
Tumbler, Water, Footed,
  5 1/4 In. 20.00

ROSE

Baker, Oval, 9 1/2 In. . . .175.00
Bowl, 5 In. . . . . .50.00 to 60.00
Goblet, Champagne 47.50
Goblet, Wine, 3 Oz. 95.00
Plate, Bread & Butter,
  6 In. 12.00
Relish, Divided 65.00
Salt & Pepper, Footed,
  Glass Cover 245.00

Sauceboat 275.00
Sherbet, High, 6 Oz.,
  6 In. 48.00
Sherbet, Low, 6 Oz.,
  4 1/4 In. 25.00
Torte Plate, 14 In. 95.00
Tumbler, Iced Tea, Footed,
  6 In. 70.00
Tumbler, Water, Footed,
  5 1/4 In. 52.50

TOPAZ

Ashtray 55.00
Berry Bowl, 5 In. 35.00
Candlestick, 3 In. 37.50
Compote, 6 In. . . . . :.85.00
Creamer, Footed 30.00
Cup, After Dinner 30.00
Cup & Saucer . .35.00 to 40.00
Finger Bowl 42.50
Finger Bowl Liner 12.00
Goblet, Champagne, 6 Oz.,
  6 In. 32.50
Goblet, Claret, 4 Oz.,
  6 In. 125.00
Goblet, Cordial, 3/4 Oz.,
  4 In. 150.00
Ice Dish Liner . .20.00 to 32.50
Mayonnaise, Footed,
  Liner . . . . . .100.00 to 120.00
Parfait 65.00
Pitcher 495.00
Plate, Dinner, 9 1/2 In. . . .45.00
Plate, Dinner, 10 1/4 In. . .32.50
Plate, Luncheon, 8 3/4 In. .18.50
Plate, Salad, 7 1/2 In. 15.00
Salt & Pepper 155.00
Saucer 8.00
Sherbet, High, 6 Oz.,
  6 In. 28.00
Sugar, Cover 225.00
Sugar & Creamer,
  Individual 150.00
Tray, Center Handle 75.00
Tumbler, Iced Tea,
  Footed, 6 In. . .47.50 to 50.00
Tumbler, Water, Footed, 9 Oz.,
  5 1/4 In. . . . . . .22.00 to 32.00
Whipped Cream Bowl . . .45.00
Whiskey, Footed 75.00

KNIFE & FORK, see Colonial

·L·

LACE EDGE

To add to the confusion in the marketplace, this pattern, which is most often called Lace Edge, has been called Loop, Old Colony, Open Lace, or Open Scallop. The pieces themselves are often confused with other similar patterns, such as Imperial's Laced Edge, and cups or tumblers may also be mixed up with Queen Mary or Coronation. The Hocking pattern, made by Hocking Glass Company in Lancaster, Ohio, from 1935 to 1938, can usually be identified by the familiar sunburst base common to many of that company's designs. Most of the pieces of Lace Edge were made in Pink, although Crystal is also found.

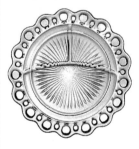

CRYSTAL

Bowl, 9 1/2 In. 27.00
Bowl, Fruit, 8 1/4 In. 40.00
Bowl, Vegetable,
  2 Sections 135.00
Butter, Cover 72.00
Candlestick, Pair 550.00
Creamer 50.00
Cup & Saucer 60.00
Grill Plate 22.00
Mayonnaise, 2 Piece 140.00
Plate, Bread & Butter,
  6 1/2 In. 25.00
Plate, Dinner,
  10 1/2 In. . . . .32.00 to 100.00

Plate, Salad, 8 1/4 In. 40.00
Platter, 12 In. 170.00
Relish, 3 Sections 28.00
Soup, Dish 100.00
Sugar 50.00
Tumbler, Water,
4 1/2 In. 70.00

PINK
Bowl, 9 1/2 In. . .22.00 to 25.00
Bowl, Cereal,
6 3/8 In. . . . . . .22.00 to 24.00
Bowl, Footed,
10 1/2 In. 100.00
Bowl, Ribbed, 9 1/2 In. . .29.00
Bowl, Salad,
7 3/4 In. . . . . . .22.00 to 24.00
Butter, Cover 65.00
Compote, Cover, Footed,
7 In. 47.50
Compote, Footed, 7 In. . . .25.00
Cookie Jar . . . . .65.00 to 72.00
Creamer 33.00
Cup . . . . .24.00 to 30.00
Cup & Saucer 37.00
Grill Plate, 10 1/2 In. 24.00
Plate, Dinner,
10 1/2 In. . . . . .20.00 to 35.00
Plate, Luncheon,
8 1/4 In. 20.00
Platter, 12 3/4 In. 26.00
Platter, 5 Sections,
12 3/4 In. . . . . .32.00 to 35.00
Relish, 3 Sections,
7 1/2 In. 65.00
Relish, 3 Sections,
10 1/2 In. . . . . .22.00 to 28.00
Saucer 10.00
Sherbet . . . . . .97.50 to 125.00
Tumbler, Juice, 5 Oz.,
3 1/2 In. 90.00
Tumbler, Water,
4 1/2 In. . . . . . .22.00 to 23.00

LACY DAISY, see No. 618

❖

**Store glasses right
side up to protect
the rims. Do not
stack glasses.**

❖

LAKE COMO

At first glance, Lake Como
looks more like a piece of
ceramic than a piece of glass . It
is Opaque White with blue
decal decorations picturing a
lake and part of an ancient ruin.
It was made by Hocking Glass
Company from 1934 to 1937.

Salt & Pepper . . .35.00 to 40.00

LAUREL

Opaque glass was used by
McKee Glass Company, Jeannette, Pennsylvania, to make
Laurel dinnerware in the 1930s.
The pattern, with a raised band
of flowers and leaves as the
only decoration, is sometimes
called Raspberry Band. A few
pieces have decals of a dog in
the center, and that group is
called Scottie Dog. The dinnerware was made in French
Ivory, Jade Green, Powder
Blue, or White Opal. A child's
set was made with a colored
rim.

FRENCH IVORY
Berry Bowl, 4 3/4 In. 6.00
Bowl, Cereal, 6 In. 9.50
Candlestick, Single 25.00
Grill Plate, 9 In. . .9.00 to 12.50
Plate, Dinner,
9 In. . . . . .9.00 to 14.00
Plate, Salad, 7 In. . .7.00 to 9.00
Plate, Sherbet,
6 In. . . . . .5.00 to 7.00

Platter, Oval, 11 In. 25.00
Sherbet 11.00

JADE GREEN
Berry Bowl, Master,
9 In. 18.00
Bowl, Cereal, 3-Footed,
6 In. 15.00
Bowl, Cereal, 6 In. 7.00
Bowl, Vegetable, Oval,
9 3/4 In. 16.00
Cheese Dish, Cover 42.00
Grill Plate, 9 In. 10.00
Plate, Dinner, 9 In. 10.00
Plate, Salad, 7 In. 7.00
Platter, Oval, 11 In. 19.00
Soup, Dish 40.00
Tumbler, Water, 9 Oz.,
4 1/2 In. 50.00

WHITE OPAL
Bowl, Vegetable, Oval,
9 3/4 In. 14.00
Cup 4.00
Salt & Pepper 55.00
Saucer 3.00

LILY MEDALLION, see American
Sweetheart

LINCOLN DRAPE, see Princess

LINCOLN INN

Lincoln Inn was made by the
Fenton Glass Company, Williamstown, West Virginia,
from 1928 until c.1936. The
ridged dinnerware sets were
made of Amber, Amethyst,
Black, Cobalt Blue, Crystal,
Green, Jadite (opaque green),
Light Blue, Pink, and Red. A
recent copy of the Lincoln Inn
pitcher was made by Fenton
Glass Company in Iridescent
carnival glass.

COBALT BLUE
Goblet, Champagne 25.00
Goblet, Water 35.00

CRYSTAL
Sherbet 10.00
Tumbler, Iced Tea, 12 Oz. 75.00

JADITE
Plate, Dinner, 12 In. 50.00

LINE 300, see Peacock & Wild Rose

LITTLE HOSTESS, see Moderntone Little Hostess Party Set

LOOP, see Lace Edge

LORAIN, see No. 615

LOUISA, see Floragold

LOVEBIRDS, see Georgian

LYDIA RAY, see New Century

MADRID

Madrid has probably had more publicity than any other Depression glass pattern. It was originally made by the Federal Glass Company, Columbus, Ohio, from 1932 to 1939, using the molds developed for Sylvan. It was made first in Green, then in Amber; Madonna Blue and Pink pieces were made for a limited time. In 1976 Federal Glass reworked the molds and made full sets of amber glass called Recollection. These can be identified by a small "76" worked into the pattern. In

1982 Crystal pieces of Recollection were made. In more recent years Blue, Pink, and Crystal pieces have been reproduced by the Indiana Glass Company. It is sometimes called Paneled Aster, Primus, and Winged Medallion.

AMBER
Berry Bowl, Master,
    9 3/4 In. 18.00
Bowl, Salad, 9 1/2 In. 30.00
Bowl, Vegetable, Oval,
    10 In. 18.00
Butter 29.00
Butter, Cover . . .62.00 to 70.00
Cake Plate,
    11 1/4 In. . . . . .13.00 to 24.00
Candlestick, 2 1/4 In.,
    Pair 22.00
Console, 11 In. 15.00
Cookie Jar . . . .35.00 to 50.00
Creamer . . . . .6.00 to 9.00
Cup . . . . .3.00 to 5.00
Cup & Saucer . .10.00 to 12.00
Mold, Jell-O . . . .13.00 to 14.00
Pitcher, 8 1/2 In. 65.00
Pitcher, Juice,
    5 1/2 In. . . . . .50.00 to 55.00
Plate, Luncheon,
    8 7/8 In. . . . . . .6.00 to 9.50
Plate, Salad, 7 1/2 In. 12.00

Plate, Sherbet,
    6 In. . . . . .4.00 to 5.50
Platter, Oval,
    11 1/2 In. . . . . .15.00 to 22.00
Relish, 2 Sections,
    10 1/4 In. 15.00
Salt & Pepper,
    Flat . . . . .45.00 to 48.00
Salt & Pepper, Footed . . .105.00
Sauce Bowl, 5 In. . .4.50 to 9.00
Sherbet . . . . .5.25 to 9.00
Soup, Cream, 4 3/4 In. . . .15.00
Soup, Dish,
    7 In. . . . . .11.00 to 16.00
Sugar, Cover . . . .45.00 to 49.50
Sugar &
    Creamer . . . . .15.00 to 16.00
Trivet 35.00
Tumbler, 5 Oz.,
    3 7/8 In. 14.00
Tumbler, 9 Oz.,
    4 1/4 In. . . . . . .11.00 to 19.50
Tumbler, 12 Oz.,
    5 1/2 In. . . . . . .14.00 to 22.50
Tumbler, Footed, 5 Oz.,
    4 In. 14.00
Tumbler, Footed, 10 Oz.,
    5 1/2 In. . . . . . .20.00 to 33.50
Tumbler, Juice, 5 Oz.,
    3 7/8 In. 55.00

CRYSTAL
Creamer 8.50
Cup 3.00
Grill Plate, 10 1/2 In. 9.00

GREEN
Bowl, Salad, 8 In. 17.00
Bowl, Vegetable, Oval,
    10 In. 17.00
Creamer 11.00
Cup 10.00
Cup & Saucer 13.00
Plate, Dinner, 10 1/2 In. . .35.00
Plate, Luncheon, 8 7/8 In. . .8.50
Plate, Sherbet, 6 In. 4.00
Platter, Oval,
    11 1/2 In. . . . . .16.00 to 18.00
Salt & Pepper 70.00
Sauce Bowl, 5 In. 6.00
Sherbet . . . . . . .5.00 to 13.00
Sugar 7.50
Sugar & Creamer 12.50

Tumbler, 9 Oz.,
4 1/4 In. 30.00

MADONNA BLUE
Plate, Dinner, 10 1/2 In. . .75.00
Salt & Pepper, Footed . . .160.00

MAGNOLIA, see Dogwood

MANHATTAN

Manhattan is another modern-looking pattern with a design made of molded circles. It was made by Anchor Hocking Glass Corporation from 1938 to 1941, primarily in Crystal. A few Green, Iridescent, Pink, and Red pieces also are known. The pattern has been called many names, such as Horizontal Fine Rib, Horizontal Ribbed, Horizontal Rounded Big Rib, Horizontal Sharp Big Rib, and Ribbed.

CRYSTAL
Ashtray, Round, 4 In. 11.00
Ashtray, Square,
4 1/2 In. 25.00
Berry Bowl, Handles,
5 3/8 In. 18.00
Bowl, Fruit, Footed, Handle,
9 1/2 In. . . . . . .35.00 to 40.00
Candlestick, Double 32.00
Candlestick,
Pair . . . . .12.00 to 15.00
Coaster, 3 1/2 In. 15.00
Compote,
5 3/4 In. . . . . . .15.00 to 30.00
Cookie Jar, Cover 35.00
Creamer 10.00
Cup . . . . .19.00 to 20.00

August is the peak month for residential burglaries. April has the fewest home break-ins. Most home burglaries occur in the daytime. The average break-in lasts 17 minutes.

Cup & Saucer 24.50
Goblet, Wine,
4 In. . . . . .2.50 to 5.00
Pitcher, Juice,
24 Oz. . . . . . .25.00 to 35.00
Plate, Dinner,
10 1/4 In. . . . . .17.00 to 20.00
Plate, Salad, 8 1/2 In. 15.00
Plate, Sherbet,
6 In. . . . . .4.00 to 7.00
Relish, 5 Sections,
14 In. 20.00
Relish, Ruby
Inserts . . . . . .50.00 to 65.00
Relish Insert 3.50
Salt & Pepper . . .18.00 to 33.00
Sandwich Tray,
14 In. . . . . . . .18.00 to 20.00
Sauce Bowl, Handles,
4 1/2 In. . . . . . . .6.00 to 9.00
Sherbet, Footed 9.00
Soup, Cream, 4 1/2 In. . . .34.00
Sugar . . . . .9.00 to 10.00
Sugar & Creamer 20.00
Tumbler . . . . . .15.00 to 18.00
Vase, 8 In. . . . . . .13.00 to 20.00

PINK
Berry Bowl, Handles,
5 3/8 In. 18.00
Bowl, Fruit, Footed,
Handle, 9 1/2 In. 37.00
Candy Dish, Footed 12.00
Compote 38.00
Salt & Pepper . . .50.00 to 55.00
Sherbet 15.00
Sugar . . . . .10.00 to 11.00
Sugar &
Creamer . . . . .18.50 to 25.00

Tumbler, Footed,
10 Oz. . . . . . . .19.00 to 22.00

RUBY
Relish Tray Insert 6.00

MANY WINDOWS, see Roulette

MARTHA WASHINGTON

The Cambridge Glass Company of Cambridge, Ohio, started manufacturing Martha Washington pattern in 1932. The glass was made in Amber, Crystal, Forest Green, Gold Krystol, Heatherbloom, Royal Blue, and Ruby.

CRYSTAL
Berry Bowl 16.00
Bowl, 9 In. 65.00
Goblet, Water, 10 Oz. 28.00
Plate, Dinner, 12 In. 40.00
Plate, Salad, 8 3/8 In. 18.00

MAYFAIR, see Rosemary

MAYFAIR FEDERAL

The Mayfair patterns can easily be recognized, but if you are buying by mail, the names are sometimes confusing. Mayfair Federal is the pattern sometimes called Rosemary Arches. It was made in Amber, Crystal, or Green by Federal Glass Company in 1934, but was discontinued because of a patent conflict with Hocking's Mayfair pattern, referred to as Mayfair Open Rose.

AMBER
Bowl, Vegetable, Oval,
10 In. 30.00

Platter, Oval, 12 In. 27.50

Saucer, 5 In. 6.50

Soup, Cream 15.00

GREEN
Creamer 14.00

Plate, Dinner, 10 In. 9.00

Platter 38.00

Tumbler, 9 Oz.,
4 1/2 In. 26.00

MAYFAIR OPEN ROSE

Mayfair Open Rose was made by Hocking Glass Company from 1931 to 1937. It was made primarily in Light Blue and Pink, with a few Green and Yellow pieces. Crystal examples are rare. The cookie jar and the whiskey glass have been reproduced since 1982.

BLUE
Bowl, 11 3/4 In. 75.00

Bowl, Fruit, Deep,
12 In. 95.00

Bowl, Oval, Divided,
11 1/4 In. 65.00

Bowl, Vegetable, 7 In. . . .50.00

Bowl, Vegetable,
10 In. . . . . .65.00 to 75.00

Bowl, Vegetable, Cover,
10 In. 100.00

Bowl, Vegetable, Oval,
9 1/2 In. 70.00

Cake Plate, Footed,
10 In. 79.00

Cake Plate, Handles,
12 In. . . . . . . .66.00 to 70.00

Candy Dish, Cover 286.00

Celery Dish, Divided,
9 In. . . . . .55.00 to 65.00

Celery Dish, Divided,
10 In. 75.00

Creamer . . . . . .75.00 to 80.00

Cup & Saucer . .75.00 to 82.00

Grill Plate, 9 1/2 In. 56.00

Pitcher, 6 In. 185.00

Plate, 5 3/4 In. 25.00

Plate, Dinner,
9 1/2 In. . . . . . .50.00 to 75.00

Plate, Luncheon,
8 1/2 In. 55.00

Plate, Sherbet,
Off-Center Indent,
6 1/2 In. . . . . . .26.00 to 30.00

Platter, Oval,
12 In. . . . . .60.00 to 75.00

Sandwich Server, Center
Handle . . . . . .75.00 to 85.00

Sherbet,
4 3/4 In. . . . . .70.00 to 110.00

Sugar 80.00

Vase, Sweet
Pea . . . . .110.00 to 135.00

CRYSTAL
Pitcher, 37 Oz., 6 In. 14.00

Platter, Handles, 5 Sections,
Oval, 12 In. . . .11.00 to 20.00

GREEN
Bowl, 11 3/4 In. .33.00 to 40.00

Bowl, Fruit, Deep,
12 In. . . . . .40.00 to 45.00

Sandwich Server, Center
Handle . . . . . .30.00 to 45.00

PINK
Bowl, 11 3/4 In. 55.00

Bowl, Cereal,
5 1/2 In. . . . . . .20.00 to 27.00

Bowl, Fruit, Deep,
12 In. 61.00

Bowl, Vegetable, 7 In. . . .28.00

Bowl, Vegetable, Handles,
10 In. . . . . . . .18.00 to 31.00

Bowl, Vegetable, Oval,
9 1/2 In. . . . . . .25.00 to 40.00

Butter, Cover . . .65.00 to 70.00

Cake Plate, Footed,
10 In. . . . . . . .28.00 to 35.00

Candy Dish, Footed,
Cover . . . . . . .50.00 to 53.00

Celery Dish, Divided,
10 In. 210.00

Cookie Jar, Cover 50.00

Creamer . . . . . .27.00 to 32.00

Cup . . . . .15.00 to 19.50

Cup & Saucer 30.00

Decanter,
Stopper . . . . .165.00 to 175.00

Goblet, Cocktail, 4 In. . .115.00

Goblet, Water, 9 Oz.,
5 3/4 In. 70.00

Grill Plate,
9 1/2 In. . . . . . .28.00 to 40.00

Pitcher, 37 Oz., 6 In. 50.00

Pitcher, 60 Oz.,
8 In. . . . . .50.00 to 60.00

Pitcher, 80 Oz.,
8 1/2 In. . . . . .95.00 to 130.00

Plate, 5 3/4 In. . . .11.00 to 12.00

Plate, Dinner,
9 1/2 In. . . . . . .50.00 to 65.00

Plate, Luncheon,
8 1/2 In. . . . . . .26.00 to 31.00

Plate, Sherbet,
6 1/2 In. . . . . . .10.00 to 14.00

Platter, Handle, Oval,
12 In. . . . . .24.00 to 26.00

Relish, 4 Sections,
8 3/4 In. . . . . . .25.00 to 27.00

Salt & Pepper, Flat 65.00

Sandwich Server, Center
Handle . . . . . .42.00 to 50.00

Saucer . . . . . . .32.00 to 34.00

Sherbet, Footed,
3 In. . . . . .15.00 to 17.00

Sherbet, Footed,
4 3/4 In. 34.00

Soup, Cream, 5 In. 42.50

Sugar 30.00

Sugar &
Creamer . . . .50.00 to 62.00

Tumbler, Footed, 10 Oz.,
5 1/4 In. 36.00

Tumbler, Footed,
Iced Tea, 15 Oz.,
6 1/2 In. . . . . . .39.00 to 42.00

Tumbler, Iced Tea,
13 1/2 Oz., 5 1/4 In. 38.00

Tumbler, Juice, Footed,
5 Oz., 3 1/2 In. 125.00

Tumbler, Water, 9 Oz.,
4 1/4 In. . . . . . .24.00 to 34.00
Vase, Sweet Pea 135.00

MEADOW FLOWER, see No. 618

MEANDERING VINE, see Madrid

MISS AMERICA

Miss America, or Diamond
Pattern, was made by Hocking
Glass Company from 1933 to
1936 in many colors, including
Crystal, Green, Ice Blue, Jadite,
Pink, Red, and Ritz Blue. It is
similar to English Hobnail but
can be distinguished by the typical Hocking sunburst base and
hobs that are more pointed than
those of the Westmoreland pattern. In 1977 some reproduction butter dishes were made of
Amberina, Crystal, Green, Ice
Blue, Pink, or Red. Saltshakers,
pitchers, and tumblers are also
being reproduced.

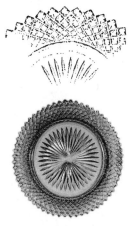

CRYSTAL
Berry Bowl, 4 1/2 In. 12.00
Bowl, Cereal,
6 1/4 In. . . . . . .6.00 to 18.00
Bowl, Curved In, 8 In. . . .20.00
Candy Jar, Cover,
11 1/2 In. . . . . .55.00 to 60.00
Celery Dish, 10 1/2 In. . . .17.00
Coaster, 5 3/4 In. 15.00

Compote, 5 In. . .10.00 to 14.00
Creamer 5.00
Cup & Saucer . .10.00 to 15.50
Goblet, Water, 5 1/2 In. . .17.00
Goblet, Wine, 3 3/4 In. . . .24.00
Grill Plate, 10 1/4 In. 11.00
Pitcher, 65 Oz.,
8 In. . . . . .35.00 to 42.00
Plate, Dinner,
10 1/4 In. . . . . .11.00 to 18.00
Plate, Sherbet 3.00
Platter, Oval, 12 1/4 In. . .14.00
Relish, 4 Sections,
8 3/4 In. . . . . . .9.75 to 12.00
Relish, 5 Sections,
11 3/4 In. . . . . .17.00 to 25.00
Salt & Pepper 30.00
Saucer 4.00
Sherbet . . . . .6.00 to 8.00
Sugar &
Creamer . . . . .16.00 to 18.00

GREEN
Berry Bowl, 4 1/2 In. 10.00
Bowl, Cereal, 6 In. 22.00
Plate, 6 3/4 In. 10.00
Salt &
Pepper . . . . .275.00 to 320.00

PINK
Bowl, Cereal,
6 1/4 In. . . . . . .22.00 to 25.00
Bowl, Curved In, 8 In. . . .97.50
Bowl, Vegetable, Oval,
10 In. . . . . . . .25.00 to 35.00
Candy Jar, Cover,
11 1/2 In. . . .140.00 to 170.00
Celery Dish,
10 1/2 In. . . . . .25.00 to 35.00
Coaster,
5 3/4 In. . . . . . .32.00 to 34.00
Compote, 5 In. . .19.00 to 37.50
Creamer . . . . . . .18.00 to 22.00
Cup . . . . .20.00 to 26.00
Cup & Saucer . .27.00 to 35.00
Goblet, Water,
5 1/2 In. . . . . . .42.00 to 54.00
Goblet, Wine,
3 3/4 In. . . . . . .73.00 to 85.00
Grill Plate,
10 1/4 In. . . . . .24.00 to 28.00
Pitcher, 8 In. 149.00

Plate, Dinner,
10 1/4 In. . . . . .27.50 to 35.00
Plate, Salad,
8 1/2 In. 25.00
Plate, Sherbet,
5 3/4 In. . . . . . .10.00 to 17.00
Platter, Oval,
12 1/4 In. . . . . .26.00 to 46.00
Relish, 4 Sections,
8 3/4 In. . . . . . .20.00 to 30.00
Salt & Pepper . . .55.00 to 70.00
Saucer . . . . .5.00 to 8.00
Sherbet . . . . . . .12.00 to 16.50
Sugar 18.50
Sugar &
Creamer . . . .32.00 to 39.00
Tumbler, Iced Tea,
5 3/4 In. 65.00
Tumbler, Juice, 4 In. 50.00
Tumbler, Water,
4 1/2 In. . . . . . .30.00 to 38.00

RED
Sherbet 220.00

MISS AMERICA, see also English
Hobnail

MODERNE ART, see Tea Room

MODERNTONE

Moderntone, or Wedding
Band, was made by Hazel Atlas
Glass Company from 1935 to
1942. The simple pattern is
popular today with Art Deco
enthusiasts. It was made of
Amethyst, Cobalt Blue, Crystal, and Pink glass. It was also
made of an opaque, almost
white glass called Platonite,
which is listed here under
Moderntone Platonite.

AMETHYST

Berry Bowl, 5 In. 25.00

Berry Bowl, Master,
  8 3/4 In. 50.00

Cup . . . . .9.00 to 12.00

Cup & Saucer 15.00

Plate, Dinner, 8 7/8 In. . . .15.00

Plate, Luncheon,
  7 3/4 In. . . . . . . .7.00 to 14.00

Plate, Sherbet,
  5 7/8 In. . . . . . . .3.00 to 6.00

Platter, Oval,
  12 In. . . . . . . .47.00 to 60.00

Saucer 5.00

Sherbet 12.50

Soup, Cream . . . .15.00 to 24.50

Sugar . . . . .6.00 to 14.00

Sugar &
  Creamer . . . . .16.00 to 22.00

Tumbler, Water, 9 Oz. . . .30.00

COBALT BLUE

Berry Bowl,
  5 In. . . . . .21.00 to 27.00

Berry Bowl, Master,
  8 3/4 In. . . . . . .35.00 to 75.00

Butter, Cover . .100.00 to 115.00

Cheese Dish, Cover 400.00

Creamer . . . . . . .10.00 to 12.00

Cup . . . . .6.25 to 11.00

Cup & Saucer . .15.00 to 18.00

Custard Cup . . . .15.00 to 22.00

Plate, Dinner,
  8 7/8 In. . . . . . .13.00 to 22.50

Plate, Luncheon,
  7 3/4 In. . . . . . . .9.50 to 14.00

Plate, Salad,
  6 3/4 In. . . . . . .10.00 to 13.00

Plate, Sherbet,
  5 7/8 In. . . . . . . .5.00 to 6.50

Platter, Oval,
  11 In. . . . . . . .39.00 to 65.00

Platter, Oval, 12 In. 80.00

Salt & Pepper . . .30.00 to 48.00

Sandwich Tray,
  10 1/2 In. . . . . .54.00 to 60.00

Check the metal strips holding any heavy wall-hung shelves. After a few years, the shelf holder may develop "creep" and gradually bend away from the wall.

Saucer . . . . .2.00 to 8.00

Sherbet . . . . . . .10.00 to 20.00

Soup, Cream,
  4 3/4 In. . . . . . .17.50 to 24.00

Soup, Cream,
  Ruffled, 5 In. 60.00

Sugar . . . . .8.75 to 10.00

Sugar &
  Creamer . . . . .18.00 to 25.00

Tumbler, Juice, 5 Oz. . . .50.00

Tumbler, Water,
  9 Oz. . . . . . . .36.00 to 45.00

Whiskey . . . . . .40.00 to 50.00

CRYSTAL

Creamer . . . . .4.00 to 7.00

Plate, Salad, 6 3/4 In. 5.00

Soup, Dish, 7 1/2 In. 8.00

PINK

Whiskey 10.00

MODERNTONE LITTLE HOSTESS PARTY SET

The Moderntone Little Hostess Party Set was also made by Hazel Atlas Glass Company in the late 1940s. This was a child's set of dishes made in Platonite with fired-on colors. We have seen Beige, Blue, Chartreuse, Gray, Green, Maroon, Orange (rust), Pink, Turquoise, Yellow, and pastels, but other colors were probably made.

BEIGE

Cup & Saucer 20.00

Plate 10.00

BLUE

Plate . . . . .9.00 to 10.00

Saucer 7.00

GRAY

Cup . . . . .10.00 to 13.00

Cup & Saucer . .19.00 to 20.00

Plate . . . . .7.00 to 10.00

GREEN

Cup 9.00

Cup & Saucer . .16.00 to 19.00

Plate . . . . .8.00 to 12.00

Saucer . . . . .2.75 to 8.00

Sugar 14.00

MAROON

Cup . . . . .13.00 to 14.00

Plate . . . . .11.00 to 12.50

Teapot 125.00

ORANGE

Creamer 12.50

Cup . . . . .12.00 to 13.00

Cup & Saucer 23.00

Plate . . . . .8.50 to 10.00

Saucer 8.00

Sugar . . . . .10.50 to 16.00

Sugar &
  Creamer . . . . .24.00 to 25.00

PASTELS

Tea Set,
  14 Piece . . . . .93.00 to 100.00

Tea Set, 16 Piece 245.00

PINK

Creamer . . . . . . .12.00 to 15.00

Cup . . . . .9.00 to 10.00

Plate . . . . .6.00 to 10.00

Saucer 7.00

Sugar 15.00

TURQUOISE

Cup 7.00

Cup & Saucer . .16.00 to 23.00

Plate . . . . .6.25 to 12.50

Saucer 7.00

Teapot,
  Cover . . . . . .120.00 to 130.00

YELLOW

Cup 3.85

Cup & Saucer . .16.00 to 22.00

Plate . . . . .8.50 to 10.00

Saucer . . . . .7.00 to 8.00

MODERNTONE PLATONITE

Moderntone Platonite was made by Hazel Atlas Glass Company from 1940 to the early 1950s. Platonite, an almost white glass, was covered with a variety of bright fired-on colors, including Black, Light or Dark Blue, Light or Dark Green, Red, Orange, Yellow, and White trimmed with a small colored rim. Clear glass pieces are listed in this book under Moderntone.

GREEN
Berry Bowl, 5 In. 3.00
Bowl, 8 In. 14.00
Bowl, Cereal, 6 1/2 In. 9.00
Cup . . . . .2.00 to 4.00
Plate, Dinner, 8 7/8 In. 3.00
Plate, Salad, 6 3/4 In. 2.00
Plate, Sherbet, 6 3/4 In. . . .4.75
Sandwich Tray,
    10 1/2 In. 7.00
Saucer . . . . .50 to 1.00
Sherbet . . . . .3.50 to 5.50
Sugar . . . . .3.00 to 5.00
Tumbler, Juice 3.00
Tumbler, Water,
    9 Oz. . . . . .9.00 to 11.00

LIGHT BLUE
Berry Bowl, No Rim,
    5 In. 7.50
Berry Bowl, Rim, 5 In. . . .25.00
Cup & Saucer . .15.00 to 16.50
Plate, Dinner,
    8 7/8 In. . . . . . . .5.50 to 17.50
Plate, Sherbet,
    6 3/4 In. . . . . . .5.00 to 12.50
Saltshaker 8.50
Saucer 15.00

Sherbet 2.50
Soup, Cream 10.00

ORANGE
Saucer 5.00

TURQUOISE
Soup, Cream 10.00

WHITE
Cup 2.00
Cup & Saucer,
    Blue Ring 7.00
Cup & Saucer,
    Green Ring 7.00
Cup & Saucer,
    Yellow Ring 7.00
Salt & Pepper, Pair 20.00
Sherbet 2.00

YELLOW
Berry Bowl, No Rim,
    5 In. 6.00
Bowl, Cereal, 6 1/2 In. 9.00
Creamer . . . . .3.00 to 5.00
Cup 2.00
Cup & Saucer 19.00
Gravy Boat, Underplate . .70.00
Plate, Dinner, 8 7/8 In. 5.50
Plate, Sherbet, 6 3/4 In. . . .2.00
Platter, 12 In. 6.00
Saucer . . . . .50 to 2.00
Sherbet . . . . .4.50 to 5.50
Soup, Cream, 5 In. 9.00

MOONDROPS

The New Martinsville Glass Manufacturing Company, New Martinsville, West Virginia, made Moondrops from 1932 to the late 1940s. Collectors like the pieces with the fan-shaped knobs or stoppers. The pattern was made in Amber, Amethyst, Black, Cobalt Blue, Crystal, Evergreen, Ice Blue, Jadite, Light Green, Medium Blue, Pink, Rose, Ruby, and Smoke.

AMBER
Bowl, Soup, 6 1/4 In. 35.00
Cup & Saucer 14.00
Goblet, Cordial,
    2 7/8 In. 23.90
Pitcher, 8 1/8 In. 200.00
Plate, Bread & Butter,
    5 7/8 In. 6.00
Plate, Luncheon,
    8 1/2 In. 10.00
Relish, 3 Sections, 8 In. . .18.00
Saucer 3.00
Sugar, 4 In. 8.00
Sugar & Creamer, 4 In. . . .19.90
Tumbler, 8 Oz.,
    4 3/8 In. 10.00
Tumbler, 9 Oz.,
    4 7/8 In. 10.00
Whiskey,
    2 3/4 In. . . . . . . .7.50 to 10.00
Whiskey, Handle,
    2 3/4 In. . . . . . .11.00 to 16.00

AMETHYST
Cup 8.00
Plate, Bread & Butter,
    5 7/8 In. 6.00

COBALT BLUE
Cup 15.00
Goblet, Cordial,
    2 7/8 In. . . . . .34.00 to 45.00
Sugar, 4 In. 15.00
Tumbler, 8 Oz.,
    4 3/8 In. 23.50
Whiskey, 2 3/4 In. 16.00

CRYSTAL
Goblet, Wine, 4 In. 20.00

LIGHT GREEN
Cup & Saucer 14.00

RUBY
Bowl, 3-Footed, Ruffled,
    9 1/2 In. 65.00
Compote, 4 In. . .25.00 to 35.00

Creamer,
   2 3/4 In. . . . . . .18.00 to 20.00
Cup . . . . .12.00 to 18.00
Cup & Saucer   . .18.00 to 21.00
Decanter Set, Juice,
   5 Piece 120.00
Goblet, Wine,
   4 In. . . . . .19.00 to 22.00
Goblet, Wine, Metal
   Stem, 5 1/8 In. 15.00
Sherbet, 2 5/8 In. 14.00
Sugar, 3 1/2 In. 13.50
Sugar & Creamer,
   2 3/4 In. 40.00
Sugar & Creamer,
   3 3/4 In. 30.00
Tumbler, 4 7/8 In. 16.50
Tumbler, 8 Oz.,
   4 3/8 In. 21.00
Tumbler, Handle,
   4 7/8 In. 13.00
Whiskey, Handle,
   2 3/4 In. . . . . . .15.00 to 16.00
Wine, 4 Oz. 20.00

MOONSTONE

The opalescent hobnails on this pattern give it the name Moonstone. It was made by Anchor Hocking Glass Corporation, Lancaster, Ohio, from 1941 to 1946. A few pieces are seen in Green. Reproductions have been made. They are listed at the end of the Depression Glass section.

CRYSTAL
Bonbon, Heart
   Shape . . . . .8.00 to 13.00
Bowl, 7 3/4 In. 14.00
Bowl,
   Cloverleaf . . . .10.00 to 12.00
Bowl, Crimped,
   9 1/2 In. . . . . . .17.00 to 25.00

Bowl, Crimped, Handle,
   6 1/2 In. 18.00
Bowl, Dessert, Crimped,
   5 1/2 In. 8.00
Candleholder,
   Pair . . . . .14.00 to 15.00
Candy, Cover,
   2 Handles . . . . .26.00 to 28.00
Cigarette Box, Cover,
   6 In. . . . . .24.00 to 25.00
Creamer 8.00
Cup . . . . .5.00 to 6.00
Cup & Saucer   . .12.00 to 13.00
Goblet, 10 Oz.   . .15.00 to 20.00
Plate, Luncheon,
   8 3/8 In. 15.00
Plate, Sherbet, 6 1/4 In. . . .5.00
Puff Box, Cover,
   4 3/4 In. 25.00
Relish, Divided,
   7 3/4 In. . . . . . . .9.00 to 15.00
Sandwich Tray,
   10 3/4 In. 25.00
Sherbet . . . . .3.00 to 7.00
Sugar 9.00
Sugar & Creamer 18.00
Vase, 5 1/2 In. 12.00

GREEN
Bowl, Crimped, Handle,
   6 1/2 In. 15.00

MT. PLEASANT

Mt. Pleasant, sometimes called Double Shield, was made by L. E. Smith Company, Mt. Pleasant, Pennsylvania, from the mid-1920s to 1934. The pattern was made in Amber; Black Amethyst, a very deep purple that appears black unless held in front of a strong light; Cobalt Blue; Crystal; Green; Pink; and White. Some pieces have gold or silver trim.

BLACK AMETHYST
Bowl, Flared, Footed,
   9 In. 28.00
Mayonnaise, 3-Footed,
   5 1/2 In. . . . . . .16.00 to 24.00
Mint Dish, Center Handle,
   6 In. 19.00
Plate, 2 Handles, 8 In. 18.00
Plate, 2 Hexagon Handles,
   7 In. 12.00
Plate, Scalloped, 8 In. 15.00
Sandwich Server, Center
   Handle, 9 In. . .19.00 to 35.00
Sugar . . . . .17.00 to 19.00
Sugar & Creamer 37.00

COBALT BLUE
Bowl, 2 Handles, Square,
   8 In. 38.00
Bowl, Fruit, Footed, Square,
   4 In. 16.00
Bowl, Fruit, Scalloped,
   10 In. 34.00
Bowl, Roll Handle, Footed,
   7 In. 18.00
Cake Plate, 2 Handles,
   10 1/2 In. . . . . .23.00 to 26.00
Creamer . . . . . . .12.00 to 22.50
Cup 14.00
Cup & Saucer   . .13.00 to 18.00
Grill Plate, 9 In. . .8.00 to 20.00
Mayonnaise, Footed,
   5 1/2 In. . . . . . .15.00 to 32.50
Plate, 2 Handles, 8 In. 13.00
Plate, Leaf Shape,
   8 In. . . . . .10.00 to 18.50
Plate, Scalloped,
   8 In. . . . . .14.00 to 16.00
Plate, Square, 8 In. 20.00
Salt & Pepper 36.00
Sherbet . . . . .12.00 to 16.50
Tumbler,
   Footed . . . . . . .15.00 to 25.00

GREEN
Creamer 18.00
Grill Plate, 9 In. 10.00

MT. VERNON

Mt. Vernon was made in the late 1920s through the 1940s by the Cambridge Glass Company, Cambridge, Ohio. It was made in Amber, Carmen (red), Crystal, Emerald Green, Heatherbloom, Royal Blue, and Violet.

AMBER
Relish, 5 Sections 35.00

CARMEN
Decanter, 40 Oz. 140.00
Whiskey 20.00

CRYSTAL
Goblet, Wine 9.00
Plate, Bread & Butter,
  6 In. 7.00
Plate, Dinner, 10 1/2 In. . .35.00

HEATHERBLOOM
Compote, 6 1/2 In. 85.00

NAVARRE

Fostoria Glass Company, Fostoria, Ohio, made Navarre pattern glass from 1937 to 1980. It is an etched pattern. Some of the pieces were made on the Baroque glass blank, others on

more modern shapes. It was originally made only in Crystal. A few later pieces were made in the 1970s in Pink, Blue, or Green.

BLUE
Goblet, Champagne, 6 Oz.,
  5 5/8 In. . . . . . .25.00 to 42.00
Goblet, Claret, 4 1/2 Oz.,
  6 1/2 In. . . . . . .55.00 to 65.00
Goblet, Water, 10 Oz.,
  7 5/8 In. . . . . . .28.00 to 52.00
Tumbler, Iced Tea, Footed,
  13 Oz., 5 7/8 In. 52.00

CRYSTAL
Bonbon, Footed,
  7 3/8 In. 30.00
Bowl, Flared, 12 In. 60.00
Cake Plate, Handle, 10 In. 50.00
Candlestick, 3-Light,
  6 3/4 In. 75.00
Candlestick, Double, 5 In.,
  Pair 75.00
Celery Dish, 9 In. 47.50
Compote,
  5 1/2 In. . . . . . .45.00 to 65.00
Creamer, Footed,
  4 1/4 In. 20.00
Cruet, Salad Dressing, Stopper,
  6 1/2 In. . . . .125.00 to 396.00
Cup & Saucer . .24.00 to 30.00
Dish, Mayonnaise, Footed,
  3 Piece . . . . . . .35.00 to 62.00
Finger Bowl, 4 1/2 In. . . .65.00
Goblet, Claret, 4 1/2 Oz.,
  6 1/2 In. 60.00
Goblet, Cocktail, 3 1/2 Oz.,
  6 In. 28.00
Goblet, Cordial, 1 Oz.,
  3 7/8 In. 50.00
Goblet, Water, 10 Oz.,
  7 5/8 In. 35.00
Goblet, Wine, 3 1/4 Oz.,
  5 1/2 In. 35.00
Ice Bucket, 4 3/8 In. 155.00

Pitcher, Water, Footed,
  48 Oz. 495.00
Plate, Breakfast,
  9 1/2 In. 45.00
Plate, Luncheon,
  8 1/2 In. 22.00
Plate, Salad,
  7 1/2 In. . . . . . .14.00 to 18.00
Relish, 2 Sections, Square,
  6 In. 32.50
Relish, 3 Sections,
  7 1/2 In. 45.00
Sherbet,
  4 3/8 In. . . . . . .20.00 to 35.00
Sugar & Creamer 45.00
Tidbit, Footed,
  8 1/4 In. 27.50
Tumbler, Juice, Footed,
  5 Oz., 4 3/8 In. 25.00
Tumbler, Water, Footed,
  10 Oz., 5 3/8 In. 28.00

NEW CENTURY

New Century used to be incorrectly called Lydia Ray by some collectors. It was made by Hazel Atlas Glass Company, a firm with factories in Ohio, Pennsylvania, and West Virginia, from 1930 to 1935. It has a series of ribs in the glass design. It is found in Amethyst, Cobalt Blue, Crystal, Green, and Pink. Ovide is sometimes incorrectly called New Century.

AMETHYST
Cup & Saucer . . .8.00 to 10.00
Tumbler, 5 Oz.,
  3 1/2 In. 12.00
Tumbler, Juice, 5 Oz.,
  3 1/2 In. 12.00

COBALT BLUE

Cup & Saucer 10.00

Tumbler, Iced Tea,
  12 Oz., 5 1/4 In. 25.00

Tumbler, Juice, 5 Oz.,
  3 1/2 In. . . . . . .15.00 to 18.00

Tumbler, Water, 9 Oz.,
  4 1/8 In. 18.00

CRYSTAL

Pitcher, Water, 80 Oz.,
  8 In. 45.00

Plate, Dinner, 10 Oz. 12.00

Plate, Luncheon, 8 1/2 In. . .9.50

Sherbet, 3 In. 10.00

GREEN

Bowl, 8 In. . . . . .22.00 to 26.00

Cup & Saucer 16.00

Decanter, Stopper 40.00

Plate, Luncheon,
  8 1/2 In. 15.00

Salt & Pepper 15.00

Soup, Cream, 4 3/4 In. . . .25.00

Tumbler, Water, 9 Oz.,
  4 1/8 In. . . . . . .12.00 to 15.00

PINK

Cup & Saucer 10.00

Saucer 4.50

Tumbler, Water, 9 Oz.,
  4 1/8 In. . . . . . .11.00 to 14.00

NEWPORT

Newport, or Hairpin, was made
by Hazel Atlas Glass Company
from 1936 to 1940. It is known
in Amethyst, Cobalt Blue,
Pink, Platonite (white), and a
variety of fired-on colors. Reproductions have been made.
They are listed at the end of the
Depression Glass section.

AMETHYST

Bowl, Cereal, 5 1/4 In. . . .30.00

Cup & Saucer 15.00

Plate, Dessert, 6 In. 6.00

Plate, Dinner,
  8 13/16 In. 30.00

Plate, Luncheon,
  8 1/2 In. . . . . . .10.00 to 15.00

Salt & Pepper 45.00

Saltshaker 20.00

Sherbet, Footed . .12.00 to 13.00

Soup, Cream,
  4 3/4 In. . . . . . .16.00 to 18.00

Sugar 13.00

Sugar &
  Creamer . . . . .15.00 to 35.00

Tumbler, Water, 9 Oz.,
  4 1/2 In. 30.00

COBALT BLUE

Bowl, Cereal,
  5 1/4 In. . . . . . .31.00 to 35.00

Creamer . . . . . . .13.00 to 15.00

Cup 10.00

Cup & Saucer . .14.00 to 17.00

Plate, Dessert,
  5 7/8 In. . . . . .7.50 to 9.00

Plate, Luncheon,
  8 1/2 In. . . . . . .15.00 to 16.50

Plate, Sherbet 9.00

Sandwich Server,
  11 1/2 In. 48.00

Saucer 7.00

Sherbet . . . . . . .13.50 to 18.50

Soup, Cream,
  4 3/4 In. . . . . . .16.00 to 18.00

Sugar & Creamer 39.50

Tumbler, Water, 9 Oz.,
  4 1/2 In. 39.00

PINK

Berry Set, 7 Piece 75.00

Cup & Saucer 15.00

Plate, Dessert, 5 7/8 In. . . .6.00

Platter, Oval, 11 3/4 In. . .47.00

PLATONITE

Creamer, Fired-On
  Yellow 8.76

Saucer 50

Sugar 1.50

Sugar, Fired-On Spruce
  Green 7.00

NO. 601, see Avocado

NO. 610

Many patterns are listed both
by the original pattern number
and by a name. No. 610 is often
called Pyramid or Rex. It was
made from 1926 to 1932 by the
Indiana Glass Company. Green
and Pink were used more than
Crystal, White, and Yellow. In
1974 and 1975 reproductions
were made in Black and Blue
by Tiara.

CRYSTAL

Berry Bowl,
  4 3/4 In. . . . . . .60.00 to 75.00

Pitcher, 1/2 Gal. 500.00

Sugar & Creamer, Tray,
  3 Piece 90.00

Tumbler, Iced Tea, Footed,
  11 Oz. 150.00

GREEN

Berry Bowl, 4 3/4 In. 65.00

Bowl, Oval, 9 1/2 In. 70.00

Ice Bucket . . .150.00 to 165.00

Pickle, 9 1/2 In. 50.00

Pitcher, 1/2 Gal. 835.00

Relish, 4 Sections,
  9 1/2 In. . . . . . .75.00 to 80.00

Tumbler, Water, Footed,
  8 Oz. 55.00

PINK

Berry Bowl, 4 3/4 In. 69.00

Berry Bowl, Master,
8 1/2 In. 30.00
Bowl, Oval, 9 1/2 In. 28.00

YELLOW
Berry Bowl,
4 3/4 In. . . . . . .55.00 to 85.00
Berry Bowl, Master,
8 1/2 In. . . . . .70.00 to 110.00
Bowl, Oval,
9 1/2 In. . . . . . .50.00 to 80.00
Pickle Dish,
9 1/2 In. . . . . . .52.00 to 55.00
Pitcher,
1/2 Gal. . . . .785.00 to 850.00
Tray, For Sugar &
Creamer 50.00
Tumbler, Iced Tea,
Footed, 11 Oz. 475.00

NO. 612

Indiana Glass Company, Dunkirk, Indiana, called this pattern No. 612, but collectors call it Horseshoe. It was made from 1930 to 1933 primarily in Green and Yellow, with a smaller number of Pink pieces. Sugar and creamer sets were also made in Crystal. Plates came in two styles, one with the center pattern, one plain.

GREEN
Berry Bowl, Master,
9 1/2 In. . . . . . .37.50 to 45.00
Bowl, Oval,
10 1/2 In. . . . . .24.00 to 70.00
Bowl, Salad, 7 1/2 In. 22.50
Creamer, Footed 17.00
Cup . . . . .10.00 to 12.00
Cup & Saucer . .11.00 to 19.00
Plate, Breakfast,
9 3/8 In. . . . . . .13.50 to 15.00
Plate, Dessert,
6 In. . . . . .5.00 to 6.00
Plate, Luncheon,
8 3/8 In. . . . . . .9.50 to 11.00
Relish, 3 Sections,
Footed 25.00
Sandwich Server,
11 1/2 In. 20.00
Saucer 5.00
Sherbet, Footed . .10.00 to 15.00
Sugar . . . . .12.00 to 17.00
Sugar & Creamer 31.50
Tumbler, Footed, Water,
9 Oz., 4 1/2 In. 22.00

YELLOW
Berry Bowl, 4 1/2 In. 70.00
Bowl, Cereal,
6 1/2 In. . . . . . .15.00 to 24.00
Bowl, Salad,
7 1/2 In. . . . . . .25.00 to 32.00
Bowl, Vegetable, Oval,
10 1/2 In. 27.50
Creamer 18.00
Cup & Saucer 17.00
Pitcher, Water, 64 Oz.,
8 1/2 In. . . . .375.00 to 850.00
Plate, Dessert, 6 In. 5.50
Plate, Luncheon,
8 3/8 In. . . . . . . .7.00 to 11.00
Platter, Oval,
10 3/4 In. . . . . .15.00 to 35.00
Relish, 3 Sections,
Footed . . . . . . .31.00 to 40.00
Sandwich Server,
11 1/2 In. . . . . .15.00 to 32.00
Saucer 4.50
Sherbet, Footed . .15.00 to 17.00
Sugar, Footed 16.00
Sugar & Creamer,
Footed . . . . . . .32.00 to 36.00
Tumbler, Water, Footed,
9 Oz. . . . . .20.00 to 25.00

NO. 615

No. 615 is often called Lorain or sometimes Basket, Bridal Bouquet, Flower Basket, or Hanging Basket. It was made by the Indiana Glass Company from 1929 to 1932 of Crystal, Green, and Yellow. Sometimes Crystal pieces have blue, green, red, or yellow borders. Reproduction pieces were made of Milk Glass or Olive Green.

CRYSTAL
Cup 9.50
Plate, Salad, 7 3/4 In. 10.00

GREEN
Bowl, Oval, 9 3/4 In. 40.00
Cup 11.00
Plate, Dinner, Square,
10 In. 40.00
Plate, Luncheon,
8 3/8 In. . . . . . .20.00 to 21.00
Plate, Salad,
7 3/4 In. . . . . . .10.00 to 11.00
Sherbet, Footed . .20.00 to 28.00
Tumbler, Water, Footed,
9 Oz., 4 3/4 In. 20.00

YELLOW
Bowl, Cereal, 6 In. 71.00
Bowl, Salad,
7 1/4 In. . . . . . .50.00 to 69.00
Bowl, Vegetable, Oval,
9 1/4 In. . . . . . .46.00 to 50.00
Creamer 20.00
Cup . . . . .12.00 to 20.00
Cup & Saucer . .20.00 to 30.00
Plate, Dinner,
10 1/4 In. . . . . .60.00 to 75.00
Plate, Luncheon,
8 3/8 In. . . . . . .16.50 to 30.00
Plate, Salad,
7 3/4 In. . . . . . .10.00 to 16.00
Plate, Sherbet, 5 1/2 In. . .11.00
Platter,
11 1/2 In. . . . . .35.00 to 50.00

Relish, 4 Sections,
8 In. . . . . .32.00 to 35.00

Saucer . . . . .4.00 to 7.00

Sherbet, Footed . .25.00 to 35.00

Sugar, Footed . . .20.00 to 22.00

Tumbler, Water, Footed, 9 Oz.,
4 3/4 In. . . . . . .28.00 to 30.00

NO. 618

Another Indiana Glass Company pattern made from 1932 to 1937 was No. 618, or Pineapple & Floral. It is also called Meadow Flower, Lacy Daisy, or Wildflower. The pattern was made of Amber, Crystal, and fired-on Green and Red. Reproductions were made in Olive Green in the late 1960s.

AMBER
Cup & Saucer . .12.50 to 14.00

Plate, Dinner, 9 3/8 In. . . .18.00

Soup, Cream, Handle 20.00

CRYSTAL
Ashtray,
4 1/2 In. . . . . . .9.75 to 16.00

Bowl, Cereal, 6 In. 25.00

Bowl, Salad, 7 In. . .2.00 to 3.00

Bowl, Vegetable, Oval,
10 In. 12.00

Cup & Saucer . .13.50 to 15.00

Plate, Dessert, 6 In. 5.00

Plate, Dinner, 9 1/2 In. . . .17.00

Plate, Indentation,
11 1/2 In. 12.00

Plate, Luncheon, 8 1/2 In. . .8.00

Platter, Closed Handle,
11 In. 18.00

Platter, Relish, Sections,
11 1/2 In. . . . . .15.00 to 18.00

Sandwich Server,
11 1/2 In. . . . . .18.00 to 25.00

Sherbet, Diamond-Shape . .6.00

Sherbet, Footed . .16.00 to 18.00

Sugar &
Creamer . . . .13.00 to 15.00

Tumbler, Water, 8 Oz.,
4 1/4 In. 35.00

NO. 620

No. 620, also known as Daisy, was made by Indiana Glass Company. In 1933 the pattern was made in Crystal, and in 1940 in Amber; in the 1960s and 1970s reproductions were made in Dark Green and Milk Glass. Some pieces have a fired-on Red color.

AMBER
Berry Bowl, 4 1/2 In. 8.00

Bowl, Oval, 10 In. 16.00

Cake Plate,
11 1/2 In. . . . . .9.00 to 13.00

Creamer, Footed 8.00

Cup 6.00

Cup & Saucer . . .5.50 to 8.00

Plate, Dessert,
6 In. . . . . .4.00 to 9.00

Plate, Dinner,
9 3/8 In. . . . . . . .8.00 to 9.00

Platter, 10 3/4 In. 14.00

Relish, 3 Sections,
8 3/8 In. . . . . .30.00 to 35.00

Saucer 3.00

Soup, Cream,
4 1/2 In. . . . . . .6.00 to 12.00

Sugar . . . . .6.00 to 9.00

Sugar &
Creamer . . . .12.50 to 14.50

Tumbler, Water, Footed,
9 Oz. . . . . . . .18.00 to 20.00

DARK GREEN
Bowl, Vegetable, Oval,
10 In. 11.00

Cup & Saucer 5.50

Plate, Dinner, 9 3/8 In. 6.50

Plate, Salad,
7 3/8 In. . . . . . . .3.50 to 6.50

Tumbler, Iced Tea, Footed,
12 Oz. 22.50

NO. 622, see Pretzel

NO. 624, see Christmas Candy

NORMANDIE

A few Depression glass patterns were made in Iridescent Marigold color, which has been collected as carnival glass. Normandie products made in this iridescence, called Sunburst, appear in the carnival glass listings as Bouquet and Lattice; when the pattern is in the other known colors, it is called Normandie. Look for it in Amber, Crystal, Pink, and Spring Green, as well as in the Iridescent color. Normandie was made by the Federal Glass Company from 1933 to 1940.

AMBER
Berry Bowl, 5 In. . .4.00 to 6.00

Bowl, Cereal, 6 1/2 In. 6.00

Creamer, Footed 16.00

Cup 7.50

Cup & Saucer . . .8.00 to 11.00

Pitcher, Water,
8 In. . . . . .75.00 to 89.00

Plate, Dessert, 6 In. 4.50

Plate, Dinner, 11 In. 27.75

Plate, Luncheon,
9 1/4 In. . . . . . .12.50 to 15.00

Plate, Salad, 7 3/4 In. 10.00

Salt & Pepper 55.00

Saucer 4.00

Sugar & Creamer 16.50

Tumbler, Iced Tea, 12 Oz.,
5 In. 50.00

Tumbler, Juice, 5 Oz.,
4 In. 38.00

Tumbler, Water, 9 Oz.,
4 1/4 In. . . . . . .20.00 to 25.00

IRIDESCENT

Berry Bowl, Master,
8 1/2 In. 10.50

Bowl, 5 In. . . . . . .3.00 to 5.00

Bowl, Cereal,
6 1/2 In. . . . . . . .6.00 to 9.00

Bowl, Vegetable, Oval,
10 In. 17.00

Creamer . . . . .6.00 to 8.00

Cup & Saucer . . . .5.75 to 9.00

Grill Plate, 11 In. . .5.50 to 9.00

Plate, Luncheon,
9 1/4 In. . . . . . .15.00 to 16.50

Plate, Sherbet,
6 In. . . . . .2.00 to 3.00

Sherbet, Footed . . . .5.00 to 7.00

Sugar &
Creamer . . . . .12.00 to 14.00

PINK

Berry Bowl, Master,
8 1/2 In. 42.00

Bowl, Vegetable, Oval,
10 In. 70.00

Cup . . . . .6.00 to 12.00

Cup & Saucer . .10.00 to 14.50

Plate, Luncheon,
9 1/4 In. 28.00

To clean wax from glass candlesticks, scrape with a wooden stick, then wash off the remaining wax with rubbing alcohol.

Plate, Salad,
7 3/4 In. . . . . . .10.00 to 14.00

Plate, Sherbet,
6 In. . . . . .7.00 to 8.00

Sherbet, Footed 8.50

Tumbler, Iced Tea, 12 Oz.,
5 In. 100.00

Tumbler, Water, 9 Oz.,
4 1/4 In. 50.00

OLD CAFE

Old Cafe is one of the few patterns with only one name. It was made by the Anchor Hocking Glass Corporation, Lancaster, Ohio, from 1936 to 1938. Pieces are found in Crystal, Pink, and Royal Ruby.

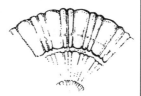

CRYSTAL

Bowl, 9 In. 9.00

Bowl, Cereal, Tab Handle,
5 1/2 In. 8.00

Candy Dish, Low, 8 In. . . .5.00

Candy Dish, Ruby
Cover 15.00

Dish, Olive, 6 In. 6.00

Tumbler, Juice, 3 In. 10.00

PINK

Bowl, 5 In. 12.00

Bowl, Closed Handles,
9 In. 10.00

Candy Dish, Low,
8 In. . . . . .9.50 to 15.00

Cup . . . . .5.00 to 6.00

Cup & Saucer 15.50

Pitcher, Water, 80 Oz. . . .80.00

Tumbler, Juice, 3 In. 16.00

Tumbler, Water, 4 In. 16.00

ROYAL RUBY

Bowl, Cereal, 5 1/2 In. . . .19.00

Candy Dish, Low,
8 In. . . . . .10.00 to 15.00

Cup 7.00

Plate, Closed Handle,
9 In. 15.00

OLD ENGLISH

Old English, or Threading, was made by the Indiana Glass Company, Dunkirk, Indiana, in the late 1920s and early 1930s. It was first made in Amber, Crystal, and Forest Green. Pink was a later color.

FOREST GREEN

Bowl, Footed, 9 In. 35.00

Creamer, Footed 15.00

Cup 10.00

Pitcher, Footed 77.00

Plate, Breakfast, 9 In. 15.00

Plate, Salad, 7 1/2 In. 17.00

Platter, Oval, 11 1/2 In. . .26.00

Sherbet, Footed 15.00

Tumbler, Juice, Footed,
4 1/2 In. 30.00

Tumbler, Water, Footed,
5 1/2 In. 42.00

OLD FLORENTINE, see Florentine No. 1

OPALESCENT HOBNAIL, see Moonstone

OPEN LACE, see Lace Edge

OPEN ROSE, see Mayfair Open Rose

OPEN SCALLOP, see Lace Edge

OPTIC DESIGN, see Raindrops

ORIENTAL POPPY, see Florentine No. 2

OVIDE

Hazel Atlas Glass Company made Ovide pattern from 1929 to the 1950s. It was made in Green at first. By 1932 it was Black and by 1935 Platonite or Opaque White glass was used with fired-on colors. Pieces were made with colored rims; overall fired-on colors; or decorations, which included things like birds, windmills, or Art Deco geometrics. Ovide is sometimes incorrectly called New Century.

BLACK
Creamer, Footed 6.50

GREEN
Plate, Breakfast, 9 In. 6.00
Sugar 4.00

PLATONITE
Bowl, Cereal, Black
   Flowers, 5 In. 10.00
Creamer, Blue Flowers 9.00
Cup & Saucer, Green
   Stripe 5.00
Eggcup, Flying Geese 22.00
Plate, Breakfast, Wide Red
   Scroll, 9 In. 6.75
Plate, Flying Geese,
   9 In. 25.00
Saucer, Green Stripe 50
Sherbet, Flying Geese,
   6 In. 15.00
Sherbet, Red & Black
   Windmill, 6 In. 14.00
Sherbet, Red Stripe, 6 In. . .4.50
Tumbler, Black Flowers . .15.00

OVIDE, see also New Century

OXFORD, see Chinex Classic

OYSTER & PEARL

Anchor Hocking Glass Corporation, Lancaster, Ohio, made only accessory pieces in the Oyster & Pearl pattern from 1938 to 1940. The first pieces were Crystal or Pink. Those with a white outside and fired-on pink or green interiors were made later, as were Royal Ruby pieces.

CRYSTAL
Bowl, Fruit, 10 1/2 In. . . .20.00
Relish, 2 Sections,
   10 1/4 In. 10.00
Sandwich Tray, 13 In. . . .20.00

PINK
Bowl, Fruit, 10 1/2 In. . . .14.00
Bowl, 2 Handles,
   6 1/2 In. 18.00
Bowl, Heart Shape,
   5 1/4 In. . . . . . . .8.00 to 15.00
Relish, 2 Sections,
   10 1/4 In. . . . . .10.00 to 15.00
Sandwich Tray,
   13 1/2 In. 34.00

ROYAL RUBY
Bowl, Fruit,
   10 1/2 In. . . . . .55.00 to 75.00
Bowl, Fruit, Handle,
   5 1/2 In. . . . . . .13.00 to 19.75
Bowl, Handle,
   6 1/2 In. . . . . . .20.00 to 23.00
Bowl, Heart Shape,
   5 1/4 In. 15.00
Candleholder, 3 1/2 In.,
   Pair . . . . .25.00 to 50.00

PANELED ASTER, see Madrid

PANELED CHERRY BLOSSOM, see
Cherry Blossom

PANSY & DORIC, see Doric &
Pansy

PARROT, see Sylvan

PATRICIAN

Federal Glass Company, Columbus, Ohio, made Patrician, sometimes called Hinge or Spoke, from 1933 to 1937. Full dinner sets were made in Golden Glo and Green, and smaller quantities in Crystal and Pink. Yellow pieces were produced later.

CRYSTAL
Berry Bowl, 5 In. 9.50
Berry Bowl, Master,
   8 1/2 In. 24.00
Cookie Jar,
   Cover . . . . . . .50.00 to 65.00
Cup . . . . .8.00 to 8.50
Grill Plate, 10 1/2 In. 13.50
Pitcher, 75 Oz., 8 In. . . .100.00
Pitcher, Applied Handle,
   75 Oz., 8 1/2 In. 150.00
Plate, Dinner, 10 1/2 In. . .13.50
Plate, Salad, 7 1/2 In. 15.00
Platter, Oval, 11 1/2 In. . .30.00
Salt & Pepper . . .57.00 to 65.00
Sherbet . . . . .10.00 to 13.00
Sugar 9.00
Sugar, Cover 64.00

❖

**Put a silver spoon in a
glass before pouring in
hot water. It will absorb
heat and keep the glass
from cracking.**

❖

❖

**Watch burning candles
in glass candlesticks.
If the candle burns
too low, the hot wax
and flame may break
the glass.**

❖

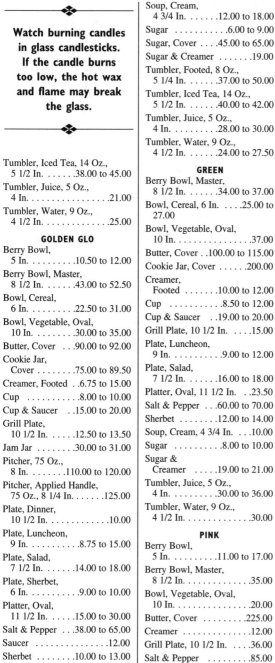

Tumbler, Iced Tea, 14 Oz.,
    5 1/2 In. . . . . . .38.00 to 45.00
Tumbler, Juice, 5 Oz.,
    4 In. 21.00
Tumbler, Water, 9 Oz.,
    4 1/2 In. 25.00

GOLDEN GLO
Berry Bowl,
    5 In. . . . . .10.50 to 12.00
Berry Bowl, Master,
    8 1/2 In. . . . . . .43.00 to 52.50
Bowl, Cereal,
    6 In. . . . . .22.50 to 31.00
Bowl, Vegetable, Oval,
    10 In. . . . . . . .30.00 to 35.00
Butter, Cover . . .90.00 to 92.00
Cookie Jar,
    Cover . . . . .75.00 to 89.50
Creamer, Footed . .6.75 to 15.00
Cup . . . . .8.00 to 10.00
Cup & Saucer . .15.00 to 20.00
Grill Plate,
    10 1/2 In. . . . . .12.50 to 13.50
Jam Jar . . . . . . .30.00 to 31.00
Pitcher, 75 Oz.,
    8 In. . . . . . .110.00 to 120.00
Pitcher, Applied Handle,
    75 Oz., 8 1/4 In. 125.00
Plate, Dinner,
    10 1/2 In. 10.00
Plate, Luncheon,
    9 In. . . . . .8.75 to 15.00
Plate, Salad,
    7 1/2 In. . . . . . .14.00 to 18.00
Plate, Sherbet,
    6 In. . . . . .9.00 to 10.00
Platter, Oval,
    11 1/2 In. . . . . .15.00 to 30.00
Salt & Pepper . . .38.00 to 65.00
Saucer 12.00
Sherbet . . . . . . .10.00 to 13.00

Soup, Cream,
    4 3/4 In. . . . . . .12.00 to 18.00
Sugar . . . . .6.00 to 9.00
Sugar, Cover . . . .45.00 to 65.00
Sugar & Creamer 19.00
Tumbler, Footed, 8 Oz.,
    5 1/4 In. . . . . . .37.00 to 50.00
Tumbler, Iced Tea, 14 Oz.,
    5 1/2 In. . . . . . .40.00 to 42.00
Tumbler, Juice, 5 Oz.,
    4 In. . . . . .28.00 to 30.00
Tumbler, Water, 9 Oz.,
    4 1/2 In. . . . . . .24.00 to 27.50

GREEN
Berry Bowl, Master,
    8 1/2 In. . . . . . .34.00 to 37.00
Bowl, Cereal, 6 In. . . . .25.00 to
27.00
Bowl, Vegetable, Oval,
    10 In. 37.00
Butter, Cover . .100.00 to 115.00
Cookie Jar, Cover 200.00
Creamer,
    Footed . . . . . . .10.00 to 12.00
Cup . . . . .8.50 to 12.00
Cup & Saucer . .19.00 to 20.00
Grill Plate, 10 1/2 In. 15.00
Plate, Luncheon,
    9 In. . . . . .9.00 to 12.00
Plate, Salad,
    7 1/2 In. . . . . . .16.00 to 18.00
Platter, Oval, 11 1/2 In. . .23.50
Salt & Pepper . . .60.00 to 70.00
Sherbet . . . . . . .12.00 to 14.00
Soup, Cream, 4 3/4 In. . . .10.00
Sugar . . . . .8.00 to 10.00
Sugar &
    Creamer . . . . .19.00 to 21.00
Tumbler, Juice, 5 Oz.,
    4 In. . . . . .30.00 to 36.00
Tumbler, Water, 9 Oz.,
    4 1/2 In. 30.00

PINK
Berry Bowl,
    5 In. . . . . .11.00 to 17.00
Berry Bowl, Master,
    8 1/2 In. 35.00
Bowl, Vegetable, Oval,
    10 In. 20.00
Butter, Cover 225.00
Creamer 12.00
Grill Plate, 10 1/2 In. 36.00
Salt & Pepper 85.00

Tumbler, Iced Tea,
    14 Oz., 5 1/2 In. 46.00
Tumbler, Water, 9 Oz.,
    4 1/2 In. 30.00

PEACH LUSTRE

Peach Lustre is both a pattern
and a color name used for Fire-
King dinnerware made by
Anchor Hocking Glass Corporation from 1952 to 1963. The
pattern has a laurel leaf design
around the edge of the plates
and bowls and the side of the
cups. The pieces are a lustrous
orange-yellow color. The same
pattern of laurel leaves was
made in 1953 in gray and was
known as Gray Laurel pattern.
Bubble and Boopie pattern
crystal stemware were made
with a similar design to go with
the dinnerware.

Bowl, Cereal,
    7 5/8 In. . . . . .3.00 to 5.00
Bowl, Fruit, 4 7/8 In. 1.50
Bowl, Vegetable,
    8 1/2 In. 7.00
Casserole, French,
    Table Lid 5.00
Casserole, Tab Handle,
    5 x 9 In. 10.00
Creamer, Footed . . .2.50 to 5.00
Cup & Saucer 3.00
Cup & Saucer, After
    Dinner 40.00
Pie Plate, 9 In. 5.00
Plate, Dinner, 9 1/8 In. 6.50
Saucer 1.00
Sugar 2.50
Sugar, Footed 6.00
Sugar & Creamer,
    Footed . . . . .7.00 to 8.00
Tom & Jerry Set,
    9 Piece 95.00
Vase, Ribbed . . . . .6.00 to 7.50

PEACOCK & ROSE, see Peacock & Wild Rose

PEACOCK & WILD ROSE

Line 300 was the name used by Paden City Glass Company, Paden City, West Virginia, for the pattern now called Peacock & Wild Rose. It was made in the 1930s of Amber, Black, Cobalt Blue, Crystal, Green, Light Blue, Pink, and Red. A few of the lists call this pattern Peacock & Rose.

BLACK
Vase, 10 In. 350.00
Vase, Elliptical, 10 In. . .600.00

CRYSTAL
Bowl, Footed, 10 1/2 In. . .95.00

GREEN
Console, Rolled Edge,
   14 In. 225.00
Vase, 10 In. 135.00
Vase, Elliptical, 10 In. . .375.00

PINK
Bowl, Footed, 10 1/2 In. . .70.00
Cake Plate, Footed,
   11 In. . . . . . .115.00 to 125.00
Vase, 10 In. 155.00

PEBBLE OPTIC, see Raindrops

PETAL SWIRL, see Swirl

PETALWARE

Macbeth-Evans Glass Company made Petalware from 1930 to 1940. It was first made in Crystal and Pink. In 1932 the dinnerware was made in Monax, in 1933 in Cremax. The pattern remained popular, and in 1936 Cobalt Blue and several other variations were made. Some pieces were handpainted with pastel bands of ivory, green, and pink. Some pieces were decorated with a gold or red rim. Flower or fruit designs in bright colors were used on others. Bright bands of fired-on blue, green, red, and yellow were used to decorate some wares. All of these patterns have their own names. These include Banded Petalware, Daisy Petals, Diamond Point, Petal, Shell, and Vivid Bands.

COBALT BLUE
Mustard,
   Underplate . . . .12.00 to 15.00

CREMAX
Berry Bowl, Master,
   9 In. . . . . .7.00 to 30.00
Cup 10.00
Cup & Saucer . . .7.00 to 14.00
Cup & Saucer, Pastel
   Bands 10.00
Plate, Dinner, 9 In. 5.50
Plate, Dinner, Gold
   Trim, 9 In. 14.00
Plate, Salad, 8 In. 3.00
Plate, Salad, Gold
   Trim, 8 In. 10.00
Plate, Salad, Pastel Bands,
   8 In. . . . . .8.00 to 9.00
Salver, 11 In. 9.00
Salver, Pastel Bands,
   11 In. 13.00
Saucer 3.50
Saucer, Pastel Bands 3.00
Sherbet, Gold Trim 12.00
Soup, Cream, 4 1/2 In. . . .16.00
Soup, Cream, Gold Trim,
   4 1/2 In. 12.00

Sugar . . . . .7.00 to 10.00

CRYSTAL
Bowl, Cereal, Gold Trim,
   5 3/4 In. 8.00
Cup & Saucer . . .4.00 to 14.00
Plate, Salad, 8 In. 10.00
Sugar & Creamer 23.50
Tumbler, Water, Red Band,
   12 Oz., 4 5/8 In. 88.50

MONAX
Berry Bowl, Master,
   9 In. . . . . .18.00 to 23.00
Bowl, Cereal,
   5 3/4 In. . . . . . . .8.00 to 11.00
Bowl, Cereal, Gold Trim,
   5 3/4 In. 8.00
Casserole, Cover, 1/2 Qt. . .5.00
Cup & Saucer . . .6.00 to 12.00
Lamp Shade . . . .9.00 to 15.00
Plate, Dinner,
   9 In. . . . . .4.00 to 13.00
Plate, Salad,
   8 In. . . . . .4.00 to 15.00
Plate, Sherbet,
   6 In. . . . . .2.00 to 6.00
Platter, Oval, 13 In. 17.00
Salver, 11 In. 10.00
Sherbet, Footed,
   4 In. . . . . .7.00 to 8.00
Soup, Cream, 4 1/2 In. . . .10.00
Soup, Dish, 7 In. 57.00
Sugar, Footed . . . . .5.00 to 9.50
Sugar, Gold Trim,
   Footed 12.00
Sugar &
   Creamer . . . . .9.75 to 10.00

PINK
Berry Bowl, Master,
   9 In. 25.00
Bowl, Cereal,
   5 3/4 In. . . . . . .8.50 to 13.00
Cake Stand, Harp 25.00
Compote, 6 In. 15.00
Creamer,
   Footed . . . . . . .13.00 to 15.00
Goblet, Water, 6 1/4 In. . .12.00
Plate, Dinner,
   9 In. . . . . .11.00 to 15.00
Plate, Salad, 8 In. 5.00
Platter, Oval,
   13 In. . . . . .15.00 to 19.00
Punch Cup 6.00

Salver, 11 In. 17.00
Saucer 2.00
Snack Set, 4 . . . . .45.00
Soup, Cream,
  4 1/2 In. . . . . . .10.00 to 18.00
Sugar 11.00
Sugar, Cover, Footed 25.00
Sugar, Footed 11.00
Tidbit, 6 Sections 30.00
Vase, 7 In. . . . . . .29.00 to 35.00

PHILBE

Philbe is a Fire-King dinnerware made by the Anchor Hocking Glass Corporation from 1937 to the 1940s. It was made in Blue, Crystal, Green, and Pink. The Blue sometimes has platinum trim. Philbe is the dinnerware pattern; the matching kitchenware is called Fire-King Oven Glass.

BLUE
Creamer 135.00
Cup . . . . . . .135.00 to 160.00
Plate, Grill, 10 1/2 In. . . .80.00
Plate, Luncheon, 8 In. . . .50.00

CRYSTAL
Bowl, Cereal,
  5 1/2 In. . . . . . .15.00 to 18.00
Cup 55.00
Bowl, Salad,
  7 In. . . . . .20.00 to 25.00
Creamer, Footed 36.00
Mug, Child's 12.00
Sugar, Cover 10.00
Tumbler, Footed,
  10 Oz., 5 In. 25.00

GREEN
Creamer, Footed,
  3 1/4 In. 110.00
Pitcher, Juice,
  6 In. . . . . . .595.00 to 695.00
Plate, 10 1/2 In. 60.00

PINK
Bowl, Salad, 7 In. 50.00
Cup 100.00
Plate, Luncheon,
  8 In. . . . . .35.00 to 40.00
Tumbler, Iced Tea,
  6 1/2 In. 75.00

PHILBE, see also Fire-King

PIE CRUST, see Cremax

PINEAPPLE & FLORAL, see No. 618

PINWHEEL, see Sierra

POINSETTIA, see Floral

POPPY NO. I, see Florentine No. 1

POPPY NO. 2, see Florentine No. 2

PORTIA

Portia was made by Cambridge Glass Company from 1932 to the early 1950s. It was made in Amber, Crystal, Green, Heatherbloom, and Yellow.

CRYSTAL
Ashtray, 5 1/2 In. 45.00
Cup 35.00
Cup & Saucer 42.50
Decanter, Footed,
  28 Oz. 295.00
Dish, Mayonnaise,
  2 Piece 72.50
Goblet, Cocktail, 3 Oz. . . .32.50
Goblet,
  Cordial . . . . .65.00 to 125.00
Goblet, Parfait, 5 Oz. 95.00
Goblet, Water, 10 Oz. 35.00
Goblet, Wine, 2 1/2 Oz. . .50.00
Jam Jar, Cover 75.00

Oyster Cocktail,
  4 1/2 Oz. 37.50
Oyster Cocktail, Icer,
  4 1/2 Oz., 2 Piece 72.50
Pitcher, Tankard 47.50
Plate, Bread & Butter,
  6 1/2 In. 14.50
Plate, Salad, 8 In. 17.50
Relish, 3 Sections, 9 In. . .55.00
Relish, 3 Sections,
  12 In. 68.00
Relish, 5 Sections,
  12 In. . . . . . . .55.00 to 75.00
Relish, Handle, 14 In. 95.00
Sherbet, Tall, 6 Oz. 25.00
Soup, Cream, Liner 30.00
Tumbler, Iced Tea, Footed,
  12 Oz. 45.00

PRETTY POLLY PARTY DISHES, see Doric & Pansy

PRETZEL

Pretzel, also called No. 622 or Ribbon Candy, was made by Indiana Glass Company, Dunkirk, Indiana, in the 1930s. Avocado, Crystal, and Teal pieces were made. Some reproductions appeared in the 1970s in Amber and Blue.

CRYSTAL
Berry Bowl, Stippled,
  Master, 9 3/8 In. 13.00
Bowl, Fruit, 4 1/2 In. 3.00
Celery Dish, 10 1/4 In. 1.50

Creamer . . . . .3.00 to 6.00

Cup . . . . .4.50 to 6.00

Cup & Saucer . . . .5.50 to 7.00

Plate, Bread & Butter,
6 In. . . . . .1.75 to 3.00

Plate, Cheese, Handle,
6 In. 7.00

Plate, Dinner,
9 3/8 In. . . . . . . .7.00 to 15.00

Plate, Indentation, Square,
7 In. 9.00

Plate, Salad, 8 3/8 In. 6.00

Relish, 3 Sections, 7 In. . . .9.00

Sandwich Server,
11 1/2 In. 8.00

Saucer 1.00

Soup, Coupe,
7 1/2 In. . . . . . . .7.00 to 10.00

Sugar . . . . .4.00 to 6.00

Sugar & Creamer . .6.50 to 9.00

Tumbler, Iced Tea,
12 Oz., 5 1/2 In. 77.50

Tumbler, Water, 9 Oz.,
4 1/2 In. 55.00

PRIMO

Green and Mandarin Yellow are the two colors of Primo advertised in the 1932 U.S. Glass Company catalog.

GREEN

Ashtray 8.75

Cake Plate, Footed,
10 In. 23.50

Cup . . . . .9.00 to 14.50

Cup & Saucer 15.00

Grill Plate, 10 In. 12.00

Plate, Dinner, 10 In. 25.50

Plate, Salad,
7 1/2 In. . . . . . .10.25 to 14.00

Saucer 3.25

Sherbet 14.25

Sugar 12.00

Tumbler, Water, 9 Oz.,
5 3/4 In. . . . . . .18.50 to 23.50

MANDARIN YELLOW

Creamer 8.50

Cup 14.50

Grill Plate, 10 In. 11.25

Sherbet 14.50

Tumbler, Water, Footed, 9 Oz.,
5 3/4 In. . . . . . .16.00 to 20.00

PRIMROSE

Primrose was a pattern made by Anchor Hocking Glass Corporation from 1960 to 1962. The white opaque glass was decorated with a red primrose.

WHITE

Baking Pan, Utility,
6 1/2 x 10 1/2 In. 5.00

Bowl, Dessert, 6 Oz. 3.00

Cake Pan, Round, 8 In. 5.00

Cup, 8 Oz. 2.00

Plate, Salad, 7 3/8 In. 2.50

Saucer 1.50

Snack Set, 2 Piece 2.50

Snack Set, 8 Piece 20.00

Sugar 2.50

Sugar, Cover 5.00

Sugar & Creamer 6.00

PRIMUS, see Madrid

PRINCESS

Hocking Glass Company, Lancaster, Ohio, made the popular Princess pattern from 1931 to 1935. The first sets were made in Green or Yellow, shaded from Apricot to Topaz, so if you are assembling a set, be careful of the color variations.

Pink was added last. There are Blue pieces found in the West. Some pieces have a frosted finish, some are decorated with hand-painted flowers. Green is sometimes trimmed with gold; other colors are trimmed with platinum. This pattern is sometimes called Drape & Tassel, Lincoln Drape, or Tassel. Reproductions have been made. They are listed at the end of the Depression Glass section.

GREEN

Ashtray, 4 1/2 In. 70.00

Berry Bowl,
4 1/2 In. . . . . . .25.00 to 29.00

Bowl, Cereal,
5 In. . . . . .25.00 to 35.00

Bowl, Hat Shape,
9 1/2 In. 42.50

Bowl, Salad, Octagonal,
9 In. . . . . .30.00 to 50.00

Bowl, Vegetable, Oval,
10 In. . . . . .28.00 to 32.00

Butter, Cover . . .50.00 to 95.00

Cake Stand, Footed,
10 In. . . . . .25.00 to 45.00

Candy Jar,
Cover . . . . . . .52.00 to 60.00

Coaster 35.00

Cookie Jar,
Cover . . . . . . .35.00 to 60.00

Creamer, Oval 15.00

Cup . . . . .8.00 to 20.00

Cup & Saucer   . .18.00 to 25.00

Grill Plate,
9 1/2 In. . . . . . .25.00 to 38.00

Grill Plate, Tab Handles,
10 1/2 In. 12.00

Pitcher, 60 Oz.,
8 In. . . . . .55.00 to 58.00

Pitcher, Juice, 37 Oz.,
6 In. . . . . .26.00 to 66.00

Plate, Dinner, 9 1/2 In. . . .26.00

Plate, Salad,
8 1/4 In. . . . . . .14.00 to 18.00

Plate, Sherbet, 5 1/2 In. . .10.00

Platter, Closed Handles,
12 In. . . . . .15.00 to 24.00

Relish, 2 Sections,
7 1/2 In. 33.00

Salt & Pepper,
4 1/2 In., Pair 69.00

Salt & Pepper, 5 1/2 In.,
Pair 40.00

Sandwich Server, Handle,
11 1/2 In. 18.50

Shaker, Spice, 5 1/2 In.,
Pair 40.00

Sherbet, Footed . .10.00 to 25.00

Sugar 10.00

Sugar, Cover . . . .30.00 to 42.00

Tumbler, Cocktail, Cone
Footed, 3 Oz., 3 In. 24.00

Tumbler, Footed, 12 1/2 Oz.,
6 1/2 In. . . . .66.50 to 135.00

Tumbler, Iced Tea, 13 Oz.,
5 1/4 In. . . . . . .32.00 to 33.00

Tumbler, Water, Cone
Footed, 9 Oz., 4 In. 35.00

Tumbler, Water, Footed,
10 Oz., 5 1/4 In. 30.00

Tumbler, Water, Square Footed,
9 Oz., 4 In. . . . .28.00 to 32.00

Vase, 8 In. . . . . . .36.00 to 45.00

PINK

Berry Bowl,
4 1/2 In. . . . . . .25.00 to 35.00

Bowl, Cereal, 5 In. 25.00

Bowl, Hat Shape,
9 1/2 In. 65.00

Bowl, Salad, Octagonal,
Handles,
9 In. . . . . .25.00 to 65.00

Bowl, Vegetable, Oval,
10 In. . . . . .30.00 to 32.00

Wipe glass dry with newspapers for a special shine.

Cake Stand,
10 In. . . . . .30.00 to 32.00

Candy Dish, Cover 65.00

Cup . . . . .9.00 to 14.00

Cup & Saucer   . .18.00 to 24.00

Grill Plate, 9 1/2 In. 16.00

Grill Plate, 10 1/2 In. 20.00

Grill Plate, Closed
Handles, 10 1/4 In. 35.00

Pitcher, Juice, 37 Oz.,
6 In. . . . . .50.00 to 75.00

Pitcher, Water, 60 Oz.,
8 In. . . . . .55.00 to 70.00

Plate, Dinner, 9 1/2 In. . . .25.00

Plate, Salad,
8 In. . . . . .14.00 to 25.00

Plate, Sherbet,
5 1/2 In. . . . . . .10.00 to 12.00

Platter, Closed Handles,
12 In. 24.00

Sherbet 22.00

Tumbler, Footed,
5 1/2 In. 34.00

Tumbler, Iced Tea, 13 Oz.,
5 1/4 In. . . . . . .42.00 to 99.00

Tumbler, Iced Tea, Footed,
12 1/2 Oz., 6 1/2 In. . . .105.00

Tumbler, Water, 9 Oz.,
4 In. 30.00

Tumbler, Water, Footed, 10 Oz.,
5 1/4 In. . . . . . .26.00 to 30.00

Vase, 8 In. 50.00

TOPAZ

Bowl, Cereal, 5 In. 24.00

Bowl, Vegetable, Oval,
10 In. 60.00

Cup . . . . .5.00 to 8.00

Cup & Saucer   . .10.00 to 12.50

Grill Plate, 9 1/2 In. 5.50

Grill Plate, Closed
Handles, 10 1/2 In. 12.00

Pitcher, Water, 60 Oz.,
8 In. . . . . .70.00 to 99.50

Plate, Dinner,
9 1/2 In. . . . . . .11.00 to 16.00

Plate, Sherbet,
5 1/2 In. . . . . .2.00 to 3.00

Salt & Pepper, 4 1/2 In. . .80.00

Sherbet, Footed . .35.00 to 40.00

Sugar & Creamer 22.50

Tumbler, Iced Tea,
13 Oz., 5 1/4 In. 26.00

Tumbler, Iced Tea, Footed,
12 1/2 Oz.,
6 1/2 In. . . . . . .10.00 to 28.00

Tumbler, Juice, 5 Oz.,
3 In. . . . . .18.00 to 28.00

Tumbler, Water, Footed,
10 Oz., 5 1/4 In. 20.00

Tumbler, Water, Square Footed,
9 Oz., 4 3/4 In. 16.00

PRISMATIC LINE, see Queen
Mary

PROVINCIAL, see Bubble

PYRAMID, see No. 610

•Q•

QUEEN MARY

Queen Mary, sometimes called
Prismatic Line or Vertical
Ribbed, was made by Anchor
Hocking Glass Corporation
from 1936 to 1943. It was made
first in Pink, later in Crystal
and Royal Ruby.

CRYSTAL

Ashtray, Oval,
2 x 3 1/4 In. 3.00

Berry Bowl, 4 In. . .3.00 to 4.00

Bowl, Cereal, 6 In. . .6.50 to 8.00

Butter, Cover 100.00

Candlestick, 2-Light,
4 1/2 In. 12.50

Candy Dish,
  Cover . . . . .20.00 to 30.00
Cigarette Jar, Oval,
  2 x 3 In. 5.50
Coaster, Square, 4 1/4 In. . .5.00
Compote, 5 3/4 In. 8.00
Creamer 6.00
Cup, Large 5.50
Cup & Saucer 6.50
Plate, 6 5/8 In. 4.00
Plate, 12 In. 9.00
Plate, Salad, 8 3/4 In. 5.00
Salt & Pepper 20.00
Sandwich Server, 12 In. . . .9.00
Saucer, Cup Ring 3.00
Sherbet, Footed 5.00

PINK

Berry Bowl,
  4 1/2 In. . . . . . . .4.75 to 6.00
Berry Bowl, 5 In. 8.50
Bowl, Cereal, 6 In. 23.00
Bowl, Handle, 4 In. 5.00
Butter, Cover 135.00
Creamer, Oval . . . .6.00 to 18.00
Cup . . . . .6.50 to 10.00
Cup, Large . . . . . .6.00 to 7.00
Cup & Saucer 10.00
Plate, 6 In. 5.50
Plate, 7 In. 8.00
Plate, Dinner,
  9 3/4 In. . . . . . .50.00 to 55.00
Saucer . . . . .5.00 to 6.00
Sherbet, Footed 9.00
Sugar, Dual 10.00
Tumbler, 5 Oz.,
  3 1/2 In. 9.00
Tumbler, 9 Oz.,
  4 In. . . . . .9.00 to 17.50
Tumbler, Footed, 10 Oz.,
  5 In. . . . . .66.00 to 75.00

RADIANCE

New Martinsville Glass Company, New Martinsville, West Virginia, made Radiance pattern from 1936 to 1939. It was made in Amber, Crystal, Emerald Green, Ice Blue, Pink, and

Red. A few rare pieces were made in Cobalt Blue. A pattern by the same name was made by Cambridge.

AMBER

Bowl, Crimped, 12 In. . . .45.00
Bowl, Flared, 12 In. 27.00
Butter, Chrome Cover 45.00
Cup & Saucer 18.00
Pitcher,
  64 Oz. . . . . .160.00 to 169.00
Salt & Pepper 50.00
Tumbler, 9 Oz. 20.00

CRYSTAL

Butter, Cover 140.00
Creamer 7.00
Cup, Footed 8.00
Plate, Luncheon, 8 In. 7.00
Punch Cup 5.00
Saucer 3.00

ICE BLUE

Bonbon, 6 In. 35.00
Candlestick, 2-Light,
  Pair 150.00
Candy Dish, Cover,
  3 Sections 125.00
Creamer . . . . . .22.00 to 25.00
Cup 18.00
Cup & Saucer 26.00
Pitcher, 64 Oz. 225.00
Plate, Luncheon, 8 In. 16.00
Punch Cup . . . . .10.00 to 17.00
Saucer 9.00
Sugar 22.00
Vase, 12 In. 50.00

RED

Bowl, Crimped, 12 In. . . .75.00
Cup & Saucer 24.00
Plate, Luncheon, 8 In. 13.00
Punch Cup 15.00
Salt & Pepper . .75.00 to 125.00

RAINDROPS

Watch out for confusion with Raindrops and another pattern called Pear Optic or Thumbprint. The rounded, fingernail-shaped impressions of the Raindrops pattern are on the inside of the pieces, the other pattern has hexagonal depressions on the outside. Federal Glass Company made Crystal and Green Raindrops luncheon sets from 1929 to 1933.

CRYSTAL

Saucer 2.00
Whiskey, 1 Oz., 1 7/8 In. . .5.00

GREEN

Berry Bowl, 7 1/2 In. 40.00
Creamer 8.00
Sugar & Creamer,
  Cover 47.00
Tumbler, 4 Oz., 3 In. 4.25
Tumbler, 5 Oz.,
  3 7/8 In. . . . . .5.00 to 6.50
Tumbler, 10 Oz., 5 In. 12.00

❖

To remove an unwanted gummed price sticker, try heating it with a hair dryer. The glue will melt a bit and it will be easier to peel off the sticker.

❖

Tumbler, 14 Oz.,
  5 3/8 In. 11.50

RASPBERRY BAND, see Laurel

REX, see No. 610

RIBBED, see Manhattan

RIBBON

Black, Crystal, Green, and Pink pieces were made in Ribbon pattern in the 1930s. It was made by the Hazel Atlas Glass Company.

GREEN
Berry Bowl, Master,
  8 In. . . . . .20.00 to 30.00

Bowl, 9 In. 27.00

Candy Dish, Cover,
  Footed . . . . . . .30.00 to 35.00

Creamer,
  Footed . . . . . . .14.00 to 15.00

Cup & Saucer 7.50

Plate, Luncheon,
  8 In. . . . . .5.00 to 10.00

Plate, Sherbet,
  6 1/4 In. . . . . . . .2.00 to 3.50

Sherbet 6.00

Sugar 12.00

Sugar &
  Creamer . . . . .25.00 to 26.00

Tumbler, Footed, 10 Oz.,
  6 In. . . . . .27.50 to 29.00

RIBBON CANDY, see Pretzel

RING

Hocking Glass Company made Ring from 1927 to 1933. The pattern, also known as Banded Ring, sometimes has colored rings added to the Crystal, Green, Mayfair Blue, Pink, or Red glass. The colored rings were made in various combinations of black, blue, orange, pink, platinum, red, and yellow. Platinum trim is on some pieces. Some solid red pieces also were made. The design is characterized by several sets of rings, each comprised of four rings. Circle, a similar Hocking pattern, has only one group of rings.

CRYSTAL
Cocktail Shaker, 11 In. . . .12.00

Creamer, Platinum Rim . . .3.50

Cup, Platinum
  Rim . . . . .2.50 to 3.00

Cup & Saucer, Platinum
  Rim 3.00

Decanter, Stopper 18.75

Goblet, Champagne,
  Platinum Rim,
  3 1/2 Oz., 4 1/2 In. 3.50

Goblet, Water, 9 Oz.,
  7 1/4 In. . . . . . . .5.00 to 18.00

Ice Tub, Multicolored
  Rings 30.00

Pitcher, 60 Oz., 8 In. 12.00

Pitcher, Platinum Rim,
  80 Oz., 8 1/2 In. 18.00

Plate, Luncheon,
  8 In. . . . . .2.00 to 7.00

Plate, Luncheon, Platinum
  Rim, 8 In. . . . . . .3.00 to 3.75

Plate, Off-Center Ring,
  6 1/2 In. . . . . . . .3.00 to 5.00

Salt & Pepper, Platinum
  Rim 40.00

Saltshaker 10.00

Sandwich Server, Center
  Handle, Platinum
  Rim . . . . .12.00 to 15.00

Sherbet, Footed,
  4 3/4 In. . . . . . . .3.75 to 5.00

Sherbet, Underplate,
  Low 20.00

Soup, Dish, Platinum
  Rim, 7 In. 9.00

Sugar, Platinum Rim 3.50

Sugar & Creamer 6.50

Tumbler, 9 Oz., 4 1/4 In. . .3.50

Tumbler, 10 Oz.,
  4 3/4 In. 5.00

Tumbler, Footed, 5 Oz.,
  3 1/2 In. . . . . . . .3.00 to 3.75

Tumbler, Footed, Platinum
  Rim, 12 Oz., 5 1/8 In. . . .6.00

Tumbler, Iced Tea, Footed,
  6 1/2 In. 6.50

Tumbler, Multicolored
  Rings, 4 Oz., 3 In. 6.00

Tumbler, Platinum Rim,
  8 Oz., 4 In. 7.00

Vase, Multicolored Rings,
  8 In. 25.00

Whiskey, Multicolored Rings,
  1 1/2 Oz., 2 In. . .4.00 to 10.00

GREEN
Berry Bowl, 5 In. 8.00

Berry Bowl, Master,
  8 In. . . . . .8.00 to 16.00

Cup 5.00

Goblet, 9 Oz.,
  7 1/4 In. . . . . . .15.00 to 19.50

Pitcher, 80 Oz., 8 1/2 In. . .36.00

Plate, Luncheon, 8 In. 9.00

Plate, Off-Center Ring,
  6 1/2 In. 4.00

Plate, Sherbet, 6 1/4 In. . . .7.00

Sandwich Server, Center
  Handle 36.00

Sherbet, Footed,
  4 3/4 In. . . . . . .11.00 to 12.00

Sherbet, Off-Center Ring
  Plate, 2 Piece 19.00

Tumbler, 5 Oz., 3 1/2 In. . .6.00

Tumbler, 10 Oz.,
  4 3/4 In. 9.50

Tumbler, 12 Oz.,
  5 1/8 In. 9.00

Tumbler, Footed, 5 Oz.,
  3 1/2 In. 15.00

ROCK CRYSTAL

Rock Crystal, sometimes called Early American Rock Crystal, was made in many solid colors by McKee Glass Company. Amber, Blue-Green, Cobalt Blue, Crystal, Green, Pink, Red, and Yellow pieces were made in the 1920s and 1930s.

CRYSTAL
Bowl, Plain Edge, 5 In. . . .16.00
Bowl, Salad, Scalloped
    Edge, 9 In. 35.00
Candelabra, 2-Light, Pair .40.00
Candelabra, 3-Light 30.00
Creamer, Footed, 9 Oz. . . .20.00
Cup . . . . .16.00 to 17.00
Goblet, 8 Oz.,
    7 1/2 In. . . . . . .9.75 to 15.00
Goblet, Champagne,
    Footed, 6 Oz. 16.00
Goblet, Cocktail, Footed,
    3 1/2 Oz. . . . . .9.00 to 16.50
Goblet, Whiskey,
    2 1/2 Oz. 18.00
Goblet, Wine,
    3 Oz. . . . . . . .18.00 to 22.50
Parfait, Low Footed,
    3 1/2 Oz. . . . . . .6.00 to 10.00
Pitcher, Scalloped Edge,
    1 Qt. 125.00
Pitcher, Tankard,
    Fancy 299.00
Plate, 8 1/2 In. . . . .7.50 to 9.00
Plate, Bread & Butter,
    6 In. 5.00
Plate, Dinner, 10 1/2 In. . .47.50
Plate, Salad, 7 1/2 In. 6.00
Relish, 2 Sections,
    11 1/2 In. 22.00
Relish, 5 Sections,
    12 1/2 In. . . . . .25.00 to 40.00

Relish, 6 Sections,
    14 In. 35.00
Sherbet, Footed,
    3 1/2 In. . . . . . .13.00 to 17.00
Vase, Footed, 11 In. 60.00

GREEN
Parfait, Low Footed,
    3 1/2 Oz. 20.00
Plate, 8 In. 15.00
Sandwich Server,
    Center Handle 50.00

PINK
Goblet, Champagne,
    Footed, 6 Oz. 24.00
Goblet, Footed, 8 Oz. 25.00
Pitcher, Cover, 9 In. 375.00
Tumbler, Juice, 5 Oz. 25.00

RED
Goblet, Champagne,
    Footed, 6 Oz. 35.00
Goblet, Footed, 7 Oz. 50.00
Goblet, Footed, 8 Oz. 60.00
Plate, 7 1/2 In. 18.00
Sherbet, Footed,
    3 1/2 Oz. 65.00
Sugar, Cover 110.00
Sundae, Low, 6 Oz. 35.00
Tumbler, Concave,
    12 Oz. 65.00
Tumbler, Straight, 9 Oz. . .50.00
Whiskey,
    2 1/2 Oz. . . . . .55.00 to 66.50

YELLOW
Cake Stand, Footed, 11 In. 30.00
Console, Footed, 12 In. . . .65.00
Goblet, Claret, 3 Oz. 65.00

ROPE, see Colonial Fluted

ROSE CAMEO

Rose Cameo was made by the Belmont Tumbler Company, Bellaire, Ohio, in 1933. It has been found only in Green and only in six different pieces, three of which are bowls.

GREEN
Bowl, Cereal, 5 In. 16.50
Plate, 7 In. 12.00
Sherbet 12.00
Tumbler, Straight, 5 In. . .17.00
Tumbler, Water, Footed,
    5 In. . . . . .20.00 to 22.50

ROSE LACE, see Royal Lace

ROSE POINT

Rose Point was made by the Cambridge Glass Company of Cambridge, Ohio, from 1936 to 1953. The elaborate pattern was made in Crystal and Crystal with gold trim. A few rare pieces were made in Red or Amber.

CRYSTAL
Ashtray Set, 5 Piece 325.00
Bowl, Footed, Oblong,
    12 In. 195.00
Bowl, Ruffled,
    10 In. . . . . . .165.00 to 295.00
Candlestick, 1-Light,
    5 In., Pair 129.00
Candlestick, Prism,
    7 1/2 In. 125.00
Candy Box, Cover,
    3 Sections, 8 In. 135.00
Compote, 5 In. 48.00
Console, Low, 7 In. 85.00
Cup & Saucer, Footed . . .55.00
Decanter, Footed,
    14 Oz. 950.00
Decanter, Sherry,
    28 Oz. 650.00
Dish, Mayonnaise,
    3 Piece 50.00
Finger Bowl 95.00
Goblet, Champagne,
    7 Oz. 33.00
Goblet, Cocktail,
    4 1/2 Oz. . . . . .35.00 to 49.00
Goblet, Cordial,
    1 Oz. . . . . .75.00 to 79.00

Goblet, Water,
10 Oz. . . . . . .45.00 to 55.00
Goblet, Wine,
2 1/2 Oz. . . . . .50.00 to 75.00
Honey Dish, Cover 345.00
Ice Pail 200.00
Ice Tub 250.00
Jam Jar, Sterling Cover, Ladle,
7 Oz. . . . . . .195.00 to 295.00
Mustard, Cover, 3 Oz. . .160.00
Oyster Cocktail, 5 Oz. . . .42.50
Pickle, Footed, 7 In. 65.00
Pitcher, Ice Lip, 76 Oz. . .450.00
Plate, Handles, 6 In. 25.00
Relish, 2 Sections, 6 In. . .35.00
Relish, 3 Sections,
6 1/2 In. 35.00
Sandwich Server, Footed,
12 In. 150.00
Sugar 37.50
Sugar &
Creamer . . . . 32.00 to 65.00
Tumbler, Footed,
2 1/2 Oz. 100.00
Tumbler, Iced Tea,
12 Oz. . . . . . . .47.50 to 50.00
Tumbler, Juice, Footed,
5 Oz. 42.50
Tumbler, Water, Low
Footed, 10 Oz. 50.00
Vase, Bud, 6 In. 85.00
Vase, Bud, Gold Encrusted,
6 In. 125.00
Vase, Footed, 11 In. 57.00

- - - - - - - - - - ❖ - - - - - - - - - -

**Be sure a copy of lists
of valuables, photographs, and other
information that will be
needed in case of an
insurance loss can be
found. Do not keep
them in your safe
deposit box because
your box key could be
lost in the fire. Give a
copy to a trusted friend.**

- - - - - - - - - - ❖ - - - - - - - - - -

Vase, Footed, 12 In. 150.00
Vase, Globe, 5 In. 145.00

ROSEMARY

Rosemary, also called Cabbage
Rose with Single Arch or
Dutch Rose, was made by
Federal Glass Company from
1935 to 1937. It was made in
Amber, Green, Iridescent, and
Pink. Pieces with bases, like
creamers or cups, are sometimes confused with Mayfair
Federal because the molds used
were those originally designed
for the Mayfair pattern. The
lower half of the Rosemary
pieces are plain, the lower half
of Mayfair Federal has a band
of arches.

AMBER
Berry Bowl, 5 In. . .4.50 to 6.00
Bowl, Cereal, 6 In. 30.00
Bowl, Vegetable, Oval,
10 In. . . . . . . .10.00 to 16.50
Creamer 9.00
Cup 6.25
Plate, Dinner,
9 1/2 In. . . . . . .5.00 to 10.00
Plate, Salad,
6 3/4 In. . . . . . . .3.50 to 6.00
Platter, Oval,
12 In. . . . . . . .10.00 to 17.50
Saucer . . . . .2.50 to 5.00
Soup, Cream, 5 In. 15.00

Sugar . . . . .6.00 to 8.25
Sugar & Creamer 19.00
Tumbler, Water, 9 Oz.,
4 1/2 In. . . . . . .25.00 to 33.00

GREEN
Bowl, Vegetable, Oval,
10 In. 37.00
Creamer 13.00
Cup 10.25
Plate, Salad, 6 3/4 In. 11.00
Platter, Oval, 12 In. 19.00
Saucer 6.50
Soup, Cream, 5 In. 28.00
Sugar 13.00
Tumbler, Water, Footed, 9 Oz.,
4 1/2 In. . . . . . .30.00 to 38.00

PINK
Berry Bowl, 5 In. 15.00
Bowl, Cereal, 6 In. 40.00
Cup 11.00
Cup & Saucer 17.00
Plate, Dinner, 9 1/2 In. . . .10.00
Saucer 6.00
Soup, Cream, 5 In. 29.00

ROSEMARY, see also Mayfair
Federal

ROULETTE

Anchor Hocking Glass Corporation made Roulette pattern
from 1935 to 1939. Primarily
Green luncheon and beverage
sets were manufactured, although some Crystal pieces
were made, as well as Pink
beverage sets. Collectors originally called the pattern Many
Windows.

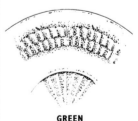

GREEN
Bowl, Fruit, 9 In. 16.00
Cup . . . . .4.50 to 6.00
Cup & Saucer . .10.00 to 12.00

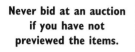

**Never bid at an auction
if you have not
previewed the items.**

Pitcher, 65 Oz., 8 In. 28.00
Plate, Luncheon,
 8 1/2 In. . . . . . . .4.50 to 7.25
Sandwich Server, 12 In. . .15.00
Saucer 5.00
Sherbet, Footed 6.00
Tumbler, Footed,
 10 Oz., 5 1/2 In. 27.00
Tumbler, Iced Tea, 12 Oz.,
 5 1/8 In. . . . . .31.00 to 45.00
Tumbler, Water, 9 Oz.,
 4 1/8 In. . . . . .22.00 to 30.00
Whiskey, 1 1/2 Oz.,
 2 1/2 In. 16.00

ROUND ROBIN

Sometimes a pattern was advertised by the wholesaler, but the
manufacturer is unknown today. One of these is Round
Robin, sometimes called Accordion Pleats. It was pictured
as a luncheon set in the catalogs
of the late 1920s and 1930s and
offered in Green, Crystal, and
Iridescent Marigold.

GREEN
Berry Bowl, 4 In. 5.50
Cup, Footed . . . . .5.00 to 8.00
Cup & Saucer 13.00
Plate, Luncheon,
 8 In. . . . . .4.50 to 7.00
Plate, Sherbet,
 6 In. . . . . .3.00 to 6.00
Sherbet, Footed, 5 Oz. . . .10.00

IRIDESCENT MARIGOLD
Berry Bowl, 4 In. 5.00

Plate, Sherbet, 6 In. 2.50
Saucer, 6 In. 2.50
Sherbet, Footed, 5 Oz. 5.00

ROYAL LACE

Royal Lace was made from
1934 to 1941. The popular pat-
tern by Hazel Atlas Glass
Company was made in Cobalt
Blue, Crystal, Green, and Pink,
and in limited quantities in
Amethyst. It is sometimes
called Gladiola or Rose Lace.
Reproductions have been made.
They are listed at the end of the
Depression Glass section.

COBALT BLUE
Berry Bowl, Master,
 10 In. . . . . . .110.00 to 120.00
Bowl, Footed,
 10 In. . . . . .59.00 to 95.00
Bowl, Rolled Edge,
 10 In. . . . .1200.00 to 1400.00
Bowl, Straight, Footed,
 10 In. 105.00
Bowl, Vegetable, Oval,
 11 In. 70.00
Butter, Cover 500.00
Cider Set, 7 Piece . . . .175.00 to
205.00
Cookie Jar,
 Cover . . . . .340.00 to 495.00
Creamer . . . . . .50.00 to 60.00
Cup . . . . .29.00 to 38.00

Cup & Saucer . .29.00 to 50.00
Grill Plate,
 9 7/8 In. . . . . .42.00 to 45.00
Pitcher, Ice Lip,
 96 Oz.,
 8 1/2 In. . . .325.00 to 495.00
Pitcher, Straight,
 48 Oz. . . . . .175.00 to 220.00
Plate, Dinner,
 9 7/8 In. . . . . . .37.00 to 55.00
Plate, Luncheon,
 8 1/2 In. . . . . . .40.00 to 47.00
Plate, Sherbet,
 6 In. . . . . .14.00 to 18.00
Salt &
 Pepper . . . . .315.00 to 325.00
Saucer . . . . . . .12.00 to 15.00
Sherbet, Footed . .42.50 to 53.00
Sherbet, Metal Holder,
 5 Piece 125.00
Soup, Cream,
 4 3/4 In. . . . . . .40.00 to 48.00
Sugar 35.00
Sugar, Cover 225.00
Sugar &
 Creamer . . . .95.00 to 110.00
Sugar & Creamer,
 Cover 295.00
Tumbler, 5 Oz.,
 3 1/2 In. 55.00
Tumbler, 9 Oz.,
 4 1/8 In. . . . . . .42.00 to 55.00
Tumbler, 10 Oz.,
 4 7/8 In. . . . .165.00 to 270.00
Tumbler, 12 Oz.,
 5 3/8 In. . . . .130.00 to 155.00

CRYSTAL
Berry Bowl, 5 In. 14.00
Bowl, Footed, 10 In. 23.00
Butter, Cover 63.00
Cookie Jar,
 Cover . . . . . . .38.00 to 45.00
Creamer 12.00
Creamer, Cover 32.00
Cup 7.50
Cup & Saucer 12.00
Pitcher, 68 Oz., 8 In. 3.00
Pitcher, 96 Oz., 8 1/2 In. . .60.00
Plate, Dinner, 9 7/8 In. . . .15.00
Plate, Luncheon,
 8 1/2 In. 10.00
Sherbet, Footed . .16.00 to 19.00
Soup, Cream . . . .12.00 to 14.00

Sugar &
Creamer .... .22.00 to 32.00
Sugar & Creamer,
Cover .... .40.00 to 45.00
Tumbler, 9 Oz.,
4 1/8 In. ...... 11.00 to 16.00

GREEN
Berry Bowl, Master,
10 In. .... .30.00 to 75.00
Bowl, Ruffled, Footed,
10 In. ..... .65.00 to 165.00
Butter, Cover . .300.00 to 325.00
Cookie Jar,
Cover .... .75.00 to 85.00
Cup 20.00
Cup & Saucer . .26.00 to 32.00
Nut Bowl 650.00
Pitcher, 86 Oz., 8 In. 205.00
Pitcher, Ice Lip,
8 1/2 In. 130.00
Pitcher, Straight,
48 Oz. .... 100.00 to 125.00
Plate, Dinner,
9 7/8 In. ..... .28.00 to 36.00
Plate, Sherbet,
6 In. .... .8.00 to 15.00
Platter, Oval,
13 In. .... .35.00 to 55.00
Salt & Pepper . .95.00 to 128.00
Saltshaker .... .60.00 to 65.00
Saucer 9.00
Sherbet, Footed . 34.00 to 36.00
Soup, Cream ... .32.00 to 37.00
Sugar .... .22.00 to 29.00
Sugar &
Creamer .... .30.00 to 45.00
Sugar & Creamer,
Cover ...... .90.00 to 132.00
Tumbler, 5 Oz.,
3 1/2 In. 37.00
Tumbler, Water, 9 Oz.,
4 1/8 In. ..... .35.00 to 44.00

PINK
Berry Bowl, 5 In. 17.00
Berry Bowl, Master,
10 In. .... .35.00 to 60.00
Bowl, Footed,
10 In. ...... .47.00 to 75.00
Bowl, Rolled Edge,
10 In. 100.00
Bowl, Ruffled, 10 In. 85.00
Candlestick, Rolled Edge,
Pair 110.00

Candlestick, Ruffled 25.00
Console Set, Footed,
Rolled Edge, 3 Piece . .265.00
Cookie Jar,
Cover .... .60.00 to 80.00
Cup .... .14.00 to 16.00
Cup & Saucer . .22.00 to 29.00
Pitcher, 64 Oz.,
8 In. ...... 120.00 to 130.00
Pitcher, 86 Oz., 8 In. 125.00
Pitcher, Straight, 48 Oz. . .95.00
Plate, Dinner,
9 7/8 In. ..... .21.00 to 27.00
Plate, Sherbet,
6 In. .... .8.00 to 12.00
Platter, Oval,
13 In. .... .30.00 to 60.00
Salt & Pepper ... .70.00 to 80.00
Saucer 6.00
Sugar, Cover 75.00
Sugar & Creamer 45.00
Tumbler, 9 Oz.,
4 1/8 In. ..... .30.00 to 39.00
Tumbler, 12 Oz.,
5 3/8 In. 60.00

ROYAL RUBY

There is no reason to picture this pattern because it is the plain shape and bright red color that identifies it. Anchor Hocking Glass Corporation made it from 1939 to the 1960s and again in 1977. The same shapes were made in green and called by the pattern name Forest Green. Reproduction tumblers were made in 1977 and 1978.

A glass vase or bowl can be cleaned with a damp cloth. Try not to wash the glass in a sink—hitting the glass on a faucet or the sink is a common cause of breakage.

Ashtray, Square, 4 1/4 In. . .6.00
Bowl, 4 1/2 In. . ..6.00 to 12.00
Bowl, 8 1/2 In. 17.50
Bowl, Cereal, 5 1/4 In. 12.00
Bowl, Fruit, Deep,
10 In. 40.00
Creamer 7.00
Cup, Round 6.00
Cup, Square 5.50
Cup & Saucer 7.50
Goblet, 5 1/4 In. . .9.00 to 15.00
Pickle, 6 In. 15.00
Pitcher, Ball, Upright,
3 Qt. 45.00
Plate, Dinner, 9 1/8 In. 9.00
Plate, Luncheon, 7 3/4 In. . .5.00
Plate, Square, 8 3/8 In. 8.00
Punch Bowl, Base 75.00
Punch Cup 3.00
Punch Set,
10 Piece .... 100.00 to 115.00
Punch Set, 14 Piece 125.00
Saucer 3.00
Sherbet, Footed .... .7.00 to 8.00
Soup, Dish,
7 1/2 In. ...... 14.00 to 18.00
Sugar 7.00
Sugar, Footed 5.00
Sugar &
Creamer ..... .12.00 to 16.00
Tumbler, 9 Oz.,
4 1/8 In. 4.75
Tumbler, 12 Oz.,
4 7/8 In. 5.00
Tumbler, 13 Oz.,
5 3/8 In. .... .6.50 to 9.00
Tumbler, Cocktail,
3 1/2 In. .... .5.50 to 12.50

Tumbler, Juice,
5 Oz., 3 In. 5.00
Vase, 6 1/2 In. . . . .7.50 to 9.00
Vase, Ball Shape, 4 In. 4.50
Vase, Bud, 7 1/2 In. 12.00

RUSSIAN, see Holiday

S PATTERN

Macbeth-Evans Glass Company
made S Pattern, or Stippled
Rose Band, from 1930 to 1935.
It was made before 1932 in
Crystal, Pink, Topaz, and Crystal with gold, blue, or platinum
trim. The 1934 listing mentions
Red, Green, and Monax. Other
pieces were made in Amber,
Ritz Blue, and Crystal with
many colors of trim including
amber, green, rose, platinum,
red, silver, or white.

AMBER
Cake Plate, 13 3/4 In. 70.00
Plate, Dinner, 9 1/4 In. 6.50
Sherbet 8.00
Tumbler, Iced Tea, 12 Oz.,
5 In. 18.00

CRYSTAL
Bowl, Cereal, Amber Band,
5 1/2 In. 6.00
Cake Plate, 11 In. 45.00
Creamer, Amber Band,
Thin 5.00
Cup, Amber Band 4.00
Cup & Saucer, Platinum
Band, Thick 4.50
Cup & Saucer, Red Band,
Thick 7.50
Cup & Saucer, Thick 4.50
Cup & Saucer,
Thin . . . . .4.50 to 5.00

Plate, Luncheon,
8 3/8 In. . . . . .3.50 to 8.00
Plate, Sherbet,
6 In. . . . . .4.00 to 4.50
Saucer, Amber Band 4.00
Saucer, Red Band 2.50
Sugar, Footed, Amber
Band 10.00
Sugar, Footed, Platinum
Band, Thick 5.00
Sugar & Creamer,
Footed, Amber Band,
Thin . . . . .10.00 to 12.00
Sugar & Creamer, Footed,
Platinum Band, Thick . .10.00
Sugar & Creamer, Footed,
Thin 8.50
Tumbler, Water, 9 Oz.,
4 In. . . . . .10.00 to 12.00

MONAX
Plate, Sherbet,
6 In. . . . . .8.00 to 10.00

YELLOW
Cup, Platinum Band 5.00
Cup & Saucer, Thin 7.00
Plate, 8 In. 5.00
Sherbet, Footed 7.00
Sugar & Creamer, Footed,
Thin 10.00

SAIL BOAT, see White Ship

SAILING SHIP, see White Ship

SANDWICH ANCHOR HOCKING

Many patterns were called
Sandwich. Each company
seemed to have one design with
that name. The most popular
were made by Anchor Hocking
Glass Corporation, Indiana
Glass Company, and Duncan &
Miller Glass Company. The
Anchor Hocking Sandwich pattern was made from 1939 to
1964 and can be distinguished
by the three lines around the
edge of each petal. Pink and
Royal Ruby were made about
1939; Crystal was made from
1939 to 1964; Forest Green and
White (opaque) date from the
1950s and 1960s; Desert Gold

from 1961 to 1964. A reproduction line was introduced in
1977 by another company in
Amber, Blue, Crystal, and
Royal Ruby.

CRYSTAL
Berry Bowl,
4 7/8 In. . . . . .3.00 to 5.00
Berry Bowl, Scalloped,
4 7/8 In. . . . . . .10.00 to 16.00
Bowl, Cereal,
6 1/2 In. . . . . .3.50 to 7.50
Bowl, Oval, 8 In. 6.00
Bowl, Scalloped,
5 1/4 In. . . . . .3.50 to 7.00
Bowl, Vegetable, Oval,
8 1/4 In. . . . . .5.00 to 6.00
Butter, Cover . . .40.00 to 48.00
Cookie Jar, Cover 36.00
Creamer 6.00
Cup 2.00
Cup & Saucer . . . .3.00 to 6.00
Custard Cup . . . . .2.00 to 3.50
Custard Cup,
Ruffled 12.00
Pitcher, Ice Lip,
1/2 Gal. . . . . . .70.00 to 90.00
Plate, Dessert, 7 In. 10.00
Plate, Dinner, 9 In. 17.00
Punch Set,
14 Piece . . . . . .58.00 to 60.00
Saucer 3.00
Sherbet, Footed . . . .7.00 to 8.00
Sugar . . . . .3.00 to 6.00
Sugar & Creamer 12.00
Tumbler, Footed, 9 Oz.,
5 1/2 In. 28.00
Tumbler, Juice, 3 Oz.,
3 3/4 In. . . . . . .14.00 to 16.00
Tumbler, Water, 9 Oz.,
4 1/2 In. . . . . . . .5.00 to 10.00

DESERT GOLD

Berry Bowl, 4 7/8 In. 6.00

Bowl, Cereal,
  6 1/2 In. . . . . . .12.00 to 17.00

Bowl, Cereal, Scalloped,
  6 1/2 In. 8.00

Cookie Jar, Cover 40.00

Cup 5.00

Cup & Saucer . . . .4.50 to 6.75

Plate, Dinner,
  9 In. . . . . .5.00 to 9.00

Sandwich Server, 12 In. . .14.00

FOREST GREEN

Berry Bowl, 4 7/8 In. 3.00

Bowl, Cereal, 6 1/2 In. . . .70.00

Bowl, Salad, 7 In. 125.00

Cup . . . . .22.00 to 24.00

Cup & Saucer 44.00

Custard Cup
  Liner . . . . .1.50 to 3.00

Pitcher, Juice, 6 In. 250.00

Plate, Dinner, 9 In. 115.00

Saucer . . . . . . .15.00 to 17.00

Sugar 25.00

Sugar & Creamer 70.00

Tumbler, Juice, 3 Oz.,
  3 3/4 In. . . . . . . .4.00 to 5.00

Tumbler, Water, 9 Oz.,
  4 1/2 In. 5.00

ROYAL RUBY

Bowl, Scalloped,
  5 1/2 In. . . . . . .15.00 to 22.00

Bowl, Scalloped, 8 In. . . .38.00

WHITE

Base, For Punch Bowl . . .12.00

Punch Cup, Gold Trim 45

Punch Set, 10 Piece 35.00

Punch Set, 13 Piece 24.00

Punch Set, Gold Trim,
  14 Piece 50.00

SANDWICH DUNCAN & MILLER

Sandwich Duncan & Miller is easy to recognize. It has long been said the pattern was designed by Mr. Heisey's son-in-law and that he added the diamond and H mark used by Heisey as part of the border design. New research suggests this is not true and that the diamon and H mark is really a mold flaw. The plates in this series have ground bottoms. The star in the center of the plate does not go to the edge of the circle. Duncan & Miller named pattern No. 41 Early American Sandwich Glass in 1925. The glass was made in Amber, Cobalt Blue, Crystal, Green, Pink, and Red. The pattern remained in production until 1955 when some of the molds were bought by other companies. Lancaster Colony made pieces in Blue, Green, and Amberina in the 1970s. Tiffin made Milk Glass pieces. Reproductions are listed at the end of the Depression Glass section.

CRYSTAL

Bowl, Footed, 10 In. 55.00

Bowl, Fruit, Flared,
  12 In. . . . . .42.50 to 45.00

Bowl, Salad, 7 In. 15.00

Candlestick, 4 In., Pair . . .35.00

Celery Dish, 10 In. 25.00

Creamer 9.00

Pickle, 7 In. 18.00

Sherbet, Footed 20.00

Sugar 8.00

Tumbler, Iced Tea, 13 Oz.,
  5 1/4 In. . . . . . .18.00 to 20.00

GREEN

Bonbon, Heart Shape,
  Handle, 5 1/2 In. 25.00

Bowl, Fruit, 5 In. 20.00

SANDWICH INDIANA

Another Sandwich pattern was made by the Indiana Glass Company, Dunkirk, Indiana, from the 1920s through the 1980s. It can be distinguished by the single line around the flower petals. Only the colors changed through the years. Amber was made from the late 1920s to the 1980s, Crystal from the late 1920s to the 1990s, Light Green and Pink from the 1920s to the 1930s, Red from 1933 to the 1970s, Teal Blue from the 1950s to the 1980s, Opaque White in the 1950s, and Smoky Blue in 1976 and 1977. The scroll design varies with the size of the plate. Tiara Home Products made Sandwich in Red (1969), Amber (1970), and Crystal (1978). They continued to make Amber, Chantilly Green, and Crystal in the 1980s. Tiara also made a few pieces from redesigned molds. A Teal Blue butter dish was also made. Reproductions are listed at the end of the Depression Glass section.

AMBER

Candlestick, 3 1/2 In.,
  Pair 12.00

Cup 2.50

CRYSTAL
Ashtray, Club Shape 1.50
Ashtray, Spade Shape 1.50
Ashtray Set, 4 Piece 12.00
Berry Bowl, 4 1/4 In. 4.00
Berry Bowl, Master,
  8 1/4 In. . . . . . .11.00 to 12.00
Butter, Cover 65.00
Cake Plate, Frosted
  Edge, 13 In. 35.00
Candlestick, 3 1/2 In.,
  Pair 18.00
Candlestick, 7 In.,
  Pair 25.00
Celery Dish 16.00
Console, Rolled Edge,
  11 1/2 In. . . . . .16.00 to 19.00
Cup . . . . .2.50 to 3.50
Cup & Saucer . . . .3.50 to 6.00
Dish, Mayonnaise,
  Flared 15.00
Goblet, Water, Footed,
  9 Oz., 5 In. 13.00
Goblet, Wine, 4 Oz.,
  3 In. 11.00
Plate, Dinner,
  10 1/2 In. . . . . . .8.50 to 10.00
Plate, Luncheon,
  8 3/8 In. . . . . .3.50 to 6.00
Plate, Sherbet, 6 In. 3.00
Sandwich Server, Center
  Handle 20.00
Sherbet, Footed . . . .3.50 to 6.00
Sugar & Creamer,
  Cover . . . . .18.00 to 30.00
Sugar & Creamer, Tray,
  3 Piece 11.00
Tidbit, 2 Tiers 30.00
Tumbler, Cocktail,
  Footed, 3 Oz. 7.50

LIGHT GREEN
Ashtray 16.00
Bowl, Cereal, 6 In. 30.00
Bowl, Hexagonal,
  6 In. 20.00
Candlestick, 3 1/2 In.,
  Pair . . . . .45.00 to 50.00
Plate, Bread & Butter,
  7 In. 12.00
Plate, Dinner,
  10 1/2 In. 20.00

Plate, Indentation, Oval,
  8 In. 15.00
Sherbet, Footed 15.00

PINK
Berry Bowl, Master,
  Scalloped, 8 1/2 In. 40.00
Berry Bowl, Scalloped,
  4 1/4 In. 10.00
Plate, Luncheon,
  8 3/8 In. 16.00

RED
Berry Bowl,
  4 1/4 In 14.00
Goblet, Water, 9 Oz.,
  5 In. 25.00

SAWTOOTH, see English
Hobnail

SAXON, see Coronation

SHAMROCK, see Cloverleaf

SHARON
Sharon, or Cabbage Rose, was
made by the Federal Glass
Company from 1935 to 1939.
The pattern was made in Am-
ber, Crystal, Green, and Pink.
A cheese dish was reproduced
in 1976 in Amber, Blue, Dark
Green, Light Green, and Pink.
Other items have been re-
produced in various colors.
They are listed at the end of the
Depression Glass section.

AMBER
Berry Bowl,
  5 In. . . . . .6.50 to 8.50
Berry Bowl, Master,
  8 1/2 In. . . . . .4.00 to 5.00
Bowl, Cereal, 6 In. 16.00
Bowl, Fruit,
  10 1/2 In. . . . . .15.00 to 22.00

Bowl, Vegetable, Oval,
  9 1/2 In. . . . . . .16.00 to 21.00
Butter, Cover . . .42.00 to 47.00
Cake Plate, Footed,
  11 1/2 In. . . . . .20.00 to 30.00
Candy Dish,
  Cover . . . . .40.00 to 47.00
Creamer 14.00
Cup . . . . .6.00 to 8.00
Cup & Saucer . .10.00 to 17.00
Jam Jar, 7 1/2 In. 30.00
Pitcher, Water, 80 Oz. . .135.00
Plate, Bread & Butter,
  6 In. . . . . .3.00 to 8.00
Plate, Dinner,
  9 1/2 In. . . . . . .8.00 to 12.00
Plate, Salad,
  7 1/2 In. . . . . . .12.00 to 16.00
Platter, Oval,
  12 1/2 In. . . . . .13.00 to 20.00
Salt & Pepper . . .30.00 to 45.00
Saucer 5.00
Sherbet, Footed . .10.00 to 12.00
Soup, Cream,
  5 In. . . . . .20.00 to 28.00
Sugar 7.00
Sugar, Cover . . . .25.00 to 31.00
Sugar & Creamer 20.00
Sugar & Creamer,
  Cover 45.00
Tumbler, Iced Tea,
  Footed, 15 Oz.,
  6 1/2 In. . . . . .95.00 to 120.00
Tumbler, Water, Thin, 9 Oz.,
  4 1/8 In. . . . . . .25.00 to 28.00

GREEN
Berry Bowl,
  5 In. . . . . .11.50 to 15.00
Bowl, Fruit,
  10 1/2 In. . . . . .33.00 to 38.00
Bowl, Vegetable, Oval,
  9 1/2 In. . . . . . .29.00 to 35.00
Butter, Cover 125.00
Creamer, Footed .17.00 to 20.00
Cup . . . . .18.00 to 19.00
Cup & Saucer 23.00
Jam Jar, 7 1/2 In. 65.00
Plate, Bread & Butter,
  6 In. . . . . .6.00 to 8.00
Plate, Dinner,
  9 1/2 In. . . . . . .19.00 to 23.00
Plate, Salad,
  7 1/2 In. . . . . . .17.00 to 21.00

Platter, Oval,
  12 1/2 In. . . . . .27.00 to 29.00
Salt & Pepper . . .69.00 to 70.00
Saucer 10.00
Sugar 16.00

PINK
Berry Bowl,
  5 In. . . . . .11.00 to 12.50
Berry Bowl, Master,
  8 1/2 In. . . . . . .27.00 to 45.00
Bowl, Cereal,
  6 In. . . . . .21.00 to 25.00
Bowl, Fruit,
  10 1/2 In. . . . . .36.00 to 40.00
Bowl, Vegetable, Oval,
  9 1/2 In. . . . . . .24.00 to 30.00
Butter, Cover . . .40.00 to 52.50
Cake Plate, Footed,
  11 1/2 In. 25.00
Candy Jar,
  Cover . . . . . . .31.00 to 50.00
Creamer,
  Footed . . . . . .17.00 to 20.00
Cup . . . . .14.00 to 19.00
Cup & Saucer . .21.00 to 27.00
Pitcher, Ice Lip,
  80 Oz. . . . .144.00 to 170.00
Plate, Bread &
  Butter, 6 In. . . . .6.00 to 14.00
Plate, Dinner,
  9 1/2 In. . . . . . .17.00 to 25.00
Plate, Salad,
  7 1/2 In. . . . . . .23.00 to 31.00
Platter, Oval,
  12 1/2 In. . . . . .24.00 to 35.00
Salt & Pepper . . .50.00 to 60.00
Saucer . . . . . . .12.00 to 15.00
Sherbet, Footed . .12.00 to 19.00
Soup, Cream,
  5 In. . . . . .41.00 to 42.00
Soup, Dish,
  7 1/2 In. . . . . . .43.50 to 53.00
Sugar . . . . .10.00 to 14.00
Sugar, Cover 39.00
Sugar & Creamer 62.00
Sugar & Creamer,
  Cover 225.00
Tumbler, Iced Tea,
  Footed, 15 Oz.,
  6 1/2 In. . . . . . .20.00 to 50.00
Tumbler, Water, Thick,
  9 Oz., 4 1/8 In. 34.00
Tumbler, Water, Thin, 9 Oz.,
  4 1/8 In. . . . . .26.00 to 40.00

Tumbler, Water, Thin, 12 Oz.,
  5 1/4 In. 42.50

SHEFFIELD, see Chinex Classic

SHELL, see Petalware

SHIPS, see White Ship

SHIRLEY TEMPLE
Shirley Temple is not really a
pattern, but the dishes with the
white enamel decoration picturing Shirley have become
popular with collectors. The
most famous were made as
giveaways with cereal from
1934 to 1942. Several companies, including Hazel Atlas
Glass Company and U.S.
Glass, made the glassware.
Sugars and creamers, bowls,
plates, and mugs were made.
The milk pitcher and mug have
been reproduced since 1982
and the bowl has been reproduced since 1986. Other items
with the Shirley Temple decal
include a Fostoria Mayfair
Green sugar bowl and tea cup,
a White mug, and an 8 7/8-inch
Moderntone Cobalt Blue plate.
In 1972 Libbey Glass Com-
pany made six different sized
tumblers.

BLUE
Bowl, Cereal,
  6 1/2 In. . . . . . .50.00 to 60.00
Creamer 45.00
Mug, 3 3/4 In. . . .50.00 to 60.00
Plate 300.00
Sugar 50.00

SIERRA
Sierra, or Pinwheel, was made
by Jeannette Glass Company
from 1931 to 1933. It is found
in Green, Pink, and Ultramarine.

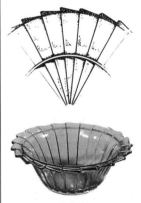

GREEN
Berry Bowl, Master,
  8 1/2 In. . . . . . .26.00 to 28.00
Bowl, Cereal,
  5 1/2 In. . . . . . .12.00 to 18.50
Butter 75.00
Creamer 22.50
Cup & Saucer . .17.00 to 24.00
Pitcher, 6 1/2 In. 150.00
Plate, Dinner,
  9 In. . . . . .18.00 to 25.00
Platter, Oval,
  11 In. 50.00

PINK
Berry Bowl, Master,
  8 1/2 In. . . . . . .30.00 to 34.50
Bowl, Cereal,
  5 1/2 In. . . . . . .12.50 to 14.00
Creamer 15.00
Cup . . . . .11.00 to 14.00
Cup & Saucer 19.00
Pitcher,
  6 1/2 In. . . . . . .75.00 to 80.00

Plate, 6 In. 8.00

Plate, Dinner,
  9 In. . . . . .17.00 to 23.00

Sandwich Server,
  10 1/4 In. 20.00

Saucer 6.00

Sherbet 15.00

Tumbler, Footed, 9 Oz.,
  4 1/2 In. . . . . . .75.00 to 80.00

SMOCKING, see Windsor

SNOWFLAKE, see Doric

SPIRAL

It is easy to confuse Spiral, a Hocking Glass Company pattern, with Twisted Optic, made by Imperial Glass Company. Ask to be shown examples of each, because even a picture will not be much help. Looking from the top to the base, Twisted Optic spirals right to left; Spiral twists left to right. There are a few pieces that are exceptions. Spiral pattern beverage and luncheon sets were manufactured from 1928 to 1930 in Crystal, Green, and Pink. It is also sometimes called Spiral Optic or Swirled Big Rib.

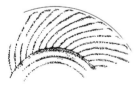

CRYSTAL
Plate, Luncheon, 8 In. 1.00

GREEN
Berry Bowl, Master,
  8 1/2 In. 17.50

Cup 5.00

Pitcher, 8 1/2 In. 22.00

Plate, Luncheon, 8 In. 3.75

Preserve, Cover 30.00

Salt & Pepper 30.00

Sherbet, Footed 4.00

Tumbler, Footed,
  5 7/8 In. 16.00

❖

To remove the remains of sticky glue and tape from antiques, try rubbing peanut butter on the sticky area until the glue is gone. Do not use this method on porous materials since the oil from the peanut butter could leave a stain.

❖

PINK
Plate, Luncheon,
  8 In. 4.50

SPIRAL FLUTES

Duncan & Miller Glass Company, Washington, Pennsylvania, made Spiral Flutes pattern. It was made of Amber, Crystal, and Green glass in 1924; Pink in 1926. A few pieces are reported with gold trim and in Blue or Vaseline-Colored glass.

AMBER
Cup & Saucer 12.00

Nut Dish, Footed 12.00

Pitcher, Water,
  1/2 Gal. 175.00

Sugar, Oval 9.00

Toothpick 27.00

CRYSTAL
Nut Dish, Footed,
  Gold Trim 12.00

Soup, Cream 10.00

GREEN
Console, Flared,
  11 3/8 In. 30.00

Goblet, Water, 7 Oz.,
  6 1/4 In. 15.00

Ice Tub, Handles 20.00

Nut Dish, Footed 12.00

Vase, 6 1/2 In. 15.00

PINK
Bouillon, 3 1/4 In. 15.00

SPIRAL OPTIC, see Spiral

SPOKE, see Patrician

SPORTSMAN SERIES

Hazel Atlas Glass Company made an unusual Depression glass pattern in the 1940s. It was made of Cobalt Blue, Amethyst, or Crystal with fired-on decoration. Although the name of the series was Sportsman, designs included golf, sailboats, hunting, angelfish, and a few strange choices like windmills. We list Windmill and White Ship separately, although they are sometimes considered part of this pattern.

COBALT BLUE
Bowl, Angelfish, 6 In. . . .67.50

Cocktail Shaker,
  Angelfish 80.00

Cocktail Shaker, Polo 65.00

Pitcher, Water,
  Angelfish 85.00

Tumbler, Juice,
  Fox Hunt 11.00

Tumbler, Water,
  Angelfish, 4 5/8 In. 10.00

SQUARE, see Charm

STARS AND STRIPES

Stars and Stripes was a clear glass pattern made about 1942 by Anchor Hocking Glass Corporation. The pieces had appropriate wartime patriotic designs of stars, stripes, and eagles.

CRYSTAL
Sherbet 14.00

STIPPLED ROSE BAND, see
S Pattern

STRAWBERRY

Strawberry and Cherry-Berry are similar patterns. The U.S. Glass Company made luncheon sets in this pattern in the early 1930s with strawberry decoration. Pink and Green were the most commonly used colors, although Crystal and Iridescent Marigold pieces were also made.

GREEN
Berry Bowl, Deep,
7 1/2 In. . . . . . .19.00 to 35.00
Sherbet, Footed 7.50
Sugar, Cover, Large 89.00
Sugar, Small 32.00

PINK
Berry Bowl,
4 In. . . . . .8.50 to 13.00
Berry Set, 7 Piece 75.00
Pitcher, 7 3/4 In. 195.00
Plate, Salad,
7 1/2 In. . . . . .11.00 to 18.00
Sherbet 7.00

STRAWBERRY, see also Cherry-Berry

SUNBURST

Crystal dinner sets were made in Sunburst pattern from 1938 to 1941 by Jeannette Glass Company of Jeannette, Pennsylvania.

CRYSTAL
Candlestick,
2-Light, Pair 25.00
Cup & Saucer 7.00
Plate, Dinner, 9 1/2 In. . . .14.00
Relish, Oval, 8 3/4 In 8.00

SUNFLOWER

Sunflower was made by Jeannette Glass Company, Jeannette, Pennsylvania, in the late 1920s and early 1930s. It is most commonly found in Pink and two shades of Green. The darker green was used for Cake Plates given as a premium in sacks of flour. Small quantities of Delphite pieces also were made.

GREEN
Ashtray, 5 In. . . .11.00 to 15.00

Cake Plate, Footed,
10 In. . . . . .8.00 to 15.00
Cup . . . . .12.00 to 15.00
Cup & Saucer . .20.00 to 27.00
Plate, Dinner,
9 In. . . . . .14.00 to 23.00
Sugar, Footed . . .18.00 to 21.00
Tumbler, Footed, 8 Oz,
4 3/4 In. 45.00

PINK
Ashtray, 5 In. 9.00
Cake Plate, Footed,
10 In. . . . . .9.00 to 20.00
Creamer, Footed 18.00
Cup 12.00
Cup & Saucer . .20.00 to 22.00
Plate, Dinner,
9 In. . . . . .15.00 to 19.00
Sugar, Footed . . .18.00 to 19.00
Tumbler, Footed, 8 Oz.,
4 3/4 In. . . . . . .25.00 to 31.00

SWANKYSWIGS

In October 1933, Kraft Cheese Company began to market cheese spreads in decorated, reusable glass tumblers. The tumbler was made in a 5-ounce size. It had a smooth beverage lip and a permanent color decoration. The designs were tested and changed as public demand indicated. Hazel Atlas Glass Company made the glasses, which were decorated by hand by about 280 girls, working in shifts around the clock. In 1937 a silk screen process was developed and the Tulip design was made by this new, faster method. The glasses were made thinner and lighter in weight. The decorated Swankyswigs were discontinued from 1941 to 1946, the war years. They were made again in 1947 and were continued through 1958. Then plain glasses were used for most of the cheese, although a few specially decorated Swankyswigs have been made since that time.

ANTIQUE NO. 1
Brown 4.00
Green . . . . .2.75 to 4.00
Red 2.00

ANTIQUE NO. 2
Blue 5.00
Orange . . . . .2.75 to 4.00
Red 2.00

BAND NO. 1
Blue & White 3.00

BAND NO. 2
Red & Black 2.50

BAND NO. 3
Blue & White . . . .3.00 to 4.00

BUSTLIN' BETSY
Blue . . . . .2.00 to 5.00
Brown . . . . .2.00 to 6.00
Green . . . . .2.00 to 4.00
Orange 4.00
Red . . . . .2.75 to 4.00
Yellow . . . . .3.00 to 4.00

CARNIVAL
Blue . . . . .6.00 to 17.00
Green . . . . .4.50 to 6.00
Red . . . . .3.00 to 4.00
Yellow 3.00

CHECKERBOARD
Red & White 25.00

CIRCLE & DOT
Black 4.25
Blue 4.25
Red 4.25

DAISY
Red, White & Green,
3 3/4 In. 2.00
Red, White & Green,
4 1/2 In. 15.00

FORGET-ME-NOT
Dark Blue . . . . . .2.00 to 7.00

Light Blue,
3 1/2 In. . . . . .2.00 to 8.00
Light Blue, 3 1/4 In. 15.00
Red . . . . .2.00 to 5.00
Yellow . . . . .2.00 to 3.00

KIDDIE KUP
Black, Duck &
Horse . . . . .2.75 to 6.00
Black, Duck &
Horse, 3 3/4 In. 15.00
Brown, Deer &
Squirrel . . . . . . .2.75 to 4.00
Green, Kitten &
Rabbit . . . . .3.00 to 4.00
Orange, Dog & Rooster,
3 1/4 In. 15.00
Orange, Dog & Rooster,
3 3/4 In. 2.75
Red, Bird & Elephant,
3 3/4 In. 15.00

POSY CORNFLOWER
No. 1, Light Blue,
3 1/2 In. . . . . .2.00 to 9.00
No. 2, Dark Blue . . .2.50 to 8.00
No. 2, Light Blue . .2.00 to 5.00
No. 2, Red 4.00
No. 2, Yellow,
3 1/2 In. . . . . .2.00 to 5.00

POSY CORNFLOWER NO. 2
Blue, 3 1/4 In. 15.00
Yellow, 3 1/4 In. 15.00

POSY JONQUIL
Yellow, 3 1/2 In. 4.00

POSY TULIP
No. 1, Blue,
3 1/2 In. . . . . .2.75 to 4.00
No. 1, Blue, 4 1/2 In. 8.50
No. 1, Green, 3 1/2 In. 2.75
No. 1, Green, 4 1/2 In. 8.00
No. 1, Red,
3 1/2 In. . . . . .2.75 to 5.00
No. 1, Red, 4 1/2 In. 15.00
No. 2, Green, 3 1/2 In. . . .22.50
No. 3, Light Blue,
3 1/4 In. 15.00
No. 3, Light Blue,
3 3/4 In. . . . . .2.75 to 3.00
No. 3, Red, 3 1/4 In. 15.00
No. 3, Red, 4 1/2 In. 15.00
No. 3, Yellow, 3 1/4 In. . .15.00

POSY VIOLET
Blue . . . . .3.00 to 5.00

SAILBOAT
No. 2, Blue, 4 1/2 In. 16.00
No. 2, Green, 4 1/2 In. . . .16.00
No. 2, Red,
4 1/2 In. . . . . . .12.00 to 16.00

STAR
Blue, 3 1/2 In. 4.00
Blue, 4 3/4 In. 15.00
Red, 3 1/2 In. 4.00
Red, 4 3/4 In. . . .11.00 to 15.00

SWEET PEAR, see Avocado

SWIRL

Swirl, sometimes called Double Swirl or Petal Swirl, was made by Jeannette Glass Company during 1937 and 1938. Ultramarine, in a variety of shades, was the most commonly used color, but Amber, Delphite, Ice Blue, and Pink were also used. Some pieces have a smooth edge while others have a flower petal rim.

DELPHITE
Bowl, Cereal,
5 1/4 In. . . . . . .13.00 to 14.00
Bowl, Salad, 9 In. 34.00
Cup & Saucer 20.00
Plate, Dinner, 9 1/4 In. . . .16.00
Plate, Sherbet, 6 1/2 In. 7.50
Platter, Oval, 12 In. 46.00

SWIRL

ICE BLUE

Sugar, Cover 12.50

PINK

Butter . . . . . . .150.00 to 170.00
Candy Dish, Footed 15.00
Coaster 15.00
Cup 4.00
Cup & Saucer 14.00
Plate, Sherbet, 6 1/2 In. . . .7.50
Saucer 1.00
Sherbet, Footed 12.00
Soup, Dish, Tab
   Handles 18.00
Sugar, Footed 10.00
Vase, Ruffled, Footed,
   6 1/2 In. 24.00

ULTRAMARINE

Bowl, Cereal,
   5 1/4 In. . . . . . .14.00 to 16.00
Bowl, Salad,
   9 In. . . . . .24.00 to 25.00
Candlestick, 2-Light,
   Pair . . . . .40.00 to 45.00
Candy Dish,
   Cover . . . . .125.00 to 175.00
Candy Dish, Footed 24.00
Console, Handles, Footed,
   10 In. . . . . . . .27.00 to 29.00
Creamer,
   Footed . . . . . .15.00 to 17.50
Cup 17.00
Cup & Saucer . .14.00 to 20.00
Plate, Dinner,
   9 1/4 In. . . . . . .16.00 to 19.00
Plate, Sherbet,
   6 1/2 In. . . . . .6.00 to 8.00
Salt & Pepper 48.00
Sandwich Server,
   12 1/2 In. . . . . .25.00 to 40.00
Soup, Dish, Tab
   Handles 32.00
Sugar, Footed 17.00
Sugar & Creamer 37.00

**All outside doors should
be made of solid wood
or metal so they are
difficult to kick in.**

Sugar & Creamer,
   Footed 27.00
Tumbler, Footed, 9 Oz.,
   4 5/8 In. . . . . . .34.00 to 45.00
Vase, Footed,
   8 1/2 In. . . . . . .18.00 to 30.00

SWIRL FIRE-KING

Swirl Fire-King is named for its wide swirled border. In the 1950s it was made in Azurite (blue), Ivory White with or without trim (later changed to Anchor White), and Pink. From 1960 to 1975 it was made in Jadite, Iridescent Lustre, and Anchor White with or without gold trim. Other related sections in this book are Alice, Charm, Fire-King, Fleurette, Game Bird, Gray Laurel, Jadite, Jane-Ray, Peach Lustre, Philbe, Turquoise Blue, and Wheat.

AZURITE

Creamer 6.00

IVORY

Cup 3.00
Mixing Bowl, 9 In. 13.00
Plate, Dinner, 10 In. 4.50
Saucer, 5 3/4 In. 1.00
Soup, Dish 8.00

JADITE

Mixing Bowl, 6 In. 12.00
Mixing Bowl, 7 In. 14.00
Mixing Bowl, 9 In. 16.00
Plate, Dinner, 10 In. 11.00
Soup, Dish, 7 5/8 In. 12.00
Sugar, Cover, Footed 49.00

PINK

Creamer 8.50
Cup 5.00
Sandwich Server, 11 In. . .20.00
Saucer 2.00

Soup, Dish, 7 5/8 In. 10.00
Sugar, Cover, Tab
   Handles 12.50

WHITE

Bowl, Vegetable,
   8 1/4 In. 8.00
Casserole, Tab Handles,
   Individual, 5 x 1 3/4 In. . .8.00
Creamer, Footed 4.00
Plate, Dinner, 10 In. 5.00
Saucer, 5 3/4 In. 1.00
Sugar, Footed, Open
   Handles 4.00
Sugar & Creamer,
   Cover . . . . .8.00 to 15.00

SWIRLED BIG RIB, see Spiral

SWIRLED SHARP RIB, see Diana

SYLVAN

Sylvan is often called Parrot or Three Parrot because of the center pattern on the plates. It was made by Federal Glass Company in 1931 and 1932 in Amber, Blue, Crystal, and Green. The molds were later used for the Madrid pattern.

AMBER

Berry Bowl, 5 In. 22.00
Bowl, Vegetable,
   Oval, 10 In. 32.00
Butter 85.00
Creamer 11.00
Cup 40.00
Cup & Saucer 17.00
Grill Plate, Round,
   10 1/2 In. . . . . .12.00 to 14.00
Plate, Dinner, 9 In. 49.00
Plate, Sherbet,
   6 In. . . . . .20.00 to 22.00
Platter, Oblong,
   11 1/4 In. 27.00
Saucer 18.00

Sherbet, Cone,
Footed . . . . . . .27.00 to 28.50

Soup, Dish, 7 In. 32.50

Tumbler, Footed,
10 Oz., 4 1/4 In. 32.00

Tumbler, Footed, 12 Oz.,
5 1/2 In. . . . . . .45.00 to 50.00

CRYSTAL

Grill Plate, Square,
10 1/2 In. . . . . .30.00 to 32.00

GREEN

Bowl, Vegetable, Oval,
10 In. . . . . .57.00 to 60.00

Butter, Cover . .350.00 to 375.00

Cup 40.00

Cup & Saucer 55.00

Hot Plate, Pointed Edge,
5 In. 900.00

Plate, Dinner, 9 In. 50.00

Plate, Salad, 7 1/2 In. 40.00

Platter, Oblong,
11 1/4 In. . . . . .50.00 to 55.00

Salt & Pepper 300.00

Saltshaker 135.00

Sugar . . . . .30.00 to 40.00

Sugar & Creamer,
Cover 285.00

Tumbler, Footed,
5 3/4 In. 175.00

TASSELL, see Princess

TEA ROOM

The very Art Deco design of
Tea Room has made it popular
with a group of collectors; it is
even called Moderne Art by
some. The Indiana Glass Company, Dunkirk, Indiana, made it
from 1926 to 1931. Dinner sets
were made of Amber, Crystal,
Green, and Pink glass.

AMBER

Pitcher,
64 Oz. . . . . .500.00 to 900.00

Sugar &
Creamer . . .200.00 to 290.00

Tumbler, Footed, 8 Oz.,
5 1/4 In. . . . .100.00 to 200.00

CRYSTAL

Relish, 2 Sections,
8 1/2 In. 20.00

Sugar & Creamer 40.00

Tumbler, Iced Tea, Footed,
11 Oz., 6 1/16 In. 50.00

Vase, Block, Frosted,
9 1/2 In. 175.00

Vase, Ruffled, 9 1/2 In. . . .50.00

Vase, Ruffled, 11 In. 175.00

GREEN

Bowl, Salad, Deep,
8 3/4 In. 150.00

Bowl, Vegetable, Oval,
9 1/2 In. . . . . . .63.00 to 75.00

Candlestick, Pair 48.00

Lamp, Electric,
9 In. . . . . . . .165.00 to 200.00

Pitcher, 64 Oz. 175.00

Salt & Pepper,
Footed . . . . . .60.00 to 75.00

Saltshaker 25.00

Sugar, Cover 295.00

Sugar, Footed,
4 In. . . . . .18.00 to 20.00

Sugar & Creamer 32.00

Sugar & Creamer,
Tray . . . . . . .65.00 to 105.00

Sundae, Footed 70.00

Vase, Ruffled, 6 1/2 In. . .145.00

Vase, Ruffled,
9 1/2 In. . . . .135.00 to 175.00

Vase, Ruffled,
11 In. . . . . . .310.00 to 350.00

Vase, Straight,
11 In. . . . . . .120.00 to 150.00

PINK

Candlestick, Pair 50.00

Pitcher, Footed, 64 Oz. . . .135.00

Salt & Pepper . . .60.00 to 75.00

Sugar & Creamer, Tray . . .87.50

Sundae,
Footed . . . . .145.00 to 150.00

Tray, Center Handle 190.00

Tumbler, 9 Oz.,
5 1/8 In. 32.00

Vase, Ruffled, 6 1/2 In. . . .125.00

Vase, Ruffled, 11 In. 145.00

Vase, Straight, 11 In. 96.00

TEAR DROP

Tear Drop, a pattern available
in full dinnerware sets, was
made by Duncan & Miller
Glass Company, Washington,
Pennsylvania, from 1934 to
1955. It was made only in
Crystal.

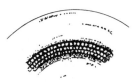

CRYSTAL

Bowl, 12 In. 24.00

Cake Stand, 13 In. 40.00

Candy Dish, Heart Shape,
7 1/2 In. 23.50

Celery Dish, Handles,
6 x 12 In. 18.00

Creamer 6.00

Cruet, Oil, 3 Oz.,
4 3/4 In. 20.00

Cup & Saucer . . .7.00 to 10.00

Dish, Mayonnaise,
Footed, Spoon 18.00

Goblet, Champagne,
5 Oz., 3 In. 7.00

Goblet, Cocktail, 3 1/2 Oz.,
4 1/2 In. . . . . . .10.00 to 15.00

Goblet, Wine, 3 Oz.,
4 1/4 In. 14.00

Jam Jar, Cover . .28.00 to 30.00

Mustard, 4 1/2 In. 30.00

Oyster Cocktail, Footed,
3 1/2 Oz., 3 3/4 In. 8.00

Pitcher, Water, Ice Lip,
64 Oz., 8 1/2 In. 110.00

Relish, 5 Sections, 12 In. .22.00

Saucer, After Dinner 3.50

Sugar 6.00

Sugar & Creamer 21.00

Sugar & Creamer, Tray,
8 In. 7.50

Tumbler, Iced Tea, 14 Oz.,
6 In. . . . . .10.00 to 18.00

THISTLE

Thistle pattern was made by
Macbeth-Evans Glass Company
from 1929 to 1930. The pattern
pictures large thistles primarily
on Pink pieces, but Green,
Crystal, and Yellow dishes also
were made. Reproductions have
been made. They are listed at
the end of the Depression Glass
section.

CRYSTAL
Plate, Luncheon, 8 In. 8.00

GREEN
Bowl, Cereal, 5 1/2 In. . . .27.00

Bowl, Fruit, 10 1/2 In. . .350.00

Cup & Saucer 37.00

Plate, Luncheon,
8 In. . . . . .23.00 to 30.00

PINK
Bowl, Cereal,
5 1/2 In. . . . . . .25.00 to 30.00

Cup . . . . .22.00 to 28.00

Cup & Saucer 36.00

Plate, Luncheon,
8 In. . . . . .15.00 to 22.50

Saucer 13.00

THREADING, see Old English

THREE PARROT, see Sylvan

TRADITION

Imperial Glass Company of
Bellaire, Ohio, made Tradition
pattern glass in the 1930s. It
was made in Amber, Amethyst,
Blue, Crystal, Green, Pink, and
Red.

AMBER
Goblet, Juice, Footed,
5 Oz. 9.00

Goblet, Water, 10 Oz. . . .10.00

Goblet, Wine, 4 Oz. 7.00

Sherbet, Footed, 4 1/8 In. . .6.50

Tumbler, Iced Tea,
12 Oz., 6 In. 7.00

AMETHYST
Goblet, Juice, Footed,
5 Oz. 7.00

Goblet, Water, 10 Oz. . . .16.00

Goblet, Wine, 4 Oz. 20.00

BLUE
Finger Bowl, 4 1/2 In. . . .35.00

Goblet, Juice, Footed,
5 Oz. 25.00

Goblet, Water, 10 Oz. . . .20.00

Goblet, Wine, 4 Oz. 30.00

Sherbet, Footed 15.00

Tumbler, Iced Tea, Footed,
12 Oz. . . . . . .22.00 to 25.00

CRYSTAL
Plate, Handles, 9 1/2 In. . .30.00

Plate, Salad, 8 In. 15.00

Salt & Pepper 17.00

GREEN
Goblet, Juice, Footed,
5 Oz. 21.00

Goblet, Water, 10 Oz. . . .12.00

Goblet, Wine,
4 Oz. . . . . .16.00 to 20.00

Sherbet, Footed 10.00

Tumbler, Iced Tea,
12 Oz. 16.00

PINK
Goblet, Water,
10 Oz. . . . . . .20.00 to 22.00

Plate, Salad, 8 In. 20.00

RED
Sherbet, Footed 16.00

TROJAN

The Fostoria Glass Company
made Trojan. The etched glass
dishes were made in Rose from
1929 to 1935, Topaz from 1929
to 1938, and Gold Tint from
1938 to 1944. It also was made
in Green. Crystal bases were
used on some pieces from 1931
to 1944.

ROSE
Lunch Tray, Center
 Handle 75.00
Plate, Luncheon, 9 In. 65.00

TOPAZ
Bowl, Dessert, Handle,
 Large 95.00
Bowl, Vegetable, Oval,
 12 In. 95.00
Candlestick, 3 In., Pair . . .65.00
Cup & Saucer . .22.00 to 24.00
Finger Bowl Liner,
 6 1/2 In. 10.00
Goblet, Water, Footed,
 9 Oz. 32.50
Parfait 65.00
Plate, Breakfast,
 7 1/2 In. 10.00
Plate, Cheese & Cracker . .60.00
Plate, Dessert, 6 In. 8.00
Plate, Lemon, Handles . . .24.00
Plate, Luncheon,
 8 1/2 In. 16.50
Soup, Dish, 7 In. 195.00
Tumbler, Juice, Footed,
 5 Oz. 19.50
Vase, Bulbous, 8 In. 395.00

TULIP
Tulip pattern pictures the side of a tulip in a very stylized border. It was made by the Dell Glass Company of Millville, New Jersey, during the 1930s. Amber, Amethyst, Blue, Crystal, and Green pieces were made. Fire-King also made a pattern called Tulip.

AMETHYST
Cup 20.00

If two tumblers get stuck when stacked, try putting cold water in the inside glass, then put both into hot water up to the lower rim.

BLUE
Cup & Saucer 24.00
Plate, Dessert, 6 In. 10.00

GREEN
Creamer 20.00
Cup & Saucer . .23.00 to 26.00
Plate, Dessert,
 6 In. . . . . .8.50 to 9.00
Plate, Dinner,
 9 In. . . . . .22.00 to 34.00
Plate, Salad,
 7 1/4 In. 15.00
Sugar 20.00

TURQUOISE BLUE
Turquoise Blue, one of the patterns made by Anchor Hocking Glass Corporation, is a plain pattern named for its color. Mixing bowls were made in 1-pt., 1-qt., 2-qt., and 3-qt. sizes. It was made in the 1950s. Related sections in this book are Alice, Charm, Fire-King, Gray Laurel, Jadite, Jane-Ray, Peach Lustre, Philbe, Swirl Fire-King, and Wheat.

Berry Bowl,
 4 1/2 In. . . . . . . .5.00 to 6.00
Bowl, 4 1/2 In. 5.00
Bowl, Cereal,
 5 In. . . . . .6.00 to 13.00
Bowl, Vegetable,
 8 In. . . . . .8.00 to 15.00
Creamer . . . . .4.00 to 5.50
Cup . . . . .2.00 to 2.50
Cup & Saucer . . . .3.50 to 6.00
Mug . . . . .4.00 to 5.75
Plate, Bread & Butter,
 7 In. 8.00

Plate, Dinner, 10 In. 27.50
Plate, Indentation, Gold
 Trim, 9 In. . . . . . .5.25 to 8.50
Plate, Salad,
 7 In. . . . . .8.00 to 11.00
Relish, 3 Sections,
 11 1/2 In. . . . . . .8.00 to 10.00
Relish, 3 Sections, Oval,
 11 1/2 In. 10.00
Saucer . . . . .1.00 to 2.00
Soup, Dish,
 6 5/8 In. . . . . . .14.25 to 20.00
Sugar 5.25
Sugar & Creamer 9.00

TWISTED OPTIC
Twisted Optic is the pattern sometimes confused with Spiral. Be sure to look at the information about that pattern. Imperial Glass Company of Bellaire, Ohio, made Twisted Optic luncheon sets from 1927 to 1930 in Amber, Blue, Canary Yellow, two shades of Green, and Pink.

GREEN
Candy Dish,
 Cover . . . . .30.00 to 35.00
Cup & Saucer 7.00
Plate, Luncheon,
 8 In. . . . . .4.00 to 7.50
Plate, Sherbet,
 6 In. . . . . .3.00 to 3.50
Vase, Footed, 2 Handles,
 8 In. 37.00

PINK
Bowl, Cereal, 5 In. 17.00
Creamer . . . . .6.00 to 11.00
Cup 6.00
Plate, Sherbet, 6 In. 3.00

Sandwich Server,
2 Handles, 8 In. 25.00
Sherbet 6.00
Vase, Footed, 2 Handles,
8 In. 37.00

VERSAILLES

Versailles by Fostoria Glass Company was made in many colors during the years of its production, 1928 to 1944. Azure Blue, Green, and Rose were made from 1928 to 1944, Topaz from 1929 to 1938, and Gold Tint from 1938 to 1944. Crystal bases were used with colored glass from 1931 to 1944.

BLUE
Candlestick, 2 In., Pair . . .55.00
Chop Plate, 13 In. 195.00
Console, Round, 11 In. . .145.00
Cup & Saucer 49.00
Finger Bowl, Liner 125.00
Goblet, Champagne 35.00
Goblet, Water 65.00
Ice Bucket 225.00
Nut Dish, Individual 65.00
Plate, Bread & Butter,
6 In. 12.50
Plate, Dinner,
10 1/2 In. 135.00
Sugar 37.50
Sugar & Creamer 75.00
Tumbler, Footed, 9 Oz. . . .35.00
Tumbler, Iced Tea, Footed,
12 Oz., 6 In. . . .50.00 to 65.00
Tumbler, Juice, Footed,
2 1/2 Oz. 45.00
Tumbler, Water, Footed . .45.00

GREEN
Finger Bowl Liner 15.00
Goblet, Champagne 37.50
Goblet, Cocktail, 3 Oz.,
5 1/4 In. 47.50
Gravy Boat, Liner 250.00
Ice Bucket 175.00
Ice Dish Liner 22.50
Pail, Whipped Cream,
Handle 125.00
Plate, Dinner, 9 In. 18.00
Platter, 12 In. 75.00
Sugar & Creamer 55.00
Sweetmeat, Loop
Handle 35.00
Tray, Service &
Lemon 375.00

ROSE
Bowl, Cereal, 6 In. 85.00
Goblet, Cocktail, 3 Oz.,
5 1/4 In. 55.00
Goblet, Cordial, Footed,
3/4 Oz., 4 In. 125.00
Goblet, Water, 9 Oz. 65.00
Goblet, Wine, 3 Oz.,
5 1/2 In. . . . . . .45.00 to 95.00
Ice Dish Liner 25.00
Pail, Whipped Cream,
Handle 275.00
Pitcher 675.00
Plate, Bread & Butter,
6 In. 4.50
Plate, Luncheon,
8 3/4 In. 18.00
Sherbet, 4 1/4 In. 37.50
Sherbet, 6 In. 19.00
Soup, Cream, Footed 75.00
Tumbler, Juice, Footed,
5 Oz., 4 1/2 In. 47.50

TOPAZ
Bowl, Footed, 12 In. 55.00

❖

If you are moving, remember there is no insurance coverage for breakage if the items are not packed by the shipper.

❖

Bowl, Fruit, 5 In. 35.00
Bowl, Whipped Cream,
Handle 35.00
Candlestick, 3 In., Pair . . .28.00
Goblet, Cordial, 3/4 Oz.,
4 In. . . . . .75.00 to 125.00
Goblet, Water, 10 Oz.,
8 1/4 In. 25.00
Sherbet, 4 1/2 In. 20.00
Sherbet, 6 In. . . . .20.00 to 25.00
Soup, Dish, 7 In. 85.00
Sugar, Individual 42.00

VERTICAL RIBBED, see Queen Mary

VESPER

Vesper was made by the Fostoria Glass Company of Ohio and West Virginia from 1926 to 1934. Dinner sets were made in Amber, Blue, and Green.

AMBER
Bowl, Footed, 10 In. 85.00
Compote, Twisted Stem,
8 In. 45.00
Cup & Saucer . .18.00 to 25.00
Finger Bowl Liner, 6 In. . .10.00
Goblet, Champagne 25.00
Goblet, Cocktail 27.50
Goblet, Water 28.00
Gravy Boat Liner 40.00
Ice Bucket, Handle 95.00
Pitcher, Footed 345.00
Plate, Dinner,
9 1/2 In. . . . . . .15.00 to 25.00
Plate, Luncheon, 8 1/2 In. . .8.00
Plate, Salad, 7 1/2 In. 6.00
Sandwich Server, Center
Handle, 11 In. 38.00
Saucer 10.00
Sherbet 15.00
Sugar & Creamer 45.00

Tumbler, Footed, 9 Oz. . . .20.00

GREEN
Candy Jar, Cover,
  1/2 Lb.. . . . . .115.00
Compote, Footed, 8 In. . . .24.00
Console, 11 In. 35.00
Cup & Saucer 18.00
Cup & Saucer, After
  Dinner 49.50
Goblet, Water 29.00
Goblet, Wine 45.00
Plate, Bread & Butter,
  6 In.. . . . . .9.00
Plate, Dinner, 9 1/2 In. 8.00
Plate, Dinner, 10 1/2 In. . .35.00
Sandwich Server, Center
  Handle 35.00
Saucer 4.50
Sherbet 15.00
Soup, Cream . . . .25.00 to 29.50

VICTORY

The Diamond Glass-Ware Company, Indiana, Pennsylvania, made Victory pattern from 1929 to 1932. It is known in Amber, Black, Cobalt Blue, Green, and Pink. A few pieces have gold trim.

AMBER
Bowl, Cereal, 6 1/2 In. 5.00
Candlestick, Gold Trim,
  3 In., Pair 22.00
Cup 4.50

GREEN
Bowl, Cereal, 6 1/2 In. . . .12.00
Creamer 11.00
Cup 6.50
Cup & Saucer . . .9.75 to 14.00
Plate, Dinner, 9 In. 18.00
Plate, Luncheon, 8 In. 7.00
Sugar 14.00

PINK
Cup 8.50
Cup & Saucer . .12.00 to 14.00

Plate, Dinner, 9 1/4 In. . . .23.50
Plate, Luncheon,
  8 In. . . . . .7.00 to 8.00
Sandwich Server, Center
  Handle . . . . . .28.00 to 30.00
Saucer 2.00

VITROCK

Vitrock is both a kitchenware and a dinnerware pattern. It has a raised flowered rim and so is often called Floral Rim or Flower Rim by collectors. It was made by Hocking Glass Company from 1934 to 1937 and resembles embossed china. It was made in White, sometimes with fired-on colors, in solid Red or Green, and with decal-decorated centers.

WHITE
Berry Bowl, 4 In. . .4.50 to 7.50
Bowl, Cereal, 6 In. 5.50
Bowl, Vegetable,
  9 1/2 In. 16.00
Canister, Tea, Screw
  Cover, 20 Oz. 27.00
Cup 4.00
Cup & Saucer 7.50
Plate, Luncheon,
  8 3/4 In. . . . . . . .4.50 to 5.00
Platter 20.00
Saucer 2.50
Soup, Cream,
  5 1/2 In. . . . . . .15.00 to 17.00

VIVID BANDS, see Petalware

WAFFLE, see Waterford

WATERFORD

Waterford, or Waffle, pattern was made by Anchor Hocking Glass Corporation from 1938 to 1944. Crystal and Pink are the most common colors; Yellow and White were used less extensively. Some of the Opaque White pieces also have fired-on pink and green. In the 1950s some Forest Green pieces were made.

CRYSTAL
Berry Bowl, 4 1/2 In. 6.00
Berry Bowl, Master,
  8 1/4 In. . . . . .8.00 to 9.00
Butter, Cover . . .23.00 to 24.00
Cake Plate, Handle,
  10 1/4 In. . . . . . . .6.00 to 8.00
Candy Dish, 2 Sections, Gold
  Trim, 6 1/2 In. 4.00
Coaster . . . . .1.50 to 4.00
Creamer . . . . .4.00 to 4.50
Cup 5.00
Cup & Saucer 8.00
Goblet, Water, 5 1/4 In. . .20.00
Pitcher, Ice Lip, Tilted,
  80 Oz. 25.00

Pitcher, Juice, Tilted,
 42 Oz. 18.00
Plate, Dinner,
 9 5/8 In. . . . . . .6.00 to 11.00
Plate, Salad,
 7 1/8 In. . . . . . . .4.00 to 6.00
Plate, Sherbet, 6 In. 3.00
Salt & Pepper,
 Large . . . . .4.00 to 9.00
Salt & Pepper,
 Small . . . . .4.00 to 8.00
Sandwich Server,
 13 3/4 In. . . . . . .8.00 to 12.00
Saucer 2.00
Sherbet, Footed . . . .2.25 to 4.00
Sugar 4.00
Sugar, Cover . . . .8.00 to 15.00
Sugar & Creamer .9.50 to 14.00
Tumbler, Footed, 10 Oz.,
 4 7/8 In. . . . . . . .9.00 to 12.00

PINK

Ashtray 3.50
Butter, Cover 200.00
Cake Plate, Handles,
 10 1/4 In. . . . . .13.00 to 21.00
Plate, Dinner, 9 5/8 In. . . .24.00
Sandwich Server,
 13 3/4 In. . . . . .30.00 to 35.00
Sherbet 12.00
Tumbler, 10 Oz. 20.00

WEDDING BAND, see
 Moderntone

WHEAT

Wheat glass was made by
Anchor Hocking Glass Corporation from 1962 to about 1967.
It is part of the Fire-King Oven
Ware line. It is a white opaque
glass decorated with a natural-
looking spray of wheat. A few
pieces were given added decoration. Another pattern of glass
called Wheat was made by
Federal Glass Company in the
1930s, but only the Anchor
Hocking glass is listed here.

Baking Pan,
 8 x 12 1/2 In. 6.00
Bowl, Dessert,
 4 5/8 In. . . . . . . .3.00 to 3.75
Casserole, 1 Qt. 6.00

Creamer 3.00
Cup 4.25
Custard, 6 Oz. 3.75
Plate, Dinner,
 10 In. . . . . .5.00 to 5.25
Platter 10.00
Platter, Oval 6.00
Snack Set, Cup, Rectangular
 Plate, 2 Piece 1.50
Soup, Dish, 6 5/8 In. 5.75
Sugar 4.25
Tray, Snack, 11 x 6 In. 5.00

WHITE SAIL, see White Ship

WHITE SHIP

White Ship, also called Sailing
Ship, Sail Boat, or White Sail,
is really part of the Sportsman
series made by Hazel Atlas
Glass Company in 1938. The
ships are enamel decorations on
Cobalt Blue, Crystal, or Amethyst glass. The enamel decorations are sometimes in color.

COBALT BLUE

Cocktail
 Shaker . . . . . .33.00 to 60.00
Ice Bowl . . . . .30.00 to 45.00
Pitcher, Ice Lip, 86 Oz. . . .64.00
Tray, Round, 12 In. 100.00
Tumbler, Iced Tea, 10 1/2 In.,
 4 7/8 In. . . . . .10.00 to 18.00
Tumbler, Juice, 5 Oz.,
 3 1/2 In. 6.00
Tumbler, Old Fashioned, 8 Oz.,
 3 5/8 In. . . . . .14.00 to 31.00
Tumbler, Roly Poly,
 4 1/2 Oz. 10.00
Tumbler, Roly Poly,
 6 Oz. 8.00
Tumbler, Water, 9 Oz.,
 3 3/4 In. . . . . . .11.00 to 16.00

❖

**A permanent record of
your collection in
the form of a video
inventory is being
offered in some cities. A
color video is recorded
in your home as your
voice describes your
antiques. Keep the
videotape in a safe
deposit box.**

❖

WILDFLOWER, see No. 618

WILDROSE, see Dogwood

**WILDROSE WITH APPLE
 BLOSSOM,** see Flower Garden
 with Butterflies

WINDMILL

Windmill, or Dutch, is a part of
the Sportsman series made by
Hazel Atlas Glass Company in
1938. Of course, it pictures a
landscape with a windmill. The
windmills are enamel decorations on Cobalt Blue, Crystal,
or Amethyst glass.

Cocktail Set, Chrome Tray,
 6 Tumblers, 8 Piece . . .175.00
Cocktail Shaker 25.00
Ice Bowl . . . . .25.00 to 30.00
Ice Bowl Set, Tumblers,
 Stirrers, Wire Carrier,
 14 Piece 130.00
Tumbler, Roly Poly,
 6 Oz. . . . . .7.50 to 10.00

Tumbler, Water, 9 Oz.,
4 5/8 In. 10.00

WINDSOR

Windsor pattern, also called
Diamond, Smocking, or Windsor Diamond, was made by
Jeannette Glass Company, Jeannette, Pennsylvania, from 1936
to 1946. The pattern is most
easily found in Crystal, Green,
and Pink, although pieces were
made in Amberina Red, Ice
Blue, and Delphite.

CRYSTAL
Berry Bowl, 4 3/4 In. 3.00
Bowl, Boat Shape,
7 x 11 3/4 In. 18.00
Bowl, Footed, 7 1/8 In. 7.00
Butter, Cover 20.00
Butter, Pointed Edge 25.00
Candlestick,
3 In. . . . . .10.00 to 12.00
Candlestick, 3 In.,
Pair . . . . .20.00 to 22.00
Chop Plate, 13 5/8 In. 32.00

Creamer 4.00
Cup 3.00
Pitcher, 16 Oz.,
4 1/2 In. . . . . . .13.00 to 15.00
Powder Jar 15.00
Relish, Oval, 11 1/2 In. . . .10.00
Sandwich Server, Closed
Handles, 10 1/4 In. 10.00
Sandwich Server,
Handles, 10 In. 5.50
Sherbet, Footed 3.00
Sugar, Cover . . . . .8.00 to 17.50
Tray, Handles, 8 1/2 In. . .13.00
Tumbler, Footed,
4 In. . . . . .5.00 to 7.00
Tumbler, Footed,
12 Oz., 5 In. 10.00

GREEN
Bowl, Vegetable, Oval,
9 1/2 In. 27.00
Butter, Cover 92.00
Chop Plate,
13 3/4 In. . . . . .40.00 to 45.00
Cup & Saucer 18.50
Pitcher, Water, 52 Oz.,
6 3/4 In. 50.00
Plate, Salad, 7 In. 27.50
Plate, Sherbet, 6 In. 8.00
Salt & Pepper . .45.00 to 50.00
Sandwich Server, Handles,
10 1/4 In. . . . . .16.00 to 18.00
Saucer 6.00
Sherbet 15.00
Sugar, Cover 37.00
Tumbler, 4 In. 29.00
Tumbler, Footed, 12 Oz.,
5 In. . . . . .34.00 to 45.00

PINK
Ashtray . . . . . .37.00 to 45.00
Berry Bowl,
4 3/4 In. . . . . . .9.00 to 12.50

Berry Bowl, Master,
8 1/2 In. . . . . . .20.00 to 22.00
Bowl, Boat Shape,
7 x 11 3/4 In. . .35.00 to 37.50
Bowl, Footed, 10 1/2 In. . .40.00
Butter, Cover . . .50.00 to 58.00
Cake Plate, Footed,
10 3/4 In. . . . . .20.00 to 25.00
Chop Plate,
13 5/8 In. . . . . .35.00 to 45.00
Compote, 6 In. 11.00
Console, 12 1/2 In. 107.00
Creamer 12.50
Cup & Saucer 14.00
Pitcher, 52 Oz.,
6 3/4 In. . . . . . .27.00 to 32.00
Plate, Dinner,
9 In. . . . . .18.00 to 24.00
Plate, Sherbet,
6 In. . . . . .4.00 to 5.00
Platter, Oval,
11 1/2 In. . . . . .20.00 to 22.00
Punch Cup 2.75
Salt & Pepper . .37.00 to 40.00
Saltshaker . . . . .18.00 to 20.00
Sandwich Server, Handles,
10 1/4 In. . . . . .12.50 to 16.00
Saucer . . . . .6.00 to 8.00
Sherbet . . . . . . .8.00 to 12.00
Sugar, Cover . . . .25.00 to 30.00
Sugar, Holiday 50.00
Tray, 2 Handles 18.00
Tumbler, 4 In. . . .12.50 to 20.00
Tumbler, 5 Oz.,
3 1/4 In. . . . . . .24.00 to 25.00
Tumbler, Footed, 12 Oz.,
5 In. 30.00

WINDSOR DIAMOND, see
Windsor

WINGED MEDALLION, see Madrid

Reproductions

PATTERN	ITEM	COLORS	DATES
Adam	Butter dish	Green, Pink	1981
American	Two-piece candle night-light	Crystal	1987
American	Almost all items have been reproduced	Crystal	1992
American	Nappy, footed punch bowl, salad bowl, torte plate	Red	1992
Avocado	Cup & saucer, handled dish, nappy, pickle, pitcher, sugar & creamer	Blue, Frosted Pink, Pink, Red, Amethyst, Yellow, Dark Green, Frosted Green	1974
Avocado	Pitcher, 64 oz.	Dark Green	1979
Avocado	Berry bowl, olive, 5 1/2-in. plate, relish, sundae, tumbler	Amber, Amethyst, Blue, Frosted Pink, Green, Pink, Red Amethyst, Red-Yellow	1974
Avocado	Pitcher, tumbler set, olive dish, cup & saucer, sugar & creamer, pickle, 6-in. & 8-in. plate, nappy, sherbet	Amber	1978–1982
Avocado	Pitcher, tumbler set, 5-piece beverage set	Pink	1973
Avocado	Pitcher, tumblers	Frosted Pink	
Avocado	Pitcher, 9 oz. tumbler, 5-piece beverage set	Purple	1975
Bubble	Square ashtray, 4-in. & 8-in. bowl, ivy ball, punch cup, 3 3/4-in. vase	Red	1977–1978
Cameo	Water set, ice bucket, tumblers, covered sugar & creamer	Pink, Yellow, Green	1996
Cameo	Children's dishes from Taiwan & China	Green, Pink, Yellow	1996

PATTERN	ITEM	COLORS	DATES
Cameo	Children's dishes called Jennifer Line	Green, Pink, Yellow	1982–1996
Cameo	Salt & pepper shakers	Green, Pink, Cobalt Blue	1982
Candlewick	Bowl, candelabra, cup & saucer, sugar & creamer, 2-handled jelly, plate, basket	Alexandrite, Blue, Pink (1987); Crystal, Cobalt Blue, Emerald Green, Red, Black (1990); Cranberry Mist (1993)	1987–1993
Cape Cod	Cruet		1986
Cape Cod	Dinner set		1978
Caprice	Bashful Charlotte, butter, sugar & creamer, footed juice, footed water tumbler, nut, relish, seashell ashtray, swan	Cobalt Blue, Light Blue; Rubina (called Sunset) (1950s)	1985
Cherry Blossom	Almost all items have been reproduced in various colors since 1972	Blue, Cobalt Blue, Delphite, Iridescent, Green, Pink, Red	1973
Cherry Blossom	Salt & pepper shakers	Pink, Green, Delphite	1977
Cherry Blossom	Pitcher	Blue	1979
Cherry Blossom	Salt & pepper shakers	Cobalt Blue, Pink, Green	1989
Cherry Blossom	Cake plate, 13-in. platter	Pink, Green, Blue, Delphite	1982
Cherry Blossom	Pitcher	Blue	1979
Cherry Blossom	Water set	Amethyst Carnival glass	1996
Colony	Reamer, 2 spouts	White, Crystal	
Diana	Bowl	Pink	1986
English Hobnail	18 pieces	Red	1980
English Hobnail	26 pieces	Pink	1982–1983
English Hobnail	Pedestal salt dip	Crystal	1986
Floral	Salt & pepper shakers, footed	Cobalt Blue, Dark Green, Pink, Red	1989
Florentine No. 1	Salt & pepper shakers, footed	Cobalt Blue, Pink, Red	1989
Florentine No. 2	Water pitcher, tumbler	Blue, Pink, Deep Opaque Green	1995
Georgian	Tumblers: 5-oz., 12-oz., & 15-oz.	Ruby	1978
Hazel Atlas Quilt	Kitchen shaker	Pink	1987
Heritage	5-in. bowl	Amber, Crystal	1987
Heritage	5-in. bowl, 9-in. footed bowl, cake plate, goblets: iced tea, 10-in. plate	Crystal	1992
Heritage	Goblets: iced tea, wine	Blue, Pink	1992

PATTERN	ITEM	COLORS	DATES
Ipswich	Candlestick	Forest Green, Ruby	1994
Iris	Candy dish (bottom only), vase	Multicolored over Crystal	1976
Iris	Various items	Crystal	1969
Iris	Various items	Milk glass & sprayed-on colors	1970
Iris	Candy dish	Crystal	1970
Iris	Vase	Crystal	1982
June	Bottom's-Up tumbler	Black, Jade, Custard	1979
June	Goblets: 4-oz., 6-oz., 9-oz., 12-oz.	Blue, Crystal, Yellow	1979
Madrid	Candleholder	Black	1977
Madrid	Candleholder, sugar & creamer	Crystal	1977
Madrid	Butter, 9 1/2-in. bowl, sugar & creamer	Amber	1977
Madrid	Covered butter dish	Crystal	1979
Madrid	Dinner set	Amber	1982
Madrid	Dinner set	Amber	1976
Madrid	Salt & pepper shakers	Crystal	1978
Madrid (called Recollection)	Various items	Amber, Blue, Crystal, Yellow, Pink, Teal, frosted & other colors later	1976–1977
Mayfair Open Rose	Cookie jar	Amethyst, Green, Pink, Cobalt Blue, Red	1982
Mayfair Open Rose	Cookie jar	Cobalt Blue	1990
Mayfair Open Rose	Juice pitcher	Cobalt Blue, Pink	1993
Mayfair Open Rose	Salt & pepper shakers	Cobalt Blue, Pink, Red	1988
Mayfair Open Rose	Salt & pepper shakers	Green, Pink	1989
Mayfair Open Rose	Whiskey	Green, Pink, Cobalt Blue	1977
Miss America	Butter dish	Amberina, Crystal, Green, Ice Blue, Pink, Red	1977
Miss America	Water pitcher, tumbler	Crystal, Cobalt Blue, Green, Ice Blue, Pink, Amberina	1970–1980
Miss America	Pitcher, tumbler	Crystal, Green, Pink	1982

PATTERN	ITEM	COLORS	DATES
Miss America	Salt & pepper shakers	Crystal, Green, Pink	1977
Miss America	Various items	Cobalt Blue	1987
Moonstone	Goblets: iced tea, wine	Dark & Light Blue	1992
Newport	Tumblers: 7-oz., 9-oz., 12-oz., 16-oz.	Cobalt Blue	1977
No. 610	Berry bowl, relish, tray, tumbler	Black, Blue	1974
Princess	Candy jar	Pink, Blue	
Princess Feather	1-piece & 2-piece reamers, "Gillespie" measuring cup	Various colors	1986
Royal Lace	5-oz. tumbler	Cobalt Blue	1996
Royal Ruby	Tumblers: 7-oz., 9-oz., 12-oz., 16-oz.	Red	1977–1978
Royal Ruby	Bread & butter plate, salad plate, 4-in. bowl, tumblers: 7-oz., 9-oz., 12-oz., 16-oz.	Red	1978
Sandwich Anchor Hocking	Covered cookie jar	Crystal	1978
Sandwich Duncan & Miller	Ashtray, basket, berry set, boxes, bowl, bridge set, candleholder, napkin holder, platter, pitcher, snack set, 3-part relish, tidbit, tumbler, vase	Amber, Light Green, Crystal	1982
Sandwich Indiana	Basket, bridge set, candle-holder, goblet, napkin holder, nappy, punch set, snack set, tidbit, vase, wine set	Amber	1982
Sandwich Indiana	Cookie jar	Crystal	1989
Sandwich Indiana	Sugar & creamer, 6-in. & 8-in. sherbet	Avocado, some frosted	1981
Sandwich Indiana	Child's set, nappy, pickle, plate, mug, bowl, 6-oz. tumbler, 5-in. pitcher (Marjorie Daw)	Avocado	1977–1985
Sandwich Indiana	Butter dish	Teal	1981
Sandwich Indiana	Basket, candleholder, snack set, wine set	Light Green	1982
Sandwich Indiana	Dinner set	Amber, Crystal, Dark Blue, Red	1969
Sandwich Indiana	Various items	Amber, Blue, Crystal, Green, Red	

PATTERN	ITEM	COLORS	DATES
Sharon	Butter dish	Amber, Blue, Dark Green, Light Green, Pink	1976
Sharon	Covered candy dish	Pink	1984
Sharon	Covered candy dish	Cobalt Blue	1976
Sharon	Cheese dish	Blue, Amber, Dark Green, Light Green, Pink	1977
Sharon	Measuring cup, candy dish	Pink	1984
Sharon	Covered sugar & creamer	Light Pink	1977
Sharon	Salt & pepper shakers	Green, Pink, & other colors	1980
Sharon	Covered sugar & creamer	Pink, Green	1983
Shirley Temple	Milk pitcher, mug	Cobalt Blue	1982
Shirley Temple	6 1/2-in. bowl	Cobalt Blue	1986
Thistle	Large bowl, pitcher, tumbler, platter	Pink	1996–1997

DEPRESSION GLASS FACTORIES, PATTERNS, AND BIBLIOGRAPHY

Kovels' Depression Glass & Dinnerware Price List is a concise guide to price and age information. This is a list that will help collectors learn more about Depression glass patterns. Each glass factory is listed separately with the location and the dates of operation. A list of books that specialize in this type of glass is also included. These books often have many color pictures of the glass, reprints of early advertising, and other information. Also included under each factory name is a list of the best-known patterns made by the firm. Not all of these are included in the main body of our book. General reference books on Depression glass are included at the end of this section.

Akro Agate Company, Clarksburg, West Virginia, 1914–1951

REFERENCE BOOKS
Archer, Margaret and Douglas. *Imperial Glass.* Paducah, Kentucky: Collector Books, 1978.

Florence, Gene. *Collector's Encyclopedia of Akro Agate.* Revised edition. Paducah, Kentucky: Collector Books, 1975. Revised 1992 prices.

Hardy, Roger and Claudia. *The Complete Line of the Akro Agate Co.* Privately printed, 1992 (10 Bailey St., Clarksburg, WV 26301-2524).

PATTERNS
Akro Agate tableware, 1932–1951

Anchor Hocking Glass Corporation, Lancaster, Ohio, 1905–present (Hocking Glass Company, 1905–1937; Anchor Hocking Glass Corporation, 1937–1969; Anchor Hocking Corporation, 1969–present)

REFERENCE BOOKS
Kilgo, Garry and Dale; Jerry and Gail Watkins. *A Collector's Guide to Anchor Hocking Fire-King Glassware.* 2nd Edition. Privately printed, 1997 (K & W Collectibles, P.O. Box 473, Addison, AL 35540).

PATTERNS

Alice, 1940s	Bubble, 1934–1965
Arctic, 1932	Burple, 1940s
Bibi, 1940s	Cameo, 1930–1934
Block Optic, 1929–1933	Chariot, 1932
Boopie, late 1940s–1950s	Charm, 1950–1954

Circle, 1930s
Colonial, 1934–1938
Coronation, 1936–1940
Dancing Girl (Sunrise Medallion), late 1920s–early 1930s
Debbra, 1931–1933
Fire-King Oven Glass, 1942–1960s
Fire-King Oven Ware, 1950s
Fleurette, 1958–1960
Forest Green, 1950–1957
Fortune, 1937–1938
Frosted Ribbon, 1940
Game Bird, c.1959–1963
Georgian, 1935
Hobnail, 1934–1936
Jane-Ray, 1945–1963
Lace Edge, 1935–1938
Lake Como, 1934–1937
Little Bo Peep, 1940
Manhattan, 1938–1941
Mayfair Open Rose, 1931–1937
Miss America, 1933–1936
Monarch, 1970s–1985
Moonstone, 1941–1946
Old Cafe, 1936–1938
Oyster & Pearl, 1938–1940

Panelled Ring-Ding, 1932
Pantryline, 1920s–1930s
Peach Lustre, 1952–1963
Philbe, 1937–1940s
Pillar Optic, 1935
Polar Bear, 1932
Primrose, 1960–1962
Princess, 1931–1935
Queen Anne, late 1930s
Queen Mary, 1936–1940
Ring, 1927–1932
Ring-Ding, 1932
Roulette, 1935–1939
Royal Ruby, 1939–1960s
Sandwich Anchor Hocking, 1939–1964
Spiral, 1928–1930
Stripe, 1932
Stars and Stripes, c.1942
Swirl Fire-King, 1955–1960s
Three Bands, 1930s
Turquoise Blue, 1950s
Vitrock, 1934–1937
Waterford, 1938–1944; 1950s
Wheat, 1960s
Whirly-Twirly, 1940s

Bartlett-Collins, Sapulpa, Oklahoma, 1914–present

REFERENCE BOOKS

Warner, Ian. *Swankyswigs: A Pattern Guide and Check List.* Privately printed, 1982 (P.O. Box 57, Otisville, MI 48463).

Weatherman, Hazel Marie. *Decorated Tumbler.* Privately printed, 1978 (P.O. Box 280, Springfield, MO 65721).

———. *Price Guide to the Decorated Tumbler.* Privately printed, 1979 (P.O. Box 280, Springfield, MO 65721).

PATTERNS

Sheraton, 1930s
Swankyswigs, 1956–1958; 1975

Twitch, early 1930s

Belmont Tumbler Company, Bellaire, Ohio, c.1920–1952

PATTERNS

ABC Stork

Belmont Ship Plate

Rose Cameo, 1933

Cambridge Glass Company, Cambridge, Ohio, 1901–1958

REFERENCE BOOKS

Cambridge Glass Co. (catalog reprint). Privately printed, 1976 (P.O. Box 416, Cambridge, OH 43725).

Fine Handmade Table Glassware (catalog reprint). Privately printed, 1978 (P.O. Box 416, Cambridge, OH 43725).

National Cambridge Collectors, Inc. *Colors in Cambridge Glass.* Paducah, Kentucky: Collector Books, 1984.

National Cambridge Collectors, Inc. *Etchings by Cambridge.* Volume 1. Privately printed, 1997 (Brookville Publishing, P.O. Box 3, Brookville, OH 45309-0003).

Smith, Bill and Phyllis. *Cambridge Glass 1927–1929.* Privately printed, 1986 (4003 Old Columbus Rd., Springfield, OH 45502).

PATTERNS

Aero Optic, 1929	Gloria, c.1930
Alpine Caprice, 1936	Imperial Hunt, 1932
Apple Blossom, 1930s	Lorna, 1930
Caprice, 1936–1953	Martha Washington, 1932
Cleo, 1930	Mt. Vernon, 1920s–1940s
Decagon, 1930s	Nautilus, 1933–1934
Diane, 1934–1950s	Portia, 1932–1950s
Elaine, 1934–1950s	Rosalie, 1920s–1930s
Everglades, 1933–1934	Rose Point, 1936–1953
	Weatherford, 1926

Consolidated Lamp & Glass Company, Coraopolis, Pennsylvania, 1894–1933; 1936–1967

PATTERNS

Catalonian, 1927–1936

Dance of the Nudes, 1920s

Dell Glass Company, Millville, New Jersey, 1930s

PATTERNS

Tulip, 1930s

Diamond Glass-Ware Company, Indiana, Pennsylvania, 1891–1931

PATTERNS
Victory, 1929–1932

Dunbar Flint Glass Corporation (Dunbar Glass Corporation), Dunbar, West Virginia, 1913–1953

PATTERNS

Aramis, 1936	Barbra, 1928
Athos, 1936	D'Artagnan, 1936

Duncan & Miller Glass Company, Washington, Pennsylvania, 1893–1955

PATTERNS

Caribbean, 1936–1955	Punties, 1931
Early American Lace, 1932	Puritan, 1929
Early American Sandwich, 1925–1949	Sandwich Duncan & Miller, 1924–1955
Full Sail, 1925	Spiral Flutes, 1924–early 1930s
Georgian, 1928	Tear Drop, 1934–1955
Kimberly, 1931	Terrace, 1935

Federal Glass Company, Columbus, Ohio, 1900–1971

PATTERNS

Colonial Fluted, 1928–1933	Mary, mid-1930s
Columbia, 1938–1942	Mayfair Federal, 1934
Corded Optic, 1928	Mutt 'N Jeff, 1928
Crossbar, mid-1930s	Normandie, 1933–1940
Daisy Spray & Lattice, 1928	Patrician, 1933–1937
Diamond Arch, 1938–1940	Pear Optic, 1929–1930
Diamond Squat, 1928	Pioneer, 1930s–1970s
Diana, 1937–1941	Raindrops, 1929–1933
Georgian, 1931–1935	Rosemary, 1935–1937
Grand Slam, 1930	Sharon, 1935–1939
Heritage, late 1930s–1960s	Squat Optic, 1928
Indian, c.1930	Sylvan, 1931–1932
Jack Frost, 1928	Tall Boy, 1928
John, mid-1930s	Trump Bridge, 1928
Lido, mid-1930s	Tudor Ring, 1928
Madrid, 1932–1939	Wheat, early 1930s

Fenton Glass Company, Williamstown, West Virginia, 1906–present

REFERENCE BOOKS

Heacock, William. *Fenton Glass: The First Twenty-five Years.* Privately printed, 1978 (Antique Publications, P.O. Box 553, Marietta, OH 45750).

———. *Fenton Glass: The Second Twenty-five Years.* Privately printed, 1980 (Antique Publications, P.O. Box 553, Marietta, OH 45750).

PATTERNS

Franklin, 1934	Lincoln Inn, 1928
Georgian Fenton, c.1930	Plymouth, 1933

Fostoria Glass Company, Fostoria, Ohio; Moundsville, West Virginia, 1887–1986

REFERENCE BOOKS

Kerr, Ann. *Fostoria: An Identification and Value Guide of Pressed, Blown & Hand Molded Shapes.* Paducah, Kentucky: Collector Books, 1994.

McGrain, Patrick, ed. *Fostoria: The Popular Years.* Privately printed, 1982 (P.O. Box 219, Frederick, MD 21701).

Piña, Leslie. *Fostoria Designer George Sakier, With Values.* Atglen, Pennsylvania: Schiffer Publishing Ltd., 1996.

———. *Fostoria: Serving the American Table 1887–1986, With Price Guide.* Atglen, Pennsylvania: Schiffer Publishing Ltd., 1995.

Weatherman, Hazel Marie. *Fostoria: Its First Fifty Years.* Privately printed, 1972 (P.O. Box 280, Springfield, MO 65721).

PATTERNS

American, 1915–1986	Legion, 1931–1940
Baroque, 1936–1966	Manor, 1931–1944
Century, 1926–1986	Midnight Rose, 1933–1957
Chantilly, late 1940s–early 1950s	Morning Glory, 1931–1944
Chateau, 1933–1940	Navarre, 1937–1980
Chintz, 1940–1972	Nectar, 1934–1943
Colony, 1920s–1970s	New Garland, 1930–1934
Fairfax, 1927–1960	Rambler, 1935–1958
Florentine, 1931–1944	Royal, 1925–1934
Fuchsia, 1931–1944	Springtime, 1933–1944
Hermitage, 1932–1945	Sunray, 1935–1944
June, 1928–1952	Trojan, 1929–1944
Kashmir, 1930–1934	Versailles, 1928–1944
Lafayette, 1931–1960	Vesper, 1926–1934

Hazel Atlas Glass Company, Washington, Pennsylvania; Zanesville, Ohio; Clarksburg, West Virginia; Wheeling, West Virginia, 1902–1956

REFERENCE BOOKS

Warner, Ian. *Swankyswigs: A Pattern Guide and Check List.* Privately printed, 1982 (P.O. Box 57, Otisville, MI 48463).

Weatherman, Hazel Marie. *Decorated Tumbler.* Privately printed, 1978 (P.O. Box 280, Springfield, MO 65721).

Weatherman, Hazel Marie. *Price Guide to the Decorated Tumbler.* Privately printed, 1979 (P.O. Box 280, Springfield, MO 65721).

PATTERNS

Afghan & Scottie Dog, 1938

Aurora, late 1930s

Cloverleaf, 1930–1936

Colonial Block, early 1930s and 1950s

Colony, 1930s

Diamond Point Columns, late 1920s–1930s

Floral Sterling, early 1930s

Florentine No. 1, 1932–1935

Florentine No. 2, 1932–1935

Fruits, 1931–1933

Hazel Atlas Quilt, 1937–1940

Homespun (Fine Rib), 1938–1940s

Moderntone, 1935–1942

Moderntone Little Hostess, 1940s

Moderntone Platonite, 1940–1950s

New Century, 1930–1935

Newport, 1936–1940

Ovide, 1929–1935

Polo, 1938

Ribbon, 1930s

Roxana, 1932

Royal Lace, 1934–1941

Shirley Temple, 1934–1942

Sportsman Series, 1940s

Starlight, 1930s

Swankyswigs, 1933–1940; 1947–1956

Tom & Jerry, 1930s

Twentieth Century, 1928–1931

White Ship, 1938

Windmill, 1938

X Design, 1928–1932

A. H. Heisey & Company, Newark, Ohio, 1896–1957

PATTERNS

Chintz, 1931–1938

Crystolite, 1938–1956

Empress, 1930–1938

Greek Key (Grecian Border), 1912–1938

Ipswich (Early American Scroll), 1931–1946; 1951–1953

Lariat, 1946–1956

Minuet, 1939–1950s

Octagon, 1925–1937

Old Sandwich (Early American Thumbprint), 1931–1956

Orchid, 1940–1957

Plantation, 1950–1956

Provincial, 1938–1956

Ribbed Octagon, 1925–1936

Ridgeleigh, 1935–1957

Saturn, 1937–1957

Twist, 1928–1937

Victorian, 1933–1953

Imperial Glass Company, Bellaire, Ohio, 1904–1982

REFERENCE BOOKS
Scott, Virginia R. *The Collector's Guide to Imperial Candlewick*. Privately printed, 1990 (275 Milledge Terr., Athens, Georgia 30606).

PATTERNS
Beaded Block, 1927–1930s
Blaise, c.1930
Block with Rose
Candlewick, 1937–1982
Cape Cod, 1932–1980s
Chesterfield, c.1930
Diamond Quilted, 1920s–1930s
Early American Hobnail, 1930s
Flora, c.1925
Fountain Swirl, 1928–1930
Hazen, c.1930
Hobstars Intaglio, c.1930
Huckabee, c.1930
Ida, c.1930
Imperial Optic Rib, 1927
Imperial Plain Octagon, 1927

Laced Edge, early 1930s
Lindburgh, c.1930
Little Jewel, late 1920s–1930
Monticello
Mt. Vernon, c.1930
New Jewel, 1931
Pillar Flute, c.1930
Scroll Fluted, c.1930
Shaffer, c.1930
Spring Flowers, 1920s
Spun, 1935
Strawflower, c.1930
Tradition, 1930s
Twisted Optic, 1927–1930
Viking, 1929
Woodbury, c.1930

Indiana Glass Company, Dunkirk, Indiana, 1907–present

PATTERNS
Avocado, 1923–1933
Artura, c.1930
Bananas, c.1930
Christmas Candy, 1937; 1950s
Cracked Ice, 1930s
Indiana Custard, 1930s–1950s
King Arthur, c.1930
Lily Pons, c.1930
Loganberry, c.1930
No. 610, 1926–1932
No. 612, 1930–1933

No. 615, 1929–1932
No. 616, 1930–1932
No. 618, 1932–1937; 1960s
No. 620, 1933–1970s
Old English, late 1920s–early 1930s
Orange Blossom, 1957
Pretzel, 1930s–1970s
Sandwich Indiana, 1920s–1980s
Soda Fountain, c.1930
Tea Room, 1926–1931

Jeannette Glass Company, Jeannette, Pennsylvania, c.1900–present

PATTERNS

Adam, 1932–1934
Anniversary, 1947–1949; 1970s
Bridget, 1925
Camellia, 1947–1951
Chantilly, 1960s
Cherry Blossom, 1930–1939
Cosmos, 1950s
Cubist, 1929–1933
Daisy J, 1926
Dewdrop, 1954–1955
Doric, 1935–1938
Doric & Pansy, 1937–1938
Floragold, 1950s
Floral, 1931–1935

Harp, 1954–1957
Hexagon Optic, 1928–1932; c.1960
Holiday, 1947–1949
Homespun, 1939–1940
Iris, 1928–1932; 1950s
Jadite, 1936–1938
Lombardi, 1938
Pretty Polly Party Dishes, 1937–1938
Sierra, 1931–1933
Sunburst, 1938–1941
Sunflower, late 1920s–early 1930s
Swirl, 1937–1938
Windsor, 1936–1946

Jenkins Glass Company, Kokomo, Indiana; Arcadia, Indiana, 1901–1932

PATTERNS

Arcadia Lace, 1901–1932
Blossoms & Band, 1927
Fieldcrest
Hob, 1927–1931
Huck Finn, c.1930
Jenkins' Basket

Ocean Wave, c.1930
Sea-Side
Twin Dolphin
Yoo-Hoo, c.1930
Yo-Yo, c.1930

Lancaster Glass Company, Lancaster, Ohio, 1908–1937

PATTERNS

Centaur, 1930s
Jane, c.1930
Jubilee, early 1930s

Patrick, c.1930
Yvonne, mid-1930s

Libbey Glass Company, Toledo, Ohio, 1892–present

PATTERNS

Shirley Temple, 1972

Liberty Works, Egg Harbor, New Jersey, 1903–1934

PATTERNS

American Pioneer, 1931–1934   Octagon Bamboo Optic, 1929
Bamboo Optic, 1929   Truman, 1930
Egg Harbor, 1929

Louie Glass Company, Weston, West Virginia, 1926–1995

PATTERNS

Chico, 1936   Semper, 1931
Groucho, 1936   Zeppo, 1936
Harpo, 1936

Macbeth-Evans Glass Company, Indiana (several factories); Toledo, Ohio; Charleroi, Pennsylvania; Corning, New York, 1899–1936 (acquired by Corning)

PATTERNS

American Sweetheart, 1930–1936   MacHOB, 1928
April, c.1930s   Oxford, 1930–1940
Bordette, 1930–1940   Petalware, 1930–1940
Chinex Classic, c.1938–1942   Pie-Crust, 1930–1940
Cremax, 1930s–1940s   Ringed Target, 1931
Crystal Leaf, 1928   S Pattern, 1930–1935
Diamond Dart, 1928   Scrabble, 1931
Dixie, 1931   Sheffield, 1930–1940
Dogwood, 1929–1934   Squirt, 1931
Fanfare, c.1930s   Thistle, 1929–1930
Ivex, 1930–1940   Yankee, 1931
Leaf, early 1930s

McKee Glass Company, Jeannette, Pennsylvania, 1853–1961

REFERENCE BOOKS

McPhee Stout, Sandra. *The Complete Book of McKee Glass*. North Kansas City, Missouri: Trojan Press, Inc., 1972.

PATTERNS

Autumn, 1934   Laurel, 1930s
Clico, 1930   Lenox, 1930s
Flower Band, 1934   Octagon Edge, 1920s–1930s

Rock Crystal, 1920s–1930s
Scallop Edge, 1920s–1930s
Scottie Dog, 1930s

Tom & Jerry, 1940s
Wiggle, 1925

Morgantown Glass Works, Morgantown, West Virginia, late 1800s–1972

PATTERNS

Art Moderne, 1929
Dancing Girl, 1920s–1930s
Hughes, 1932
Krinkle, 1924
Langston, 1932
Marilyn, 1929
Melon, 1932
Millay, 1932

Palm Optic, 1929
Peacock Optic, 1929–1930
Pineapple Optic, 1929
Primrose Lane, 1929
Simplicity, 1920s–early 1930s
Sommerset, 1932
Square, 1928

New Martinsville Glass Manufacturing Company, New Martinsville, West Virginia, 1901–1944

REFERENCE BOOKS

Measell, James. *New Martinsville Glass, 1900–1944.* Privately printed, 1994 (Antique Publications, P.O. Box 553, Marietta, OH 45750).

PATTERNS

Moondrops, 1932–1940s

Radiance, 1936–1939

Paden City Glass Manufacturing Company, Paden City, West Virginia, 1916–1951

REFERENCE BOOKS

Barnett, Jerry. *Paden City: The Color Company.* Astoria, Illinois: Stevens Publishing, 1978.

PATTERNS

Cupid, 1930s
Line 191, 1928
Nora Bird, 1929–1930s
Orchid, early 1930s
Peacock & Wild Rose, 1930s

Peacock Reverse, 1930s
Penny Line, 1932
Popeye & Olive, early 1930s
Wotta Line, 1933

L. E. Smith Glass Company, Mt. Pleasant, Pennsylvania, 1907–present

PATTERNS

By Cracky, late 1920s
Do-Si-Do, 1930s
Gothic Arches, 1920s
Hammered Band, early 1930s

Homestead, 1930s
Mt. Pleasant, mid-1920s–1934
Soda Shop, mid-1920s

Standard Glass Manufacturing Company, Lancaster, Ohio, 1924–c.1984
(became subsidiary of Hocking/Anchor Hocking in 1940)

PATTERNS

Blanche, c.1930
Grape, 1930s

Rose, c.1930
Trudy, c.1930

Tiffin Glass Company, Tiffin, Ohio, 1888–1980 (Factory R of U.S. Glass Company)

REFERENCE BOOKS

Bickenheuser, Fred. *Tiffin Glassmasters*. Privately printed, 1979 (Glassmasters Publications, P.O. Box 524, Grove City, OH 43123).

PATTERNS

Cadena, early 1930s
Cherokee Rose, 1940s–1950s
Classic, 1913–1930s
Flanders, mid-1910s–mid-1930s

Fuchsia, 1937–1940
June Night, 1940s–1950s
Velva, late 1930s

U.S. Glass Company (United States Glass Company), Pennsylvania (several factories); Tiffin, Ohio; Gas City, Indiana; West Virginia, 1891–1963

PATTERNS

Aunt Polly, late 1920s–1935
Bee Hive, 1926
Cherry-Berry, early 1930s
Comet, mid-1920s
Craquel, 1924
Deerwood, 1920s–1930s
Diner, 1927
Flanders, 1914–1935
Floral & Diamond Band, 1920s
Flower Garden with Butterflies,
    late 1920s

Fuchsia, 1930s–1940s
Lariette, 1931
Octagon, 1927–1929
Primo, 1932
Shirley Temple, 1934–1942
Strawberry, 1930s
Thorn, 1930s
U.S. Swirl, late 1920s

Westmoreland Glass Company, Grapeville, Pennsylvania, 1890–1985

REFERENCE BOOKS

Grisel, Ruth Ann. *Westmoreland Glass: Our Children's Heirlooms.* Privately printed, 1993 (FSJ Publishing Co., P.O. Box 122, Iowa City, IA 52244).

Kovar, Lorraine. *Westmoreland Glass, 1950–1984.* Privately printed, 1991 (Antique Publications, P.O. Box 553, Marietta, OH 45750).

———. *Westmoreland Glass, 1950–1984.* Volume II. Privately printed, 1991 (Antique Publications, P.O. Box 553, Marietta, OH 45750).

Newbound, Betty and Bill. *Collector's Encyclopedia of Milk Glass Identification & Values.* Paducah, Kentucky: Collector Books, 1995.

Wilson, Chas West. *Westmoreland Glass Identification & Value Guide.* Paducah, Kentucky: Collector Books, 1996.

PATTERNS

Della Robbia, 1920s–1930s

Doreen, 1924

English Hobnail, 1920–1970s

Lotus, 1920s–1930s

Marguerite, 1924

Orphan Annie, 1925

Princess Feather, 1939–1948; 1960s

Scramble, 1924

Wagner, 1924

Wakefield, 1933–1960s

Woolworth, early 1930s

General Reference Books

Florence, Gene. *Collectible Glassware from the 40s, 50s, 60s: An Illustrated Value Guide.* 4th edition. Paducah, Kentucky: Collector Books, 1998.

————. *Collector's Encyclopedia of Depression Glass.* 13th edition. Paducah, Kentucky: Collector Books, 1998.

————. *Elegant Glassware of the Depression Era.* 7th edition. Paducah, Kentucky: Collector Books, 1998.

————. *Kitchen Glassware of the Depression Years.* 5th edition. Paducah, Kentucky: Collector Books, 1995.

————. *Very Rare Glassware of the Depression Years.* 5th series. Paducah, Kentucky: Collector Books, 1995.

Kovel, Ralph and Terry. *Kovels' Antiques & Collectibles Price List.* 30th edition. New York: Crown Publishers, 1998.

————. *Kovels' Guide to Selling, Buying, and Fixing Your Antiques and Collectibles.* New York: Crown Publishers, 1995.

————. *Kovels' Know Your Collectibles.* New York: Crown Publishers, 1981, updated 1992.

Luckey, Carl F., with Mary Burris. *Identification & Value Guide to Depression Era Glassware.* 3rd edition. Iola, Wisconsin: Books Americana/Krause, 1994.

Rogove, Susan Tobier, and Marcia Buan Steinhauer. *Pyrex by Corning.* Privately printed, 1993 (Antique Publications, P.O. Box 553, Marietta, OH 45750).

Washburn, Kent G. *Price Survey.* 4th edition. Privately printed, 1994 (8048 Midcrown, Suite 26, San Antonio, TX 78218-2334).

Weatherman, Hazel Marie. *Colored Glassware of the Depression Era 1.* Privately printed, 1970 (Weatherman Glassbooks, P.O. Box 280, Ozark, MO 65721).

————. *Colored Glassware of the Depression Era 2.* Privately printed, 1974 (Weatherman Glassbooks, P.O. Box 280, Ozark, MO 65721).

————. *Price Trends to Colored Glassware of the Depression Era 1.* Privately printed. (Weatherman Glassbooks, P.O. Box 280, Ozark, MO 65721).

————. *Supplement & Price Trends for Colored Glassware of the Depression Era Book 2.* Privately printed. (Weatherman Glassbooks, P.O. Box 280, Ozark, MO 65721).

Whitmyer, Margaret and Kenn. *Bedroom & Bathroom Glassware of the Depression Years.* Paducah, Kentucky: Collector Books, 1990.

Yeske, Doris. *Depression Glass: A Collector's Guide.* Atglen, Pennsylvania: Schiffer Publishing Ltd., 1997.

DINNERWARE

DINNERWARE

Introduction

This book has changed to reflect the collecting trends of the late 1990s. The inexpensive dinnerware sets made in America are the main focus of this section. We also included sets made in other countries, but sold in quantity in America. Azalea pattern, made in Japan, and Liberty Blue, made in England, are two of these new entries. We list the prices for the most popular everyday sets being collected today. Formal dinnerwares made by firms like Lenox or Royal Worcester are not included.

Because dishes were made by so many manufacturers, there is a problem with variations in vocabulary. Most sugar bowls made for these dinnerware sets had covers. Today many have lost their original covers and are sold as open sugars. We do not include the word *open* in the description, but we do indicate if there is a cover. A gravy boat with a liner is a gravy boat with the oval tray that it rests on. Sometimes the liner is permanently attached to the gravy boat. A mayonnaise bowl may also have a liner.

A lug soup is a bowl with a flat handle called a lug. Other soup bowls may have pierced handles or no handles. Oatmeal bowl and cereal bowl are both names for a bowl about 6 inches in diameter. We use the name cereal bowl. We list both a pickle dish and a pickle tray. The tray is flat. An after-dinner coffee cup is larger than a demitasse but smaller than a coffee cup. A few mixing bowls have covers. The covers are very rare and sell for high prices. We list the bowls with and without the covers. A French baker or fluted baker is a bowl with straight sides.

One strange size indication is often used by dealers. A piece is "36s." When the dinnerware was made it was packed in barrels. The words 30s or 36s refers to the number of pieces that would fit in a barrel. The larger the number, the smaller the size of the piece. If that is the common way the piece is described today, we have included it in the listing. The height of a pitcher or jug is one indication of size; the number of liquid ounces it holds is also important. We have tried to list both. Wherever possible, we have used both the name of the piece and the size, so the listing is "plate, dinner, 10 in." Although most dinner plates are 10 inches in diameter, a few are smaller and we have listed the actual size in each case.

The terms "kitchenware" and "dinnerware" are used in the original sense. A dinnerware set includes all the pieces that might have been used on a dinner table, including dishes, bowls, platters, tumblers, cups, pitchers, and serving bowls. A kitchenware set has bowls and storage dishes of the type used in a kitchen and does not include dinner plates or cups. Kitchenware includes rolling pins, pie servers, and other kitchen utensils. A few kitchenware bowls are listed, but other pieces are not.

Colors often were given romantic names, and, whenever possible, we have used these original factory names. Some colors, such as Camellia (rose), Cadet (light blue), Indian Red (orange), or Dresden (deep blue), are explained in the paragraph descriptions.

It is important to remember that the descriptions of dinnerware may include many strange names. Some are the factory names, some refer to the pattern (decorations applied to the piece), and many were used by the factory to describe the shape. For example, Taverne is a pattern; Laurel is the shape of the dish used to make that pattern; and Taylor, Smith, and Taylor is the name of the company that made the dinnerware. Sometimes a name refers to both a pattern and a shape.

Pieces of American dinnerware are constantly being discovered in attics, basements, garage sales, flea markets, and antiques shops. The publications that offer them through the mail use descriptions that often include both the pattern and the shape name. Learn to recognize the shapes that were used by each maker. Authors of some of the other books about dinnerwares have arbitrarily named the pieces. Sometimes these names, although referring to the same piece, are different in different books. We have tried to cross-reference these names so you can locate them in any of the books.

This year we have included the bibliography of dinnerware books in a new form. It is not a traditional bibliography. Instead we have made it more "user friendly." Look up the factory that made your dinnerware pattern. (If you don't know the factory name, you will find it in the paragraph listing prices in the main section of the book.) Under the factory name is a list of the most collectible patterns made by that factory. We have changed to this form because so many dinnerware pieces are marked with the name of the maker, not the name of the pattern. Some of the patterns are priced in this book, some are not. The listing also includes the books that picture or discuss your pattern. General books about pottery marks and dinnerware are listed separately. Some companies have changed their names during the years of dinnerware production. Gladding, McBean & Company became Franciscan Ceramics, Inc., and eventually was purchased by the Water-

The Changing Styles and Colors
of
DEPRESSION GLASS AND DINNERWARE

DEPRESSION GLASS

This Waterford, or Waffle, 2-handled plate is an example of a popular clear glass pattern.

Clear and pastel-colored glassware in matching sets became popular about 1925. The Fostoria Glass Company of Fostoria, Ohio, made the first of these glass sets, which included dinner plates, coffee cups, and other pieces to be used at a dinner table. The glassware was expensive and its popularity led to similar pieces being made by other companies that were able to produce a less expensive glass.

Inexpensive glass was made by a method called tank molding. Silica sand, soda ash, and limestone were heated, and the molten glass mixture was passed through pipes to the automated pressing mold. Patterns were acid-etched or tooled into the mold so the finished glassware had a design. Because the pressing process made a glass that often had flaws or bubbles, patterns used as decoration

This Princess cookie jar was made in light green, a common pastel color.

The Floral pattern features a lacy-type design of poinsettias. This is a pink sugar bowl that was originallly sold with a cover.

This pink Hobnail cup gets its name from the bumpy 19th-century glassware of the same name.

Indiana Glass Company's Sandwich pattern is similar to glass made in the 19th century by the Sandwich Glass Works of Sandwich, Massachusetts; hence the name.

were often lacy in appearance to help hide the flaws.

During the late 1960s, interest in the inexpensive pastel glass led to several books, and the term "Depression glass" came into general use, even though the glassware was made before, during, and after the Depression. The name has gradually come to include other glassware made from 1925 through the 1970s: lacy types, pseudo-Sandwich glass patterns, hobnail variations, solid-colored wares of ruby, cobalt, or green, and many opaque-glass patterns. In the past few years another term, "elegant glassware of the Depression era," has come into use. This refers to the better-quality glass made at the same time. There is much overlap between these types of glass, and even the exact name to use for a pattern may be in doubt.

Depression glass designs can be divided into groups. The pseudo-etched designs, like Adam or Cherry Blossom, were made first, from about 1925 to 1935, in pastel colors.

Pseudo-etched designs, like the one on this green Adam bowl, were made in the mold. They hid the flaws in inexpensive molded glass.

Raised designs, often with fruit and flower patterns, such as Open Rose and Sharon, were made in the mid-1930s. At the same time other patterns were made of deep colors like cobalt blue or Royal Ruby or Forest Green. Opaque glass, pastels, and clear glass were also popular.

Geometric wares, such as Hobnail and Ribbon, were made during the late 1920s, and again in the late 1930s and early 1940s. Simple outlines and bold colors predominated. Art Deco–influenced geometric designs included Cubist, Imperial Octagon, and U.S. Octagon.

Enameled or silk-screened patterns were developed during the 1940s. White-enameled designs were added to cobalt blue, Royal Ruby, Forest Green, and clear glass. Shirley Temple pieces, originally given away with cereal, and Windmill are among the most popular with collectors today.

A few patterns, Windsor Diamond and Floral & Diamond Band, for example, were designed to resemble the cut glass of the 19th century or the Lacy Sandwich patterns made by the Sandwich, Massachusetts, glassworks. About ten pseudo-Sandwich patterns were sold, most of which were referred to as Sandwich in the manufacturers' catalogs.

Opaque glass was popular in the 1930s. Each of the colors was given a special name by the

Anchor Hocking made glassware in strong, solid colors like these Royal Ruby cups and this Forest Green pitcher.

This Iris pattern covered butter features a raised design.

The Art Deco era is characterized by geometric designs, like this Cubist bowl.

company that produced it. Monax or Ivrene are opaque white glasswares. So are Azurite, Chinex, Clambroth, and Cremax. Opaque green glass was known by a variety of names, including Jade-ite by Anchor Hocking and Jadite by Jeannette Glass Company. Jade green is a generic name used by many companies. Delphite is an opaque blue glass.

The famous Swankyswigs, glasses that held cheese spread, first made in 1933, were made with enamel decorations of many colors. But the 1940s and after was the the time of color-added decoration on other glasswares. Bands or stripes were used on some patterns; colorful stylized flowers were added to opaque white wares. Some pieces were even colored to look like solid-color pottery.

This Windmill sugar bowl, made in the 1940s, features a white enamel design on cobalt blue glass. White Ship and the Sportsman Series are related patterns made by the Hazel Atlas Company.

The Windsor Diamond pattern provides an inexpensive alternative to cut glass. This salt and pepper set was made by the Jeanette Glass Company.

Some pieces, like Cherry Blossom, were made in clear pastel colors or of opaque glass. This plate is Delphite, an opaque blue. Other colors include green, jadite (opaque green), pink, and red.

Depression glass dinner sets are popular with collectors, but so are the utility wares that date from the same period. Utility dishes were meant to be used in the kitchen and not on the table, and included leftover dishes, lemon reamers, cookie jars, and canister sets.

Swankyswigs, small glasses that were made to hold cheese spread, are decorated with colorful enamel designs.

The Ring pattern features multicolored enameled stripes.

A word of warning about the use of these dishes. Most can be used in a microwave and dishwasher with no problem. But patterns with designs that change the thickness of the glass may have stress points that will pop in a microwave. And dishes with decals like White Sails or with an iridescent finish will be harmed by the high temperatures of a dishwasher. Ceramic dinnerware and the prices for these pieces can be found in the second half of this book.

Fire King used several decorations on its opaque white lines. This cup and saucer feature the Bachelor Button design.

These mugs by Fire-King are colored to look like solid-color pottery.

DINNERWARE

The first ceramic pots made in the American colonies were redware. In the 1600s local red clay was dug, worked, and fired to make utilitarian pots and dishes. Salt-glazed pottery, a ware that did not chip as easily, was developed by the 1700s. Transfer-printed wares made in England were popular in America in the 19th century, and American factories, many near clay beds in Ohio and New Jersey, began to make inexpensive pottery dishes. Other popular dishes of the 19th century included iron-

Noritake's Azalea-pattern cake plate competed with similar American wares.

stone china, luster-decorated pieces, and colorful majolica. But it was not until the late 1920s that the "modern" dish styles evolved. Expensive and inexpensive dishes were made in thousands of different designs.

Many dinnerware sets were made in America from the 1930s through the 1960s. Some collectors refer to these sets as "Depression dinnerware," but the name used by manufacturers was "American dinnerware," which is

Friendly Village dinnerware, first made in 1953, is still made by the English company Johnson Brothers.

Colorful Fiesta is probably the most popular Homer Laughlin pattern.

the name still used by most collectors and dealers. Not all dishes were American made, however. There were also some popular dinnerware patterns marketed like the American pieces, such as Azalea, made by the Japanese company Noritake, and Friendly Village, made by Johnson Brothers in England.

Pottery, porcelain, semi-porcelain, ironstone, and other ceramic wares are included in the category of dinnerware. Most were made in potteries located in southern Ohio and in West Virginia near the Ohio River. Each

Riviera is another Homer Laughlin line.

Color is again the main focus of Homer Laughlin's Harlequin line.

El Patio pattern, produced from 1936 to 1956 by Franciscan Ceramics of California, was made in twenty solid colors.

Here are a sugar and creamer in the traditional Willow pattern by the Buffalo China Company of Buffalo, New York.

factory made many patterns for sale to gift shops and department stores. The potteries also made special patterns for use as premiums and free giveaways or to sell for low prices as store promotions. Dishes were given away at movies, stuffed into soap and cereal boxes and bags of flour, or sold for very low prices at grocery stores.

Dinnerware patterns fall into many categories. The first patterns to be rediscovered by collectors of the 1980s and 1990s were the solid-colored pottery lines such as Fiesta, Riviera, and Harlequin. Some colorful dinnerware was also made in California potteries before 1960. One

Liberty pattern made by an English company in the Staffordshire district of England features historical scenes, such as this plate picturing Washington at Valley Forge.

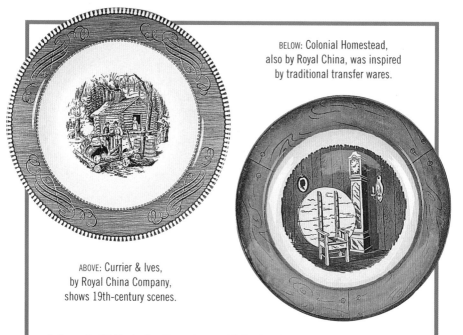

BELOW: Colonial Homestead, also by Royal China, was inspired by traditional transfer wares.

ABOVE: Currier & Ives, by Royal China Company, shows 19th-century scenes.

of these is El Patio by Franciscan. El Patio dishes are heavy and have a handcrafted look. Sets were sold in mix-and-match colors. These dishes have remained popular, and pieces were made in the 1990s in new colors.

Traditional-looking pieces reminiscent of the 19th century, including Willow and Liberty, have also remained popular. Some traditional patterns, like Currier & Ives and Colonial Homestead, are modern interpretations of older transfer patterns.

Nocturne was made by Southern Potteries, also called Blue Ridge by collectors.

BELOW: Hilda is another Blue Ridge floral design.

ABOVE: Blueberry was one of many fruit designs made by Stangl Pottery.

Many manufacturers in the 1930s preferred hand-painted, peasantlike decorations on their dinnerware. Included in this group are the pieces made by Southern Potteries under the name Blue Ridge; the pottery by Stangl of New Jersey picturing fruit, flowers, or birds; and the pieces by Gladding McBean (Franciscan), Metlox, and Red Wing.

Cameo Ware is an unusual type of dinnerware made about 1935 by Harker and others. To make Cameo Ware, a solid-colored plate was embel-

California Provincial is a pattern in the Poppy Trail line by Metlox.

Franciscan's Desert Rose
pattern is still popular.

This Bob White pitcher by
Red Wing Potteries, made from
1956 to 1967, incorporates
modern shapes with
hand-painted bird decorations.

Harker's Ivy Wreath plate
is part of the Cameo Ware line.

lished with a white decoration that in the finished product appears to be cut into the colored glaze. Cameo dinnerware pieces usually picture flowers and leaves, and some special children's wares have nursery rhyme animals or birds.

Realistically shaped pieces resembling corn were produced by several makers about 1955. The most important are Corn King and Corn Queen by the Shawnee Pottery Company. Green and yellow dishes were made in full sets. Other dishes were made in three-dimensional shapes. Most famous is

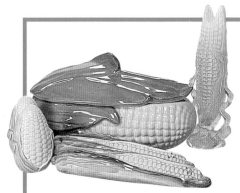

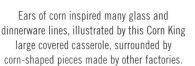

Ears of corn inspired many glass and dinnerware lines, illustrated by this Corn King large covered casserole, surrounded by corn-shaped pieces made by other factories.

Hull made this figural Red Riding Hood salt and pepper set.

the Red Riding Hood line first manufactured by Hull in 1943. Figural cookie jars, a few figural teapots, and salt and pepper shakers were made by both dinnerware firms and those who specialized in kitchen wares.

Most of the dinnerware made after the 1930s was decorated with decal designs. These colored, printed patterns were applied to the dishes, and often the same decal was used on several differently shaped plates or bowls. The most famous of these designs, Autumn Leaf, was made for and sold by the Jewel Tea Company after 1936. Reproductions of Autumn Leaf are being made today.

Mexican-inspired designs such as Mexicana by Homer Laughlin and Patio by Paden City were popular during the late 1930s. At least twenty different sets were made that picture cacti, haciendas, or sleeping Mexicans.

An Autumn Leaf ball pitcher made by Hall for the Jewel Tea Company.

Patio is a Mexican-inspired decoration on Paden City's Shell-Crest shape.

Red Poppy is one
of Hall's floral lines.

Hall also made Crocus,
another flower-inspired pattern.

The Hall China Company made many decal-decorated wares, including Poppy, Red Poppy, and Crocus. These dishes were often made with matching kitchen pieces, including coffeepots, stove-top salt and pepper shakers, cookie jars, leftover jars, and mixing bowls. Black silhouette designs on light-colored dishes were popular in the 1930s. Silhouette pictures to hang on the wall were very much in style. Silhouette pattern dishes by the Crooksville China Company and Taverne by the Hall China Company are the best known.

This is a Silhouette teapot made by Crooksville China Company.

American Modern is Russel Wright's most famous dinnerware.

Some dishes with innovative shapes and subtle earth-tone colors became favorites in the 1940s and 1950s. Important industrial designers, such as Russel Wright, who created American Modern and Iroquois; Walter Dorwin, who designed Conversation for Taylor, Smith, and Taylor; and Ben Seibel, who designed Raymor for Roseville, made these dishes. American Modern, the most famous dinnerware by Russel Wright, is said to be the best-selling dinnerware of all time.

Even more modern-looking dinnerware was made by Eva Zeisel (Hallcraft, Century, and Tomorrow's Classic for Hall) and other industrial designers and company art directors in the 1950s and 1960s. These include Starburst by Franciscan and California Contempora by Metlox. Many of the modern shapes and decorations used in this dinnerware were copied by other factories.

This Iroquois syrup with the Improptu design is another line by Russel Wright.

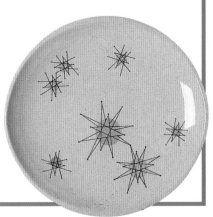

Starburst is one of Franciscan's modern lines.

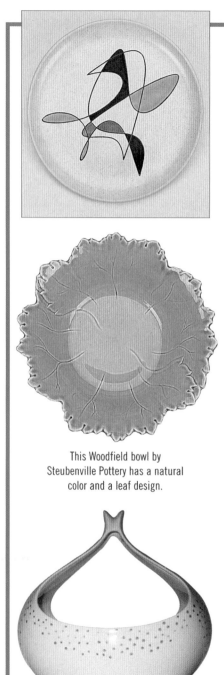

Metlox's California Contempora
pattern has a free-form design.

This Woodfield bowl by
Steubenville Pottery has a natural
color and a leaf design.

Eva Zeisel created the
Hallcraft line for Hall.
This serving bowl features
the Dawn design on a
Hallcraft shape.

The 1950s saw another trend: casual entertaining and outdoor living became popular. The dishes designed for these pastimes were often made in realistic forms of leaves and flowers or were colored in the subdued tones of nature. Woodfield by Steubenville was typical.

Because plastic dinnerware like Melmac didn't break easily, its popularity grew in the 1960s. However, plastic dinnerware did scratch, and it eventually lost favor to Pyroceram, a ceramiclike glass substance made by Corning for its baking dishes and Corelle dinnerware. Even though Corelle dinnerware is still popular today, the American dinnerware era was over by the 1970s. Unable to compete with cheaper wares made in Asia, most American potteries closed in the 1960s and 1970s. Today most of our dishes are made in England or in countries such as Sri Lanka or Thailand.

ford Wedgwood Group. We use the name that was in use most of the time the pattern was made.

Although hundreds of patterns are included in this book, many patterns were not seen at sales this year and are not included. Prices listed in this book are actual prices asked by dealers at shows, shops, and through national advertising. It is not the price you would pay at a garage sale or church bazaar. Prices are not estimates. If a high and low are given, we have recorded several sales. There is a regional variation in the prices, especially for the solid-colored wares. In general, these pieces are high priced in the East and West, lower in the center of the country.

There have been a few reissues of dinnerware. Harlequin was put back into production in 1979 for the Woolworth Company, the sole distributor. Complete dinner sets were made in the original colors, except that the salmon is a deeper color than the original. The sugar bowls were made with closed handles. Fiesta was reissued by Homer Laughlin China Company in 1986. The original molds and marks were used. The new Fiesta has a china body that shrinks a little more than the semivitreous clay body used before. This means that most new pieces are slightly smaller than the old ones. Dinner plates, soup bowls, and cereal bowls were made slightly larger to accommodate modern tastes. New molds were made for these pieces. The dinner plates are 10 1/2 inches. The new dishes were first made in cobalt blue (darker than the original), black, white, apricot, and rose. Other colors have been added. A few of the pieces have been slightly redesigned since 1986, with variations in handles and bases. A special line was added with cartoon decorations. A Fiesta lookalike has been made by Franciscan since 1978 under the name Kaleidoscope and a line called Cantinaware has been sold by Target stores. We have tried to indicate in the paragraphs in the main section if any reproductions of a pattern have been made.

This book is a report of prices for pieces offered for sale during the past year. Most of the patterns included in earlier books are found here because the collectors still buy these patterns. Many newly popular patterns are also included.

Depression glass and prices for these pieces can be found in the first half of this book.

Particular patterns can be found by using either the Depression Glass or Dinnerware main listings, both of which are arranged alphabetically. Depression Glass begins on page 11 and Dinnerware on page 121.

Clubs and Publications

CLUBS

Abingdon Pottery Collectors Club, *Abingdon Pottery Collectors Newsletter* (newsletter), R.R. 1, Box 145, Abingdon, IL 61410.

Blue & White Pottery Club, *Blue & White Pottery Club* (newsletter), 224 12th Street NW, Center Point, IA 52405.

Currier & Ives Dinnerware Collectors, *Collectors' Newsletter* (newsletter), 29470 Saxon Rd., Toulon, IL 61483.

Fiesta Collector's Club, *Fiesta Collector's Quarterly* (newsletter), P.O. Box 471, Valley City, OH 44280.

Fiesta Club of America, Inc., *Fiesta Club of America Newsletter* (newsletter), P.O. Box 15383, Loves Park, IL 61132-5383.

Franciscan Collectors Club, *Franciscan Newsletter* (newsletter), 8412 5th Ave. NE, Seattle, WA 98115, e-mail: gmcb1@aol.com

Frankoma Family Collectors Association, *Pot & Puma* (newsletter); *Prairie Green Sheet* (newsletter), 5632 NW 58th Terr., Oklahoma City, OK 73122-7329.

Hall China Collector Club, *Hall China Collector Club Newsletter* (newsletter), P.O. Box 360488, Cleveland, OH 44136.

Homer Laughlin Collectors Club, *The Homer Laughlin Glaze* (newsletter), P. O. Box 16174, Loves Park, IL 61132-6174.

National Autumn Leaf Collectors Club, *Autumn Leaf Newsletter* (newsletter), P.O. Box 1, Mira Loma, CA 91752-0001.

Novelty Salt & Pepper Shakers Club, *Novelty Salt & Pepper Shakers Club Newsletter* (newsletter), 581 Joy Road, Battle Creek, MI 49017.

Red Wing Collectors Society, *Red Wing Collectors Newsletter* (newsletter), P.O. Box 50, Red Wing, MN 55066.

Shawnee Pottery Collector's Club, *Exclusively Shawnee* (newsletter), P.O. Box 713, New Smyrna Beach, FL 32170-0713.

Stangl/Fulper Collectors Club, *Stangl/Fulper Times* (newsletter), P.O. Box 538, Flemington, NJ 08822.

Watt Collectors Association, *Watt's News* (newsletter), P.O. Box 184, Galesburg, IL 61402-0184.

Watt Pottery Collectors USA, *Spoutings* (newsletter), P.O. Box 26067, Fairview Park, OH 44126.

Wedgwood Society of New York, *Ars Ceramica* (magazine), 5 Dogwood Ct., Glen Head, NY 11545.

PUBLICATIONS

Antique Trader Weekly (newspaper), P.O. Box 1050, Dubuque, IA 52004-1050.

Bauer Quarterly (newsletter), P.O. Box 2524, Berkeley, CA 94702, e-mail: bauerpot@ix.netcom.com

California Pottery Trader (newsletter), P.O. Box 844, Cambria, CA 93428.

Currier & Ives Quarterly (newsletter), P.O. Box 504, Riverton, KS 66770 (Currier & Ives dinnerware by Royal China Company).

Daze (newsletter), P.O. Box 57, Otisville, MI 48463.

Fiesta Collector's Quarterly (newsletter), P.O. Box 471, Valley City, OH 44280.

Hull Pottery News (newsletter), 15-H Fiedler Ct., Fenton, MO 63026.

***Kovels on Antiques and Collectibles* (newsletter), P.O. Box 22200, Beachwood, OH 44122.**

Laughlin Eagle (newsletter), 1270 63rd Terr. S., St. Petersburg, FL 33705.

Lu-Ray Relay (newsletter), 204 S. Veitch, #3, Arlington, VA 22204, e-mail: mforbes@lewin.com (Taylor, Smith and Taylor's Lu-Ray Pastels and other dinnerware lines).

***Matching Services: China, Silver, Crystal* (leaflet), Ralph and Terry Kovel (P.O. Box 22900, Beachwood, OH 44122).**

National Blue Ridge Newsletter (newsletter), 144 Highland Dr., Blountville, TN 37617-5404.

Pottery Collectors Express (newsletter), P.O. Box 221, Mayview, MO 64071-0221.

Purinton Pastimes (newsletter), P.O. Box 9394, Arlington, VA 22219, e-mail: lhinterl@aol.com

Vernon Views (newsletter), P.O. Box 945, Scottsdale, AZ 85252.

Willow Word (magazine), P.O. Box 13382, Arlington, TX 76094-0382.

·A·

AMBERSTONE

Fiesta is a popular dinnerware pattern found in solid colors. In 1967, Amberstone was made by the Homer Laughlin China Company of Newell, West Virginia, using the Fiesta shapes. The pieces were glazed a rich brown. Some pieces had black machine-stamped underglaze patterns. The pieces were used for supermarket promotions and were called Genuine Sheffield dinnerware. Full sets of dishes were made.

Creamer	10.00
Cup & Saucer	5.00 to 8.00
Pie Plate	85.00
Plate, Dessert, 6 In.	2.00
Plate, Dinner, 10 In.	7.00
Plate, Luncheon, 8 In.	4.00
Sugar	16.00

AMERICAN MODERN

Russel Wright was a designer who made dinnerware in modern shapes for many companies, including Iroquois China Company, Harker Pottery Company, Steubenville Pottery, Paden City Pottery (Justin Tharaud and Sons), Sterling China Company, Edwin M. Knowles China Company, and J.A. Bauer Pottery Company. American Modern was made by the Steubenville Pottery Company, Steubenville, Ohio, from 1939 to 1959. The original dishes were made in Bean Brown (a shaded brown), Chartreuse, Coral, Granite Gray, Seafoam (blue-green), and White. The brown was replaced with Black Chutney (dark brown) during World War II. Cantaloupe, Cedar Green, and Glacier Blue were added in the 1950s. Matching linens and glassware were made.

Russel Wright
MFG. BY
STEUBENVILLE

BEAN BROWN

Bowl, Fruit, 1 Lug, 6 1/4 In.	18.00 to 20.00
Bowl, Salad	50.00
Casserole, Cover	45.00 to 55.00
Celery Dish	40.00 to 45.00
Cup & Saucer, After Dinner	50.00
Plate, Dinner, 10 In.	14.00
Plate, Salad, 8 In.	18.00 to 20.00
Platter, 13 3/4 In.	32.00 to 38.00
Refrigerator Jar	200.00

BLACK CHUTNEY

Bowl, Vegetable, Cover, 10 In.	70.00
Casserole, Cover	55.00
Coffeepot	225.00 to 245.00
Cup	5.00
Pitcher, Water	100.00 to 125.00
Platter, Square, 13 In.	32.50
Soup, Dish, Lug	20.00
Sugar & Creamer	42.00
Teapot	145.00

CANTALOUPE

Pitcher	275.00
Plate, Dinner, 10 In.	22.00

CEDAR GREEN

Bowl, Vegetable, Divided, 10 In.	100.00
Carafe, Jug	135.00
Celery Dish	16.00 to 20.00
Chop Plate	47.00
Cup	5.00
Cup, Coffee, Cover	22.00
Pitcher, Cover	700.00
Plate, Dinner, 10 In.	6.00 to 12.00
Relish	225.00
Teapot	145.00 to 175.00
Tumbler, Child's	55.00

CHARTREUSE

Bowl, Vegetable, 10 In.	8.00
Butter	150.00
Carafe	85.00
Celery Dish	20.00
Chop Plate, 13 In.	20.00 to 30.00
Coffeepot	125.00
Coffeepot, After Dinner	68.00
Creamer	7.50 to 15.00
Cup	2.50
Cup & Saucer	9.00 to 18.00
Goblet, 4 In.	36.00
Gravy Boat	20.00
Pepper Shaker	12.00
Pitcher, Cover	350.00
Pitcher, Water	70.00
Plate, Bread & Butter, 6 In.	5.00
Plate, Dinner, 10 In.	9.00
Plate, Salad, 8 1/2 In.	7.00
Platter, 13 1/2 In.	20.00
Relish, Divided	22.00
Salt Shaker	10.00

Saucer 3.00
Sherbet, 2 1/2 In. 22.00
Sugar, Cover 10.00
Teapot 85.00

CORAL
Bowl, Fruit, Lug 12.00
Bowl, Salad, Serving 85.00
Bowl, Vegetable, 10 In. . .18.00
Carafe . . . . .135.00 to 145.00
Casserole, Cover, 12 In. . .75.00
Celery Dish . . . .15.00 to 30.00
Cup, After Dinner 17.00
Cup, Child's 20.00
Cup & Saucer . . .6.00 to 8.00
Cup & Saucer, After
  Dinner . . . . . .20.00 to 24.00
Dish, Pickle 20.00
Gravy Boat 22.00
Pitcher,
  7 1/2 In. . . . . .65.00 to 75.00
Pitcher, Water 110.00
Plate, Bread & Butter,
  6 1/4 In. . . . . . . .2.50 to 5.00
Platter,
  13 3/4 In. . . . . .18.50 to 20.00
Relish, Divided, Reed-Wrapped
  Handle 275.00
Relish, Rosette 225.00
Salt & Pepper 20.00
Saucer 3.00
Soup, Dish, Child's 45.00
Soup, Dish, Lug 7.50
Stack Set 275.00
Sugar, Cover 16.00
Sugar & Creamer,
  Cover . . . . . . .24.00 to 30.00
Teapot 75.00
Tumbler, Iced Tea 35.00

GRANITE GRAY
Bowl, Vegetable,
  Divided 58.00
Bowl, Vegetable, Open . . .22.00
Butter, Cover 175.00
Casserole,
  Cover . . . . . . .45.00 to 55.00
Coaster, Pair 18.00
Coffeepot, After Dinner . .85.00
Creamer . . . . .9.00 to 12.00
Cup, After Dinner 17.00
Cup, Coffee, Cover 22.00
Cup & Saucer . . .6.00 to 12.00

Cup & Saucer, After
  Dinner . . . . . .28.00 to 30.00
Gravy Boat 25.00
Plate, Bread & Butter,
  6 1/4 In. . . . . . . .2.50 to 5.00
Plate, Dinner, 10 In. 10.00
Plate, Salad, 8 In. 12.00
Platter, 13 3/4 In. 20.00
Relish, Divided, Rattan
  Handle 275.00
Salt & Pepper 16.00
Soup, Dish, Lug 15.00
Sugar, Cover 20.00

SEAFOAM
Bowl, Salad 100.00
Bowl, Vegetable,
  Cover, 12 In. 50.00
Coffeepot, After
  Dinner 120.00
Cup . . . . .8.00 to 12.00
Cup, After
  Dinner . . . . . .12.00 to 18.00
Cup & Saucer 24.00
Cup & Saucer, After
  Dinner 6.00
Plate, Bread & Butter,
  6 In. . . . . .3.00 to 6.00
Plate, Dinner, 10 In. 8.00
Relish, Divided, Rattan
  Handle 185.00
Salt & Pepper 10.00
Saucer 3.00
Sherbet 15.00
Soup, Dish, Lug 10.00
Sugar, Cover . . . .12.00 to 14.00
Teapot 135.00

WHITE
Bowl, Salad 140.00
Chop Plate 75.00
Coffeepot, Cover 65.00
Cup & Saucer 48.00
Pitcher, Ice Lip 195.00
Teapot 145.00

ANTIQUE GRAPE
Antique Grape is a pattern introduced by Metlox Potteries in 1964. The firm had been making a pattern called Sculptured Grape with a raised grapevine border in natural col-

ors. Antique Grape is the same shape but according to the brochure has carved grapes and leaves raised on a soft beige antique finish against a warm white background. It was made until at least 1975.

Bowl, Divided, 8 1/2 In. . .35.00
Creamer 18.00
Gravy Boat, 1 Pt. 32.00
Platter, 9 In. 32.00
Salt & Pepper 20.00
Sugar, Cover 20.00
Teapot 95.00

ANYTIME
Anytime is the name of both a shape and pattern made by Vernon Kilns from 1956 to 1958. It has abstract streaks of gray, green, mocha, and yellow. The pattern and name rights were purchased by Metlox Potteries in 1958 and Anytime continued to be produced.

Chowder 8.00
Pitcher, 2 Qt. 35.00
Relish 25.00
Tumbler 28.00

APPLE BLOSSOM

Two companies made patterns called Apple Blossom. Crooksville China Company of Crooksville, Ohio, made a pink flowered pattern. The pattern listed here was made by Homer Laughlin China Company of Newell, West Virginia, from 1935 to 1955. It has a flowered border and gold trim.

Bowl, 13 In. 95.00
Compote, 7 In. 85.00
Grill Plate, 10 In. 55.00
Pitcher 395.00
Plate, 11 1/2 In. 65.00
Relish, 4 Sections 135.00
Sandwich Server,
   2 Handles 45.00

APPLE FRANCISCAN

Gladding, McBean & Company made Apple pattern dishes, one of its Franciscan Ceramics "Classics" designs, beginning in 1940. The pattern is still being made, but Franciscan Ceramics is now part of Waterford Wedgwood USA. Several other factories also made patterns called Apple.

Ashtray . . . . . .18.00 to 20.00
Berry Bowl 3.00
Bowl, Cereal,
   6 In. . . . . .10.00 to 15.00
Bowl, Fruit,
   5 1/4 In. . . . . . .8.00 to 13.00
Bowl, Salad,
   10 In. . . . . . .115.00 to 145.00
Bowl, Salad, Crescent 30.00
Bowl, Vegetable,
   8 1/2 In. . . . . . .15.00 to 25.00

Bowl, Vegetable, 9 In. . . .50.00
Bowl, Vegetable, Oval,
   Divided, 10 1/2 In. 45.00
Bowl, Vegetable, Scalloped,
   8 1/4 In. . . . . . .25.00 to 32.00
Butter, Cover, 1/4 Lb. 40.00
Cake Plate, 12 1/2 In. 35.00
Casserole,
   Cover . . . . . . .65.00 to 95.00
Chop Plate,
   12 In. . . . . .38.00 to 60.00
Chop Plate, 14 In. 100.00
Cigar Box, Cover 95.00
Cigarette Box . .95.00 to 125.00
Coaster 50.00
Compote, Footed,
   8 In. . . . . .60.00 to 85.00
Cookie Jar,
   Cover . . . . .280.00 to 300.00
Creamer, Individual 30.00
Cup 5.00
Cup, After Dinner 40.00
Cup & Saucer . . .8.00 to 18.50
Cup & Saucer, After
   Dinner . . . . . .35.00 to 60.00
Eggcup . . . . . . .20.00 to 35.00
Gravy Boat . . . .35.00 to 45.00
Gravy Boat, Underplate . .50.00
Grill Plate 90.00
Mixing Bowl, Medium . .165.00
Mixing Bowl, Small 115.00
Mixing Bowl Set,
   3 Piece 500.00
Mug, 7 Oz. 25.00
Mug, 10 Oz. 65.00
Pitcher, Iced Tea,
   5 1/4 In. 30.00
Pitcher, Milk,
   6 1/4 In. . . . . . .60.00 to 95.00
Pitcher, Syrup . . .75.00 to 90.00
Pitcher, Water 80.00
Plate, 12 In. 76.00
Plate, Bread & Butter,
   6 1/2 In. . . . . . . .4.00 to 8.00
Plate, Breakfast,
   9 1/2 In. . . . . . .10.00 to 16.00
Plate, Child's,
   Sections . . . .125.00 to 195.00
Plate, Dinner,
   10 1/2 In. . . . . .16.00 to 25.00
Plate, Salad,
   8 1/2 In. . . . . . .9.00 to 14.00

Plate, Salad, Crescent 25.00
Plate, Steak 150.00
Platter,
   12 1/2 In. . . . . .48.00 to 50.00
Platter, 14 In. . . .33.00 to 75.00
Platter, 19 In. 245.00
Relish,
   3 Sections . . . .55.00 to 70.00
Relish, Oval . . . .23.00 to 25.00
Salt & Pepper . . .20.00 to 25.00
Salt & Pepper, Tall 60.00
Saucer 2.00
Sherbet, Footed 24.00
Soup, Dish . . . . .20.00 to 28.00
Sugar, Cover 40.00
Sugar, Cover, Small 20.00
Sugar & Creamer,
   Cover . . . . . . .35.00 to 38.00
Sugar & Creamer, Cover,
   Large 60.00
Teapot, Cover 70.00
Tumbler . . . . . . .25.00 to 28.00
Tureen, Soup, Large 375.00

APPLE PURINTON

Apple pattern was also made by Purinton Pottery of Shippenville, Pennsylvania. The hand-decorated dinnerware was made in the early 1940s. It was designed by William Blair. The apple was colored red with yellow and brown highlights, the stems and leaves were green, blue, and dark brown. The trim colors were red, cobalt blue, or blue-green.

Bean Pot, Cover, Individual,
   3 3/4 In. . . . . . .50.00 to 75.00
Bowl, Fruit,
   12 In. . . . . .35.00 to 45.00
Canister, Coffee, Blue . . .65.00

Canister, Coffee, Red 55.00
Canister, Flour 35.00
Canister Set, Cobalt Trim,
 4 Piece 475.00
Casserole, Cover 65.00
Chop Plate,
 12 In. . . . . . . .35.00 to 40.00
Chop Plate, Scalloped
 Border, 12 In. 58.00
Coffeepot, 8 Cup 90.00
Cookie Jar, Red Trim 64.00
Creamer 15.00
Ginger Jar, Cover, Paper
 Label 45.00
Grill Plate 60.00
Jug, Dutch, 5 Pt. 75.00
Jug, Petals, Honey 45.00
Lazy Susan Set,
 7 Piece . . . . . .85.00 to 130.00
Mug 20.00
Oil & Vinegar,
 Cobalt Trim 275.00
Oil & Vinegar,
 Red Trim . . . .75.00 to 125.00
Plate, Dinner, 10 In. 20.00
Plate, Salad, 7 1/2 In. 8.00
Platter, 2 Sections,
 12 1/4 In. . . . . .35.00 to 55.00
Platter, Meat, 12 In. 40.00
Relish, 3 Sections 50.00
Salt & Pepper 25.00
Saucer . . . . .3.00 to 5.00
Sugar, Cover 25.00
Sugar, Open 10.00
Sugar & Creamer 40.00
Sugar & Creamer,
 Miniature 25.00
Tea & Toast Set, Snack . .25.00
Tumbler, Iced Tea, 12 Oz. 28.00

APPLE WATT

The Watt Pottery Company was incorporated in Crooksville, Ohio, in 1922. They made a variety of hand-decorated potteries. The most popular is Apple pattern, sometimes called Red Apple. Dinnerware sets and kitchenware were made beginning in 1952. The company burned to the ground in 1965.

Baker, Cover, No. 67 . . .140.00
Baker, Cover, No. 96 . . .125.00
Baker, No. 85, 3-Leaf,
 Rectangular 1000.00
Bean Pot, 2 Handles,
 No. 76 . . . . .200.00
Bowl, Cover, No. 601,
 Ribbed, 8 3/4 In. 80.00
Bowl, Salad, No. 73 . . . . .95.00
Bowl, Salad, No. 74,
 2-Leaf . . . . . .30.00 to 40.00
Bowl, Spaghetti, No. 24,
 3-Leaf . . . . . .85.00 to 175.00
Canister, No. 72 . . . . . .600.00
Canister, Sugar, No. 81 . .650.00
Casserole, Cover, No. 5,
 2-Leaf 60.00
Casserole, Stick Handle,
 No. 18, Individual 150.00
Chop Plate,
 No. 49 . . . . .300.00 to 350.00
Coffee Server, Cover,
 No. 115 . .2350.00 to 3000.00
Cookie Jar, No. 503 . . . .495.00
Creamer, No. 62,
 2-Leaf . . . . .115.00 to 130.00
Ice Bucket, No. 59 . . . . .325.00
Mixing Bowl, No. 5,
 2-Leaf 45.00
Mixing Bowl, No. 5,
 Ribbed 60.00
Mixing Bowl, No. 6,
 Ribbed 55.00

❖

**Don't put china with
gold designs in the
dishwasher. The gold
will wash off.**

❖

Mixing Bowl, No. 7,
 Ribbed 55.00
Mixing Bowl Set, No. 63,
 No. 64, No. 65,
 Nested 185.00
Mug,
 No. 121 . . . .175.00 to 200.00
Mug, No. 501 . . . . .265.00
Mug, No. 701 . . . . .475.00
Nappy, No. 04 . . .60.00 to 70.00
Pie Plate, No. 33 . . . . . .100.00
Pitcher, No. 16, 2-Leaf . . .60.00
Pitcher, No. 17, Ice Lip,
 8 In. 175.00
Plate, Dinner, No. 29,
 10 In. 250.00
Salad, Cover, No. 73 . . . .190.00
Salad, No. 73, Green
 Band 100.00
Salt & Pepper, Barrel . . .425.00
Salt & Pepper,
 Hourglass . . .150.00 to 225.00
Sugar, Cover, No. 98 . . .400.00
Sugar & Creamer, No.
 98, No. 62, 3-Leaf 595.00
Teapot, No. 505 . . . . . .4000.00

ARCADIA

Arcadia has a hand-painted brown and mustard laurel leaf border and was made by Vernon Kilns of Los Angeles, California, from 1942 to 1955.

Cup & Saucer, After
Dinner 16.00
Gravy Boat 22.00
Plate, Breakfast, 9 1/2 In. .12.00

AUTUMN FOLIAGE

Autumn Foliage was made by the Watt Pottery Company from 1959 to 1965. It has brown leaves on brown stems. It is also called Brown Leaves.

Bean Pot, No. 76 . . . . . .145.00
Cookie Jar, No. 76 . . . . . .80.00
Creamer, No. 62 . . . . . . .195.00
Cruet Set, No. 126 . . . . .625.00
Sugar, Cover, No. 98 . . .140.00
Teapot, No. 505 . . . . . . .980.00

AUTUMN LEAF

One of the most popular American dinnerware patterns, Autumn Leaf was made for the Jewel Tea Company, a grocery chain, beginning in 1936. Hall China Company of East Liverpool, Ohio; Crooksville China Company of Crooksville, Ohio; Harker Pottery Company of Chester, West Virginia; and Paden City Pottery of Paden City, West Virginia, made dishes with this design. The Autumn Leaf pattern always has the same shades of dark yellow and rust leaves. The shape of the dish varies with the manufacturer. Several special terms are used to describe these shapes, such as "bud-ray," which describes a bowl lid with a knob surrounded by raised rays. Collectors can find Autumn Leaf pattern tinware, plastic tablecloths, glassware, clocks, even painted furniture. There are several books about Autumn Leaf and a collectors club listed at the back of this book. The Jewel Tea pattern is listed here. Reproductions using the Autumn Leaf decoration have been made since 1990. These, unlike the originals, are marked "Limited Edition."

It is easy to glue pieces of broken china. Use a new, fast-setting but not instant glue. Position the pieces correctly, then use tape to hold the parts together. If the piece needs special support, lean it in a suitable position in a box filled with sand.

Baker, French, 4 1/2 In. . .70.00
Baker, Oval, 7 x 5 x
1 1/2 In. 270.00
Bean Pot, 2 Handles 150.00
Bean Pot, Cover,
2 Handles 360.00
Bean Pot, Cover,
Handle . . . .995.00 to 1100.00
Bowl, 2 Sections, Oval . .170.00
Bowl, 9 In. . . . . .25.00 to 30.00
Bowl, Fruit, 5 In. . .4.00 to 8.00
Bowl, Salad 36.00
Bowl, Vegetable,
2 Sections, 10 1/2 In. . .175.00
Bowl, Vegetable, Cover, Oval,
10 1/2 In. . . . . .69.00 to 80.00
Bowl, Vegetable, Round,
9 In. 75.00
Butter, Square,
1/4 Lb. 500.00
Cake Plate,
9 1/2 In. . . . . . .18.50 to 35.00
Cake Plate, Metal Base . .265.00
Candy Dish, Gold
Trim . . . . . .525.00 to 545.00
Casserole, Cover,
10 Oz. 35.00
Casserole, Cover, 2 Qt. . . .22.00
Coaster, 3 1/4 In. 12.00
Coffeepot,
Electric . . . . .395.00 to 435.00
Coffeepot, Metal Drip,
8 Cup . . . . . . .85.00 to 120.00
Cookie Jar, Big Ear 275.00
Cookie Jar,
Tootsie . . . . .285.00 to 350.00

Creamer, Rayed 36.00
Cup, Ruffled 30.00
Cup & Saucer, After
  Dinner 50.00
Custard Cup 12.00
Drip Jar, Cover 36.00
French Baker, 10 Oz.,
  4 1/2 In. . . . . .50.00 to 70.00
French Baker, Flute,
  3 Pt. 30.00
Gravy Boat . . . .25.00 to 50.00
Jam Jar 40.00
Jug, Ball . . . . . .40.00 to 50.00
Mixing Bowl,
  3 Piece . . . . .55.00 to 110.00
Mug, Irish Coffee 200.00
Pie Baker 55.00
Plate, Dinner, 10 In. 17.00
Platter, Oval, 11 3/8 In. . . .8.50
Platter, Oval, 13 1/2 In. . .29.00

❖

Salt & Pepper, Left Hand
  Salt 44.00
Salt & Pepper,
  Range . . . . . . .25.00 to 35.00
Salt & Pepper,
  Ruffled . . . . . . .26.00 to 28.00
Soup, Cream . . . .36.00 to 45.00
Stack Set, 4 Piece 200.00
Sugar, Cover, Rayed 50.00
Teapot, Aladdin 65.00
Teapot, Aladdin,
  Insert . . . . . .98.00 to 120.00
Teapot, Donut 110.00
Teapot, Long Spout,
  Sunshine . . . .90.00 to 120.00
Teapot, New York 1000.00
Teapot, Newport 350.00
Tidbit, 3 Tiers 200.00
Warmer, Oval 150.00
Warmer, Round 240.00

AZALEA

Azalea pattern was made for
Larkin Company customers
from 1918 to 1941. Larkin, the
soap company, was in Buffalo,
New York. The dishes were
made by Noritake China Company of Japan. Each piece of
the white china was decorated
with pink azaleas.

Ashtray 32.00
Berry Bowl, 5 1/2 In. 25.00
Bowl, 4 3/4 In. . .18.00 to 24.00
Bowl, Fruit, 11 3/4 In. . .155.00
Cup & Saucer 14.00
Plate, Dessert, 6 In. 6.00
Plate, Dinner,
  10 In. . . . . . . .18.00 to 37.00
Sauce Bowl, 5 1/4 In. 8.00
Saucer 5.00
Saucer, After Dinner 12.00

Sugar & Creamer, Cover .30.00
Trivet 40.00

BALLERINA

Solid-colored pottery was popular in the 1950s. Universal
Potteries of Cambridge, Ohio,
made Ballerina from 1947 to
1956. Ballerina was very modern in shape and had solid-
colored glazes. A later line was
decorated with abstract designs. The original solid-
colored Ballerina dinnerware
was offered in Dove Gray, Jade
Green, Jonquil Yellow, and
Periwinkle Blue. In 1949 Chartreuse and Forest Green were
added. By 1955 Burgundy,
Charcoal, and Pink were added,
while some other colors had
been discontinued. There was
also a line called Ballerina
Mist, which was a pale blue-
green with decal decorations.

DOVE GRAY
Bowl, Vegetable, Round,
  7 In. 12.00

**Protect your home and
antiques from theft. Use
a timer on your lights
even when you are at
home. This will set a
pattern of certain lights
going on and off each
day. When you are
away, the house will
appear to have normal
activity. Also park a car
near the front of the
house. The car will block
the driveway so a
burglar cannot load up
through the garage.
Have someone keep
your trash cans filled.
This will make the house
look occupied. Keep the
grass mowed and the
snow shoveled. Stop
your mail and news-
paper deliveries.**

❖

Plate, Dinner, 10 In. 12.50
Relish 5.00

JADE GREEN
Bowl, 36s 8.00
Eggcup . . . . .10.00 to 12.00
Plate, 6 In. 3.00
Platter, Round, Lug,
   10 In. 14.00

PINK
Cup 6.00
Plate, Dinner, 10 In. 12.00

BALLERINA MIST

The shapes of Ballerina Mist are those used for the Ballerina pattern also made by Universal Potteries of Cambridge, Ohio. This 1950s pattern was pale blue-green with decal decorations.

Pitcher, Ice Lip   15.00
Pitcher, Juice 12.50
Stack Set, Cover .40.00 to 45.00

BEEHIVE, see Ring

BLUE BOUQUET

Standard Coffee of New Orleans, Louisiana, gave Blue Bouquet pattern dinnerware and kitchenware as a premium from the early 1950s to the early 1960s. Although it was made by the Hall China Company, East Liverpool, Ohio, it is most easily found in the South. The pattern is very plain with a thin blue border interrupted by roses. Blue Ridge also made a pattern called Blue Bouquet, but the pattern listed here is by Hall China Company.

Bean Pot 175.00
Bowl, Fruit, 5 1/2 In. 12.00
Bowl, Radiance, 6 In. 25.00
Bowl, Radiance, 7 In. 30.00
Bowl, Radiance, 9 In. 45.00
Bowl, Salad, 9 In. 30.00
Bowl, Vegetable, 9 In. . . .30.00
Casserole 75.00
Coffeepot 100.00
Creamer, Boston 20.00
Cup 18.00
French Baker 25.00
Pie Baker 30.00
Plate, Bread & Butter,
   7 In. 12.00
Plate, Breakfast, 9 In. 18.00
Plate, Dessert, 6 In. 8.00
Platter, Oval, 11 In. 30.00
Saucer 4.00
Soup, Dish 20.00
Teapot, Aladdin 80.00

BLUE WILLOW, see Willow

BLUEBERRY

Stangl Pottery of Trenton, New Jersey, made Blueberry (pattern No. 3770) before 1942. The heavy red pottery dishes were glazed with a yellow border and a sgraffito decoration of blueberries in the center.

Cup & Saucer 16.00
Plate, Bread & Butter, 6 In. 2.50

BOB WHITE

Bob White was made by Red Wing Potteries from 1956 to 1967. It was one of the most popular dinnerware patterns made by the factory. The pattern, a modern hand-painted design, shows a stylized bird and background.

Bowl, Cereal, 6 In. 25.00
Bowl, Salad, 12 In. 50.00
Bread Tray, 24 In. 100.00
Butter Warmer, Cover,
   1/4 Lb. . . . . . . .75.00 to 95.00
Carafe 195.00
Casserole, Cover,
   2 Qt. . . . . .40.00 to 45.00
Casserole, Cover,
   4 Qt. . . . . .50.00 to 52.00
Creamer 20.00
Cruet 30.00
Cup & Saucer . .10.00 to 25.00
Gravy Boat,
   Cover . . . . .47.50 to 55.00
Jug, 60 Oz. 45.00
Lazy Susan, 5 Piece 125.00
Mug 80.00
Pitcher, Water, 60 Oz.,
   6 3/4 In. . . . . . .25.00 to 38.00

Pitcher, Water, 112 Oz.,
12 In. 60.00
Plate, Bread & Butter,
6 1/2 In. 9.50
Plate, Dinner,
10 1/2 In. . . . . .10.00 to 17.50
Plate, Salad,
6 1/2 In. . . . . . . .6.00 to 8.00
Platter, 13 In. 90.00
Platter, 20 In. 100.00
Relish,
3 Sections . . . .47.50 to 55.00
Salt & Pepper,
Bird Shape . . . .32.00 to 50.00
Salt & Pepper, Hourglass
Shape, 6 In. 25.00
Sugar & Creamer,
Cover 40.00
Teapot 75.00
Teapot, Stand . .95.00 to 120.00
Tray, Cocktail 40.00

BOW KNOT

Bow Knot is a variation of the
Whirligig pattern. It has a
piecrust rim on a Colonial
shape. It was made by Blue
Ridge in the 1950s. Bow Knot
is colored chartreuse and
brown, Whirligig is red and
light blue.

Cornucopia, 7 1/2 In. . . .125.00
Cup 14.00
Flowerpot, 6 1/2 In. 160.00
Plate, Salad, 7 In. 15.00
Tumbler 25.00
Wall Pocket, 8 In. 175.00

CALICO

Calico is one of the plaid
designs made by Vernon Kilns
of Vernon, California. The design was pink and blue with a
blue border. Other related
plaids are Coronation Organdy
(gray and rose), Gingham
(green and yellow), Homespun
(cinnamon, yellow, and green),
Organdie (brown and yellow),
Tam O'Shanter (rust, chartreuse, and dark green), and
Tweed (yellow and gray-blue).

Berry Bowl 9.00
Creamer 20.00
Cup & Saucer 42.00
Plate, Bread & Butter,
6 In. 9.00
Salt & Pepper 35.00

CALIFORNIA IVY

California Ivy was one of the
most popular patterns made by
the Metlox Potteries of Manhattan Beach, California. It was
introduced in 1946. The pattern
was named for its ivy vine
border.

Berry Bowl, 5 1/2 In. 9.00
Bowl, 2 Sections, 11 In. . .45.00
Bowl, Round, 9 In. 40.00
Bowl, Salad, 11 1/4 In. . . .50.00
Bowl, Vegetable, Round,
10 In. 25.00
Coaster 16.00
Creamer 14.00
Cup . . . . .6.00 to 12.00
Cup & Saucer 12.00
Plate, 9 1/4 In. 11.00
Plate, Dinner,
10 In. . . . . .9.00 to 12.00
Plate, Luncheon,
9 1/4 In. 12.00
Plate, Salad, 6 In. . .5.00 to 7.00

❖

**Don't store dishes for
long periods of time
in old newspaper
wrappings. The ink can
make indelible stains on
the china.**

❖

Platter, Oval,
    13 In. . . . . . . .36.00 to 50.00
Relish 25.00
Saucer 3.00
Sugar & Creamer 35.00

CALIFORNIA PROVINCIAL

California Provincial dinnerware pictures a rooster in the center. The rooster is maroon, green, and yellow. The border is green and coffee brown. It was made by Metlox Potteries beginning in 1950. A similar design, in different colors, was called Red Rooster.

Basket, Vegetable, Round,
    8 1/2 In. 50.00
Bowl, 10 In. 80.00
Bowl, Vegetable,
    2 Sections, 10 In. 48.00
Bread Basket . . .55.00 to 68.00
Butter, Cover 55.00
Canister, Coffee 55.00
Canister, Sugar 70.00
Canister, Tea 70.00
Casserole, Individual 22.00
Chop Plate, 12 In. 75.00
Coaster 20.00
Coffee Carafe &
    Warmer 275.00
Coffeepot 115.00
Condiment Set, Cover 65.00
Cup, 6 Oz. 12.00
Cup & Saucer 16.00
Dish, Hen On Nest 95.00
Jam Jar 55.00
Mug, Cocoa . . . .35.00 to 38.00
Mug, Cover, Large 65.00

Pitcher, Figural,
    Rooster 275.00
Plate, Dinner, 10 In. 16.00
Plate, Luncheon, 9 In. 32.00
Platter, 12 In. 28.00
Platter, Oval, 13 1/2 In. . .55.00
Salt & Pepper 27.00

CALIFORNIA STRAWBERRY

California Strawberry dinnerware pictures a red strawberry on an avocado green vine. It is one of the Poppytrail lines made by Metlox Potteries from 1961 to 1980.

Bowl, Divided, Round,
    9 In. 40.00
Bowl, Fruit, 5 1/2 In. 10.00
Bowl, Salad, 11 In. 50.00
Bowl, Vegetable,
    Cover, 11 1/4 In. 35.00
Butter, Cover 45.00
Casserole, 7 In. 55.00
Coffeepot 75.00
Creamer 15.00
Cup & Saucer 10.00
Fork & Spoon Set 55.00
Gravy Boat, Fast Stand . . .30.00
Plate, Bread & Butter,
    6 In. 6.00
Plate, Dinner,
    10 In. . . . . . . .10.00 to 15.00
Plate, Salad,
    8 In. . . . . .8.00 to 10.00
Platter, Oval, 13 In. 30.00
Salt & Pepper 20.00
Soup, Dish, 6 3/4 In. 15.00
Sugar, Cover 18.00
Sugar & Creamer,
    Cover 40.00

Teapot 80.00
Vegetable, Cover, 2 Qt. . .25.00

CAMEO ROSE HALL

Cameo Rose made by Hall China Company has gray and white decal decorations and a gold trim. It was not made by the cameo process used for cameo shellware and other designs. Reproductions using the Cameo Rose decoration have been made since 1997. These, unlike the originals, are marked "Limited Edition."

Butter 50.00
Plate, Dinner, 10 In. 12.00
Plate, Salad, 8 In. 10.00
Teapot 50.00

CAMEO ROSE HARKER, see also
    Cameo Shellware

CAMEO SHELLWARE

Another cameo pattern, Cameo Shellware, has the same design as Cameo Rose, but the dishes are fluted.

Creamer . . . . . . .8.00 to 10.00
Cup & Saucer 10.00
Plate, Dinner, 9 1/2 In. . . .10.00
Plate, Square, 7 1/2 In. 6.00

CARNIVAL

One pattern named Carnival was made by Stangl Pottery, Trenton, New Jersey, from 1954 to 1957. It is decorated with abstract star patterns.

Bowl, Salad, 10 In. 32.00
Creamer 18.00

❖

Be careful loading the dishwasher. Metal utensils that touch ceramic dishes may leave marks on china. Dishes can also show black marks if rubbed against a stainless steel sink. The marks can be removed with a wet sponge and a bit of silver polish or other mild abrasive.

❖

Plate, Dinner, 10 In. 10.00
Platter, 12 1/2 In. 25.00
Platter, 14 1/2 In. 35.00

CASUAL CALIFORNIA
Vernon Kilns made Casual California, a very popular solid-color dinnerware, from 1947 to 1956. It was made in Acacia Yellow, Dawn Pink, Dusk Gray, Lime Green, Mahogany Brown, Mocha Brown, Pine Green, Sno-white, and Turquoise Blue.

MOCHA BROWN
Platter, 13 In. 60.00

PINE GREEN
Plate, Dinner, 10 In. 22.00

CAT-TAIL
Cat-Tail pattern dishes must have been found in most homes in America in the 1940s. Sears, Roebuck and Company fea-

tured the pattern from 1934 to 1956. It was made by the Universal Potteries of Cambridge, Ohio. The red and black cattail design was used for dinnerware and matching tinware, kitchenware, glassware, furniture, and table linens.

Cake Plate, Handle,
   12 1/2 . . . . . .15.00 to 20.00
Cup & Saucer 14.00
Grill Plate 18.00
Sugar 17.00
Plate, Dinner,
   10 In. 12.00

CENTURY
Century pattern was made by the Homer Laughlin China Company. The ivory dinnerware had floral decals.

Batter Set, Marked Wells,
   18K Gold Banding 350.00

Casserole 75.00
Jug, Gold Trim,
   2 1/2 Pt. 65.00

CHATELAINE
Vernon Kilns of Los Angeles and Vernon, California, introduced the solid-colored Chatelaine pattern in 1953. Pieces were square with leaf handles. It was made in Bronze, Topaz, Jade with a leaf decoration, and Platinum with a leaf decoration.

JADE
Cup & Saucer . .20.00 to 22.00
Plate, Dinner,
   10 In. 20.00
TOPAZ
Plate, Salad,
   7 1/2 In. . . . . . .10.00 to 12.00

CHESTERTON
Chesterton was a pattern produced by Harker Pottery Company of Chester, West Virginia, from 1945 to 1965. The pieces had a gadroon border. They were made in Blue, Gray, Green, Pink, or Yellow.

GRAY

Cup & Saucer 5.00
Plate, Breakfast, 9 In. 8.00

CHINTZ

Chintz is a floral decorated pattern made by Vernon Kilns in about 1942 and again in 1950. The pattern in red, blue, yellow, green, and maroon resembled the English dinnerware patterns of the early nineteenth century. Another pattern named Chintz was made by Blue Ridge. Many English manufacturers made overall patterns now called Chintz by collectors. Only the Vernon Kilns chintz pattern is listed here.

Bowl, Chowder 13.00
Cup & Saucer 25.00
Plate, Bread & Butter,
  6 In. 10.00
Plate, Dinner, 9 1/2 In. ...50.00
Plate, Salad, 7 1/2 In. 14.00
Sugar & Creamer 26.00

❖

**Don't keep a house key
in an obvious spot in
the garage or yard.**

❖

COLONIAL HOMESTEAD

Colonial Homestead was one of many patterns made by Royal China Company of Sebring, Ohio. The dinnerware was made from about 1951 and was offered by Sears, Roebuck and Company all through the 1960s. It was designed by Gordon Parker. The Royal China Company closed in 1986. A different pattern by the same name was made by Metlox Potteries.

Bowl, 5 1/2 In. 3.00
Canister, Cookie, Cover ..40.00
Canister, Flour, Cover ...32.00
Casserole, Cover 15.00
Cup & Saucer 4.00
Gravy Boat, Underplate ..21.00
Plate, Bread & Butter,
  6 In. 1.50
Plate, Dinner, 10 In. 8.50
Plate, Salad, 7 In. 2.50
Plate, Sherbet, 6 1/2 In. ...1.25
Salt & Pepper 10.00
Soup, Dish, 8 1/2 In. 11.00
Teapot, Cover ...23.50 to 60.00

COORS, see Rosebud

CORAL REEF

Coral Reef was designed by Don Blanding for Vernon Kilns in 1938. The tropical fish in the design were colored blue, mustard, and maroon on a cream background.

MAROON
Cup 45.00
MUSTARD
Cup & Saucer 60.00
Plate, Dinner, 9 In. 55.00

CORN KING

Dishes shaped like ears of corn? This novel idea became a popular reality when Corn King pattern was sold by Shawnee Pottery Company, Zanesville, Ohio, before 1954. The green and yellow pieces, three-dimensional representations of ears of corn, ranged from dinner plates to small salt and pepper shakers. Corn King has darker yellow corn kernels and lighter green leaves than a later pattern called Corn Queen.

Bowl, Cereal,
  No. 94 ......45.00 to 55.00

Bowl, No. 92, 5 In. 37.00

Butter, Cover,
No. 72 . . . . . .65.00 to 75.00

Casserole, Cover,
No. 74, 11 In. . .60.00 to 85.00

Casserole, Individual, No. 73,
9 Oz. . . . . . .15.00 to 125.00

Creamer,
No. 70 . . . . . .24.00 to 40.00

Cup & Saucer, No. 90,
No. 91 . . . . . .55.00 to 65.00

Mixing Bowl, No. 5,
5 In. . . . . .25.00 to 40.00

Mixing Bowl, No. 6,
6 1/2 In. . . . . . .35.00 to 50.00

Mixing Bowl, No. 8,
8 In. 65.00

Mug, No. 69,
8 Oz. . . . . . . .45.00 to 55.00

Pitcher, No. 71,
40 Oz. . . . . . .85.00 to 95.00

Plate, No. 68,
10 In. . . . . . . .32.00 to 45.00

Plate, No. 93, 8 In. 40.00

Platter, No. 96,
11 3/4 In. 41.00

Relish, No. 79 . . .25.00 to 40.00

Salt & Pepper,
No. 76 . . . . . .20.00 to 34.00

Salt & Pepper,
No. 77 . . . . . .32.00 to 35.00

Sugar, Cover,
No. 78 . . . . . .30.00 to 45.00

Sugar & Creamer, No. 78,
No. 70 . . . . . .65.00 to 75.00

Teapot, Cover, No. 75,
30 Oz. . . . . . .97.00 to 125.00

❖

Use half the amount of detergent the manufacturer recommends. Most dishwashing products contain trisodium phosphate, which may dull the glaze on some dishes.

❖

Teapot, No. 65,
10 Oz., Individual . .250.00 to 325.00

CORN QUEEN

Corn King was redesigned slightly by Shawnee Pottery Company, Zanesville, Ohio, and continued to be marketed from 1954 to 1961. The kernels of the new line were lighter yellow and the foliage was a deeper green. It was called Corn Queen.

Bowl, Fruit, No. 92,
6 In. 35.00

Bowl, Vegetable, No. 95,
9 In. 52.00

Butter, Cover,
No. 72 . . . . . .48.00 to 55.00

Cookie Jar, No. 66 . . . . .198.00

Creamer, No. 70,
15 Oz. . . . . . .14.00 to 30.00

Mixing Bowl, No. 5,
5 In. 35.00

Mixing Bowl, No. 6,
6 1/2 In. 40.00

Mixing Bowl, No. 8,
8 In. 45.00

Mug, No. 69, 8 Oz. 45.00

Pitcher, Coffee,
No. 71, Qt. 80.00

Plate, No. 68, 10 In. 19.00

Plate, No. 91, 8 In. 11.00

Platter, No. 96, 12 In. 49.00

Relish, No. 79 . . . . .32.00

Salt & Pepper, No. 76,
3 1/4 In. . . . . . .19.00 to 20.00

Salt & Pepper, No. 77,
5 1/4 In. . . . . . .35.00 to 48.00

Saucer, No. 91,
5 1/2 In. 20.00

Sugar, Cover, No. 78 . . . .24.00

Teapot, Cover,
No. 75 . . . . .125.00 to 180.00

CORONADO

Franciscan dinnerware was made by Gladding, McBean in Los Angeles, California. Coronado, also called Swirl, was a popular plain-colored art ware made from 1935 to 1942. At least fifty different shapes and fifteen different glossy and matte colors were made. Another pattern called Coronado was made by Vernon Kilns. The Franciscan pieces are listed in this book.

AQUA
Plate, Bread & Butter,
6 1/2 In. 4.00

Plate, Breakfast, 9 In. 6.50

Plate, Salad, 7 In. 4.50

CORAL
Cereal, 2 Handles 10.00

WHITE
Butter Dish, Cover 30.00

Cup & Saucer 5.00

Plate, 6 1/2 In. 3.50

Soup, Dish 6.00

COTTAGE, see Petit Point House

COUNTRY GARDEN

Three raised flowers are pictured on the Country Garden dinnerware. The pattern was made by Stangl Pottery of Trenton, New Jersey, from 1956 to 1974. Country Garden was also made by Blue Ridge and Red Wing Potteries, but only the Stangl pattern is listed here.

Bowl, Salad,
  12 In. . . . . . . .40.00 to 45.00
Bread Tray 40.00
Cruet, Stopper 35.00
Cup 5.00
Plate, Luncheon, 8 In. 10.00
Salt & Pepper 20.00
Saucer 13.00
Server 10.00

CRAZY RHYTHM

Crazy Rhythm was a hand-painted abstract pattern made by Red Wing Potteries on the Futura shape in 1960.

Bowl, Vegetable,
  Divided . . . . .25.00 to 40.00
Creamer 20.00

Platter, 13 In. 30.00
Sugar 20.00

CROCUS

Crocus was a popular name for dinnerware patterns. Prices listed are for the Crocus pattern by Hall China Company of East Liverpool, Ohio, in the 1930s. The decal-decorated dinnerware was sometimes called Holland. The design was a border of oddly shaped crocuses in black, lavender, red, green, and pink. Most pieces have platinum trim. Other firms, including Stangl Pottery and Blue Ridge, had very different-looking dinnerwares called Crocus. Reproductions using the Crocus decoration have been made since 1993. These, unlike the originals, are marked "Limited Edition."

Bowl, Radiance, 7 In. 30.00
Bowl, Radiance, 9 In. 45.00
Coffee Dispenser, Metal . .25.00
Coffeepot, Terrace 100.00
Jug, Ball 195.00
Teapot, Banded 175.00

Tureen, Soup 395.00
CURIOSITY SHOP, see Old Curiosity Shop

CURRIER & IVES

Currier & Ives was made by the Royal China Company of Sebring, Ohio, from 1949 until about 1983. It was designed by Gordon Parker and is based on the old Currier & Ives prints. Early pieces were date coded. It is a blue and white or pink and white pattern that was popular as a store premium. The Royal China Company closed in 1986. Currier & Ives patterns were also made by Homer Laughlin and Scio. Some serving pieces were made by Harker Pottery Company. Only the Royal China pattern is listed here.

Ashtray . . . . . . .8.00 to 10.00
Bowl, Cereal, 6 In. 8.50
Bowl, Fruit,
  5 1/2 In. . . . . . . .3.00 to 8.00
Bowl, Vegetable, Round,
  9 In. . . . . .18.00 to 20.00
Bread Tray, Round 5.00
Cake Plate, Tab Handle,
  10 In. . . . . . . .20.00 to 28.00

❖

Don't put crazed pottery or porcelain in the dishwasher. It may be damaged even more.

❖

Casserole,
   Cover . . . . .75.00 to 85.00
Chop Plate, 12 In. 25.00
Coffee Mug 23.00
Creamer 7.50
Cup . . . . .2.50 to 3.00
Cup & Saucer 4.00
Gravy Boat 20.00
Gravy Boat,
   Underplate . . . .24.00 to 28.00
Hostess Set, 9 Piece 100.00
Pie Plate 20.00
Plate, 12 In. 24.00
Plate, Bread & Butter,
   6 In. . . . . .2.25 to 5.00
Plate, Calendar, 1983 . . . .22.00
Plate, Dinner,
   10 In. . . . . .4.00 to 5.00
Plate, Luncheon,
   8 In. . . . . .12.00 to 25.00
Plate, Salad,
   7 In. . . . . .6.00 to 10.00
Platter, 13 In. 28.00
Platter, Oval,
   13 x 10 In. . . . .33.00 to 37.00
Salt & Pepper . . .15.00 to 20.00
Saucer 1.00
Soup, Dish . . . . .10.00 to 12.00
Sugar, Cover 12.00
Sugar & Creamer 2.50
Sugar & Creamer,
   Cover 24.00
Teapot 125.00

·D·

DAISY

Daisy, or Hawaiian 12-point Daisy, is a Fiesta Casual pattern made by the Homer Laughlin China Company of Newell, West Virginia. It was first made in 1962 and discontinued in 1968. Daisy pattern, on the familiar Fiesta shape, has a turquoise rim and turquoise and brown daisies in the center. Patterns named Daisy were also made by Red Wing, Stangl, and Taylor, Smith, and Taylor. Only the Homer Laughlin pattern is listed here.

Cup & Saucer 15.00
Plate, Dinner, 10 In. 20.00

DESERT ROSE

Desert Rose by Franciscan is a popular pattern with today's collectors. It was introduced in 1942 by Gladding, McBean's Franciscan Ceramics. Franciscan Ceramics was purchased by Waterford Wedgwood USA in 1979, and the pattern is still being made. The flowers on the dishes are a soft pink.

Ashtray, Individual 20.00
Ashtray, Oval,
   9 In. . . . . .65.00 to 85.00
Berry Bowl,
   5 1/4 In. . . . . . .8.00 to 10.00
Bowl, Cereal,
   6 In. . . . . .12.00 to 13.00
Bowl, Footed, 10 In. 90.00
Bowl, Microwave,
   Square 245.00
Bowl, Salad, 10 In. 110.00
Bowl, Vegetable,
   8 In. . . . . .37.00 to 38.00
Bowl, Vegetable,
   10 1/2 In. 85.00
Bowl, Vegetable, 12 In. . .70.00
Bowl, Vegetable,
   2 Sections, 10 In. . . . .35.00 to
   45.00
Bowl, Vegetable, Cover,
   8 x 4 1/2 In. . . .45.00 to 50.00
Bowl, Vegetable, Round,
   9 In. . . . . .32.00 to 40.00
Box, Heart Shape 165.00
Butter, Cover,
   1/4 Lb. . . . . . .45.00 to 50.00
Candleholder, 3 In.,
   Pair . . . . .75.00 to 95.00
Candy Dish 100.00
Casserole, Cover,
   1 1/2 Qt. . . . . . .90.00 to 95.00
Celery Dish 35.00
Chop Plate,
   14 In. . . . . . . .82.00 to 95.00
Cigarette Box 125.00
Coffeepot,
   Cover . . . . . . .95.00 to 150.00
Compote, Footed,
   8 In. . . . . .65.00 to 75.00
Cookie Jar, Cover,
   10 1/2 In. 295.00
Creamer, Individual 45.00
Cup & Saucer . . .8.00 to 10.00
Cup & Saucer, After
   Dinner . . . . . . .50.00 to 65.00
Cup & Saucer, Tea, Low . .8.50
Eggcup . . . . .26.00 to 35.00
Goblet, 6 1/2 In. 15.00
Gravy Boat, 2 Spout 50.00
Gravy Boat,
   Underplate . . . .30.00 to 35.00
Grill Plate . . . .90.00 to 125.00
Jam Jar, Cover 90.00

Mixing Bowl,
9 In. . . . . . .175.00 to 195.00
Mug, 10 Oz. 35.00
Mug, 12 Oz. . . . .40.00 to 45.00
Mug, 16 Oz., 4 1/2 In. . . .50.00
Pitcher, Milk, 1 Qt. 90.00
Pitcher, Syrup, 1 Pt.,
6 1/4 In. . . . . .65.00 to 75.00
Pitcher, Water,
2 1/2 Qt. . . . .100.00 to 125.00
Plate, Bread & Butter,
6 1/2 In. . . . . . . .6.00 to 8.00
Plate, Breakfast,
9 1/2 In. . . . . . .10.00 to 12.00
Plate, Crescent Shape,
8 1/2 In. . . . . . .27.50 to 30.00
Plate, Dinner,
10 1/2 In. . . . . .12.00 to 19.00
Plate, Divided, Child,
Square 190.00
Plate, Luncheon,
8 In. . . . . .7.00 to 10.00
Plate, Sandwich,
11 1/2 In. 50.00
Platter, Oval,
12 1/2 In. . . . .32.00 to 45.00
Platter, Oval,
14 In. . . . . . . .35.00 to 65.00
Platter, Sandwich,
11 1/2 In. 75.00
Platter, Turkey, 19 In. . . .300.00
Relish, 11 In. 40.00
Relish, 3 Sections,
12 In. . . . . . . .65.00 to 70.00
Salad, Footed, 10 In. 90.00
Salt & Pepper, 6 In.,
Pair . . . . .50.00 to 65.00
Salt & Pepper
Mill . . . . . .250.00 to 295.00
Sherbet, Footed . .20.00 to 30.00
Soup, Dish, Flat
Rim . . . . .16.00 to 26.00
Soup, Dish, Footed,
5 1/2 In. 32.00
Sugar, Individual 75.00

❖

**Glue broken china
with invisible mending
cement that is
waterproof.**

❖

Sugar & Creamer,
Cover . . . . . . .35.00 to 50.00
Teapot, Cover . .95.00 to 120.00
Tile, Square, 6 In. 65.00
Tureen, Soup, Large 500.00
Vase, Bud, 6 In. 55.00

EARLY CALIFORNIA

In the late 1930s, Vernon Kilns
of Vernon, California, made a
solid-color line of dinnerware
called Early California. The
dishes, in Blue, Brown, Green,
Orange, Pink, Turquoise, or
Yellow, were made to be used
as mix-and-match sets. The
dishes are marked with the
name of the pattern.

BLUE
Cup & Saucer 13.00
Tumbler 20.00

BROWN
Creamer . . . . . .10.00 to 12.00
Plate, Dinner, 10 1/2 In. . .10.00

TURQUOISE
Egg Cup 16.00
Plate, Salad, 6 1/2 In. 5.00

BLUE
Plate, Dinner, 10 1/2 In. . .11.00

EGGSHELL NAUTILUS

Eggshell Nautilus is a shape
that was made by Homer
Laughlin China Company from
1937 to the 1950s. The nautilus
shell motif can be seen in the
handles. The shape was decorated in many different ways.

Bowl, Gold Rim,
5 1/4 In. . . . . .1.00 to 3.00
Bowl, Gold Rim,
8 1/4 In. 10.00
Creamer 10.00
Cup 1.00
Plate, Breakfast, 9 In. 9.50
Plate, Luncheon, 8 In. 6.00
Plate, Salad, 6 In. 5.00
Sugar & Creamer,
Cover 18.50

EL PATIO

El Patio is one of many solid-
color dinnerware patterns made
by Franciscan Ceramics from
1936 to 1956. It comes in
twenty colors.

CORAL
Bowl, Round, 8 1/2 In. . . .30.00
Cup & Saucer 10.00
Plate, Dinner, 10 1/2 In. . .12.00
Plate, Luncheon,
9 1/4 In. 10.00
Sugar & Creamer 22.00
Teapot 75.00

IVORY
Plate, Breakfast, 9 1/4 In. .10.00
Plate, Dessert, 6 1/4 In. . . .5.00

TURQUOISE

Plate, Dessert, 6 1/4 In. 5.00
Plate, Dinner, 10 1/2 In. . .12.00
Plate, Luncheon,
9 1/4 In. 10.00

YELLOW

Plate, Luncheon, 8 1/4 In. . .9.00
Platter, 13 In. 45.00

·F·

FESTIVE FRUIT, see Fruit Stangl

FIESTA

Fiesta ware was introduced in 1936 by the Homer Laughlin China Company, Newell, West Virginia. It was originally designed by Frederick Hurten Rhead. The line was redesigned in 1969 and withdrawn in 1973. The design was characterized by a band of concentric circles, beginning at the rim. The complete Fiesta line in 1937 had 54 different pieces. Rarities include the covered onion bowl, the green disk water jug, the 10-inch cake plate, and the syrup pitcher. Cups had full-circle handles until 1969, when partial-circle handles were made. The original Fiesta colors were Dark Blue, Fiesta Red, Light Green, Old Ivory, and Yellow. Later, Chartreuse, Forest Green, Gray, Medium Green, Rose, and Turquoise were added. From 1970 to 1972 the redesigned Fiesta Ironstone was made only in Antique Gold, Mango Red, and Turf Green. Homer Laughlin reissued Fiesta in 1986 using new colors but the original marks and molds. The new colors were Apricot, Black, Cobalt Blue, Rose (pink), and White. In 1989 the company added three other colors—Periwinkle Blue, Turquoise, and Yellow. See American Dinnerware In-

troduction for more information. Most Fiesta ware was marked with the incised word Fiesta. Some pieces were hand-stamped before glazing. The word genuine was added to the mark in the 1940s. The Fiesta shape was also made with decal decorations, but these are not considered Fiesta by collectors; instead, they are collected by the pattern names. There is also a Fiesta Kitchen Kraft line, a group of kitchenware pieces made in the early 1940s in Blue, Green, Red, or Yellow. These were bake-and-serve wares. Glassware and linens were made to match the Fiesta colors.

CHARTREUSE

Ashtray . . . . . . .65.00 to 95.00
Bowl, Cereal,
5 1/2 In. . . . . . .30.00 to 31.00
Bowl, Dessert,
6 In. . . . . .40.00 to 42.00
Bowl, Fruit, 4 3/4 In. 30.00

Casserole, Cover, 2 Handles,
10 In. . . . . . .225.00 to 300.00
Chop Plate, 13 In. 56.00
Coffeepot . . . .585.00 to 785.00
Cup & Saucer, After
Dinner 625.00
Mug,
Tom & Jerry . .75.00 to 95.00
Pitcher, Water, Disk 275.00
Plate, Bread & Butter,
7 In. 13.00
Plate, Dessert,
6 In. . . . . .9.00 to 12.00
Plate, Dinner,
10 In. . . . . . . .32.00 to 36.00
Plate, Luncheon,
9 In. . . . . .16.00 to 19.00
Platter, Oval,
12 In. . . . . . . .40.00 to 50.00
Sauceboat 55.00
Saucer . . . . .7.00 to 8.00
Soup, Cream 75.00
Sugar, Cover 65.00
Sugar & Creamer, Tray,
3 Piece . . . . .275.00 to 280.00
Teapot, Medium, 6 Cup .100.00

COBALT BLUE

Chop Plate, 13 In. 35.00
Marmalade, Cover 268.00
Plate, Dinner, 10 In. 38.00
Saucer 4.00
Sugar 20.00

DARK BLUE

Ashtray 95.00
Bowl, Dessert,
6 In. . . . . .35.00 to 37.00
Bowl, Fruit, 4 3/4 In. 25.00
Bowl, Fruit, 11 3/4 In. . .485.00
Bowl, Salad, Footed 625.00
Candleholder, Bulb,
Pair 100.00
Candleholder, Tripod,
Pair . . . . . .400.00 to 950.00
Carafe . . . . . .125.00 to 375.00
Casserole, Cover 295.00
Chop Plate, 13 In. 45.00
Chop Plate, 15 In. 50.00
Coffeepot 200.00
Coffeepot, After
Dinner 550.00
Compote, Footed, Low,
12 In. . . . . . .115.00 to 120.00

Compote,
Sweets . . . . . .80.00 to 150.00

Cover, Mixing Bowl,
No. 1, 5 In. 575.00

Creamer 20.00

Creamer, Stick Handle . . .55.00

Cup 20.00

Cup & Saucer 85.00

Cup & Saucer, After
Dinner 68.00

Eggcup . . . . . . .56.00 to 58.00

Grill Plate, 10 1/2 In. 42.00

Grill Plate, 12 In. 65.00

Marmalade, Cover 265.00

Mixing Bowl, No. 1,
5 In. 95.00

Mixing Bowl, No. 2,
6 In. 195.00

Mixing Bowl, No. 3,
7 In. 120.00

Mixing Bowl, No. 4,
8 In. . . . . . . .115.00 to 125.00

Mixing Bowl, No. 6,
10 In. 215.00

Mug 60.00

Mug,
Tom & Jerry . .50.00 to 55.00

Mustard . . . . .190.00 to 325.00

Nappy,
8 1/2 In. . . . . . .35.00 to 50.00

Pitcher, 2 Pt. 120.00

Pitcher, Ice Lip 155.00

Pitcher, Juice, Disk,
30 Oz. . . . . .135.00 to 165.00

Pitcher, Water, Disk 150.00

Plate, Dessert, 6 In. 9.00

Plate, Dinner, 10 In. 38.00

Platter, Oval, 12 In. 30.00

Relish Tray 300.00

Sauceboat 65.00

Saucer 4.00

Soup, Cream . . . .50.00 to 55.00

Soup, Onion,
Cover . . . . . .450.00 to 550.00

Sugar & Creamer, Cover,
Individual 350.00

Sugar & Creamer,
Pair . . . . .50.00 to 75.00

Syrup 300.00

Teapot, Large,
8 Cup . . . . . .225.00 to 335.00

Tray, Utility 30.00

Tumbler, Juice,
5 Oz. . . . . .35.00 to 45.00

Tumbler, Water,
10 Oz. . . . . . . .55.00 to 60.00

Vase, 8 In. . . . .550.00 to 820.00

Vase, 10 In. . .525.00 to 1150.00

Vase,
12 In. . . . .1150.00 to 1600.00

Vase, Bud,
6 1/2 In. . . . . . .90.00 to 125.00

FIESTA RED

Ashtray . . . . . .45.00 to 65.00

Bowl, Cereal,
5 1/2 In. . . . . . .25.00 to 28.00

Bowl, Dessert, 6 In. 38.00

Bowl, Fruit, 4 3/4 In. 35.00

Bowl, Fruit,
11 3/4 In. . . .155.00 to 175.00

Bowl, Salad, Footed 625.00

Bowl, Salad, Individual,
7 1/2 In. 48.00

Cake Plate, 10 In. 50.00

Candleholder, Bulb,
Pair . . . . . . .85.00 to 120.00

Candleholder, Tripod . . .950.00

Carafe . . . . .190.00 to 325.00

Casserole 295.00

Casserole, Cover,
2 Handles, 10 In. 200.00

Chop Plate,
15 In. . . . . . . .40.00 to 57.00

Coffeepot . . . .195.00 to 225.00

Coffeepot, After
Dinner 360.00

Compote, Footed, Low,
12 In. . . . . . . .90.00 to 100.00

Compote,
Sweets . . . . . .60.00 to 70.00

Cover, Mixing Bowl,
No. 1 . . . .1000.00 to 1400.00

Cover, Mixing Bowl,
No. 4 . . . . .850.00

Creamer,
Individual . . .185.00 to 350.00

❖

**Some tea and coffee
stains can be removed
by rubbing dishes with
damp baking soda.**

❖

Creamer, Stick
Handle . . . . . . .48.00 to 65.00

Cup & Saucer . .25.00 to 75.00

Cup & Saucer, After
Dinner . . . . . .85.00 to 130.00

Marmalade 235.00

Mixing Bowl, No. 1,
5 In. . . . . . .260.00 to 275.00

Mixing Bowl, No. 2,
6 In. 75.00

Mixing Bowl, No. 3,
7 In. 55.00

Mixing Bowl, No. 5,
9 In. 120.00

Mixing Bowl, No. 6,
10 In. 150.00

Mug . . . . .65.00 to 70.00

Mug, Tom & Jerry 70.00

Mustard 365.00

Nappy, 8 1/2 In. 35.00

Pitcher, Juice, Disk,
30 Oz. . . . . .340.00 to 410.00

Pitcher, Water,
Disk . . . . . . .158.00 to 175.00

Plate, Bread & Butter,
7 In. . . . . .6.00 to 10.00

Plate, Deep,
8 In. . . . . .30.00 to 42.00

Plate, Dessert, 6 In. 4.00

Plate, Dinner,
10 In. . . . . . . .40.00 to 60.00

Plate, Luncheon, 9 In. 20.00

Platter, Oval,
12 In. . . . . . . .40.00 to 46.00

Relish 425.00

Salt & Pepper 26.00

Sauceboat . . . . . .50.00 to 60.00

Saucer . . . . .2.00 to 4.00

Saucer, After Dinner 12.00

Soup, Cream . . . .58.00 to 75.00

Soup, Onion,
Cover . . . . . .460.00 to 690.00

Sugar & Creamer 35.00

Syrup . . . . . . .300.00 to 450.00

Teapot, Large,
8 Cup . . . . . .165.00 to 285.00

Teapot, Medium,
6 Cup 160.00

Tray, Utility 48.00

Tumbler, Juice,
5 Oz. . . . . .40.00 to 50.00

Tumbler, Water,
10 Oz. . . . . . . .60.00 to 75.00

Vase, 8 In. . . . .925.00 to 985.00
Vase, 10 In. . . .799.00 to 895.00
Vase, 12 In. 1700.00
Vase, Bud,
6 1/2 In. . . . .100.00 to 125.00

FOREST GREEN

Ashtray . . . . . .72.00 to 90.00
Bowl, Cereal,
5 1/2 In. . . . . .27.00 to 32.00
Bowl, Dessert,
6 In. . . . . .40.00 to 42.00
Bowl, Fruit, 4 3/4 In. 30.00
Casserole,
Cover . . . . .300.00 to 435.00
Chop Plate, 13 In. 75.00
Chop Plate, 15 In. 125.00
Coffeepot . . . .228.00 to 230.00
Creamer 30.00
Cup & Saucer, After
Dinner 625.00
Cup & Saucer, Tea 40.00
Mixing Bowl, No. 3,
7 In. 120.00
Mixing Bowl, No. 4,
8 In. 100.00
Mug . . . . .50.00 to 85.00
Mug,
Tom & Jerry . .65.00 to 85.00
Nappy, 8 1/2 In. 65.00
Nut Dish 125.00
Pitcher, Juice, Disk,
30 Oz. . . . . .265.00 to 365.00
Plate, Deep, 8 In. 45.00
Plate, Dessert, 6 In. 9.00
Plate, Luncheon, 9 In. 11.00
Saltshaker 10.00
Sauceboat . . . . .35.00 to 90.00
Saucer 3.00
Soup, Cream . . . .40.00 to 55.00
Teacup 20.00
Teapot, Medium,
6 Cup . . . . .395.00 to 475.00
Tumbler, Water, 10 Oz. . .50.00

GRAY

Ashtray 95.00
Bowl, Cereal, 5 1/2 In. . . .24.00
Bowl, Dessert,
6 In. . . . . .28.00 to 40.00
Bowl, Fruit,
4 3/4 In. . . . . . .24.00 to 30.00
Bowl, Salad, 7 1/2 In. 43.00

Casserole,
Cover . . . . . .195.00 to 375.00
Chop Plate,
13 In. . . . . . . .60.00 to 95.00
Chop Plate, 15 In. 70.00
Coffeepot 540.00
Creamer . . . . . .25.00 to 35.00
Cup & Saucer, After
Dinner 625.00
Eggcup 135.00
Mug . . . . .80.00 to 85.00
Mug,
Tom & Jerry . .80.00 to 95.00
Nappy, 8 1/2 In. . .45.00 to 60.00
Pitcher, Juice, Disk,
30 Oz. 145.00
Pitcher, Water, Disk,
2 Qt. . . . . . . .250.00 to 370.00
Plate, Deep,
8 In. . . . . .48.00 to 50.00
Plate, Dessert, 6 In. 6.00
Plate, Dinner, 10 In. 37.00
Plate, Luncheon,
9 In. . . . . .17.00 to 19.00
Platter, Oval, 12 In. 52.00
Salt & Pepper 41.00
Saltshaker 25.00
Sauceboat 75.00
Soup, Cream . . . .65.00 to 95.00
Sugar, Cover 75.00
Teapot, Medium,
6 Cup 325.00
Tumbler, Juice, 5 Oz. 30.00

LIGHT GREEN

Ashtray . . . . . .32.00 to 65.00
Bowl, Cereal,
5 1/2 In. . . . . .20.00 to 26.00
Bowl, Fruit, 4 3/4 In. 18.00
Bowl, Salad, Footed 575.00
Candleholder, Bulb, Pair . .88.00

Stains on porcelain can be removed by soaking in a mixture of two tablespoons of Polident denture cleaner in a quart of tepid water.

Candleholder, Tripod,
Pair 300.00
Carafe . . . . . .265.00 to 330.00
Casserole, Cover 130.00
Chop Plate,
13 In. . . . . . . .30.00 to 38.00
Coffeepot, After
Dinner 175.00
Coffeepot, Cover, Stick
Handle, After
Dinner . . . . .275.00 to 475.00
Compote, 12 In. 68.00
Creamer, Stick Handle . . .50.00
Cup 20.00
Cup & Saucer . .50.00 to 62.00
Eggcup . . . . . . .35.00 to 50.00
Jug, 2 Pt. 150.00
Marmalade 300.00
Mixing Bowl, Cover,
No. 1 . . . . .1150.00
Mixing Bowl, No. 1,
5 In. 230.00
Mixing Bowl, No. 3,
7 In. . . . . . . .95.00 to 120.00
Mixing Bowl, No. 4,
8 In. . . . . .75.00 to 155.00
Mixing Bowl, No. 5,
9 In. . . . . . .115.00 to 175.00
Mixing Bowl, No. 7,
11 In. 215.00
Mustard . . . . .150.00 to 250.00
Nappy, 8 1/2 In. 54.00
Plate, Bread & Butter,
7 In. . . . . .9.00 to 12.00
Plate, Deep, 8 In. 35.00
Plate, Dinner,
10 In. . . . . . . .22.00 to 34.00
Plate, Luncheon,
9 In. . . . . .8.00 to 12.00
Platter, Oval, 12 In. 22.00
Platter, Oval, 13 In. 75.00
Relish 225.00
Salt & Pepper 20.00
Saltshaker 16.00
Sauceboat 35.00
Soup, Onion 950.00
Sugar 45.00
Syrup . . . . . .225.00 to 375.00
Teapot, Medium,
6 Cup . . . . . .120.00 to 145.00
Tray, Utility 30.00
Tumbler, Water,
10 Oz. . . . . . . .50.00 to 55.00

Vase, 8 In. . . . .475.00 to 675.00
Vase, 10 In. . . .500.00 to 700.00
Vase,
  12 In. . . . .1250.00 to 1400.00
Vase, Bud, 6 1/2 In. 50.00

MEDIUM GREEN

Ashtray . . . . .175.00 to 260.00
Bowl, Cereal,
  5 1/2 In. . . . . .45.00 to 75.00
Casserole, Cover,
  2 Handles, 10 In. 560.00
Chop Plate, Metal & Rattan
  Handle, 13 In. 220.00
Cup, Tea 195.00
Cup & Saucer . .58.00 to 95.00
Mug . . . . .95.00 to 145.00
Plate, Bread & Butter,
  7 In. . . . . .30.00 to 45.00
Plate, Deep,
  8 In. . . . . . .110.00 to 135.00
Plate, Dessert,
  6 In. . . . . .13.00 to 35.00
Plate, Dinner,
  10 In. . . . . . .80.00 to 150.00
Plate, Luncheon,
  9 In. . . . . .36.00 to 65.00
Platter, Oval,
  12 In. . . . . . .170.00 to 175.00
Salt &
  Pepper . . . . .110.00 to 270.00
Sauceboat . . . .220.00 to 250.00
Sugar & Creamer 95.00
Teapot, Large,
  8 Cup 1650.00
Teapot, Medium,
  6 Cup . . . . .950.00 to 1000.00

OLD IVORY

Ashtray 75.00
Bowl, Cereal,
  5 1/2 In. . . . . .25.00 to 28.00
Bowl, Dessert,
  6 In. . . . . .35.00 to 45.00
Bowl, Fruit,
  4 3/4 In. . . . . . .20.00 to 22.00
Bowl, Fruit, 11 3/4 In. . .165.00
Bowl, Salad, 9 1/2 In. 30.00
Bowl, Salad, Footed . . .625.00
Candleholder, Bulb,
  Pair 100.00
Candleholder, Tripod,
  Pair 950.00
Carafe . . . . . .225.00 to 375.00
Chop Plate, 13 In. 30.00

Chop Plate,
  15 In. . . . . .60.00 to 70.00
Coffeepot 135.00
Coffeepot, Cover, After
  Dinner . . . . .432.00 to 440.00
Compote, 12 In. 225.00
Cover, Mixing Bowl,
  No. 3, 7 In. 612.00
Creamer . . . . . . .18.00 to 20.00
Creamer, Stick
  Handle . . . . . . .38.00 to 55.00
Cup & Saucer, After
  Dinner . . . . . . .60.00 to 90.00
Eggcup . . . . . . .48.00 to 90.00
Marmalade . . .175.00 to 325.00
Mixing Bowl, No. 1,
  5 In. 350.00
Mixing Bowl, No. 2,
  6 In. . . . . . .100.00 to 230.00
Mixing Bowl, No. 4,
  8 In. 225.00
Mixing Bowl, No. 5,
  9 In. 275.00
Mixing Bowl, No. 6,
  10 In. 360.00
Mug, Tom & Jerry,
  Gold Trim . . . .45.00 to 65.00
Mustard, Cover 155.00
Nappy, 8 1/2 In. 45.00
Pitcher, Ice Lip,
  2 Qt. . . . . . . .120.00 to 125.00
Plate, Bread & Butter,
  7 In. 9.00
Plate, Calendar, 1954,
  10 In. . . . . .42.00 to 45.00
Plate, Deep, 8 In. 40.00
Plate, Dessert,
  6 In. . . . . .10.00 to 12.00
Plate, Dinner,
  10 In. . . . . . . .29.00 to 40.00
Plate, Luncheon,
  9 In. . . . . .9.00 to 12.00
Relish 175.00
Relish, Cobalt Blue
  Center 350.00
Relish, Red Center 350.00
Salt & Pepper 26.00
Sauceboat 48.00
Saucer 2.00
Soup, Cream 60.00
Soup, Onion,
  Cover . . . . .510.00 to 950.00
Sugar & Creamer 80.00

Syrup . . . . . . .600.00 to 650.00
Teapot, Medium,
  6 Cup 140.00
Tumbler, Juice,
  5 Oz. . . . . .42.00 to 45.00
Tumbler, Water,
  10 Oz. . . . . . . .48.00 to 60.00
Vase, 8 In. . . . .435.00 to 895.00
Vase, 10 In. . .895.00 to 1185.00
Vase,
  12 In. . . . .1400.00 to 1500.00
Vase, Bud, 6 1/2 In. 65.00

ROSE

Ashtray 95.00
Bowl, Fruit,
  4 3/4 In. . . . . . .25.00 to 28.00
Casserole . . . .135.00 to 375.00
Chop Plate,
  15 In. . . . . . . .95.00 to 150.00
Coffeepot 450.00
Creamer 38.00
Creamer, Stick Handle . . .28.00
Cup & Saucer, After
  Dinner 625.00
Eggcup 135.00
Mug . . . . .80.00 to 95.00
Nappy, 8 1/2 In. 40.00
Pitcher, Water, Disk 310.00
Plate, Bread & Butter,
  7 In. 15.00
Plate, Deep, 8 In. 55.00
Plate, Luncheon,
  9 In. . . . . .19.00 to 23.00
Saucer . . . . .4.00 to 8.00
Soup, Cream . . . .60.00 to 95.00
Teapot, Medium,
  6 Cup . . . . . .350.00 to 450.00

TURQUOISE

Ashtray . . . . .34.00 to 50.00
Bowl, Cereal, 5 1/2 In. . . .22.00
Bowl, Fruit,
  4 3/4 In. . . . . . .18.00 to 20.00
Bowl, Fruit, 11 3/4 In. . .200.00
Bowl, Salad, 7 1/2 In. 72.00
Bowl, Salad, Footed 575.00
Cake Plate,
  10 In. . . . . . .600.00 to 605.00
Candleholder, Bulb,
  Pair . . . . . .100.00 to 110.00
Candleholder, Tripod,
  Pair 890.00
Carafe . . . . . .215.00 to 380.00

Casserole . . . . .75.00 to 135.00
Casserole, Cover,
  2 Handles, 10 In. 110.00
Chop Plate, 13 In. 35.00
Chop Plate, 15 In. 40.00
Coffeepot 225.00
Creamer . . . . . . .21.00 to 25.00
Creamer, Stick
  Handle . . . . . .55.00 to 115.00
Cup 16.00
Cup & Saucer 29.00
Cup & Saucer, After
  Dinner . . . . . .62.00 to 115.00
Eggcup 55.00
Marmalade . . .178.00 to 325.00
Mixing Bowl, No. 1,
  5 In. 275.00
Mixing Bowl, No. 2,
  6 In. . . . . . . .115.00 to 210.00
Mixing Bowl, No. 3,
  7 In. 225.00
Mixing Bowl, No. 4,
  8 In. . . . . . . .120.00 to 225.00
Mixing Bowl, No. 5,
  9 In. . . . . . . .120.00 to 250.00
Mixing Bowl, No. 7,
  11 1/2 In. 200.00
Mug 46.00
Mug, Tom &
  Jerry . . . . 45.00 to 52.00
Mustard 275.00
Nappy, 8 1/2 In. 24.00
Nappy, 9 1/2 In. 60.00
Pitcher, Ice Lip,
  2 Qt. . . . . . . .132.00 to 195.00
Pitcher, Syrup 275.00
Pitcher, Water,
  Disk . . . . . . .85.00 to 100.00
Plate, Bread & Butter,
  7 In. 12.00
Plate, Dessert, 6 In. 8.00
Plate, Dinner,
  10 In. . . . . . . .22.00 to 60.00
Plate, Luncheon, 9 In. 14.00
Platter, Oval, 12 In. 40.00
Relish, 5 Multicolored
  Sections 200.00
Salad, 7 1/2 In. 70.00
Salt & Pepper 16.00
Saltshaker 12.00
Sauceboat 30.00
Saucer 8.00

❖

**Put foam or paper
plates between the
china plates stacked
for storage.**

❖

Soup, Cream 45.00
Soup, Onion, Cover 900.00
Sugar, Cover . . . .35.00 to 36.00
Syrup . . . . . .500.00 to 585.00
Teapot, Large,
  8 Cup . . . . .140.00 to 280.00
Teapot, Medium,
  6 Cup . . . . . .45.00 to 110.00
Tray,
  Figure 8 . . . .240.00 to 245.00
Tray, Utility 30.00
Tumbler, Juice, 5 Oz. 50.00
Tumbler, Water,
  10 Oz. . . . . . .50.00 to 75.00
Vase, 8 In. 595.00
Vase, 10 In. . .600.00 to 1000.00
Vase, 12 In. 1400.00

YELLOW

Ashtray 50.00
Bowl, Cereal, 5 1/2 In. . . .20.00
Bowl, Dessert, 6 In. 26.00
Bowl, Fruit,
  4 3/4 In. . . . . . .18.00 to 20.00
Bowl, Fruit, 5 1/2 In. 20.00
Bowl, Fruit, 11 3/4 In. . .350.00
Bowl, Salad, 7 1/2 In. 69.00
Bowl, Salad, Footed 575.00
Cake Plate,
  10 In. . . . . . .490.00 to 500.00
Candleholder, Bulb,
  Pair . . . . . . .98.00 to 100.00
Candleholder, Tripod . . .215.00
Carafe . . . . . .190.00 to 330.00
Casserole . . . . .65.00 to 125.00
Casserole, French, Cover, Stick
  Handle . . . . .215.00 to 225.00
Chop Plate,
  13 In. . . . . .17.50 to 35.00
Chop Plate, 15 In. 70.00
Coffeepot . . . .135.00 to 175.00
Compote, Footed, Low,
  12 In. 50.00
Creamer 18.00

Creamer,
  Individual . . . . .45.00 to 75.00
Creamer, Stick
  Handle . . . . . . .30.00 to 45.00
Cup 18.00
Cup & Saucer . .20.00 to 26.00
Cup & Saucer, After
  Dinner . . . . . . .55.00 to 85.00
Eggcup . . . . .43.00 to 50.00
Mixing Bowl, Cover,
  No. 4 . . . .1300.00 to 1400.00
Mixing Bowl, No. 1,
  5 In. . . . . . .250.00 to 325.00
Mixing Bowl, No. 2,
  6 In. . . . . .62.00 to 80.00
Mixing Bowl, No. 4,
  8 In. 145.00
Mixing Bowl, No. 5,
  9 In. 165.00
Mixing Bowl, No. 6,
  10 In. 285.00
Mug . . . . .45.00 to 50.00
Mug, Tom & Jerry 60.00
Mustard 200.00
Nappy,
  8 1/2 In. . . . . . .37.50 to 40.00
Pitcher, Ice Lip,
  2 Qt. 85.00
Pitcher, Juice, Disk,
  30 Oz. . . . . . . .40.00 to 50.00
Pitcher, Water, Disk 75.00
Pitcher Set, Juice,
  7 Piece 350.00
Plate, Bread & Butter,
  7 In. . . . . .6.00 to 12.00
Plate, Calendar, 1954,
  10 In. 30.00
Plate, Deep,
  8 In. . . . . .35.00 to 40.00
Plate, Dessert, 6 In. 5.00
Plate, Dinner,
  10 In. . . . . . . .18.50 to 25.00
Plate, Luncheon,
  9 In. . . . . .8.00 to 14.00
Platter, Oval, 12 In. 25.00
Salt & Pepper . . .10.00 to 18.00
Saltshaker 12.00
Saucer 3.00
Soup, Cream . . . .35.00 to 40.00
Soup, Onion 950.00
Syrup . . . . . . .425.00 to 565.00
Teapot, Large, 8 Cup . . .155.00
Teapot, Medium, 6 Cup . .95.00

Tray, Relish 160.00
Tray, Utility 25.00
Tumbler, Juice,
  5 Oz. . . . . .30.00 to 45.00
Tumbler, Water,
  10 Oz. . . . . . . .50.00 to 60.00
Vase, 8 In. 400.00
Vase, 10 In. . . .795.00 to 860.00
Vase, 12 In. 1250.00
Vase, Bud, 6 1/2 In. 60.00

FIESTA, see also Amberstone;
  Fiesta Kitchen Kraft

FIESTA CASUAL, see Daisy

FIESTA KITCHEN KRAFT

Fiesta Kitchen Kraft was a bake-and-serve line made in the early 1940s by Homer Laughlin China Company, Newell, West Virginia. It was made in Red, Yellow, Green, and Blue.

KITCHEN KRAFT

BLUE
Cake Server 275.00
Casserole, Cover,
  Individual 75.00
Fork 150.00
Jar, Cover,
  Medium . . . .175.00 to 250.00

❖

**Pack plates to be moved
vertically with a pad
under and between the
plates. The weight of a
stack of plates can crack
the bottom plates.**

❖

Jar, Cover, Small 200.00
Mixing Bowl, 6 In. 100.00
Mixing Bowl, 8 In. 100.00
Pie Plate, 9 In. 65.00
Platter, Frame 60.00
Spoon . . . . . . .130.00 to 170.00

GREEN
Cake Plate, 11 In. 50.00
Cake Server, Original
  Label . . . . .150.00 to 250.00
Casserole, Cover,
  Individual . . .145.00 to 185.00
Fork . . . . .100.00 to 130.00
Jar, Cover, Large 325.00
Jar, Cover, Medium 325.00
Jar, Cover, Small,
  Sticker 375.00
Leftover, Cover,
  Stacking 225.00
Pie Plate, 10 In. 50.00
Platter, 13 In. 70.00
Salt & Pepper 90.00

IVORY
Stack Unit 175.00

RED
Cake Plate 70.00
Cake Server 180.00
Carafe 299.00
Casserole, 8 1/2 In. 135.00
Fork 180.00
Jar, Cover, Large 325.00
Jar, Cover,
  Small . . . . .200.00 to 325.00
Jug, Cover 385.00
Pie Plate, 9 In. 60.00
Salt & Pepper 90.00
Spoon . . . . . . .110.00 to 180.00

YELLOW
Cake Plate, 11 In. 50.00
Cake Server . .150.00 to 190.00
Casserole, Cover 225.00
Casserole, Cover,
  Individual . . .115.00 to 185.00
Fork 210.00
Jar, Cover,
  Medium . . . .325.00 to 360.00
Jar, Cover, Small 325.00
Jug, Cover 75.00
Pie Plate, 9 In. . . .25.00 to 35.00
Pie Plate, 10 In. . .35.00 to 50.00
Platter, 13 In. 70.00

FRIENDLY VILLAGE

Friendly Village is made by Johnson Brothers, Ltd. of Hanley, England, now part of the Waterford Wedgwood Group. The pattern has been made since 1953 and is still being made. It is decorated with a black transfer design tinted in pastel colors and features scenes of rural life.

Plate, Bread & Butter 4.00
Plate, Dinner, 10 In. 8.00
Platter, 11 3/4 In. 18.00
Platter, Turkey, 20 In. . . .125.00
Sugar & Creamer,
  Cover . . . . . . .45.00 to 50.00

FRUIT & FLOWERS

Fruit & Flowers pattern, No. 4030, was made by Stangl Pottery, Trenton, New Jersey, from 1957 to 1974. The design shows a mixed grouping of flowers, leaves, grapes, and fanciful shapes. Pieces have a colored border. Universal Potteries also made a pattern called Fruit & Flowers, but only the Stangl pattern is listed here.

Bowl, Vegetable, 8 In. . . .35.00
Cup 15.00

Gravy Boat, Liner 45.00
Pitcher, 12 Oz. 20.00
Pitcher, Pt. 35.00
Pitcher, Qt. 18.00
Plate, Luncheon, 8 In. 18.00
Salt & Pepper 24.00
Vegetable, 8 In. 35.00

FRUIT PURINTON

Fruit patterns were very popular in the 1940s and sets of dishes called Fruit were made by Franciscan Ceramics, Purinton Pottery, Red Wing Potteries, and Stangl Pottery. The Fruit pattern listed here was made by Purinton from 1936 to about 1950. It pictures large fruits.

Bowl, 5 In. 15.00
Bowl, Vegetable,
   Divided 40.00
Gravy Boat 25.00
Plate, Luncheon, 8 In. 15.00
Sugar & Creamer 25.00

·G·

GINGHAM

Vernon Kilns, Vernon, California, made six different plaid patterns. Each plaid was given a special name. Gingham is the pattern with a dark green border and green and yellow plaid. Other related plaids are Calico (pink and blue), Coronation Organdy (gray and rose), Homespun (cinnamon, yellow, and green), Organdie (brown and yellow), Tam O'Shanter (rust, chartreuse, and dark green), and Tweed (yellow and gray-blue).

Canister Set, Revolving . .78.00
Lazy Susan 125.00
Salt & Pepper, Jug 16.00
Teapot, 4 Cup 45.00
Teapot, 6 Cup 45.00

FRUIT STANGL

Stangl Pottery, Trenton, New Jersey, made Fruit pattern from 1942 to 1974. The dishes had center designs that were different fruits. Some pictured apples, some pears, grapes, or

other fruit. This pattern, No. 3697, was sometimes called Festive Fruit. It was marked Terra Rose.

Bowl, Deep, 5 In. 14.00
Casserole, Cover,
   Individual 28.00
Chop Plate,
   12 In. . . . . .20.00 to 40.00
Creamer 9.00
Eggcup 18.00
Pitcher, 2 Pt. 36.00
Plate, Luncheon, 9 1/2 In. . .5.00
Plate, Sherbet, 6 In. 9.00
Saucer 4.00
Sugar & Creamer 8.00
Tumbler, 5 1/2 In. 20.00

GOLDEN HARVEST

Golden Harvest was made by Stangl Pottery from 1953 to 1973. The pattern pictured yellow flowers on a gray background.

Chop Plate, 14 1/2 In. 25.00
Cup 4.00
Cup & Saucer . . .6.00 to 12.00
Plate, 14 1/2 In. 35.00
Shaker 4.00

❖

**The best defense
against a burglary is a
nosy neighbor.**

❖

GRASS

Grass is a pattern designed by Russel Wright for E. M. Knowles from 1957 to 1962. The gray dinnerware has a few abstract lines of gold and dark gray strewn across the pieces. It is one of the few pieces by Wright that is not just a solid color.

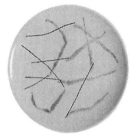

BOWL

Salad, 5 In. . . . . .10.00 to 15.00
Vegetable, 8 In. 17.00
Plate, 6 In. 6.00

HACIENDA

A Mexican-inspired pattern, Hacienda was made by Homer Laughlin China Company, Newell, West Virginia, in 1938. The dinnerware was made on the Century shape. A decal showed a bench, cactus, and a portion of the side of a Mexican home. Most pieces have red trim at the handles and at the edge of the plate. After 1936, Franciscan Ceramics also made a dinnerware pattern called Hacienda, but only Hacienda by Homer Laughlin is listed here.

HOMER LAUGHLIN

Bowl, Oval, Red Trim,
9 In. 15.00
Bowl, Square, Red Trim . .15.00
Cup & Saucer 24.00
Nappy 40.00
Platter, Red Trim 15.00

HALL TEAPOT

Teapots of all sizes and shapes were made by the Hall China Company of East Liverpool, Ohio, starting in the 1920s. Each pot had a special design name such as Airflow or Boston. Each shape could be made in one of several colors, often with names like Cadet (light blue), Camellia (rose), Canary (yellow), Dresden (deep blue), Delphinium (medium purple-blue), Green Lustre (dark green), Indian Red (orange), Mahogany (dark brown), and Marine (dark purple-blue). An infuser is an optional piece that was usually sold separately. It held the tea leaves while the water was poured through them. Coffeepots were also made by Hall. Reproduction teapots have been made since 1992. These, unlike the originals, are marked "Limited Edition."

AIRFLOW
Canary, Gold, 6 Cup 55.00
Chinese Red, 8 Cup 120.00
Cobalt 50.00
Cobalt, Gold . . .95.00 to 100.00
Emerald 55.00
Indian Red 200.00
Turquoise, Gold 95.00
Warm Yellow, Gold,
8 Cup 55.00

ALADDIN
Black, Gold, 6 Cup 60.00
Canary, Gold . . .35.00 to 45.00
Canary, Gold, Infuser 58.00
Cobalt, Gold 45.00
Cobalt, Gold, Oval
Infuser 120.00
Cobalt, Oval Infuser 85.00
Emerald 145.00
Maroon 18.00
Maroon, Gold 75.00
Pink, Infuser 45.00

ALBANY
Emerald, Gold 35.00

AUTOMOBILE
Canary 675.00
Emerald, Platinum 575.00
Turquoise, 6 Cup 600.00

BALTIMORE
Warm Yellow 50.00

BASKET
Cadet 375.00
Canary, 6 Cup 185.00
Emerald, 6 Cup 200.00

BASKETBALL
Black 550.00
Chinese Red 950.00
Warm Yellow 775.00

BIRD CAGE
Maroon, Gold 650.00

BOSTON
Canary 55.00
Emerald, Gold, 2 Cup 40.00
Mahogany, With Trivet . .60.00
Pink, 2 Cup 40.00

CLEVELAND
Emerald 65.00

CUBE
Stock Brown, 1 Cup 60.00
Turquoise, 1 Cup 125.00
Turquoise, 2 Cup 140.00
Warm Yellow, 1 Cup . . .250.00

DONUT
Maroon 425.00
Warm Yellow, Gold 475.00

FOOTBALL
Maroon . . . . .500.00 to 625.00

FRENCH
Canary, Gold 70.00
Ivory, Gold 4.00
Rose 40.00
Rose, Gold 40.00

GLOBE
Cadet, Dripless 45.00
Canary 80.00
Emerald, 6 Cup . .90.00 to 95.00

HOLLYWOOD
Emerald, 8 Cup . .40.00 to 55.00
Green Lustre, 6 Cup 40.00
Ivory, Gold, 6 Cup 45.00
Maroon 45.00
Maroon, Gold Trim 45.00

HOOK COVER
Cadet, Gold . . . .48.00 to 55.00
Dresden, Gold 35.00
Red 135.00
Silver 250.00

If you discover a cache of very dirty antiques and you are not dressed in work clothes, make a temporary cover-up from a plastic garbage bag.

Turquoise, 6 Cup 40.00
Warm Yellow, Gold 55.00

KANSAS
Emerald, Gold 375.00

LOS ANGELES
Cobalt, Gold 65.00

MCCORMICK
Emerald, Infuser 80.00
Maroon, Infuser 80.00
Turquoise, 2 Cup 110.00

MELODY
Chinese Red 325.00
Ivory, 6 Cup 350.00
Turquoise, Gold 250.00
Warm Yellow, Gold,
   6 Cup 350.00

MODERNE
Chinese Red, 6 Cup 695.00

NAUTILUS
Canary, Gold Trim 135.00
Emerald 280.00
Emerald, Gold Trim 225.00
Warm Yellow, Gold 280.00

NEW YORK
Marine 25.00
Red Poppy 85.00
Turquoise, Gold Trim,
   6 Cup 25.00

OHIO
Mahogany 240.00
Warm Yellow, Gold
   Polka Dots 425.00

PARADE
Canary, 6 Cup 40.00
Canary, Gold, 6 Cup 50.00
Turquoise 35.00

PHILADELPHIA
Daffodil, Gold 75.00
Stock Green, Gold,
   6 Cup . . . . . . .60.00 to 75.00

RONALD REAGAN
White 120.00

SAF-HANDLE
Canary . . . . . . .70.00 to 75.00
Chinese Red 350.00

STAR
Cobalt, Gold 90.00
Delphinium, 6 Cup 75.00
Emerald, Gold 60.00

Maroon, 6 Cup 35.00
Turquoise, Gold 50.00

STREAMLINE
Chinese Red . .135.00 to 190.00
Delphinium, Gold 70.00
Emerald . . . . . .70.00 to 75.00

T-BALL
Maroon, Square 85.00

TWINSPOUT
Canary, Gold 95.00
Cobalt, Ribbed 115.00
Emerald 80.00
Ivory 80.00
Warm Yellow, Gold 125.00

WINDSHIELD
Camellia, Gold 40.00
Ivory, Gold Dot .80.00 to 85.00
Maroon, Gold Dot 85.00
Turquoise, 6 Cup 55.00
White, Gold Dot 75.00

HARLEQUIN

Harlequin, a solid-color dinnerware made by Homer Laughlin China Company of Newell, West Virginia, was less expensive than Fiesta. It was made from 1938 to 1964 and sold unmarked in Woolworth stores. The rings molded into the plate were at the edge of the plate well, and the rim was plain. Dishes were made in Chartreuse, Forest Green, Gray, Green (light green), Deep Maroon (sometimes called red), Mauve (blue), Rose, Spruce Green (dark green), Tangerine (red), Turquoise, and Yellow.

CHARTREUSE
Bowl, 10 1/2 In. 45.00
Casserole, Cover 240.00

Plate, Deep, 8 In. 20.00
Salad, Individual 25.00
Sugar 9.50
Teapot . . . . . . .75.00 to 165.00

FOREST GREEN
Bowl, Deep, 5 1/2 In. 25.00
Bowl, Fruit, 10 1/2 In. . . .45.00
Bowl, Oatmeal, 36s 20.00
Creamer, Individual 125.00
Cup 14.00
Cup & Saucer 13.00
Cup & Saucer,
   After Dinner 80.00
Nut Dish 125.00
Pitcher 75.00
Plate, Deep, 8 In. 25.00
Sauceboat . . . . . .28.00 to 35.00
Saucer 4.00
Soup, Cream 40.00
Sugar & Creamer 90.00
Teapot 125.00
Tumbler, Antique Car 45.00

GRAY
Creamer, Novelty 95.00
Cup 10.00
Eggcup, Double 24.50
Pitcher, Water 125.00
Plate, Deep, 8 In. 38.00
Plate, Dessert,
   6 In. . . . . .3.50 to 4.00
Plate, Dinner, 10 In. 45.00
Plate, Luncheon, 9 In. . . .15.00
Sauceboat 45.00
Sugar, Cover 45.00
Teapot 185.00

GREEN
Bowl, Oatmeal 15.00
Creamer 15.00
Cup 15.00
Cup & Saucer 24.00
Plate, Bread & Butter,
   7 In 18.00
Plate, Deep, 8 In. 95.00
Plate, Dinner, 10 In. 35.00
Plate, Luncheon, 9 In. . . .20.00
Salad, Individual 175.00
Saucer 16.00

MAROON
Candleholder, Pair 595.00
Casserole 130.00

❖

**When stacking
dinner plates, put a
piece of felt or paper
between each plate.
Never put more than
24 in one stack.**

❖

Casserole, Cover 215.00
Eggcup, Double 38.00
Nut Cup 22.00
Plate, Deep, 8 In. 35.00
Plate, Dinner, 10 In. 55.00
Salad, Individual 50.00
Sugar, Cover 45.00
Sugar & Creamer 110.00
Tumbler 40.00

MAUVE
Bowl, 10 1/2 In. 24.00
Creamer, High
   Lip . . . . . . 275.00 to 375.00
Creamer, Individual 23.00
Creamer, Novelty 45.00
Cup & Saucer 10.00
Cup & Saucer, After
   Dinner 150.00
Eggcup, Double 25.00
Nut Cup 16.00
Pitcher, Water 45.00
Pitcher, Water,
   Ball . . . . .70.00 to 75.00
Pitcher, Water, With
   Decal 95.00
Plate, Dessert, 6 In. 4.00
Platter, 11 In. 12.00
Sauceboat 35.00
Sugar, Cover 25.00
Sugar & Creamer, After
   Dinner 150.00
Teapot . . . . . .95.00 to 120.00
Tumbler 50.00

ROSE
Bowl, Deep,
   8 In. . . . . .30.00 to 35.00
Bowl, Fruit, 5 1/2 In. 7.00
Bowl, Individual,
   7 1/4 In. 27.00

Bowl, Oatmeal, 36s 18.00
Candleholder, Pair 600.00
Casserole 110.00
Cup . . . . .6.50 to 9.00
Cup & Saucer . .10.00 to 13.00
Cup & Saucer, After
   Dinner . . . . .80.00 to 115.00
Eggcup,
   Double . . . . . .24.50 to 45.00
Nut Dish 125.00
Pitcher, Water,
   Ball . . . . .46.00 to 95.00
Plate, Bread & Butter,
   7 In. 3.00
Plate, Dessert, 6 In. 6.00
Plate, Dinner, 10 In. 11.00
Plate, Luncheon,
   9 In. . . . . .10.00 to 20.00
Plate, Salad, 7 In. 5.00
Platter, Oval, 13 In. 13.00
Salt & Pepper 15.00
Sauceboat 19.00
Saucer 6.00
Soup, Cream 22.00
Sugar, Cover 30.00
Sugar & Creamer,
   After Dinner 115.00
Teapot . . . . . . .65.00 to 75.00

SPRUCE GREEN
Casserole, Cover 215.00
Creamer, Individual 25.00
Cup, After Dinner 95.00
Cup & Saucer, After
   Dinner 195.00
Eggcup, Double 25.00
Nut Cup 22.00
Pitcher, Ball 95.00

TANGERINE
Ashtray . . . . . .85.00 to 90.00
Creamer, Individual 16.50
Cup 7.50
Cup & Saucer 9.50
Cup & Saucer, After
   Dinner . . . . .80.00 to 130.00
Eggcup 20.00
Marmalade 190.00
Pitcher, Water 70.00
Sugar & Creamer, After
   Dinner 130.00
Teapot 125.00

TURQUOISE
Bowl, 6 In. 15.00
Bowl, Cereal, 5 1/2 In. 7.00
Bowl, Vegetable, Round,
    8 1/2 In. 18.00
Creamer . . . . . . .10.00 to 18.00
Cup & Saucer . . .7.50 to 10.00
Eggcup 20.00
Eggcup, Double 15.00
Jug, 22 Oz. 25.00
Marmalade 170.00
Nappy, 9 In. 18.50
Plate, Bread & Butter,
    7 In. 6.00
Plate, Deep, 8 In. 24.00
Plate, Dessert,
    6 In. . . . . .3.50 to 6.00
Plate, Dinner, 10 In. 10.00
Plate, Luncheon, 9 In. 12.00
Platter, 10 In. 10.00
Platter, 13 In. 15.00
Salad,
    Individual . . . . .12.00 to 15.00
Salt & Pepper 15.00
Saucer 6.00
Soup, Cream 16.00
Spoon Rest . . .225.00 to 265.00
Sugar & Creamer,
    Cover 30.00

YELLOW
Bowl, Cereal, 5 1/2 In. 4.50
Bowl, Fruit, Footed,
    11 3/4 In. 155.00
Casserole 80.00
Cup . . . . .7.50 to 11.00
Cup & Saucer . . . .7.00 to 9.50
Cup & Saucer, After
    Dinner 60.00
Eggcup 20.00
Eggcup, Double . .15.00 to 20.00
Jug, 22 Oz. 38.00
Marmalade 160.00
Nappy, 9 In. 18.50
Pitcher, Ball . . . .48.00 to 75.00
Plate, Deep, 8 In. 20.00
Plate, Dessert,
    6 In. . . . . .3.50 to 4.00
Plate, Dinner, 10 In. 10.00
Plate, Luncheon, 9 In. 7.00
Saltshaker 6.00
Sauceboat 25.00

Sugar 30.00
Sugar, Cover, 100th
    Anniversary 34.00
Sugar & Creamer 3.00
Syrup, Cover 185.00

HAWAIIAN DAISY, see Daisy

HAWAIIAN FLOWERS
Hawaiian Flowers was a well-known Vernon Kilns, Vernon, California, tableware designed by Don Blanding. It was first made in 1939.

BLUE
Chop Plate, 14 In. 110.00
Salt & Pepper 45.00

MAROON
Chop Plate,
    12 In. . . . . . .135.00 to 145.00
Chop Plate, 14 In. 95.00
Salt & Pepper 35.00

HOLLAND, see Crocus

HOMESPUN
Homespun, a yellow, green, and reddish brown plaid pattern, was made by Vernon Kilns, Vernon, California. Other related plaids are Calico (pink and blue), Coronation Organdy (gray and rose), Gingham (green and yellow), Organdie (brown and yellow), Tam O'Shanter (rust, chartreuse, and dark green), and Tweed (yellow and gray-blue).

Bowl, Vegetable,
    9 In. . . . . .8.00 to 14.00
Bowl, Vegetable,
    Divided 20.00
Carafe . . . . . . .37.50 to 42.50
Chop Plate,
    12 In. . . . . . . .20.00 to 30.00
Coaster 30.00
Creamer, Cover 17.00
Cup & Saucer . . . .5.00 to 6.00
Flowerpot, Small 35.00
Gravy Boat 16.00
Jug, Small 25.00
Mixing Bowl, 5 In. 25.00
Mixing Bowl, 8 In. 35.00
Pitcher, 2 Qt. 35.00
Plate, Bread & Butter 1.25
Plate, Dessert,
    6 In. . . . . .1.25 to 4.00
Plate, Dinner,
    9 1/2 In. . . . . . . .5.00 to 9.00
Platter,
    12 1/2 In. . . . . . .9.00 to 10.00

Salt & Pepper 8.00

Salt & Pepper,
Small ....10.00 to 15.00

Saucer ....3.00 to 5.00

Soup, Dish, Rim 10.00

Sugar & Creamer 20.00

Tidbit, Metal Handle,
3 Tiers 26.00

Tumbler,
5 1/2 In. ......15.00 to 18.00

Water Set, 2 Qt. Pitcher,
6 Tumblers, 14 Oz.,
5 In. 150.00

HOMESTEAD PROVINCIAL

Homestead Provincial is one of the Poppytrail patterns by Metlox Potteries. The designs are based on Early American folk art themes. Homestead Provincial is dark green and burgundy. The same design was made by the factory in other colors. Colonial Homestead is red and brown, and Provincial Blue is blue.

Bowl, 6 In. 10.00

Box, Cigarette 65.00

Bread Tray 38.00

Butter 60.00

Canister Set, Cover,
4 Piece 295.00

Casserole, Cover 75.00

Coffeepot 65.00

Creamer 20.00

Cup & Saucer ..10.00 to 12.00

Gravy Boat 45.00

Mug, Beer 15.00

Mug, Cover, Spout 95.00

Plate, Bread & Butter,
6 3/8 In. ....4.00 to 7.00

Plate, Dinner, 10 In. 12.00

Plate, Salad,
7 1/2 In. ....8.00 to 9.00

Platter, 14 In. 50.00

Platter, 22 1/2 In. 140.00

Salt & Pepper ...20.00 to 30.00

Snack Plate, Cup 85.00

Soup, Dish 18.00

Sugar, Cover 28.00

Sugar & Creamer 30.00

Sugar & Creamer,
Cover ....42.00 to 65.00

Teapot 115.00

HOUSE, see listings under Petit Point

IROQUOIS

Russel Wright was an important industrial designer. His dinnerwares were made by at least four companies. Iroquois Casual China was a Russel Wright modern design made by Iroquois China Company, Syracuse, New York. The dinnerware was less expensive than American Modern, heavier and less breakable. It was advertised as cook-and-serve. The first pieces were marked China by Iroquois with the signature of Russel Wright. In the 1950s the ware was redesigned and the mark was changed to Iroquois Casual China by Russel Wright. The dishes were made in a number of colors, designed to be mixed and matched. Sets were often sold with pieces in several colors. The original Iroquois was glazed Avocado Yellow, Ice Blue, Lemon Yellow, Nutmeg Brown, Parsley (green), or Sugar White. In 1951 more colors were added, including Aqua, Brick Red, Cantaloupe, Charcoal, Lettuce Green, Oyster (gray), Pink Sherbet, and Ripe Apricot. In 1959 some

Iroquois pieces were decorated with patterns and sold under other names. Glass tumblers were made in matching colors.

AVOCADO YELLOW

Bowl, Vegetable,
8 In. ....22.00 to 35.00

Bowl, Vegetable,
Divided, 10 In. 40.00

Butter 25.00

Carafe ......125.00 to 140.00

Gravy Boat, Fast Stand ...75.00

Sugar & Creamer,
Stacking ......25.00 to 50.00

CANTALOUPE

Bowl, Fruit, Redesigned ..24.00

Bowl, Salad, 5 In. 15.00

Cup & Saucer 25.00

Plate, Dinner, 10 In. 35.00

Plate, Salad, 7 1/2 In. 12.00

Sugar, Cover,
Redesigned 50.00

CHARCOAL

Casserole, Cover, 4 Qt.,
8 In. 145.00

Casserole, Divided,
10 In. 40.00

Cup 8.00

Plate, Dinner, 10 In. 8.00

Sugar & Creamer 10.00

ICE BLUE

Bowl, Cover, 5 In. 15.00

Bowl, Gumbo 25.00

Bowl, Salad, 5 In. 6.00

Bowl, Vegetable,
8 In. ....12.00 to 15.00

Bowl, Vegetable,
Divided, 10 In. 20.00

Butter 95.00

Carafe 110.00

Casserole, Cover, 8 In. . . .45.00

Casserole, Divided,
Round 20.00

Coffeepot, After
Dinner . . . . . .75.00 to 135.00

Creamer 11.00

Cup & Saucer 10.00

Mug 60.00

Plate, Bread & Butter,
6 In. . . . . .3.00 to 4.00

Plate, Dinner, 10 In. 45.00

Plate, Luncheon, 9 In. 8.00

Plate, Salad,
7 1/2 In. . . . . .5.00 to 6.00

Platter, 12 1/2 In. 15.00

Platter, Oval,
14 1/2 In. . . . . .20.00 to 30.00

Salt & Pepper 20.00

Soup, Dish, Cover,
18 Oz. 15.00

Sugar & Creamer 25.00

Sugar & Creamer,
Stacking 20.00

LEMON YELLOW

Ashtray 95.00

Bowl, Vegetable, 10 In. . .35.00

Butter 70.00

Teapot 125.00

LETTUCE GREEN

Bowl, Vegetable, Cover,
Divided, 10 In. 40.00

Carafe 90.00

Casserole, Cover, 6 Qt. . . .95.00

Cup 3.00

Plate, Dinner, 10 In. 8.00

Plate, Salad, 7 1/2 In. 4.00

Platter, 12 3/4 In. 15.00

Sugar, Stacking 20.00

NUTMEG BROWN

Bowl, Vegetable, Divided,
10 In. 20.00

Bowl, Vegetable, Open,
10 In. 18.00

Carafe 125.00

Mug 60.00

Plate, Salad, 7 1/2 In. 8.00

Soup, Dish, 11 1/2 Oz. . . .20.00

OYSTER

Bowl, Salad, 5 In. 8.00

Casserole, 10 In. 40.00

Cup 6.00

Cup & Saucer 12.00

Plate, Dinner, 10 In. 10.00

Platter, Oval, 14 1/2 In. . .45.00

PARSLEY

Bowl, Vegetable, Open,
8 In. 22.00

Casserole, Avocado
Yellow Cover, 2 Qt. . . .40.00

Coffeepot, After Dinner . .30.00

Creamer 12.00

PINK SHERBET

Bowl, Salad, 5 In. 6.00

Bowl, Vegetable,
8 In. . . . . .20.00 to 32.00

Bowl, Vegetable, Cover,
Divided 40.00

Carafe . . . . .125.00 to 170.00

Casserole, 4 Qt. 90.00

Casserole, Cover, 2 Qt. . . .20.00

Casserole, Cover,
Redesigned, 2 Qt. 60.00

Cup & Saucer 10.00

Mug 65.00

Plate, TV 48.00

Platter, 12 1/2 In. 15.00

Saucepan,
Cover . . . . .175.00 to 195.00

Saucer, After Dinner 30.00

RIPE APRICOT

Bowl, Salad, 5 In. 8.00

Bowl, Vegetable, Divided,
10 In. 20.00

Bowl, Vegetable, Divided,
Cover, 10 In. 40.00

Bowl, Vegetable, Open,
8 In. 22.00

Butter 80.00

Casserole, 4 Qt. 85.00

Casserole, Cover,
Round 40.00

Creamer, Redesigned 15.00

Pitcher, 5 1/4 In. 45.00

Plate, Bread & Butter,
6 In. 3.00

Plate, Dinner, 10 In. 9.00

SUGAR WHITE

Bread & Butter, 6 In. 4.00

Butter 125.00

Casserole, Cover, 4 Qt.,
8 In. 145.00

Cup & Saucer 12.00

Fry Pan, Cover 175.00

Pitcher, Cover 145.00

Plate, Dinner,
10 In. . . . . .9.00 to 15.00

IVY

Ivy is a hand-painted pattern
made by Franciscan Ceramics
from 1948. Harker Pottery
Company and Paden City Pottery also made patterns called
Ivy, but only Franciscan Ivy is
listed here.

Ashtray 20.00

Bowl, 7 1/2 In. . .25.00 to 50.00

Bowl, Cereal, 6 In. 18.00

Bowl, Fruit,
5 1/4 In. . . . . . .15.00 to 18.00

Bowl, Salad, Footed,
11 In. 150.00

Bowl, Vegetable,
7 1/4 In. 50.00

Bowl, Vegetable,
8 1/4 In. 60.00

Bowl, Vegetable, Divided,
12 In. . . . . . . .55.00 to 60.00

Butter, Cover 85.00

Casserole, Cover,
Handles 145.00

Chop Plate,
12 In. . . . . . . .95.00 to 100.00

Creamer . . . . . .25.00 to 35.00

Cup & Saucer . .20.00 to 34.00

Gravy Boat, Attached
Liner . . . . . . .75.00 to 85.00

Jar, Range, Cover 45.00

Mixing Bowl 40.00

Pickle, Oval,
10 1/2 In. . . . . .30.00 to 65.00

Plate, Bread & Butter,
6 In. . . . . .7.00 to 12.00

Plate, Dinner,
10 In. . . . . . . .25.00 to 27.00

Plate, Luncheon, 8 In. 20.00

Platter, 11 1/2 In. 75.00

Platter,
13 3/4 In. . . . .85.00 to 100.00

Relish, 11 In. 55.00

Salt & Pepper 25.00

Saucer 4.00

Saucer, Jumbo 10.00

Sherbet 28.00

Soup, Dish, Flat 30.00

Soup Dish, Footed,
5 1/2 In. 18.00

Sugar & Creamer,
Cover . . . . . . .45.00 to 70.00

Tray, TV 145.00

Tumbler, Water . .30.00 to 40.00

·L·

LEI LANI

Lei Lani was made by Vernon Kilns from 1938 to 1942 and again from 1947 to 1955. The pattern was a maroon printed lotus flower.

Chop Plate,
14 In. . . . . . .175.00 to 195.00

Chop Plate, 17 In. 275.00

Creamer, Short 35.00

Cup 18.00

Cup & Saucer 32.00

Plate, Breakfast,
9 1/2 In. 40.00

Plate, Dinner,
10 1/4 In. . . . . .55.00 to 65.00

Plate, Salad, 7 In. 30.00

Platter, 12 In. 125.00

LIBERTY BLUE

A & P grocery commissioned the Liberty Blue dishes to tie in with the 1776-1976 bicentennial celebration of America's independence. They were made by Enoch Wedgwood in the Staffordshire district of England, in the tradition of the 19th-century Staffordshire historical blue china. They have a floral wreath border and central transfer designs of scenes from American history. The dishes were sold beginning in April 1977. There was a different center design on each plate.

Bowl, Cereal,
6 1/2 In. . . . . . . .7.00 to 11.00

Bowl, Fruit, 5 In. . .5.00 to 5.50

Bowl, Vegetable,
Oval . . . . .30.00 to 45.00

Butter, Cover 25.00

Casserole, Cover 75.00

Coaster 8.00

Creamer 15.00

Cup & Saucer . . . .5.00 to 6.50

Gravy Boat, Underplate . .45.00

Mug . . . . .10.00 to 15.00

Pitcher, Milk, 7 1/2 In. . .115.00

Plate, Bread & Butter,
6 In. . . . . .2.00 to 3.50

Plate, Dinner,
10 In. . . . . .5.50 to 8.00

Plate, Luncheon,
8 1/2 In. . . . . . .11.00 to 15.00

Plate, Salad,
7 1/2 In. . . . . .6.00 to 9.00

Platter, 12 In. 30.00

Platter, 14 In. . . .45.00 to 65.00

Salt & Pepper . . .25.00 to 28.00

Saucer 2.00

Soup, Dish 12.00

Sugar & Creamer,
Cover . . . . . . .35.00 to 45.00

Teapot 85.00

Tureen, Soup,
Cover . . . . . .385.00 to 595.00

LITTLE RED RIDING HOOD, see
Red Riding Hood

LU-RAY

The characteristic slightly speckled glaze of the solid-colored Lu-Ray makes it easy to identify. Taylor, Smith, and Taylor of Chester, West Virginia, made this pattern after 1938. Pastel colors include Chatham Gray, Persian Cream, Sharon Pink, Surf Green, and Windsor Blue.

CHATHAM GRAY
Soup, Dish, Tab Handle . .65.00

Teapot 145.00

PERSIAN CREAM

Bowl, 36s 60.00
Bowl, 5 In. . . . . . .4.00 to 6.50
Bowl, 9 In. 15.00
Butter, Cover, 1/4 Lb. 35.00
Cake Plate 110.00
Creamer 6.00
Creamer, After Dinner . . .50.00
Cup & Saucer . . . .5.00 to 8.50
Eggcup . . . . . . .13.00 to 25.00
Grill Plate 30.00
Nut Dish 125.00
Pitcher 135.00
Plate, Bread & Butter,
  6 In. 1.00
Plate, Breakfast, 9 In. 7.50
Plate, Luncheon, 8 In. 20.00
Soup, Cream,
  Underplate 110.00
Soup, Dish 11.00
Tumbler, Juice 70.00

SHARON PINK

Bowl, 5 In. . . . . . .3.00 to 4.00
Bowl, 9 In. 12.00
Bowl, Vegetable 20.00
Cake Plate 110.00
Casserole, Cover 140.00
Chop Plate 30.00
Coffeepot, After
  Dinner 135.00
Creamer 6.00
Creamer, After Dinner . . .50.00
Cup & Saucer . . . .5.00 to 8.50
Eggcup 13.00
Epergne 145.00
Nappy 11.00
Nut Dish 125.00
Pitcher 135.00
Plate, 11 1/2 In. 12.00
Plate, 13 In. 14.00

❖

**Cups are best stored by
hanging them on cup
hooks. Stacking cups
inside one another can
cause chipping.**

❖

Plate, Bread & Butter,
  6 In. . . . . .1.00 to 4.00
Plate, Breakfast,
  9 In. . . . . .7.50 to 18.00
Plate, Dinner,
  10 In. . . . . .18.50 to 20.00
Plate, Luncheon,
  8 1/2 In. . . . . . .20.00 to 22.00
Plate, Salad, 7 1/4 In. 6.00
Platter, Oval, 14 In. 15.00
Soup, Cream 80.00
Soup, Dish . . . . .11.00 to 14.00
Teapot, Flat Spout 80.00
Tumbler, Juice . .40.00 to 70.00

SURF GREEN

Bowl 60.00
Cake Plate, Round,
  11 In. 45.00
Casserole, Cover 140.00
Chop Plate, 15 In. 25.00
Creamer . . . . .5.00 to 6.00
Cup, After Dinner 25.00
Cup & Saucer 5.00
Cup & Saucer, After
  Dinner 45.00
Eggcup . . . . . . .13.00 to 45.00
Grill Plate 30.00
Nut Dish 125.00
Pitcher, Footed 135.00
Plate, Bread & Butter,
  6 In. . . . . .1.00 to 6.00
Plate, Luncheon,
  9 In. . . . . .7.50 to 18.00
Platter, 13 1/2 In. 15.00
Relish, 4 Sections 110.00
Soup, Dish 11.00
Tumbler, Juice 70.00

WINDSOR BLUE

Bowl, 5 In. 4.00
Bowl, Vegetable, Oval,
  10 In. 18.00
Cake Plate 125.00
Casserole, Cover 140.00
Creamer 6.00
Cup 6.00
Cup & Saucer . . . .5.00 to 9.50
Cup & Saucer, After
  Dinner 35.00
Eggcup 13.00
Epergne 145.00

Gravy Boat 22.00
Grill Plate 30.00
Pitcher, Juice . .175.00 to 225.00
Pitcher, Water 75.00
Plate, Bread & Butter,
  6 In. . . . . .2.50 to 6.00
Plate, Breakfast, 9 In. 7.50
Plate, Luncheon,
  8 1/2 In. 22.00
Platter, 11 1/2 In. 11.00
Platter, 13 1/2 In. 15.00
Relish, 4 Sections 75.00
Salt & Pepper 15.00
Soup, Cream,
  Underplate 110.00
Soup, Dish 11.00
Soup, Dish, Tab Handle . .22.00
Teapot 98.00
Tumbler, Water 95.00
Underplate, For Cream
  Soup 30.00
Vase, Bud 130.00

LUTE SONG

Lute Song is a Red Wing
Potteries pattern made in the
1960s. It was decorated with
stylized pictures of musical
instruments in pastel colors.
The dishes were china, not pottery like many Red Wing patterns, and were one of the eight
patterns made in 1960.

Bowl, 5 In. 11.00

Plate, Bread & Butter,
 7 In. 9.00

Saucer 3.00

Sugar & Creamer 10.00

MAGNOLIA

A wide, bright, cranberry-red band borders Magnolia pattern by Stangl Pottery, Trenton, New Jersey. The pattern, No. 3870, was made from 1952 to 1962. Another version of Magnolia by Red Wing Potteries does not have the banded edge. It was made in 1947. Both are listed here.

Magnolia Stangl

Magnolia Red Wing

Bowl, Fruit,
 Stangl . . . . . . .9.00 to 12.00

Bowl, Vegetable, Round,
 8 In., Red Wing 24.00

Bowl, Vegetable, Round,
 10 In., Red Wing 28.00

Chop Plate, Stangl,
 14 1/2 In. 40.00

Cup, Red Wing 5.00

Planter, Red Wing,
 No. 1322 . . . . .40.00

Plate, Bread & Butter,
 Red Wing, 6 In. 6.00

Plate, Dinner, Stangl,
 10 In. 10.00

Plate, Luncheon, Stangl,
 8 In. 12.00

Salt & Pepper,
 Stangl . . . . . .20.00 to 22.50

Saucer, Red Wing . .1.50 to 3.50

Sugar & Creamer, Red
 Wing 7.00

Sugar & Creamer,
 Stangl 45.00

MARDI GRAS

Southern Potteries, Erwin, Tennessee, made Mardi Gras, a hand-painted dinnerware. A large blue daisy and a large pink-petaled flower are surrounded by leaves and buds. The design is placed so that only parts of the flowers are seen on the plate.

Blue Ridge
Hand Painted
Underglaze
Southern Potteries, Ino.
MADE IN U. S. A.

Cake Plate, 12 In. 35.00

Creamer 10.00

Pie Baker 28.00

Platter, 11 1/2 In. 48.00

MAYAN-AZTEC

Mayan-Aztec pattern made by Frankoma Pottery was introduced in 1948. It was made in Desert Gold, Prairie Green, White Sand, and Woodland Moss and has a Mayan geometric border. The names were simplified, and on the 1994 price list the pattern called Aztec was available in Gold, Green, and White.

DESERT GOLD
Creamer 18.50

Cup 14.50

Gravy Boat 38.50

Shaker 16.50

PRAIRIE GREEN
Bowl, 14 Oz. 4.00

Mug, 8 Oz. 6.00

Plate, Ada Clay, 5 In. 8.00

Plate, Ada Clay, 9 In. 15.00

WHITE SAND
Mug, 14 Oz. 7.50

WOODLAND MOSS
Bowl, Serving, Sapulpa
 Clay . . . . .10.00 to 12.00

Butter, Cover, Sapulpa
 Clay 30.00

Cup, Sapulpa Clay, Large . .7.00

Plate, Dinner, Sapulpa
 Clay, 10 In. 40.00

Plate, Salad, Sapulpa
 Clay, 7 In. 9.00

Platter, Sapulpa Clay,
 13 In. 12.00

Salt & Pepper, Sapulpa
 Clay 12.00

Saucer, Sapulpa Clay 3.00

Sugar & Creamer, Sapulpa
 Clay 24.00

MAYFLOWER

Mayflower listed here is a pattern by Southern Potteries (Blue Ridge) of Erwin, Tennessee. The pattern was made in the 1950s. Another Mayflower pattern was made by Edwin M. Knowles from 1957 to 1963. May Flower is a pattern by Vernon Kilns.

Bowl, 9 In. 22.00
Bowl, Tab Handle,
  6 1/8 In. 8.00
Chop Plate, 12 In. 25.00
Cup & Saucer 15.00
Plate, Breakfast, 9 In. 12.00
Plate, Salad, 7 1/2 In. 6.00
Platter, 13 1/2 In. 20.00
Salt & Pepper 15.00
Sugar & Creamer, Cover .25.00

MEADOW ROSE

Meadow Rose was a pattern made by Franciscan Ceramics of Los Angeles, California, in 1977. It is a variation of the Desert Rose pattern. The flowers are colored yellow instead of pink.

Bowl, Cereal 18.00
Bowl, Salad, Side 45.00
Butter, Cover 65.00
Goblet . . . . .125.00 to 175.00
Microwave Baker,
  Rectangular, Large . . .165.00
Platter, 14 In. 38.00
Saucer 5.00
Snack Plate 165.00
Teapot 195.00
Tumbler, Juice, 4 Oz.,
  3 3/4 In. 40.00
Tumbler, Water, 10 Oz.,
  5 1/2 In. 40.00

MEXICANA

The first of the Mexican-inspired patterns that became popular as a dinnerware in the 1930s was Mexicana. This decal-decorated set, designed by Frederick Hurten Rhead, was first offered in 1938. The design shows a collection of orange and yellow pots with a few cacti. The edge of the dish well is rimmed with red or occasionally yellow, green, or blue. Almost all of the pieces are Century line, a popular Homer Laughlin China Company dinnerware shape.

Cup & Saucer 28.00
Jug, Cover, Kitchen
  Kraft 200.00
Nappy 48.00
Plate, Bread & Butter,
  6 In. 12.00
Plate, Luncheon,
  9 In. 26.00
Platter, 15 In. 48.00

MOBY DICK

Moby Dick was a high-priced line made by Vernon Kilns in 1939. Rockwell Kent, the famous illustrator, had illustrated Herman Melville's classic story *Moby Dick*. These illustrations were adapted for the dinnerware. Plates pictured whaling ships, other pieces showed ships and whales. The printed design was available in one of four colors: Dark Blue, Maroon, Walnut Brown, or Yellow (orange-yellow). The Ultra shape was used.

DARK BLUE
Bowl,
  Chowder . . . . .30.00 to 50.00
Bowl, Fruit 25.00
Chop Plate,
  12 1/2 In. . . .125.00 to 150.00
Cup & Saucer, After
  Dinner 50.00
Plate, Bread & Butter,
  6 1/2 In. . . . . . .35.00 to 40.00
Plate, Dinner,
  10 1/2 In. . . . . .55.00 to 95.00
Teapot 175.00
Tumbler . . . . . .75.00 to 115.00

MAROON
Jam Jar, Notched Lid . . .250.00
Mug 95.00
Plate, Luncheon,
  9 In. 40.00
Sugar, Cover 75.00

WALNUT BROWN
Pitcher, 2 Qt. 425.00

MONTEREY

J.A. Bauer Pottery Company made a solid-color pottery line from 1934 to the early 1940s. The Los Angeles, California, pottery sold full dinnerware sets with matching serving pieces. It was a mix-and-match set made in Black, Brown, Burgundy, Canary Yellow, Chartreuse, Gray, Ivory, Monterey Blue, Olive Green, Orange, Pink, Turquoise Blue, and White. A series of molded rings was used on plates, vases, cups, pitchers, and bowls.

CANARY YELLOW
Cake Plate   . . .185.00 to 195.00
Casserole, Individual 30.00
Chop Plate, 13 In. 45.00

MONTEREY BLUE
Chop Plate, 13 In. 45.00
Teapot 95.00

ORANGE
Cake Plate, Pedestal 375.00
Chop Plate, 13 In. 45.00
Jug, Ice Lip 125.00
Sugar & Creamer 40.00

TURQUOISE BLUE
Jug, Ice Lip 325.00
Teapot 60.00

MT. VERNON

Mt. Vernon is a pattern made by the Hall China Company for Sears, Roebuck and Company in the 1940s. It has pink and green flowers in the design.

Bowl, Fruit, 5 In. 8.00
Creamer . . . . . .10.00 to 14.00
Cup . . . . .8.00 to 10.00
Gravy Boat   . . .20.00 to 25.00
Plate, Dinner, 10 In. 14.00

Saucer 3.00
Sugar 24.00

·O·

OLD CURIOSITY SHOP

The Old Curiosity Shop is one of many patterns made by Royal China Company of Sebring, Ohio, from the late 1940s until the late 1960s. It was designed by Gordon Parker. It pictures a view of the shop and an elaborate border. The design comes in green or pink. The Royal China Company closed in 1986.

GREEN
Berry Bowl, 4 In. 3.00
Bowl, 5 1/2 In. 3.00
Bowl, 9 1/4 In. 18.00
Cup & Saucer 4.00
Plate, Bread & Butter,
   6 1/2 In. . . . . . . .1.25 to 2.50
Plate, Dinner, 10 In. 9.50

PINK
Bowl, 9 1/4 In. 18.00
Bowl, Fruit, 5 1/2 In. 3.50
Bowl, Vegetable, Round,
   9 In. 14.00
Bowl, Vegetable, Round,
   10 In. 16.50

Cake Plate, 2 Handles 15.00
Cup & Saucer 4.00
Plate, Bread & Butter,
   6 1/2 In. . . . . . . .2.00 to 2.50
Plate, Dinner, 10 In. 4.00
Soup, Dish, Flat, 8 1/2 In. . .6.00
Sugar & Creamer,
   Cover 15.00

ORANGE POPPY, see Poppy

ORGANDIE

Organdie is one of six different plaid patterns made by Vernon Kilns, Vernon, California, in the 1940s and 1950s. It is an overall brown pattern with a yellow and brown plaid border. Other related plaids are Calico (pink and blue), Gingham (green and yellow), Homespun (cinnamon, yellow, and green), Tam O'Shanter (rust, chartreuse, and deep green), and Tweed (yellow and gray-blue). Organdie was originally the name for a group of plaid designs made in 1937. One of these was Coronation Organdy (gray and rose).

Berry Bowl 9.00
Bowl, Fruit,
   5 1/2 In. . . . . .3.00 to 5.00

Bowl, Salad, 10 1/2 In. . . .60.00
Bowl, Vegetable, 9 In. . . .20.00
Butter . . . . .22.00 to 30.00
Casserole, 8 In. 65.00
Chicken Pot Pie, Cover . . .30.00
Chop Plate,
　12 In. . . . . . . .25.00 to 28.50
Chop Plate, 16 5/8 In. . . .425.00
Coffee Server 25.00
Creamer 9.00
Creamer, Tall 24.00
Cup 8.00
Cup, After Dinner 18.00
Cup & Saucer 6.00
Eggcup 25.00
Flowerpot, 5 In. 40.00
Gravy Boat 18.00
Jug, 2 Qt. 65.00
Mug 15.00
Plate, Bread & Butter,
　7 In. . . . . .4.00 to 10.00
Plate, Dessert, 6 In. 3.00
Plate, Dinner,
　9 1/2 In. . . . . . .6.00 to 11.00
Plate, Salad, 7 1/2 In. 5.00
Platter, 12 In. . . .15.00 to 24.00
Platter, 14 In. 30.00
Salt & Pepper . . .10.00 to 18.00
Saucer 2.50
Server, 2 Tiers 20.00
Soup, Dish, 8 In. 10.00
Sugar & Creamer, Cover .18.00
Teapot, Cover 40.00
Tumbler 28.00

·P·

PETIT POINT

Petit Point was an idea that was used by many makers. The pattern had a center design that looked as if it had been stitched of colored wool. Petit Point patterns were made by Crown Pottery of Evansville, Indiana, in 1941; Leigh Potters of Alliance, Ohio, in 1936 for Montgomery Ward; and Taylor, Smith, and Taylor of Taylor, West Virginia, and East Liver-

pool, Ohio. Other similar patterns with "stitched" designs were called Petit Point Basket, Petit Point House, etc. The prices for all of the patterns are very similar, and so only one price listing is given for all Petit Point patterns.

Bowl, 5 1/4 In. 3.50
Bowl, 6 In. 4.00
Bowl, House, 5 1/4 In. 3.50
Bowl, House, 6 In. 4.00
Cake Lifter 20.00
Cake Plate 30.00
Casserole, Cover,
　8 1/2 In. 10.00
Casserole, Cover,
　Stacking 55.00
Creamer, House 3.00
Plate, Dinner,
　10 In. . . . . .2.00 to 10.00
Plate, Dinner, House,
　10 In. 2.00
Plate, Salad, House, 6 In. . .3.00
Saucer 1.00
Saucer, House 1.00

PLAINSMAN

Plainsman is a pattern made by Frankoma Pottery. It was originally named Oklahoma. The pattern started in 1948 and is still being made. It is available in Autumn Yellow, Black, Brown Satin, Desert Gold, Flame, Peach Glow, Prairie Green, Robin's Egg Blue, White Sand, and Woodland. The 1994 catalog offered 22 pieces of Plainsman with the simplified color names of

Brown, Country Blue, Gold, Green, Forest, and Navy.

BROWN SATIN
Bowl, Salad, Sapulpa
　Clay 5.00
Salt & Pepper 6.00
Salt & Pepper, Sapulpa
　Clay 6.00
Sugar & Creamer,
　Cover, On Tray 35.00
Tumbler, 6 Oz. 4.00

DESERT GOLD
Cup, 5 Oz. 8.00
Cup, Sapulpa Clay, 5 Oz. . .8.00
Cup, Sapulpa Clay, 7 Oz. . .6.00
Lazy Susan, Base,
　Sapulpa Clay 75.00
Mug, Sapulpa Clay,
　10 Oz. 10.00
Plate, Bread & Butter,
　Sapulpa Clay, 7 In. 5.00
Plate, Breakfast, 9 In. 5.00
Plate, Dinner, 10 1/2 In. . .12.00
Plate, Dinner, Sapulpa
　Clay, 10 1/2 In. 12.00
Platter, Sapulpa Clay,
　13 In. 20.00

FLAME
Creamer 5.00

PRAIRIE GREEN
Casserole, Ada Clay,
　Individual 35.00
Casserole, Sapulpa Clay,
　Large 25.00

Cup, After Dinner 5.00
Cup, After Dinner,
  Ada Clay 10.00
Jug, Sapulpa Clay, 3 Qt. . .20.00
Mug, 12 Oz. 8.00
Platter, 13 In. 8.00
Salt & Pepper,
  Sapulpa Clay 6.00
Sauceboat, Ada Clay 25.00
Vase, Pod, Sapulpa
  Clay, 9 In. 24.00

WHITE SAND
Bowl, Divided, 13 In. 7.50

POPPY

Poppy, sometimes called Orange Poppy by collectors, was made by the Hall China Company, East Liverpool, Ohio, from 1933 through the 1950s. The decals picture realistic groups of orange poppies with a few leaves. Another Hall pattern called Red Poppy has bright red stylized flowers with black leaves and trim. Poppy is a name used by at least five companies but listed here are Poppy pattern pieces by Hall. Reproductions using the Poppy decoration, but called Orange Poppy, have been made. These, unlike the originals, are marked "Limited Edition."

Bean Pot 150.00
Berry Bowl, 5 In. 10.00
Bowl, 9 1/4 In. 25.00
Bowl, 10 In. 50.00
Bowl, Vegetable, Round,
  9 1/4 In. . . . . . .25.00 to 36.00
Cake Plate 36.00
Cake Safe 75.00

Canister, Coffee 325.00
Canister Set, 4 Piece . . .1000.00
Casserole, Oval, 8 In. 65.00
Casserole, Oval, 9 In. 55.00
Casserole,
  Sunshine . . . . .35.00 to 40.00
Coffeepot 45.00
Coffeepot, S-Lid 55.00
Cup & Saucer 60.00
Custard,
  Individual . . . .3.00 to 10.00
Gravy Boat 85.00
Plate, Breakfast, 9 In. 8.00
Plate, Dinner, 10 In. 60.00
Platter, 9 In. 35.00
Platter, Oval, 14 In. 36.00
Salt & Pepper, Teardrop . .38.00
Sandwich Server 8.00
Spoon 130.00
Sugar, Cover 85.00
Teapot, Aladdin 93.00
Teapot, Boston 350.00
Teapot, Melody,
  Streamline . .240.00 to 300.00
Teapot, Windshield 300.00
Vase, 6 1/2 In. 100.00

POPPY & WHEAT

Poppy & Wheat is a design that was introduced after 1933. It was made by Hall China Company, East Liverpool, Ohio. The design shows a realistic spray of orange flowers and wheat heads. It is sometimes called Wheat or Wild Poppy.

Bean Pot 225.00
Bowl, 5 In. 16.00
Coffeepot, Washington,
  10 Cup 395.00
Cookie Jar, Banded 295.00

Creamer, Radiance,
  Large 40.00
Jug, Cover, No. 6,
  Radiance 175.00
Plate, 14 In. 36.00
Sugar, Handles 75.00
Tea Tile, Round, 6 In. 70.00
Teapot, Manhattan,
  6 Cup 395.00
Teapot, New York,
  4 Cup 175.00
Teapot, New York,
  6 Cup 395.00

POPPY TRAIL

Metlox Potteries of California made many dinnerwares marked with the word Metlox or Poppytrail (Poppy Trail). Solid-colored wares and hand-decorated pieces were made. Listed here are solid mix-and-match pieces marked Metlox Poppy Trail. This is the 1934 pattern known to the company as the 200 Series. The original eight colors were Canary Yellow, Cream, Delphinium Blue, Old Rose, Poppy Orange, Rust, Sea Green, and Turquoise Blue. Later, seven pastel colors were added: Opaline Green, Pastel Yellow, Peach, Petal Pink, Powder Blue, Satin Ivory, and Satin Turquoise.

"Poppy trail"
MADE IN
CALIFORNIA
U.S.A.

CANARY YELLOW
Bowl, 6 In. 10.00
Bowl, Salad, 9 1/2 In. 17.00
Plate, Bread & Butter,
  6 In. 5.00
Plate, Dinner, 10 In. 9.00

DELPHINIUM BLUE
Bowl, 6 In. 10.00
Plate, Dinner, 10 In. 9.00

Platter, Round,
12 1/2 In. 25.00

OLD ROSE

Bowl, 6 In. 10.00
Plate, Bread & Butter,
6 In. 5.00
Plate, Dinner, 10 In. 5.00

TURQUOISE BLUE

Cup & Saucer 7.00
Plate, Bread & Butter,
6 In. 5.00
Plate, Dinner,
10 In. . . . . .8.00 to 9.00

PROVINCIAL BLUE

Provincial Blue is a Metlox
Potteries pattern that was made
from 1950 to about 1968. It is
decorated with blue scenes of
farm life. A similar pattern,
Homestead Provincial, has the
designs in other colors.

Bowl, Round, 10 In. 44.00
Coffeepot 100.00
Creamer 24.00
Plate, 6 In. 8.00
Plate, 10 In. 14.00
Platter, Casual 35.00
Salt & Pepper 24.00

❖

**For emergency repairs
to chipped pottery,
try coloring the spot
with a wax crayon or
oil paint. It will look
a little better.**

❖

QUEEN ESTHER

Queen Esther is a Homer
Laughlin China Company pattern. It is on the Liberty shape
designed by Frederick Hurten
Rhead about 1928. The pattern
is decorated with a large pink
rose decal.

Bowl, 8 3/4 In. 14.00
Bowl, Dessert, 5 3/4 In. . .45.00
Creamer 10.00
Cup & Saucer 9.00
Plate, Bread & Butter,
6 In. 3.00
Plate, Dinner, 9 1/2 In. 7.00
Platter, 13 3/4 In. 18.00

·R·

RAFFIA

Raffia is a pattern made by
Vernon Kilns about 1950. It is
green brushed with brownish-
red to give a textured effect.
Barkwood and Shantung are
the same pattern in different
colors.

Butter 30.00
Casserole, Cover 20.00
Chop Plate 20.00

Creamer 10.00
Cup & Saucer,
Colossal 200.00
Eggcup 20.00
Pitcher, 2 Qt. 45.00
Syrup, Dripcut 45.00

RAYMOR

Many collectors search for
pieces in the Raymor pattern.
It is a stoneware made by
Roseville Pottery Company
of Zanesville, Ohio, in 1952
and 1953. It was designed by
Ben Siebel. Pieces were made
in Autumn Brown, Avocado
Green, Beach Gray, and Terra
Cotta (rust) in either plain
or mottled versions, and in
Contemporary White. Some
Avocado Green pieces are mis-
takenly called black. Later,
Chartreuse and Robin's Egg
Blue were added to the line.

AUTUMN BROWN

Bowl, Fruit 14.00
Cup, After Dinner 45.00
Eggcup 22.00
Jam Jar, Cover 65.00
Platter, Meat, 20 In. 110.00
Sugar & Creamer,
After Dinner 110.00

AVOCADO GREEN

Bowl, Fruit 12.00
Eggcup, Double 25.00
Plate, Salad, 7 In. 8.00

Be sure you have
photographs and
descriptions of your
collections in case of a
robbery. Keep them in a
safe place away from
your house.

Soup, Dish, Lug,
No. 155 . . . . .25.00
Sugar & Creamer,
After Dinner 75.00

BEACH GRAY
Bowl, Divided, No. 165 . .55.00
Casserole, Cover 145.00
Cup 12.00
Pitcher, Water 125.00
Platter, Oval, 13 In. 45.00

CONTEMPORARY WHITE
Platter, 12 In. 50.00
Ramekin, Cover,
Individual, No. 156 . . . .30.00

TERRA COTTA
Bowl, Fruit 12.00
Casserole, Cover 90.00
Creamer, Individual 18.00
Cup, After Dinner 40.00
Plate, Bread & Butter,
6 In. 6.00
Plate, Breakfast, 9 In. 10.00
Soup, Cream 24.00
Soup, Dish, Lug,
No. 155 . . . . .25.00

RED POPPY

Bright red flowers and black
leaves were used on this popular Hall China Company pattern called Red Poppy. The
pattern, made in East Liverpool, Ohio, from 1930 through
1950, was a premium item for
Grand Union Tea Company.
Matching metal pieces, such as
wastebaskets and bread boxes,
were made, and glass tumblers
are known. Reproductions using the Red Poppy decoration

have been made since 1993.
These, unlike the originals, are
marked "Limited Edition."

Baker, French Flute 35.00
Bowl, Fruit 8.00
Bowl, Vegetable, Round,
9 1/2 In. 30.00
Casserole,
Cover . . . . . . .39.00 to 45.00
Cup . . . . .9.00 to 10.00
Custard 19.00
Drip Jar 30.00
Jug 33.00
Jug, Ball 40.00
Mixing Bowl, Pair 38.00
Plate, Breakfast, 9 In. 9.00
Salt & Pepper, Eggdrop,
Pair 44.00
Salt & Pepper, Handle,
Pair 28.00
Salt & Pepper, Pair 22.00
Soup, Dish 15.00
Teapot, New York 65.00

RED RIDING HOOD

One of the easiest patterns of
American dinnerware to recognize is Red Riding Hood. Three-
dimensional figures of the little
girl with the red hood have
been adapted into saltshakers,
teapots, and other pieces. The
pattern was made by the A.E.
Hull Pottery Company, Crooksville, Ohio, from 1943 to 1957.

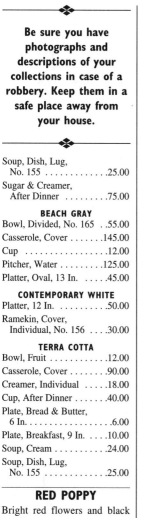

*Hull Ware
Little Red Riding Hood
Patent Applied For
U.S.A.*

Bank, Wall 2800.00
Butter, Cover 425.00
Cookie Jar, Cover 195.00
Creamer, Open 150.00
Creamer, Tab Handle . . .300.00
Matchbox Holder 545.00
Mustard 300.00
Pitcher, Top Pour,
8 In. . . . . . . .375.00 to 475.00
Salt & Pepper,
3 1/4 In. . . . . . .65.00 to 95.00
Salt & Pepper, Range,
5 1/2 In. . . . .145.00 to 250.00
Sugar & Creamer 300.00
Sugar & Creamer,
Creeping, Rose Decal, Tab
Handle . . . . .650.00 to 700.00
Teapot . . . . . .300.00 to 395.00
Wall Pocket 450.00

RED ROOSTER

Red Rooster by Metlox Potteries is one of the Poppytrail
line made beginning in 1955. It
is easy to identify because the
center design is a large red
rooster. The same design was
made by Metlox in different
colors and included Rooster
Bleu and California Provincial.
Some of the pieces look as if
they have rivets.

Ashtray, 8 In. 30.00
Basket, Vegetable,
Round, 8 In. 25.00

Bowl, Cereal,
7 1/4 In. . . . . . .12.00 to 18.00

Bowl, Fruit, 6 In. 8.00

Bowl, Salad, 11 1/2 In. . . .95.00

Bowl, Vegetable,
Divided, 7 7/8 In. 38.00

Bowl, Vegetable, Divided,
Handle, 12 In. 48.00

Bowl, Vegetable, Open,
Round, 10 In. 30.00

Bowl, Vegetable, Stick Handle,
2 Pt., 8 1/2 In. 45.00

Bread Server, 9 1/2 In. . .150.00

Butter, Cover 55.00

Canister Set,
8 Piece . . . . .200.00 to 275.00

Casserole, Kettle, Cover,
Handle 35.00

Chop Plate,
Round . . . . . .40.00 to 65.00

Coffeepot,
6 Cup . . . . . . .60.00 to 95.00

Cookie Jar, Cylinder 75.00

Cruet Set, 5 Piece 225.00

Cruet Set, Oil &
Vinegar 80.00

Cup & Saucer . . .6.00 to 10.00

Eggcup 38.00

Gravy Boat, Handle 30.00

Mug, 8 Oz. 22.00

Mug, Handle, 2 Pt. 30.00

Mustard, Cover 45.00

Plate, Bread & Butter,
6 In. 6.00

Plate, Dinner, 10 In. 12.00

Plate, Luncheon, 8 In. 10.00

Platter,
13 1/2 In. . . . . .20.00 to 25.00

Salt & Pepper 12.00

Saucer 4.00

◆

China can be washed in warm water with mild soapsuds. The addition of ammonia to the water will add that extra sparkle.

◆

Soup, Dish, 8 In. 18.00

Soup, Dish, Lug, 5 In. . . .15.00

Soup, Tureen, Ladle 575.00

Sugar 19.00

Teapot, 5 Cup . . .60.00 to 80.00

Tumbler, 11 Oz. 15.00

REFRIGERATOR WARE

Refrigerator sets were made by the Hall China Company, East Liverpool, Ohio, from the late 1930s. For Westinghouse, the company made Phoenix (Patrician) in 1938, General (Emperor) in 1939, Hercules or Peasant Ware (Aristocrat) in 1940-1941, and Adonis (Prince) in 1952. Hall also made King and Queen ovenware to match the Refrigerator ware. Sears, Roebuck; Montgomery Ward; Hotpoint; and General Electric also used Hall Refrigerator ware. In addition, the company made some pieces sold with the Hall name: Bingo in the late 1930s, Plaza in the 1930s to the 1960s, and Norris.

Made Exclusively for WESTINGHOUSE By The Hall China Co. MADE IN U.S.A.

GENERAL ELECTRIC
Leftover, Cover, Blue,
Yellow, 4 x 8 In. 22.00

Leftover, Cover, Blue,
Yellow, 8 x 8 In. 34.00

Water Server, Adonis,
Blue, Yellow 55.00

Water Server, Adonis, Gray,
Yellow . . . .45.00 to 55.00

HOTPOINT
Leftover, Gray, Square,
4 3/4 In. 40.00

MONTGOMERY WARD
Leftover, Ivory,
Rectangular 60.00

WESTINGHOUSE
Butter, General,
Dark Green 40.00

Butter, Hercules,
Yellow . . . . . .30.00 to 40.00

Casserole, Cover, Blue . . .40.00

Casserole, Cover, Ridged,
Yellow 40.00

Leftover, Delphite 16.00

Leftover, General,
Orange 30.00

Leftover, General,
Yellow 30.00

Leftover, Hercules,
Green 30.00

Leftover, Hercules,
Ivory 30.00

Leftover, Hercules,
Yellow 30.00

Leftover, Phoenix, Blue . .30.00

Pitcher, Donut, Ivory 90.00

Water Server, General,
Green 95.00

Water Server, Phoenix,
Blue 45.00

RHYTHM

Rhythm is a solid-color dinnerware made by Homer Laughlin China Company from about 1951 to 1958. It is a pattern with simple, modern shapes. The dishes were made in many of the Harlequin colors, including Chartreuse, Forest Green, Gray, Maroon, and Yellow. Other companies also made patterns named Rhythm, but only Homer Laughlin Rhythm is listed here.

BURGUNDY
Plate, Dinner, 10 In. 18.00

Platter, Oval, 11 1/2 In. . .15.00

Soup 14.00	
Sugar 18.00	

CHARTREUSE
Creamer 6.50
Cup & Saucer ..10.00 to 12.00
Plate, Dinner, 10 In. 18.00
Salt & Pepper 22.00

FOREST GREEN
Spoon Rest 310.00

HARLEQUIN YELLOW
Teapot 60.00

RING

Ring, sometimes called Bee-hive, was made by J. A. Bauer Pottery Company, Los Angeles, California, from 1932 to 1962. It was made in many colors including Black, Burnt Orange (orange red), Chartreuse, Chinese Yellow (light yellow), Dark Blue, Gray, Green, Ivory, Jade Green, Light Brown, Maroon, Olive Green, Orange, Pale Blue, Pink, Red Brown, Turquoise, White, and Yellow.

BLACK
Bowl, Vegetable, 8 In. ...65.00
Chop Plate,
   12 1/2 In. ...195.00 to 250.00
Creamer 120.00
Cup & Saucer 50.00
Mixing Bowl, No. 12,
   9 1/2 In. 250.00
Mixing Bowl, No. 36,
   5 In. 95.00
Platter, 12 1/2 In. 225.00
Punch Cup ...115.00 to 125.00
Salt & Pepper,
   Barrel .....250.00 to 295.00

Vase, Cylinder, 8 In. 180.00

BURNT ORANGE
Ashtray, Square, 4 In. 75.00
Bean Pot, Cover 45.00
Bowl, Salad, 12 In. 155.00
Butter, Cover,
   Round ....145.00 to 165.00
Carafe, Copper
   Handle .....65.00 to 125.00
Casserole, 9 1/2 In. 80.00
Casserole, Cover, Rack ..255.00
Chop Plate, 12 In. 40.00
Chop Plate, 13 In. 95.00
Chop Plate, 14 In. 65.00
Cookie Jar ..800.00 to 995.00
Goblet 145.00
Grill Plate, 10 1/2 In. 75.00
Jug 295.00
Mixing Bowl, No. 9,
   10 1/2 In. 155.00
Mug 65.00
Pitcher, 1 Qt. ...75.00 to 125.00
Pitcher, 3 Qt. 225.00
Plate, Dinner, 10 1/2 In. ..95.00
Plate, Luncheon, 8 In. 15.00
Sandwich Server,
   17 In. 100.00
Sugar, Cover 65.00
Sugar &
   Creamer ..100.00 to 125.00
Sugar Shaker, Low 15.00
Teapot, 2 Cup 95.00
Teapot, 6 Cup 125.00
Tumbler, 6 Oz. 20.00
Tumbler, 12 Oz. 45.00
Tumbler, Barrel,
   Handle ....125.00 to 225.00

CHARTREUSE
Mixing Bowl, No. 9,
   10 1/2 In. 110.00
Pitcher, 2 Qt. 250.00
Punch Bowl, 9 In. 450.00
Syrup, 1 Pt. 120.00

DARK BLUE
Butter, Cover, Round ...145.00
Carafe 75.00
Chop Plate, 13 In. 85.00
Goblet .....140.00 to 225.00
Gravy Boat 125.00
Pickle 55.00
Punch Bowl, 14 In. 1295.00

Teapot, 6 Cup 350.00
Tumbler, 12 Oz. 45.00
Vase, 6 In. 75.00
gray
Berry Bowl, 4 In. 10.00
Mixing Bowl, No. 36,
   5 In. 40.00
Tumbler, 12 Oz. 75.00

GREEN
Berry Bowl, 4 In. 50.00
Bowl, Vegetable, 8 In. ...55.00
Carafe 30.00
Chop Plate, 12 In. 65.00
Chop Plate, 17 In. 265.00
Coffeepot 120.00
Goblet 225.00
Mixing Bowl, No. 12,
   9 1/2 In. 50.00
Pie Plate, 10 In. 45.00
Plate, Dinner, 10 1/2 In. ..95.00
Plate, Salad, 7 1/2 In. 12.00
Stack Set, Cover 95.00
Sugar
   Shaker .....350.00 to 395.00
Teapot 225.00

IVORY
Chop Plate, 12 In. 145.00
Mixing Bowl, No. 36,
   5 In. 55.00
Plate, Dinner, 10 1/2 In. ..75.00
Sugar & Creamer 350.00

MAROON
Berry Bowl, 4 In. 10.00
Chop Plate, 13 In. 250.00
Gravy Boat 145.00
Mug 40.00
Punch Cup 55.00
Teapot 325.00

PALE BLUE
Bowl, Salad, Low,
   9 In. 65.00
Butter, Cover,
   Round .....125.00 to 225.00
Carafe, Copper Handle ..275.00
Chop Plate, 13 In. 60.00
Nappy, Handle, 7 In. 16.00
Pitcher, 1 Qt. 165.00
Pitcher, 2 Qt. 275.00
Plate, Dinner, 10 1/2 In. ..95.00
Plate, Luncheon, 8 In. 36.00
Punch Cup 55.00

Saucer 15.00
Tumbler, 6 Oz. 35.00
Vase, Cylinder, 10 In. 80.00

TURQUOISE
Beater Bowl, 5 In. 100.00
Vase, Cylinder, 8 In. 85.00

WHITE
Bowl, Salad, 12 In. 375.00
Carafe, Wooden
  Handle 350.00
Punch Bowl, Pedestal,
  14 In. 2000.00
Vase, Cylinder, 10 In. . . .110.00

YELLOW
Bean Pot, 2 Qt. 125.00
Bowl, Fruit, 5 In. 55.00
Bowl, Salad, 12 In. 125.00
Carafe 65.00
Casserole, Rack,
  7 1/2 In. . . . . .70.00 to 125.00
Chop Plate, 12 In. 65.00
Creamer 45.00
Cup & Saucer 40.00
Mixing Bowl, No. 9,
  10 1/2 In. 125.00
Mug 165.00
Mustard 525.00
Nappy, 9 In. 50.00
Plate, Dinner, 10 1/2 In. . .95.00
Punch Bowl, Pedestal,
  14 In. 995.00
Punch Cup 55.00
Sugar Shaker 15.00
Syrup, 1 Pt. 85.00
Teapot, 2 Cup 225.00
Teapot, 6 Cup 85.00
Tumbler, Barrel,
  Handle 300.00

◆

**Bauer Ringware pattern
can be dated from the
mark. "Bauer" or
"Bauer Los Angeles"
were the earliest.
"Bauer Made in USA" or
"Bauer USA" were used
in the mid-1930s.**

◆

RIVIERA

Riviera was solid-color ware made by Homer Laughlin China Company, Newell, West Virginia, from 1938 to 1950. It was unmarked and sold exclusively by the Murphy Company. Plates and cup handles were squared. Colors were Ivory, Light Green, Mauve Blue, Red, Yellow, and, rarely, Dark Blue.

DARK BLUE
Platter, Oval,
  11 1/4 In. . . .135.00 to 200.00

IVORY
Bowl, Fruit, 5 1/2 In. 8.00
Bowl, Oatmeal,
  6 In. . . . . .5.00 to 16.00
Bowl, Utility 40.00
Butter, 1/2 Lb. 155.00
Casserole 65.00
Creamer . . . . . . .7.00 to 10.00
Cup . . . . .7.00 to 8.00
Cup & Saucer, After
  Dinner . . . . . .45.00 to 95.00
Jug, Batter, Cover 160.00
Plate, Luncheon, 9 In. 12.00
Platter, Oval,
  11 1/4 In. . . . . .12.00 to 15.00
Soup, Cream 45.00
Sugar & Creamer 65.00
Syrup, Cover 125.00

LIGHT GREEN
Bowl, Oatmeal, 6 In. 85.00
Bowl, Sugar, Cover 20.00

Butter, 1/4 Lb. 65.00
Casserole, Cover 95.00
Creamer 9.00
Cup 11.00
Jug, Batter, Cover 160.00
Nappy, 9 In. 20.00
Plate, Dessert,
  6 In. . . . . .6.50 to 9.50
Plate, Dinner,
  10 In. 95.00
Plate, Luncheon,
  9 In. 12.00
Saucer 3.00
Shaker 8.00
Sugar & Creamer,
  Cover 30.00
Tumbler, Handle 80.00

MAUVE BLUE
Bowl, Sugar, Cover 25.00
Casserole,
  Cover . . . . . .85.00 to 110.00
Creamer 7.00
Cup . . . . .7.00 to 11.00
Cup, Tea 10.00
Nappy, 9 In. 18.00
Pitcher,
  Juice . . . . . .325.00 to 350.00
Plate, Dessert,
  6 In. . . . . .5.50 to 6.00
Plate, Luncheon,
  9 In. 12.00
Platter, 13 1/4 In. 25.00
Saltshaker 8.00
Sugar 20.00
Tumbler, Handle 75.00

RED
Bowl, Fruit,
  5 1/2 In. 8.00
Bowl, Oatmeal, 6 In. . . .29.00
Butter, 1/2 Lb. 135.00
Cup 7.00
Plate, Dessert, 6 In. 9.50
Plate, Luncheon,
  9 In. 12.00
Saucer 5.00
Soup, Cream 32.00
Syrup, Cover 150.00
Teapot 75.00

YELLOW
Bowl, Fruit, 5 1/2 In. 8.00
Bowl, Oatmeal, 5 In. 8.00

Casserole,
Cover . . . . . . .75.00 to 150.00
Cup . . . . .7.00 to 10.00
Cup & Saucer 11.00
Juice Set, 5 Piece 500.00
Pitcher, Juice . . .75.00 to 160.00
Plate, Deep 65.00
Plate, Dessert,
6 In. 6.00
Plate, Dinner,
10 In. . . . . . . .85.00 to 95.00
Plate, Luncheon,
9 In. . . . . .10.00 to 12.00
Platter,
11 1/4 In. . . . . .15.00 to 22.00
Salt & Pepper 15.00
Sugar 8.00
Teapot 150.00
Tumbler,
Handle . . . . . . .42.50 to 55.00

ROOSTER WATT

Rooster pattern was introduced
by Watt Pottery Company of
Crooksville, Ohio, in 1955. It
was made until at least 1958.
The factory closed in 1965.

Baker, Cover,
No. 67 . . . . .160.00
Baker, No. 85,
Rectangular 1400.00
Casserole, Cover,
No. 18, Individual 425.00
Creamer, No. 62 . . . . . .295.00
Crock, Cheese,
No. 80 . . . . .1500.00
Mixing Bowl, No. 5,
Ribbed 80.00
Mug, No. 701 . . . . . . .1000.00
Pitcher, No. 15 . . . . . . .150.00
Salt & Pepper, Barrel,
No. 45 & No. 46 . . . . .295.00

❖

**Take off your rings and
bracelets before you
start to wash dishes.**

❖

ROSE PARADE

The Hall China Company, East
Liverpool, Ohio, sometimes
made surprising color- and
decal-decorated wares. Rose
Parade has a solid Cadet Blue
body with contrasting Hi-white
knobs and handles. A rose
decal was added to the white
spaces. Sometimes the flower
is pink, sometimes blue. The
pattern was made from 1941
through the 1950s. Serving
pieces, not dinnerware sets,
were made. Pert is a shape.

Brown, Mug, Footed 4.00
Jug, Pert, 5 In. 32.50
Salt & Pepper 24.00
Salt & Pepper, Pert,
Pair . . . . .25.00 to 27.50

ROSE WHITE

Rose White, first made in 1941
by Hall China Company, is
similar to Rose Parade. The
same shapes were used, but the
pieces were all white with a
slightly different rose-decal
decoration. There is silver trim
on many pieces. Pert is a shape.

Bean Pot, Cover 115.00
Pitcher, Pert,
Small 29.00
Salt & Pepper,
Pert 30.00

ROSEBUD

Rosebud was made by Coors
Porcelain, Golden, Colorado,
from 1934 to 1942. It is a solid-
colored ware with a stylized
flower and leaves on the edge
of plates or sides of cups. It was
made in Blue, Green (tur-
quoise), Ivory, Maroon, Orange,
and Yellow.

BLUE
Plate, 9 1/4 In. 30.00
GREEN
Plate, 7 In. 15.00

It is safe to wash most dishes in the dishwasher if they are undamaged and have no gold overlay. For best results, be sure the water temperature is between 140 and 160 degrees and use a rinse agent that causes the water to flow off the dishes in sheets.

IVORY
Pitcher 250.00

MAROON
Plate, 7 In. 15.00
Tumbler, Handle 145.00

MAROON & GREEN
Salt & Pepper 60.00

ORANGE
Baker, Large 85.00
Cake Knife . . .100.00 to 175.00
Cake Plate 55.00
Cookie Jar 85.00

YELLOW
Honey Pot,
   Cover 200.00

ROUNDUP
RoundUp is a hand-painted Red Wing Potteries pattern made from January 1958. It was made on the Casual shape and decorated with cowboys and desert scenes in tones of browns, blues, and greens. It was very similar to Chuck Wagon, which was sold by mail.

Butter, Cover . . .95.00 to 175.00
Cup 25.00
Cup & Saucer 40.00
Pitcher,
   12 In. . . . . . .185.00 to 250.00
Salt & Pepper 75.00

RUSSEL WRIGHT, see American Modern; Grass; Iroquois; Sterling; White Clover

---

SALAMINA
Salamina is an important pattern made by Vernon Kilns in 1939. The pattern pictures a girl from Greenland. Each piece has a different scene. The designs were adapted from the drawings in the book *Salamina* by Rockwell Kent. It is the story of a girl. The dinnerware was hand-colored.

Chop Plate, 12 In. 265.00
Chop Plate, 14 In. 375.00
Pitcher, 2 Qt. 825.00
Plate, Dinner, Salamina
   Kneeling, 10 1/2 In. . . .125.00

SCULPTURED DAISY
Sculptured Daisy was made by Metlox Potteries of Manhattan Beach, California, as part of the Poppy Trail line in 1964. The pattern features raised white daisies and green leaves.

Bowl, 12 In. 70.00
Bowl, Handle, 7 In. 28.00
Bowl, Handle, 8 In. 35.00
Casserole, Cover,
   1 1/2 Qt. 85.00
Coffeepot 50.00
Creamer 18.00
Cup & Saucer 12.00
Gravy Boat, Handle,
   1 Pt. 32.00
Mug 18.00
Plate, 7 1/2 In. 8.00
Soup, Dish, 7 In. 12.00
Sugar, Cover 24.00

SCULPTURED GRAPE
Sculptured Grape is a pattern made by Metlox Potteries as part of the Poppy Trail line from 1963 to 1975. The pattern had a raised grapevine colored blue, brown, and green.

Bowl, 9 1/2 In. 27.00
Bowl, 12 In. 90.00
Bowl, Cereal, 7 3/8 In. . . .15.00
Bowl, Vegetable 23.00
Canister Set, 4 Piece 240.00

Casserole, Cover, 1 Qt. . . .85.00
Cup & Saucer 16.00
Gravy Boat 42.50
Plate, Dinner,
  10 1/2 In. 17.00
Plate, Luncheon,
  7 1/2 In. 10.00
Platter, Oval, 10 In. 30.00
Platter, Oval, 12 In. 40.00
Salad Fork, Spoon 45.00
Sugar, Cover 22.00
Sugar & Creamer 45.00

SCULPTURED ZINNIA

Sculptured Zinnia is a pattern
made by Metlox Potteries as
part of the Poppy Trail line
made from 1964 to 1980. The
Sculptured Zinnia shape was
made in three color variations
named Sculptured Zinnia, Lavender Blue, or Memories.

Bowl, 12 In. 48.00
Bowl, Cereal, 7 3/8 In. . . .13.00
Bowl, Fruit, 6 In. 11.00
Bowl, Vegetable, 8 In. . . .30.00
Cup & Saucer 13.00
Plate, Bread & Butter,
  6 In. 5.50
Plate, Dinner, 12 In. 14.00
Plate, Luncheon, 8 In. 10.00
Plate, Salad, 7 1/2 In. 7.00
Platter, 12 In. 37.50
Platter, Oval, 11 In. 28.00
Platter, Oval, 14 In. 32.00
Salt & Pepper 16.00
Saucer 1.00
Sugar & Creamer 9.50

SERENADE

There are three patterns named
Serenade. The Homer Laughlin
China Company dishes made
from 1939 to the 1940s listed

here are plain, made in Blue,
Green, Pink, or Yellow. The
Hall China Company dishes are
decorated with sprigs of orange
flowers. Another pattern called
Serenade was made by Edwin
M. Knowles China Company.

BLUE
Casserole, Cover 100.00
Saucer 4.00

GREEN
Casserole, Cover 100.00
Cup & Saucer 16.00
Plate, Bread & Butter, 6 In. 6.00

PINK
Bowl, Fruit, 5 1/2 In. 10.00
Chop Plate, 13 In. 40.00
Creamer 12.00
Cup & Saucer 16.00
Plate, Dinner, 10 In. 20.00
Plate, Salad, 7 In. 8.00

YELLOW
Cup 10.00

SHELLWARE, see Cameo
  Shellware

SILHOUETTE

Silhouette looks just like its
name. The 1930s pattern shows
a black silhouette of two people
eating at a table and a dog beg-
ging for food in front of the
table. The plates are trimmed in
platinum. The pattern, made by
Crooksville China Company,
Crooksville, Ohio, is similar to
Taverne, but Taverne has no
dog. Matching metal pieces and
glasswares were made. At least
five companies called their patterns Silhouette. Reproductions
called Silhouette but using the
Taverne decal with no dog have

been made since 1993. These,
unlike the originals, are marked
"Limited Edition."

Bowl, Vegetable, Oval . . .30.00
Plate, Bread & Butter,
  6 In. 7.00
Plate, Salad, 7 In. 10.00
Platter, Oval, 11 In. 35.00
Salt & Pepper 58.00

STANHOME IVY

Stanhome Ivy is a Blue Ridge
pattern made on the Skyline
shape after 1954. It is decorated
with a stylized green ivy sprig.

Cup & Saucer, Skyline 5.00
Plate, Skyline, 6 In. 2.00
Plate, Skyline, 9 1/2 In. . . .4.00

STARBURST

Starburst pattern was made by Franciscan Ceramics of Los Angeles, California, in 1954. The company started in 1934 and became part of what is now Waterford Wedgwood USA in 1979. They stopped making Starburst in 1985.

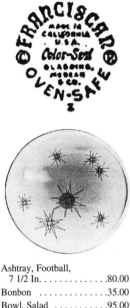

Ashtray, Football, 7 1/2 In.	80.00
Bonbon	35.00
Bowl, Salad	95.00
Bowl, Vegetable, Divided, Round, 8 1/2 In.	38.00
Butter, Cover	45.00 to 50.00
Canister, Flour	200.00
Cruet Set, Oil & Vinegar, 2 Piece	135.00
Cup & Saucer	5.00
Gravy Boat	38.00
Ladle	35.00
Mug	25.00
Pitcher, Milk	75.00 to 82.00
Pitcher, Water, 10 In.	115.00
Plate, Bread & Butter, 6 In.	4.00 to 5.00
Plate, Dinner, 11 In.	9.00 to 12.00
Plate, Luncheon, 9 1/2 In.	20.00
Plate, Salad, 7 In.	6.00
Platter, Oval, 15 In.	55.00
Salad, Crescent	25.00 to 45.00
Saucer	4.00
Snack Tray, Cup Rest, 12 1/2 In.	65.00

STARFLOWER

Starflower by Watt Pottery Company was made in the early 1950s in several variations. One type has either 4-petal or 5-petal red flowers with green leaves on a cream background. Other variations have two or three green leaves. Similar patterns with different names were made in several color combinations. There is another pattern named Star Flower by Stangl Pottery.

Baker, Cover, No. 67	160.00
Bowl, Spaghetti, No. 24	100.00
Casserole, Tab Handles, No. 18, Individual	100.00
Cookie Jar, No. 21	155.00
Creamer, No. 62	180.00 to 250.00
Jar, Grease, No. 01	350.00
Jug, No. 15, 5-Petal	85.00
Jug, No. 17, 4-Petal, Ice Lip	110.00 to 175.00
Mug, Barrel, No. 501	75.00 to 90.00
Mug, No. 121, White On Red	1100.00
Pepper Shaker, No. 46, Barrel	65.00
Plate, Dinner, 10 In.	13.00
Platter, No. 31, Round, 15 In.	50.00

Salt & Pepper, Barrel, No. 45 & No. 46	135.00 to 185.00
Salt & Pepper, Hourglass, No. 117 & No. 118	295.00

STERLING

Sterling by Russel Wright is a heavy restaurant china made by the Sterling China Company in 1949. It was made in Ivy Green, Shell Pink, Straw Yellow, Suede Gray, and Cedar Brown.

IVY GREEN

Ashtray	125.00
Grill Plate, Child's, Astronaut, 8 In.	60.00
Platter, Oval, 7 1/2 In.	22.00

SHELL PINK

Plate, 7 1/2 In.	6.00
Plate, 10 In.	12.00
Plate, 11 1/2 In.	25.00
Platter, Oval, 7 1/2 In.	20.00

STRAW YELLOW

Ashtray	95.00
Plate, 7 1/2 In.	12.00
Plate, 9 In.	14.00

•T•

TAM O'SHANTER

Tam O'Shanter is one of the many plaid patterns made by Vernon Kilns, Vernon, California. It is a rust, chartreuse, and dark green plaid with forest green border. Other related plaids are Calico (pink and blue), Coronation Organdy (gray and rose), Gingham (green and yellow), Homespun (cinnamon, yellow, and green), Organdie (brown and yellow), and Tweed (yellow and gray-blue).

Bowl, Salad, Individual . .25.00
Bowl, Vegetable,
  Divided 18.00
Butter 40.00
Cup, After Dinner 15.00
Eggcup . . . . . . .12.00 to 18.00
Plate, Bread & Butter,
  6 In. . . . . .4.00 to 10.00
Plate, Dinner, 10 1/2 In. . .15.00
Plate, Luncheon, 9 1/2 In. . .8.00
Platter, 14 In. 30.00

TAMPICO

Tampico is a pattern with browns, greens, and pinks picturing watermelon slices. The pattern, on a Futura shape, was made by Red Wing Potteries of Red Wing, Minnesota. This modern design was introduced in 1955. Many other patterns were also made on the Futura bodies.

Bowl, 12 In. 75.00
Creamer 25.00
Gravy Boat . . . .40.00 to 60.00
Nut Bowl, 5 Sections . . .125.00
Pitcher, 2 Qt. . . . .85.00 to 90.00
Plate, Dinner,
  10 1/2 In. 17.00
Platter, 13 In. 90.00

TAVERNE

Taverne serving pieces were made by the Hall China Company of East Liverpool, Ohio, in the 1930s. Matching dinnerware was made by Taylor, Smith, and Taylor of Chester, West Virginia. A rolling pin was made by Harker Pottery Company. The silhouetted figures eating at a table are very similar to those seen on the pattern Silhouette, but there is no dog in this decal. In some of the literature, Taverne is called Silhouette. Reproductions using the Taverne decoration have been made. These, unlike the originals, are marked "Limited Edition."

Baker, French,
  8 In. . . . . .30.00 to 45.00
Bowl, Medallion,
  6 In. 20.00
Bowl, Salad, 9 In. 25.00
Coffeepot,
  5 Band . . . . .125.00 to 150.00
Drip Jar 24.00
Drip Jar, Cover 40.00
Jug, No. 3 . . . . .45.00
Leftover, Square 75.00
Pretzel Jar, Cover 165.00
Saucer 10.00
Teapot, Medallion 125.00

THISTLE

Thistle, or No. 3847, is a pattern made by Stangl Pottery, Trenton, New Jersey. The hand-painted decoration is a purple thistle and green spiked thistle leaves. The dishes were made from 1951 to 1967. Thistle pattern was made by four companies, but only the Stangl pattern is listed here.

Bowl, 10 In. . . . .40.00 to 45.00
Bowl, 12 In. 50.00
Bowl, Fruit, 5 1/2 In. 10.00
Bowl, Vegetable,
  Divided 40.00
Casserole, Individual 10.00
Cup 6.00

Cup & Saucer 11.00
Eggcup 7.50
Mixing Bowl, 5 1/2 In. ...10.00
Plate, Bread & Butter,
6 In................5.00
Plate, Luncheon, 8 In. 10.00
Sugar & Creamer 22.00

TICKLED PINK

Tickled Pink is a pattern made by Vernon Kilns from 1955 to 1958. It features small squares and crosses in pink and charcoal on most pieces. Cups, lids, and a few serving pieces are made of solid pink. The pattern and name rights were purchased by Metlox Potteries in 1958 and Tickled Pink continued to be produced. Blue Ridge also made a pattern called Tickled Pink.

Bowl, Vegetable, 9 In. ...22.50
Bowl, Vegetable, Solid
Pink, 7 In. 14.00
Coffeepot 45.00
Creamer ......12.00 to 14.00
Cup 9.50
Cup & Saucer 12.00
Mug 38.00
Plate, 13 In. 25.00
Plate, Bread & Butter,
7 In................8.00
Plate, Dinner,
10 In. ....7.00 to 10.00
Platter, 11 In. ...15.00 to 26.00
Platter, 14 In. 30.00
Platter, Oval, 13 In. 20.00
Saucer 6.50
Teapot 65.00
Tumbler,
14 Oz. ....18.00 to 35.00

TOM & JERRY

Tom & Jerry sets were made to serve the famous Christmas punch. A set was usually a punch bowl and six matching cups or mugs.

BLACK
Punch Set, Cover,
8 Cup 200.00
Punch Set, Footed Bowl,
18 5-Oz. Cups 250.00

IVORY
Punch Set, Footed Bowl,
Gold Letters,
7 Piece .....100.00 to 120.00

TOWN & COUNTRY RED WING

Town & Country by Red Wing Potteries was designed by Eva Zeisel in 1947 and was made until 1954. Pieces are decorated with glossy or matte glaze. Sets were sold in mixed colors. Colors include Chalk White, Chartreuse, Dusk Blue, Forest Green, Gray, Metallic Brown, Rust, and Sandy Peach. Town & Country was also made by Stangl.

DUSK BLUE
Coffeepot 65.00
Mustard Set, Stopper,
3 Piece 295.00
Plate, 10 1/2 In. 25.00
Platter 75.00
Sugar, Cover 45.00
Syrup ....65.00 to 75.00
Teapot 200.00

FOREST GREEN
Bowl, Dessert 12.00
Butter, Cover 40.00
Casserole, 3 Qt. 50.00

Cup 10.00
Jug Set, 4 Mugs,
1 1/2 Pt. 75.00
Pitcher, 2 1/2 Qt. 37.50

METALLIC BROWN
Bean Pot 50.00
Bowl, 7 3/4 In. 50.00
Bowl, 10 In. 50.00
Salt & Pepper 80.00
Sugar, Cover 35.00

RUST
Mug 40.00
Saucer 10.00
Teapot 130.00

TOWN & COUNTRY STANGL

Stangl Pottery made Town & Country pattern in a variety of colors in the 1970s. The design looks like the sponged stoneware made in the nineteenth century, but the pattern was made in many colors. Black, Blue-Green, Brown, Honey Beige, and Yellow were used. Town & Country was also made by Red Wing Potteries.

BLUE-GREEN
Pitcher & Wash Basin,
2 Piece 150.00

BROWN
Bowl, 7 3/4 In. 50.00
Butter, Cover 60.00
Candleholder, 7 1/2 In.,
Pair 50.00
Creamer 20.00
Cup & Saucer 20.00
Flowerpot, 4 3/4 In. 25.00
Jello Mold, 7 In. 35.00
Ladle 15.00
Nappy 25.00
Plate, Bread & Butter,
6 In.................8.00
Plate, Dinner, 10 1/2 In. ..18.00
Plate, Salad, 8 1/2 In. 12.00
Platter, Oval, 11 1/2 In. ..60.00

Salt & Pepper	.18.00
Spoon Rest	.25.00
Sugar, Cover	.35.00
Tumbler, 8 Oz., 3 3/4 In.	.25.00

HONEY BEIGE
Bowl, 13 In. 125.00

YELLOW
Bowl, Cereal, 5 1/2 In.	. . . .8.00
Bundt Mold, Swirl, 7 1/2 In., Pair	.35.00
Casserole, Cover, 3 Qt.	.15.00

TULIP HALL
Tulip is a 1930s pattern made by Hall China Company, East Liverpool, Ohio. It remained popular until the 1950s. Most of the pieces were distributed by Cook Coffee of Cleveland, Ohio. Pale yellow and purple tulips were applied by decal. The ware is trimmed with silver. The same design is found on a Harker Pottery pattern called Pastel Tulip.

Bowl, 6 In.	.27.00
Bowl, 7 1/2 In.	.36.00
Bowl, Fruit, 5 1/2 In.	.10.00
Bowl, Oval, 10 1/2 In.	.35.00

Creamer	.15.00
Mixing Bowl, 6 In.	.27.00
Mixing Bowl, 7 1/2 In.	.36.00
Plate, Dinner, 10 In.	.15.00
Plate, Luncheon, 9 In.	.16.00
Platter, Oval, 13 1/4 In.	.42.00
Sugar, Cover	.25.00

TULIP WATT
Watt Pottery Company of Crooksville, Ohio, made a pattern called Tulip that was sold in Woolworth's stores. It was made about 1963. The pattern featured a red and a blue tulip with green leaves. Other patterns called Tulip were made by Hall China Company; Stangl Pottery; Edwin H. Knowles China Company; Paden City Pottery; Universal Potteries; Leigh Potters; and Royal Pottery. Other patterns called by the plural name Tulips were made by Homer Laughlin China Company; Pottery Guild; Taylor, Smith, and Taylor; and Blue Ridge.

Baker, Cover, No. 600, Ribbed	.340.00
Baker, Cover, No. 601, Ribbed	.150.00
Bean Pot, No. 76	.100.00
Bowl, Salad, No. 73	.140.00
Bowl, Spaghetti, No. 39	.100.00
Cookie Jar, No. 503	.280.00 to 450.00
Creamer, No. 62	.185.00 to 225.00
Mixing Bowl, No. 63	.65.00 to 110.00
Mixing Bowl, No. 64	.100.00

Don't brag about the value of your collection to strangers. It might lead to extra interest by the local burglary group.

Pitcher, No. 16	.225.00
Pitcher, No. 17, Ice Lip	.200.00 to 250.00

TWEED
Tweed is one of the group of six plaid patterns made by Vernon Kilns from 1950 to 1955. The patterns are the same except that the colors used for the plaid pattern are different. Tweed is a yellow and gray-blue plaid. The other five related designs are Calico (pink and blue), Coronation Organdy (gray and rose), Organdie (yellow and brown), Gingham (green and yellow), Homespun (cinnamon, yellow, and green), and Tam O'Shanter (rust, chartreuse, and dark green).

Cup & Saucer	.14.00
Creamer, Open	.15.00
Plate, 10 In.	.16.00

•V•

VILLAGE GREEN
Village Green by Red Wing Potteries was first made in 1953. It is a heavy pottery set which is brown on the outside and green inside. In 1955 they came out with a related set called Village Brown, which was solid brown.

Casserole, Cover	.20.00
Mug, Coffee, 5 In.	.10.00
Pitcher, 7 In.	.20.00
Salt & Pepper	.15.00

VIRGINIA ROSE

Virginia Rose is the name of a shape of dishes made by Homer Laughlin China Company, Newell, West Virginia. The shapes were decorated with a variety of decal decorations. The dishes with a design of a spray of roses and green leaves is the pattern most often called Virginia Rose by collectors.

Bowl, Oatmeal 5.00
Butter, Cover . . .75.00 to 95.00
Casserole 95.00
Pitcher 98.00
Plate, Luncheon, 8 In. 35.00
Platter, 11 1/2 In. 15.00
Salt & Pepper 140.00
Sauceboat, Liner 25.00
Soup, Coupe 22.00

VISTOSA

Taylor, Smith, and Taylor of Chester, West Virginia, made a solid-colored dinnerware about 1938 called Vistosa. The plates had piecrust edges, and the other pieces had some bands or ridges. The glaze colors were Cobalt Blue, Deep Yellow, Light Green, and Mango Red. Pieces were marked with the name Vistosa and the initials T.S. & T. Co. U.S.A.

COBALT BLUE
Bowl, Vegetable 45.00
Creamer 20.00
Cup & Saucer . .15.00 to 18.00
Eggcup 25.00
Plate, Dinner,
    10 In. . . . . .15.00 to 22.00
Sugar 15.00
Water Jug 75.00

DEEP YELLOW
Cup & Saucer . .15.00 to 17.00
Cup & Saucer,
    After Dinner 45.00
Salt & Pepper 22.00
Teapot 100.00

LIGHT GREEN
Bowl, Salad, Footed,
    12 In. 185.00
Chop Plate, 12 In. 40.00
Cup & Saucer . .15.00 to 18.00
Plate, Dinner,
    10 In. . . . . .15.00 to 22.00
Plate, Luncheon,
    9 In. . . . . .15.00 to 20.00
Salt & Pepper . . .20.00 to 30.00
Sauceboat 125.00
Teapot 95.00

MANGO RED
Chop Plate, 14 In. 50.00
Cup & Saucer . .16.00 to 20.00
Pitcher, Water 85.00
Plate, Bread &
    Butter . . . . .6.00 to 10.00
Plate, Luncheon,
    9 In. . . . . .15.00 to 20.00
Soup, Coupe . . . .20.00 to 25.00
Sugar, Cover 25.00
Teapot 85.00

·W·

WAGON WHEEL

Wagon Wheel was made from 1941 to 1983 by Frankoma Pottery. A few pieces are still being made. Many of the pieces in this pattern are shaped like wagon wheels. Most pieces were made in Desert Gold and Prairie Green, a few were made in other colors.

DESERT GOLD
Baker, Sapulpa Clay,
    3 Qt. 40.00
Bean Pot, Sapulpa Clay,
    Individual 40.00
Bowl, Chili, Ada Clay . . .10.00
Bowl, Dessert,
    Ada Clay 8.00
Bowl, Fruit, Ada Clay,
    Small 10.00
Candleholder, Ada Clay . .25.00
Casserole, Sapulpa Clay . .35.00
Cup 20.00
Cup, Ada Clay 10.00
Mug, Ada Clay, 16 Oz. . . .12.00
Pitcher, Ada Clay 45.00
Plate, Breakfast, Ada
    Clay, 9 In. 13.00
Plate, Dinner, Ada
    Clay, 10 In. 10.00
Plate, Dinner, Sapulpa
    Clay, 10 In. 10.00
Plate, Luncheon, Ada
    Clay, 8 In. 8.00
Punch Bowl, Ada Clay,
    10 Qt. 100.00
Saucer, Ada Clay . .5.00 to 7.00
Server, Divided, Sapulpa
    Clay 25.00
Sugar & Creamer, Sapulpa
    Clay 25.00

Teapot, Cover,
Ada Clay 35.00

PRAIRIE GREEN

Cup 8.00

Mug, Ada Clay 15.00

Pitcher, 7 In. 18.00

Plate, Dinner, 10 In. 20.00

Plate, Salad, Ada Clay,
7 In. 8.00

Platter, Sapulpa Clay,
13 In. 16.00

Salt & Pepper, Ada
Clay . . . . .14.00 to 15.00

Sugar, Individual,
Ada Clay 10.00

Wall Pocket 30.00

WHEAT, see Poppy & Wheat

WHITE CLOVER

White Clover is a dinnerware
that was designed by Russel
Wright for Harker Pottery
Company of East Liverpool,
Ohio. It had the very sleek
modern shapes inspired by his
other design, American Modern, but a sprig of clover decoration was added. It was made
in four colors: Charcoal, Coral
Sand, Golden Spice, and Meadow Green. The dinnerware
was advertised as ovenproof,
chip-resistant, and detergent-
resistant. The pattern was discontinued in 1955.

Russel Wright

CHARCOAL
Plate, Bread & Butter,
Harker, 6 In. 2.50

GOLDEN SPICE
Platter, 13 In. 50.00
Saltshaker, 4 In. 12.00

MEADOW GREEN
Clock Face, Harker 12.50
Plate, 9 3/4 In. 8.00
Salt & Pepper 40.00

WILD POPPY, see Poppy &
Wheat

WILDFIRE

Great American Tea Company
gave Wildfire pattern as a premium. This Hall China Company pattern of the 1950s has a
Hi-white body and flower garland decal decoration.

Bowl, 6 In. 8.00
Bowl, 8 1/2 In. 12.00
Bowl, Oval, 10 1/2 In. . . .20.00
Bowl, Salad, 9 In. 12.00
Pitcher, 6 In. 3.00
Plate, Bread & Butter,
6 In. 3.00
Plate, Salad, 7 In. 6.00
Salt & Pepper 50.00
Soup, Dish, 8 1/2 In. 12.00

WILDFLOWER

Franciscan made Wildflower
pattern in 1942. Other patterns
named Wildflower were made
by Blue Ridge and Edwin M.
Knowles. Pieces listed here are
by Franciscan Ceramics.

Ashtray, Mariposa Lily . .100.00
Bowl, 6 1/2 In. 75.00
Bowl, 8 1/2 In. 95.00
Casserole 675.00
Chop Plate, 12 In. 275.00

Platter, Oval, 14 In. 425.00
Sugar, Cover 250.00

WILLOW

Willow pattern pictures a
bridge, three figures, birds,
trees, and a Chinese landscape.
The pattern was first used in
England by Thomas Turner in
1780 at the Caughley Pottery
Works. It was inspired by an
earlier Chinese pattern. The
pattern has been copied by
makers in almost every country. It was made in the United
States by Homer Laughlin
China Company, Sebring, and
others. Pieces listed here are
blue unless another color is
mentioned. Blue and pink willow was made by the Royal
China Company of Sebring,
Ohio, from the 1940s through
the 1960s.

Bowl, 5 In. 3.00
Bowl, Fruit, Royal,
5 1/2 In. 2.00
Bowl, Royal, 10 1/4 In. . .10.00
Bowl, Vegetable,
Ridgway 15.00
Child's Set, 26 Pieces . . .325.00
Chop Plate, Occupied
Japan 40.00
Creamer 20.00
Creamer, Angular Handle,
Royal 5.00

Creamer, Occupied Japan,
Medium 20.00

Creamer, Pointed Handle,
Royal, 3 In. 19.00

Creamer, Round Handle,
Royal 5.00

Creamer, Shenango,
Individual 25.00

Cup & Saucer, Buffalo . . .30.00

Cup & Saucer, Handleless,
Buffalo 50.00

Gravy Boat, Double Spout,
Royal 8.00

Mug 15.00

Mug, Inside Decal 20.00

Mug, Occupied Japan 15.00

Oil & Vinegar, Stopper,
Tall 90.00

Pie Plate, Shallow 40.00

Pitcher, Iced Tea, Ice Lip,
Japan 115.00

Plate, Bennett, Brown,
9 In. 5.00

Plate, Bread & Butter,
Royal, 6 In. . . . .2.00 to 4.00

Plate, Buffalo, 5 In. 20.00

Plate, Child's, 4 3/8 In. 9.00

Plate, Dinner, Homer
Laughlin, 10 In. 12.00

Plate, Dinner, Ridgway,
10 In. . . . . .13.00 to 22.00

Plate, Dinner, Royal,
10 In. . . . . .5.00 to 7.00

Plate, Handle, Royal,
10 1/2 In. 10.00

Plate, Luncheon, Bennett,
Pink, 8 In. 4.00

Plate, Luncheon, Ridgway,
9 In. 11.00

Plate, Luncheon, Royal,
9 In. 5.00

Plate, Salad, 7 In. 5.00

Plate, Salad, Ridgway,
7 In. 13.00

Plate, Salad, Royal,
7 1/4 In. 3.50

Platter, Oval, Japan,
12 1/2 In. 24.00

Platter, Rectangular, Bennett,
Brown, 15 In. 50.00

Platter, Round, Royal,
12 1/4 In. 10.00

Platter, Round, Royal,
13 1/4 In. 12.00

Saltshaker, Barrel 10.00

Saucer, Buffalo 10.00

Saucer, Ridgway 1.00

Shaker, Barrel, Occupied
Japan 10.00

Soup, Dish, Japan,
7 1/2 In. 12.00

Soup, Dish, Ridgway 22.00

Soup, Dish, Royal,
8 3/8 In. 8.00

Soup, Lug, Royal, 7 In. . . .7.00

Sugar, Cover, Pointed
Handle, Royal 24.00

Sugar, Cover, Round
Handle, Royal 6.00

Sugar & Creamer, Angular
Cover, Royal 5.00

Sugar & Creamer, Cover .40.00

Sugar & Creamer, Cover,
Lug, Royal 13.00

Sugar & Creamer,
Occupied Japan 30.00

Tumbler, Juice, Flat,
3 1/2 In. 6.00

Tumbler, Water . .18.00 to 20.00

Tumbler, Water, Footed,
5 In. 9.00

WINNIE

Winnie is a pattern made in the
1950s by Blue Ridge. It is decorated with off-center red flowers on the Skyline shape.

Berry Bowl 5.00

Bowl, 9 In. 18.00

Creamer 10.00

Cup & Saucer 10.00

Plate, Bread & Butter,
6 In. 5.00

Plate, Dinner, 10 In. 15.00

Platter, 13 In. 25.00

Soup, Dish 10.00

Sugar, Cover 15.00

·Z·

ZEISEL

Eva Zeisel designed the Century and Tomorrow's Classic
shapes for Hall China Company's Hallcraft line in 1952. It
remained popular until the
1960s. The solid white dinnerware, sometimes decorated
with decals, is marked with her
name.

Bowl, 5 3/4 In. 5.00

Bowl, Vegetable, Square,
Large 50.00

Coffeepot 170.00

Cup & Saucer 8.00

Gravy Boat, Ladle 100.00

Plate, Bread & Butter,
6 1/2 In. 4.00

Soup, Dish, 7 In. 30.00

Teapot 245.00

DINNERWARE FACTORIES, PATTERNS, AND BIBLIOGRAPHY

Kovels' Depression Glass & Dinnerware Price List is a concise guide to price and age information. This is a list that will help collectors learn more about dinnerware patterns. Each pottery factory is listed separately with the location and the dates of operation. A list of books that specialize in this type of dinnerware is also included. These books often have many color pictures of dinnerware, reprints of early advertising, and other information. Also included under each factory name is a list of the best-known patterns made by the firm. Not all of these are included in the main body of our book. General reference books on dinnerware are included at the end of this section.

Abingdon Potteries, Abingdon, Illinois, 1908–1951

REFERENCE BOOKS

Paradis, Joe. *Abingdon Pottery Artware 1934–1950: Stepchild of the Great Depression.* Atglen, Pennsylvania: Schiffer Publishing Ltd., 1997.

Rehl, Norma. *Abingdon Pottery.* Privately printed, 1981 (P.O. Box 556, Milford, NJ 08848-0556).

PATTERNS

Abingdon, 1935

J. A. Bauer Pottery Company, Los Angeles, California, c.1923–c.1958 (Bauer Pottery, 1909–c.1923)

REFERENCE BOOKS

Chipman, Jack, and Judy Stangler. *Bauer Pottery: 1982 Price Guide.* Privately printed, 1982 (16 E. Holly St., Pasadena, CA 91003).

Tuchman, Mitch. *Bauer Classic American Pottery.* San Francisco, California: Chronicle Books, 1995.

PATTERNS

Brushes	Los Angeles
Cal-Art	Monterey, 1934–early 1940s
California Pottery	Modern, 1935
El Chico	Monterey Moderne, 1948–1962
Hi-Fire, 1930s	Moon Song
La Linda, 1939–1940s	Ring, 1932–1962

Russel Wright, 1945   Speck Ware, 1946
Smooth, 1936–1937

Blair Ceramics, Ozark, Missouri, 1946–1950s

PATTERNS

Autumn Leaf   Gay Plaid
Bamboo   Rick-Rack
Bird   Yellow Plaid

Blue Ridge, see Southern Potteries

Brusché Ceramics (mark used by J.A. Bauer Pottery Company, c.1950)

PATTERNS

Al Fresco, 1950s   Contempo, 1952

Buffalo Pottery, Buffalo, New York, established by the Larkin Company after 1902 (Buffalo China Company from 1956, now part of Oneida, Ltd.)

PATTERNS

Beverly   Dresden
Blue Willow   Gaudy Willow
Bungalow   Glendale
Coin Gold Band   Pink Rose

Caribe-Sterling, Vega Baja, Puerto Rico, early 1950s–1977

PATTERNS

Bonita, 1950s–1963   El Vuelo, 1950s–1963
Caribe Casual, 1950s–1963

Catalina Pottery, Catalina Island, California, c.1927–1947 (name purchased by Gladding McBean Company in 1937; Catalina name remained in use until 1947)

REFERENCE BOOKS

Catalina Art Pottery Price List and General Sales Instructions, 1942 (catalog reprint). Privately printed, 1982 (Delleen Enge, 912 N. Signal, Ojai, CA 93023).
Fridley, A. W. *Catalina Pottery: The Early Years 1927–1937*. Privately printed, 1977 (P.O. Box 7723, Long Beach, CA 90807).

PATTERNS

Arabesque, 1935

Art Deco, early 1930s

Octagon, 1930s

Rope Edge, 1936

Trojan, 1930–1940s

Coors Porcelain, Golden, Colorado, 1910–present (stopped making dinnerware in the 1950s)

REFERENCE BOOKS

Carlton, Carol and Jim. *Collector's Encyclopedia of Colorado Pottery.* Paducah, Kentucky: Collector Books, 1994.

Schneider, Robert. *Coors Rosebud Pottery.* Privately printed, 1984 (P.O. Box 10382S, Pike Place Station, Seattle, WA 98101).

PATTERNS

Glencoe, 1920s

Golden, 1930s

Mello-Tone, late 1930s

Rockmount, late 1930s

Rosebud, 1934–1942

Thermo-Porcelain

Crooksville China Company, Crooksville, Ohio, 1902–c.1960

PATTERNS

Apple Blossom

Autumn Leaf

Avenue

Black Tulip, 1950s

Blossom Time

Blossoms

Blue Blossoms

Border Bouquet

Border Rose

Brilliance

Calico Chick

Calico Flowers

California James Poppy

Carnival

Country Home

Flamingo

Flower Fair

Gold Drape

Homestead

Hunting

Ivy Vine

Jessie

Kaleidoscope

Little Bouquet

Meadow Flowers

Medallion

Petit Point House

Petit Point Leaf

Pheasant

Pink Border

Posies

Queen Rose

Rose Garden

Rose Garland, 1920s

Roses

Rust Bouquet

Scotch Plaid

Silhouette, 1930s

Southern Belle

Spray

Spring Blossom, 1940s
Swirl
Trellis, 1929

Trotter
Veggies
Willow

Crown Pottery, Evansville, Indiana, 1882–1962

PATTERNS

Autumn Leaf
Blue Bird, 1941
Bouquet
Carriage
Croydon, 1941
Dresden, 1941
Garland, 1941
Hawthorne

Laurel, 1941
Navajo
Petit Point, 1941
Poppy
Swedish
Wild Rose, 1941
Windmill

Franciscan Ceramics Inc., Los Angeles, California, 1934–present (a dinnerware line made by Gladding, McBean & Company, which operated from 1875 to 1984. Franciscan Ceramics has been part of Waterford Wedgwood Group since 1979)

REFERENCE BOOKS

Enge, Delleen. *Franciscan: Embossed Hand Painted.* Privately printed, 1992 (E. El Roblar Dr., Suite #10, Ojai, CA 93023).

———. *Franciscan Ware.* Paducah, Kentucky: Collector Books, 1981.

Enge, Delleen, and Merrianne Metzger. *Franciscan, Plain & Fancy.* Privately printed, 1997 (121 E. El Roblar Dr., Suite #10, Ojai, CA 93023).

Snyder, Jeffrey B. *Franciscan Dining Services: A Comprehensive Guide with Values.* Atglen, Pennsylvania: Schiffer Publishing Ltd., 1996.

PATTERNS

Amapola, 1973
Apple, 1940–present
Arcadia, 1941
Autumn, 1955
Canton, 1950
Cherokee Rose, 1941–1942
Coronado, 1936–1956
Coronado Swirl, 1936–1956
Daisy, 1960
Daisy Wreath, 1975

Del Mar, 1937
Desert Rose, 1941–present
Dogwood, 1975
Duet, 1956
Duotone, 1940
El Patio, 1934–1954
Elsinore, 1946
Floral, 1971
Fruit, 1931–1942
Garden Party, 1974

Gingersnap, 1974
Hacienda, 1964
Hawthorne, 1938–1942
Ivy, 1948
Jamoca, 1973
Lorraine, 1946
Mango, 1937–1938
Mariposa, 1949
Maypole, 1974
Meadow Rose, 1977
Mesa, 1950
Mirasol, 1975
Montecito, 1957
Monterey, 1949
Nut Tree, 1970
Oasis, 1955

October, 1977
Palo Alto, 1950
Pebble Beach, 1969
Picnic, 1973
Poppy, 1950
Rancho, 1937–1941
Starburst, 1954
Strawberry Fair, 1979
Tiempo, 1949
Tiger Flower, 1937–1942
Trio, 1954
Wheat, 1951–1953
Wild Flower, 1942
Willow, 1937–1940
Zinnia, 1967

Frankoma Pottery, Sapulpa, Oklahoma, 1936–present

REFERENCE BOOKS

Bess, Phyllis and Tom. *Frankoma Treasures*. Privately printed, 1983 (14535 E. 13th St., Tulsa, OK 74108).

———. *Suggested Values for Frankoma Treasures*. Privately printed, 1990 (14535 E. 13th St., Tulsa, OK 74108).

Cox, Susan N. *Collectors Guide to Frankoma Pottery, Book Two*. Privately printed, 1982 (P.O. Box 2674, La Mesa, CA 92041).

Schaum, Gary V. *Collector's Guide to Frankoma Pottery: 1933–1990*. Gas City, Indiana: L-W Book Sales, 1997.

PATTERNS

Lazybone, 1953
Mayan-Aztec, 1948
Plainsman, 1948

Wagon Wheel, 1941–1983
Westwind, 1962

French Saxon China Company, East Liverpool, Ohio, 1935 (bought by Royal China Company in 1964)

PATTERNS

Aloha
Granada, 1939–1940

Rancho
Thistle

W. S. George Company, Kittanning, Pennsylvania, 1880–1959

PATTERNS

Argosy, 1930

Bird

Blossoms

Blossomtime

Bluebird

Breakfast Nook

Bridle Rose

Country Gentleman

Cynthia

Dogwood

Floral

Flower Rim

Gascon

Iroquois Red

Lido Dalrymple

Mexicana

Mexi-Gren, 1930s

Mexi-Lido

Neville

Peach Blossom

Petalware, late 1930s

Petit Point Rose

Plain-Jane, 1949–present

Poppy

Pussy Willow

Rainbow, late 1930s

Rosita

Rust Floral

Sailing

Shortcake

Springtime, 1940s

Wampum

Wheat

Gonder Ceramic Art Company, Zanesville, Ohio, 1941–1957

PATTERNS

La Gonda, 1950s

Haeger Potteries, Dundee, Illinois, 1914–present (also called Royal Haeger)

REFERENCE BOOKS

Garmon, Lee, and Doris Frizzell. *Collecting Royal Haeger: A Comprehensive Illustrated Price Guide.* Paducah, Kentucky: Collector Books, 1989.

PATTERNS

Country Classics

Hall China Company, East Liverpool, Ohio, 1903–present

REFERENCE BOOKS

Cunningham, Jo. *Autumn Leaf Story Price Guide.* Privately printed, 1979 (P.O. Box 4929, Springfield, MO 65808).

Duke, Harvey. *Superior Quality Hall China: A Guide for Collectors.* Privately printed, 1977 (12135 N. State Rd., Otisville, MI 48463).

Miller, C. L. *Jewel Tea Sales and Houseware Collectibles with Value Guide*. Atglen, Pennsylvania: Schiffer Publishing Ltd., 1995.

Miller, C. L. *The Jewel Tea Company: Its History and Products*. Atglen, Pennsylvania: Schiffer Publishing Ltd., 1994.

Whitmyer, Margaret and Kenn. *Collector's Encyclopedia of Hall China*. 2nd edition. Paducah, Kentucky: Collector Books, 1994.

PATTERNS

Acacia

Adonis, 1952

Airflow Teapot, 1940

Aladdin Teapot, 1939

Albany Teapot, 1930

Albert, 1940s

Alma Teapot

Apple Teapot, 1950s

Automobile Teapot, 1938

Autumn Leaf, 1936–present

Baltimore Teapot, 1930s

Banded, 1937

Basket, 1932–1960

Basketball Teapot, 1938

Basket Teapot, 1938

Bellevue (or Bellvue) Teapot,
    1920s–present

Benjamin Teapot, early 1940s

Big Boy

Birch Teapot, early 1940s

Birdcage Teapot, 1939

Bittersweet

Black Beauty, 1935

Blue Blossom, 1939

Blue Bouquet, 1950–1960s

Blue Garden, 1939

Boston Teapot, 1920

Bouquet, 1950s–1960s

Bowknot, early 1940s

Bowling Ball Teapot, late 1930s

Cactus, 1937–1940s

Cameo Rose, 1970s

Caprice, 1952–1957

Carraway

Cattail, 1927

Cleveland Teapot, 1930s

Clover, 1940–1960

Coffee Queen

Colonial Teapot, 1932

Columbia Teapot

Connie Teapot, early 1940s

Coverlet Teapot

Cozy Cover

Crocus, 1930s

Cube Teapot

Cut-A-Way, 1930

Deca-Flip

Disraeli Teapot, 1940s

D-Line, 1936

Donut Teapot, 1938

Eggshell Polka Dot, 1934

English Countryside

E-Style Teapot

Fantasy, 1930s–1940s

Flamingo

Flare Ware Gold Lace, 1960s

Floral Lattice

Flowerpot

Flute, 1935

Football Teapot, 1938–1940

Forman

French Teapot, 1920

Fuji

Fuzz Ball, 1930s

General, 1939

General Electric

Gladstone, 1940
Globe Teapot
Gold Label, 1950s
Grape
Grape Teapot, 1950s
Harlequin
Heather Rose
Hercules, 1940–1941
Hollywood Teapot, late 1920s
Hook Cover Teapot, 1940
Hotpoint
Illinois Teapot, 1920s–early 1930s
Indiana Teapot
Irongate
Johnson Teapot
J-Sunshine
Kansas Teapot
Lipton Teapot
Los Angeles Teapot, 1926
Manhattan Teapot
Marylou
McCormick Teapot, 1907
Meadow Flowers, 1938
Melody Teapot, 1939
Miss Terry
Moderne Teapot, 1930s
Monk's Head
Monticello, 1941–1959
Morning
Morning Glory, 1942–1949
Mountain Flower, 1940
Mt. Vernon, 1940s
Mums, 1930s
Murphy Teapot, early 1940s
Naomi Teapot
Nautilus Teapot, 1939
New York Teapot, 1920
Newport Teapot, early 1930s
Nora, 1950s
Ohio Teapot
Parade Teapot, 1942

Pastel Morning Glory, 1930s
Peach Blossom
Pert Teapot
Petunia, 1932–1969
Philadelphia Teapot, 1923
Phoenix, 1938
Pink Morning Glory
Pink Mums, 1930s
Plain
Plaza, 1930s–1960s
Plum Pudding
Plume Teapot, early 1940s
Polka Dot, 1942
Poppy, 1933–1950s
Poppy & Wheat, 1933
Provincial, 1938
Radiant Ware, 1940s
Rainbow
Red Dot
Red Poppy, 1930–1950
Regal
Regal Teapot, 1950s
Rhythm Teapot, 1939
Richmond, 1941
Ridged
Rio Rose, 1950s
Ronald Reagan Teapot, 1970s
Rose Parade, 1941–1950s
Rose White, 1941
Royal
Royal Rose, late 1940s–early 1950s
Royal Teapot, 1950s
Rutherford Teapot
Saf-Handle Teapot, 1938–1960s
Sani-Grid, 1941
Serenade
Shaggy Tulip, mid-1930s–mid-1940s
Silhouette, 1930s
Sprig Crocus
Springtime
Starlight

Starlight Teapot, 1950s
Star Teapot, 1940
Step-Down
Step-Round
Streamline Teapot, 1937
Sundial Teapot
Sunshine, 1933
Surfside Teapot, 1939
Taverne, 1930s
T-Ball Teapot, 1948
Tea for Two/Tea for Four Teapot
Teataster Teapot, late 1940s
Thistle
Thorley

Tom & Jerry, 1930s
Tritone, 1950s
Tulip, 1930s–1950s
Twinspout Teapot, late 1940s
Twin-Tee Teapot
Victoria, early 1940s
Wildfire, 1950s
Windcrest, 1940s
Windcrest Teapot, 1950s
Windshield Teapot, 1941
World's Fair Teapot
Yellow Rose
Zeisel, 1952–1960s
Zephyr, late 1930s

Harker Pottery Company, Chester, West Virginia, and East Liverpool, Ohio, 1890–1972

REFERENCE BOOKS
Colbert, Neva W. *Collector's Guide to Harker Pottery U.S.A.* Paducah, Kentucky: Collector Books, 1992.

PATTERNS
Amy
Autumn Leaf
Basket
Becky
Birds and Flowers
Blue Rhythm, 1959
Bouquet
Boyce
Brim
Calico Tulip
Cameo Rose, 1940s
Cameo Shellware, 1940s
Cherry
Cherry Blossom
Cherry Trim
Chesterton, 1945–1965
Children's Plates
Colonial Lady
Cottage

Countryside
Deco-Dahlia
Enchantment
Engraved Rooster
Forest Flower
Forever Yours
Fruits
Garden Trail
Heritance
Ivy
Ivy Vine
Jessica
Laurelton
Leaf and Flower
Leaf Swirl
Lotus, 1960s
Mallow
Modern Tulip, 1930s
Pansy

Pastel Tulip
Pate Sur Pate
Petit Point Rose
Pine Cone
Provincial Tulip, 1959
Provincial Wreath
Puritan
Quaker Maid, 1960s
Rawhide, 1960s
Red Apple 1
Red Apple 2
Rooster
Rose Spray
Rosettes
Royal Rose

Ruffled Tulip
Shellridge
Silhouette
Slender Leaf
Springtime
Sun-Glo, 1955
Taverne (Rolling Pin)
Teal Rose, 1952
Vine
Vintage, 1947–1949
Wheat, 1961
White Clover, until 1955
White Rose, 1940s
Wood Song

Harmony House, see Sears, Roebuck and Co.

Homer Laughlin China Company, East Liverpool, Ohio, 1877–1929, and Newell, West Virginia, 1905–present

REFERENCE BOOKS

Homer Laughlin China Company: A Fiesta of American Dinnerware. Newell, West Virginia: Homer Laughlin China Co., 1985.

Huxford, Sharon and Bob. *Collector's Encyclopedia of Fiesta.* 7th edition. Paducah, Kentucky: Collector Books, 1992.

Jasper, Joanne. *The Collector's Encyclopedia of Homer Laughlin China: Reference & Value Guide.* Paducah, Kentucky: Collector Books, 1993.

Nossaman, Darlene. *Homer Laughlin China: An Identification Guide.* Revised edition. Privately printed, 1994 (5419 Lake Charles, Waco, TX 76710).

Riederer, LaHoma, and Charles Bettinger. *Fiesta III: A Collector's Guide to Fiesta Dinnerware.* Privately printed, 1980 (P.O. Box 2733, Monroe, LA 71201).

Snyder, Jeffrey B. *Fiesta: Homer Laughlin China Company's Colorful Dinnerware.* Atglen, Pennsylvania: Schiffer Publishing Ltd., 1997.

PATTERNS

Amberstone, 1967
American Provincial
Apple Blossom, 1935–1955
April
Aristocrat
Bermuda, 1977–1978

Bimini, 1977–1978
Blue Dresden, 1949
Blue Medallion, 1920
Blue Symphony
Bolero, 1977–1978
Briar Rose, 1933

Brittany, 1936–1950s
Call Rose
Capri
Carnation Beauty, 1920
Carnival, late 1930s–early 1940s
Cashmere
Casualstone, 1970
Cavalier, 1950s–1970s
Century, 1931–present
Chateau
Chinese Buddha, 1950s
Clive
Columbine, 1950s
Conchita, 1938
Conchita Kitchen Kraft, 1930s
Coronet, 1935
Country Road, 1977–1978
Crazy Quilt, 1977–1978
Currier & Ives, 1950s
Daisy, 1962–1968
Debutante, 1948–early 1960s
Dick Tracy, 1950
Dogwood, 1960s
Duraprint, 1950s
Early American, 1960s
Eggshell, 1930s–1950s
Eggshell Georgian, 1933–1960s
Eggshell Nautilus, 1937–1950s
Eggshell Theme, 1940s
Elegant Modern
Empress, 1919–1940s
English Garden, 1933
Epicure, 1955
Fiesta, 1936–1972
Fiesta Ironstone, 1970–1972
Fiesta Kitchen Kraft, 1939–early 1940s
Fiesta Wood
Fleur de Lis
Flight of the Swallows, 1930s
Flower Power, 1977–1978
Flowers of the Dell, 1930s

Flying Bluebird, 1920
Fruit Basket, 1977–1978
Gold & Cobalt, 1920
Gold Floral Band, 1920
Gold Garland, 1920
Gold Lace over Cobalt Blue, 1920
Golden Wheat, 1953–1958
Green Valley, 1977–1978
Hacienda, 1938
Harlequin, 1938–1964; 1979
Hollyhock
Jubilee, 1948; 1977–1978
June Rose, 1935
Kitchen Bouquet
Kitchen Kraft, 1930s
Kwaker, 1901–1940s
Lady Alice
Lady Greenbriar
Lady Stratford
Lexington
Liberty, 1928–1950s
Lido, 1977–1978
Louise
Madrid, 1977–1978
Magnolia
Margaret Rose
Marigold, 1930s–1960s
Max-i-cana, 1930s
Mexicana, 1930s
Mexicana Kitchen Kraft, 1938
Mirador, 1977–1978
Nassau
Nautilus, 1930s–1950s
New Art, 1930s
Newell, 1927–1937
Nordic, 1977-1978
Norway Rose
Old English
Orange Tree
Orbit, 1960s
Organdy

Paradise
Petitpoint, 1960s
Piccadilly, 1940s–1950s
Pinecone Spray
Pink Moss Rose, 1920
Pink Rose, 1920
Pink Rose & Daisy, 1920
Priscilla, 1940s–1950s
Queen Esther, 1928
Rambler Rose
Ravenna
Raymond, 1926
Red Tulip
Republic, 1900–1940s
Rhythm, 1951–1958
Rhythm Rose, mid-1940s–1950s
Riviera, 1938–1950
Romance
Rose & Lattice, 1920
Rose Garland Border, 1920
Rosetta
Royal Harvest
Serenade, 1939–1940s
Silver Rose, 1960s
Skyblue, 1977–1978
Skytone
Snowflake, 1920
Sonesta, 1977–1978
Sorrento, 1977–1978

Spring Song
Stardust, 1940s–1950s
Sun Gold, 1953
Sun Porch
Swing, 1938–1950s
Tango, 1930s
Theme, 1939–1990s
Tom Thumb & the Butterfly
Tulip Tree, 1977–1978
Tulip Wreath
Tulips, 1930s
Violet Spray, 1920
Virginia Rose, 1935–1960
Waverly, 1977–1978
Wells, 1930–1935
White & Gold, 1920
White & Gold Carnation, 1920
White & Green Persian, 1920
Wild Bouquet, 1977–1978
Wild Rose
Wild Rose & Flower, 1920
Willow, 1942
Winged Streamliner
Yellow Carnation, 1962–1968
Yellow Matte Gold, 1920
Yellow Matte Gold Band, 1920
Yellowstone, 1927
Zinnia, 1977–1978

A. E. Hull Pottery Company, Crooksville, Ohio, 1905–1986 (Hull Pottery Company, 1952–1986)

REFERENCE BOOKS

Hull, Joan Gray. *Hull Shirt Pocket Price List.* Privately printed, 1994 (1376 Nevada SW, Huron, SD 57350).

―――. *Hull: The Heavenly Pottery.* 2nd edition. Privately printed, 1992 (1376 Nevada SW, Huron, SD 57350).

Roberts, Brenda. *Roberts' Ultimate Encyclopedia of Hull Pottery.* Privately printed, 1992 (Rt. 2, Highway 65 S., Marshall, MO 65340).

―――. *Collectors Encyclopedia of Hull Pottery.* Paducah, Kentucky: Collector Books, 1980.

————. *Companion Guide to Roberts' Ultimate Encyclopedia of Hull Pottery.* Privately printed, 1992 (Route 2, Highway 65 S., Marshall, MO 65340).

PATTERNS

Crestone   Red Riding Hood, 1943–1957

Iroquois China Company, Syracuse, New York, 1905–1969

PATTERNS

Carrara Modern, 1955   Intaglio
Casual China (Russel Wright), 1946   Iroquois, 1959–mid 1960s
Impromptu, 1956

James River Potteries, Hopewell, Virginia, 1922–1938

PATTERNS

Isle of Palms   Pocahontas

Jewel Tea Company, see Hall Autumn Leaf

Johnson Brothers, Ltd., Hanley, England 1883–present (now part of Waterford Wedgwood Group)

REFERENCE BOOKS

Finegan, Mary J. *Johnson Brothers Dinnerware Pattern Directory & Price Guide.* Privately printed, 1993 (Marfine Antiques, P.O. Box 3618, Boone, NC 28607).

PATTERNS

Friendly Village, 1953–present

Edwin M. Knowles China Company, Chester, West Virginia, 1900–1931, and Newell, West Virginia, 1913–1963. (The trademark was sold to another company in Chester, West Virginia, that makes "collector plates," 1975–present)

PATTERNS

Allure, 1960   Botanica, 1955–1962
Ambassador, 1948   Breath O'Spring, 1960
Bench   Brown Leaf, 1954
Berkeley, 1955   Buttercup, 1948
Black-Eyed Susan, 1959   Caprice, 1954
Blossomtime, 1958   Carlton, 1955
Blue Bells, 1954   Carmen, 1958
Border Rim   Cattails, 1955

Celeste, 1961–1963

Celestial, 1955

Chalet, 1955

Choreography, 1955

Classic, 1954–1955

Columbia, 1948

Coral Pine, 1954

Cornflower Blue, 1930s

Coronado, 1948

Corsage, 1954

Country Fair, 1955

Daisies

Damask Rose, 1954

Dawn Rose, 1958

Deanna

Debussy, 1961–1963

Delft, 1957

Dubarry, 1948

Dubonnet, 1955

Duet, 1961–1963

Ebonite, 1954

Eldorado, 1948

Equation, 1955

Evening Song, 1960

Fantasy, 1955

Feather Fantasy, 1955

Festival, 1955; 1957

Fjord, 1959

Fleur de Lis, 1955

Fleurette, 1959

Flight, 1957

Flora, 1948–1955

Florence, 1933–1934

Florida, 1948

Flower Basket

Foliage, 1961–1963

Four Seasons White, 1959–1963

Frosted Leaves, 1955

Fruits

Garden Magic, 1960

Garland, 1948

Golden Foliage, 1960–1963

Golden Laurel, 1930

Golden Wheat, 1936

Golden Wreath, 1960

Gourmet, 1956

Grass, 1957–1962

Green Wheat

Greenbriar, 1959

Happy Days, 1957

Hen Party, 1954

High Sierra, 1955

Highlands, 1957

Hors-d'Oeuvres, 1955

Ingrid, 1954

Isobella, 1948

Jamestown, 1961–1963

Knowles, 1955

Lacquer Blossom, 1957

Leaf Ballet, 1953–1954

Leaf Dane, 1960–1963

Leaf Spray

Lido, 1948

Lucerne, 1960

Mantilla, 1961–1963

Mayfair, 1957

Mayflower, 1957–1963

Meadow Gold, 1954

Ming Tree, c.1954

Mini Flowers

Modern Classic, 1960–1963

Moss Rose, 1954

Navarra, 1955

Nordic Flower, 1959

Oakleaf, 1955

Oslo, 1954

Palm Tree

Pantry Shelf

Park Lane, 1955

Peach Blossom, 1955

Penthouse

Picket Fence

Pink Dogwood, 1960
Pink Pastel
Poppy, 1948
Pretty Pinks, 1957
Provincial Bouquet, 1961–1963
Queen Anne's Lace, 1955–1962
Rambler Rose, 1930s
Reflection, 1960–1963
Rhonda, 1958
Ribbon, 1954
Ring-A-Round, 1959–1963
Romance, 1955
Rose
Rose Bouquet, 1933–1934
Rose Tree, 1955
Rosemont, 1948
Royal Brocade, 1957
Scandia, 1954
Scroll, 1955
Sea Fare, 1957
Seeds, 1956–1962
September Song, 1959
Sequoia, late 1930s
Serenade, 1960
Silver Spray, 1954
Simplicity, 1955
Skiffs
Skylark, 1959
Sleeping Mexican
Snowflower, 1956
Solar, 1957–1966
Southwind, 1959
Star Bright, 1957

Stratosphere, 1955–1957
Suburbia, 1956
Sun Glow, 1958
Sunburst, 1959
Sunnybrook Farm, 1957
Symmetry, 1959
Tea Rose, 1954
Tia Juana
Tiffany, 1955
Tradition, 1948
Tulip
Tuliptime, 1961–1963
Twin Oaks, 1954
Vestal Rose, 1930s
Victoria, 1959
Vintage, 1953–1954
Vistosa, 1936
Water Lily
Weather Bloom, 1933–1934
Weathervane, 1957
Wheat, 1954
Wheat Sheaf, 1955
Wild Oats, 1955
Wild Rose, Regent shape, 1948
Wild Rose, Floral Edge shape,
    1933–1934
Wildflower, 1933–1934
Williamsburg, 1961–1963
Wood Echo, 1957
Wood Violets, 1954
Wrightwood, 1930s
Yellow Trim Poppy
Yorktown, 1936

Leigh Potters, Inc., Alliance, Ohio, 1926–1938 (Crescent China Company, 1920–1926)

PATTERNS

Basket
Clio
Fuchsia

Glenedon
Green Wheat
Housetops

Indian Tree
Iris Bouquet
Madison
Manhattan

Mayfair
Petit Point, 1936
Tower
Tulip

Limoges, see Sebring Pottery Company

Metlox Potteries, Manhattan Beach, California, 1935–1989

REFERENCE BOOKS
Gibbs, Carl, Jr. *Collector's Encyclopedia of Metlox Potteries.* Paducah, Kentucky: Collector Books, 1996.

PATTERNS
Antique Grape, 1964
Blue Dahlia, 1969
Blueberry Provincial, 1962
Blues, 1978
Bottle Brush, 1979
Calico, 1977
California Contempora, 1955
California Apple, 1949
California Aztec, 1955
California Brownstone, 1976
California Confetti, 1955
California Del Rey, 1955
California Freeform, 1954
California Fruit, 1949
California Geranium, 1958
California Golden Blossom, 1953
California Ivy, 1946–1980
California Mobile, 1954
California Palm, 1958
California Peach Blossom, 1952
California Provincial, 1950–1980
California Rose, 1959
California Strawberry, 1961–1980
California Tempo, 1960s
California Whitestone, 1975
Camellia
Cape Cod, 1961

Central Park, 1953
Chantilly Blue, early 1980s
Colonial Heritage, 1956
Colorbands, 1979
Colorstax, 1978–1984
Country Side, 1950s
Della Robbia, 1965
Dill, 1979
Eucalyptus, 1979
Fleur-de-lis, 1964
Floralace, 1975
Geranium, 1976
Gold Dahlia, 1968
Golden Fruit, 1960
Golden Scroll, 1962
Grape Arbor, 1975
Happy Time, 1950s
Homestead Provincial, 1950–1980
Impression Series, 1971
Indiana Summer, 1953
Iris, 1978
Jamestown, 1957
Lavender Blue, 1980
Lotus, 1974
Luau, 1959
Macrame, 1977
Mardi Gras, 1955

Marguerite, 1978
Matilija, 1974
Mayan Necklace, 1964
Memories, early 1980s
Mission Gold, 1966
Mission Verde, 1966
Navajo, 1956
Oh' Susanna, 1975
Painted Desert, 1960
Palm Springs, 1962
Pepper Tree, 1957
Pink Lady, 1965
Pintoria, c. 1937
Pomegranate, 1976
Poppy Trail, 1934–1942
Primary Blue, 1977
Primary Blue Daisies, 1978
Primary Red, 1977
Primary Red Daisies, 1978
Primary Yellow, 1978
Primary Yellow Daisies, 1978
Provincial Blue, 1950–1968
Provincial Flower, 1962
Provincial Fruit, 1961–1980
Provincial Rose, 1958

Provincial Whitestone, 1977
Red Rooster, 1956–1980
Rhythm, 1978
Rooster Bleu, 1966
Sculptured Daisy, 1964
Sculptured Grape, 1963–1975
Sculptured Zinnia, 1964–1980
Shoreline, 1953
Silver Dollar, 1979
Strawflower, 1977
Street Scene, 1956
Tiffany, 1976
Tiffany Yellow, 1976
Tropicana, 1960
True Blue, 1965
Vine Yard, 1965
Vintage Pink, 1965
Wicker Strawberry, 1982
Wicker White, 1982
Wild Poppy, 1972
Wildflower, 1977
William, 1977
Winter Scene, 1950s
Woodland Gold, 1959
Yorkshire, 1939

Montgomery Ward (sold by Montgomery Ward)

PATTERNS

Blueberry, 1921
Cascade, 1936
Chartreuse, 1936
Corn Gold, 1921
Emerald, 1921
Fashion White, 1936
Floral Border, 1936
Gold Band, 1920–1936
Gold Initial, 1921

Gold Stripe, 1936
Petit Point, 1936
Pink Print, 1936
Red & Gold, 1936
Snowflake, 1936
Spring Bouquet, 1936
Ward's Garland, 1936
White and Embossed, 1920

Noritake China, Japan, 1904–present

REFERENCE BOOKS

Melvin, Florence, and Rodney and Wilma Bourdeau. *Noritake Azalea China: A Reference in Color for Collectors.* Privately printed, 1975 (Red White and Blue Shop, 2 Starr St., Danbury, CT 06810).

Stevenson, Ferne and David. *Noritake Azalea China,* Privately printed, 1987 (730 North 5th St., Hamburg, PA 19526).

PATTERNS

Azalela, 1918–1941 (made for Larkin Company)

Paden City Pottery, Paden City, West Virginia, 1914–1963

PATTERNS

Acacia Flowers

American Beauty

Arabian Night

Autumn Leaf

Blossoms

Bluebell

Caliente, 1940s

Capri, 1933

Corn

Corn Is Green

Duchess, 1942

Far East

Flaming Rose

Floral

Grandiose, 1952

Highlight, 1948

Ivy

Jonquil

Modern Orchid

Morning Glory

Nasturtium, 1940s

Orange Blossom

Paden Rose

Patio, 1907–1950s

Poppy

Posies

Red Rose

Rhythm, 1936

Rite of Spring

Rococo, 1933

Rust Tulip

Sea Shell

Springblossom

Strawberry

Touch of Black

Tulip

Wild Rose

Yellow Rose, 1952

Pope-Gosser China, Coshocton, Ohio, 1902–1958

PATTERNS

Florence, 1940s

Rose Point

Pottery Guild, New York, New York, 1937–1946

PATTERNS

Apples	Peach
Calico Flower	Pear
Calico Fruit	Sombrero
Hostess Pantry Ware, 1954	Tulips

Purinton Pottery, Wellsville, Ohio, 1936–1941; Shippenville, Pennsylvania, 1941–1951

REFERENCE BOOKS

Bero-Johnson, Jamie, and Jamie Johnson. *Purinton Pottery with Values.* Atglen, Pennsylvania: Schiffer Publishing Ltd., 1997.

Dole, Pat. *Purinton Pottery.* Privately printed, 1984 (P.O. Box 4782, Birmingham, AL 35206).

————. *Purinton Pottery Book II.* Privately printed, 1990 (142 W. Salisbury St., P.O. Box 308, Denton, NC 27239-0308).

Morris, Susan. *Purinton Pottery.* Paducah, Kentucky: Collector Books, 1994.

PATTERNS

Apple, 1940s–1959	Normandy Plaid, 1950s
Chartreuse, 1949–1959	Palm Tree, 1936–1959
Crescent	Palm Tree Intaglio
Fruit, 1940s	Peasant Garden
Harmony, 1949–1959	Pennsylvania Dutch, 1936–1959
Heather Plaid, 1950s	Petals, late 1940s–1959
Intaglio, 1950–1959	Provincial Fruit, 1950s
Maywood, 1950–1959	Saraband, early 1950s–1959
Ming Tree, 1950s	Seaform, mid-1950s–1959
Mountain Rose, 1940s–1959	Tea Rose, mid-1950s–1959

Red Wing Potteries, Inc., Red Wing, Minnesota, 1878–1967

REFERENCE BOOKS

Bougie, Stanley J., and David A. Newkirk. *Red Wing Dinnerware.* Privately printed, 1980 (Rt. 3, Box 141, Monticello, MN 55362).

Dollen, B. L. *Red Wing Art Pottery Identification & Value Guide, 1920s–1960s.* Paducah, Kentucky: Collector Books, 1997.

Newkirk, David A. *Guide to Red Wing Prices.* Privately printed, 1982 (Rt. 3, Box 146, Monticello, MN 55362).

Reiss, Ray. *Red Wing Art Pottery, Including Pottery Made for RumRill: Classic American Pottery from the 30s, 40s, 50s, & 60s.* Chicago: Property Publishing, 1996.

————. *Red Wing Dinnerware Price and Identification Guide.* Chicago: Property Publishing, 1997.

Simon, Dolores. *Red Wing Pottery with Rumrill.* Paducah, Kentucky: Collector Books, 1980.

PATTERNS

Adobestone, 1967

Ardennes, 1941

Blossom Time, 1941

Blue Shadows, 1964

Bob White, 1956–1967

Brittany, 1941

Brocade, 1964

Bud, 1941

Capistrano, 1953–1967

Caprice, 1952

Charstone Bleu, 1967

Chevron, 1935

Chrysanthemum, 1941

Chuck Wagon, 1955

Colonnes, 1960

Country Garden, 1953

Crazy Rhythm, 1960

Crocus, 1960

Daisy Chain, 1960

Damask, 1964

Delta Blue, 1951

Desert Sun, 1962

Driftwood, 1953

Ebb Tide, 1965

Fantasy, 1941

Flight, 1962

Fondoso, 1938

Frontenac, 1960

Fruit, 1941

Golden Viking, 1960

Granada, 1960

Greenwichstone, 1967

Harvest, 1941

Hearthside, 1955

Hearthstone, 1961

Heatherstone, 1967

Heatherstone Beige, 1967

Heatherstone Orange, 1967

Iris, 1941

Ivanhoe, 1937

Kashmir, 1964

Kermis, 1957

Labriego, 1942

Lanterns, 1941

Lexington, 1942

Lotus, 1941

Lupine, 1960

Lute Song, 1960s

Magnolia, 1941

Majestic, 1960

Mediterrania, 1960

Merrileaf, 1960

Midnight Rose, 1953

Montmartre, 1960

Morning Glory, 1941

Nassau, 1941

Normandy, 1941

Northern Lights, 1960

Orleans, 1941

Pepe, 1963

Picardy, 1951

Pink Spice, 1953

Plain, 1935

Plum Blossom, 1949

Pompeii, 1962

Provincial, 1951

Quartette, 1941

Random Harvest, 1961

Red Wing Rose, 1960

Reed, 1935

RoundUp, 1958

Smart Set, 1955

Spring Song, 1941
Spruce, 1956
Tahitian Gold, 1962
Tampico, 1955
Tip Toe, 1955
Town & Country, 1947–1954
Turtle Dove, 1962
Tweed Tex, 1953

Two Step, 1951
Village Brown, 1951
Village Green, 1951
Vintage, 1960
White and Turquoise, 1956
Willow Wind, 1941
Zinnia, 1941

Roseville Pottery Company, Zanesville, Ohio, 1892–1954

REFERENCE BOOKS
Huxford, Sharon and Bob. *The Collectors Encyclopedia of Roseville Pottery.* Paducah, Kentucky: Collector Books, 1976. Updated 1993 values.

PATTERNS
Raymor, 1952–1953

Royal China Company, Sebring, Ohio, 1933–1986

REFERENCE BOOKS
Aupperle, Eldon R. *A Collector's Guide for Currier & Ives Dinnerware.* Privately printed, 1996 (29470 Saxon Rd., Toulon, IL 61483).

PATTERNS
Bluebell, 1940s
Brentwood
Casa del Sol
Casablanca
Clear Day
Colonial Homestead, 1950–1952
Currier & Ives, 1940s–1986
Dynasty
Hidden Valley
Medici

Memory Lane
Middlebury
Night Song
Old Curiosity Shop, 1940s
Overture
Sunny Day
Triple Treat
Tulip
Willow, 1960s

Sabin Industries, McKeesport, Pennsylvania, 1946–1979

PATTERNS
Floral Birdsong, 1946
Golden Crown
Jacobean, 1946
Pastel Garden

Pompadour, 1946
Regal Rings, 1946
Tudor Rose

Salem China Company, Salem, Ohio, 1898–1967

PATTERNS

Anniversary, 1943
Aristocrat
Basket
Basket of Tulips
Basket Petit Point
Bluebird
Breeze, 1948
Bridge
Bryn-Mawr
Cadet Series
Cherry, 1951
Colonial
Commodore
Dominion
Dutch Petit Point
Formal
Fruit Basket
Garden Design, 1940s
Goldtrim, 1952
Indian Tree
Jane Adams, 1950s
Jeanette
Jonquil
Landscape, 1940s
Mandarin Red
Mandarin Tricorne

Maple Leaf
Midsummer
Monogram
Moon Flower
Parsley
Petit Point Basket
Polo
Red Berry
Rio, 1943
Rose-Marie
Royal Windsor, 1950s
Rust Tulip
Sailing
Sampler
Sandra, 1950s
Sheffield, 1943
Standard
Summer Day
Tricorne, 1934
Tulip
Victory
Vienna, 1940s
Windmill
Woodhue
Woodland
Yellowridge

Scio Pottery Company, Scio, Ohio, 1932–1985

PATTERNS

Currier & Ives
Dorset

Hazel

Sears, Roebuck and Company (sold by Sears, Roebuck and Company; pieces usually marked Harmony House or Sunrise)

PATTERNS

Acorn
Cat-Tail, made by Universal Potteries, 1934–1956

Colonial Homestead, made by Royal China Company, 1960s

Monticello, made by Hall China
Company, 1941–1959

Mt. Vernon, made by Hall China
Company, 1940s

Sebring Pottery Company, Sebring, Ohio, 1887–1955 (Sebring Pottery
Company, American Limoges China Company, and Salem China Company combined under same management, c.1940)

PATTERNS

Asbury, 1940s

Blue Willow

Buddah

Casino, c.1954

Chateau-France

Doric

Federal, 1942

Gadroon

Heirloom

Jade Ware, 1940s

Joan of Arc

Karen, 1940

Meerschaum, c.1940s

Midsummer, 1940

New Princess

Old Dutch

Old Mexico

Old Virginia Fashionware, 1942

Posey Shop, 1944–1945

Red Poppy Head

Red Sails, c.1940s

Rose Marie

Royal Marina, 1944–1945

Ship Ahoy, 1940s

Square

Tahiti, 1938

Thin Swirl

Toledo Delight, 1941–1942

Triumph

Trojan

Vermillion Rose

Waldorf, 1939

Wheatfield

White Gold Ware, 1940s

Shawnee Pottery Company, Zanesville, Ohio, 1936–1961

REFERENCE BOOKS

Curran, Pamela Duvall. *Shawnee Pottery: The Full Encyclopedia with Value Guide.*
Atglen, Pennsylvania: Schiffer Publishing Ltd., 1995.

Mangus, Jim and Bev. *Shawnee Pottery: An Identification & Value Guide.* Paducah,
Kentucky: Collector Books, 1994.

Simon, Dolores. *Shawnee Pottery.* Paducah, Kentucky: Collector Books, 1977.

Supnick, Mark E. *Collecting Shawnee Pottery.* Revised edition. Gas City, Indiana:
L-W Book Sales, c.1989. Revised 1997 price guide.

Vanderbilt, Duane and Janice. *The Collector's Guide to Shawnee Pottery.* Paducah,
Kentucky: Collector Books, 1992.

PATTERNS

Corn King, 1954

Corn Queen, 1954–1961

Lobster Ware, 1954–1956

Southern Potteries, Inc. (Blue Ridge), Erwin, Tennessee, 1917–1957

REFERENCE BOOKS

Keillor, Winnie. *Dishes What Else? Blue Ridge of Course!* Privately printed, 1983
(5731 Gorivan Rd., Frankfort, MI 49635).

Newbound, Betty and Bill. *Southern Potteries Incorporated: Blue Ridge Dinnerware.*
3rd edition. Paducah, Kentucky: Collector Books, 1989.

Ruffin, Frances and John. *Blue Ridge China Today: A Comprehensive Identification
and Price Guide for Today's Collector.* Atglen, Pennsylvania: Schiffer Publishing
Ltd., 1997.

PATTERNS

Abundance
Alexandria
Alleghany
Aloaha, 1950s
Amarylis
Amherst
Anemone
Antique Leaf
Appalachian Spring
Apple & Pear, 1950s
Apple Crisp, 1950s
Apple Crunch, 1948
Apple Jack, 1950s
Arlene
Arlington Apple, 1950s
Ashland
Astor Fruit
Atlanta, 1950s
Aurora
Autumn Apple, 1941
Autumn Breeze, 1950s
Autumn Laurel
Bamboo, 1950s
Barbara
Bardstown, 1950s
Basketweave, 1950s
Beaded Apple
Beatrice, 1950s
Becky
Belle Haven, 1950s
Bellemeade
Berea Blossom
Berry Patch, 1950s
Berryville
Bethany Berry, 1950s
Betty, 1950s
Big Apple
Bittersweet, 1950s
Black Ming, 1950s
Blackberry Lily
Bleeding Heart
Blossom Tree, 1950s
Blue Bouquet
Blue Flower
Blue Heaven
Blue Moon
Blue Tango
Blue Willow
Bluebell Bouquet
Bluefield
Bonsai, 1950s
Bosc
Bountiful
Bouquet
Bourbon Rose
Bow Knot
Bramwell
Breckenridge
Briar Patch
Bridal Bouquet

Bristol Bouquet
Bristol Lily
Brittany
Brownie
Brunswick
Buttercup
Butterfly and Leaves
Cactus
Cadenza, 1948
Caladium, 1950s
Calais
Calico
Calico Farm, 1950s
California Poppy, 1950s
Callaway, 1948
Camelot, 1948
Candied Fruit
Cantata, 1948
Carlise
Carnival
Caroline, 1950s
Carretta Cattail, 1950s
Cassandra
Cattails, 1950s
Champagne Pinks, 1940s–1950s
Chanticleer, 1950s
Cheerio, 1950s
Cherokee Rose, 1950s
Cherries Jubilee
Cherry Blossom
Cherry Cobbler
Cherry Coke
Chicken Feed, 1950s
Chicken Pickins, 1950s
Chickory
Chintz
Christmas Doorway, 1950s
Christmas Tree
Chrysanthemum
Cinnabar
Clairborne

Clover, 1947–1954
Cock o' the Morn, 1950s
Cock o' the Walk, 1948
Cock-a-Doodle, 1950s
Cocky-Locky
Colonial Birds No. 1
Colonial Birds No. 2
Colonial Rose
Color Stitch
Columbine, 1950s
Concorde
Confetti
Constance
Coreopsis
Corsage
Cosmos, 1950s
Country Fruit, 1950s
Country Garden
Country Road
County Fair
Cowslip
Crab Apple, 1930–1957
Crab Orchard
Cradle
Crocus
Cross Stitch
Cumberland, 1948
Cynthia, 1949
Daffodil, 1948
Dahlia, 1948
Dandridge Dogwood, 1950s
Daydream
Deep Purple
Delft Rose
Delicious
Della Robbia, 1948
Desert Flower, 1950s
Dewberry
Dixie Harvest (No. 3913), 1949
Dogwood, 1950s
Dream Flower

Dreambirds
Dresden Doll
Duff
Dutch Bouquet
Dutch Iris
Dutch Tulip
Edgemont
Eglantine
Evening Flower, 1950s
Eventide, 1950s
Fairmede Fruits
Fairmount, 1950s
Fairy Bells
Fairy Tale
Falling Leaves
Falmouth, 1950s
Fantasia, 1950s
Fantasy Apple, 1950s
Farmer Takes a Wife
Farmhouse, 1950s
Farmyard, 1950s
Fayette Fruit
Feathered Friends, 1950s
Festive, 1950s
Field Daisy
Fireside, 1950s
Fisherman
Flight, 1950s
Flirt, 1950s
Flounce
Flower Bowl
Flower Fantasy, 1954
Flower Ring
Flower Wreath
Floweret, 1950s
Flowering Berry
Fluffy Ruffles
Forest Fruits, 1950s
Fox Grape
Foxfire, 1950s
Frageria, 1950s

French Peasant
Fruit Cocktail
Fruit Fantasy
Fruit Punch
Fruit Ring
Fruit Salad
Fruit Sherbet
Fruitful
Fuchsia
Full Bloom
Gaity
Garden Flowers
Garden Lane
Garden Pinks, 1950s
Garland
Gingham Fruit, 1950s
Gooseberry
Grandfather's Clock
Grandmother's Garden
Granny Smith Apple, 1950s
Grape Salad
Grass Flower, 1950s
Green Briar, 1948
Green Eyes, 1950s
Greensville, 1950s
Gumdrop Tree
Gypsy
Gypsy Dancer
Ham 'n Eggs
Harvestime, 1950s
Hawaiian Fruit, 1948
Heirloom
High Stepper
Highland Ivy, 1949
Hilda
Hollyberry
Hollyhock
Homeplace, 1950s
Homestead, 1950s
Honolulu
Hopscotch

Jan
Jellico, 1950s
Jessamine, 1948
Jessica
Jigsaw, 1950s
Joanna
Jonquil
Joyce
June Apple, 1950s
June Bouquet
June Bride
June Rose
Karen
Kate
Kimberly, 1950s
Kingsport
Kitchen Shelf
Language of Flowers
Laura
Laurie
Lavalette, 1950s
Lavender Fruit
Leaves of Fall, 1950s
Ledford
Lenore
Lexington
Little Violet
Liz
Louisiana Lace
Love Song
Madras
Magic Flower
Magnolia, 1948
Manassas
Maple Leaf, 1950s
Mardi Gras, 1943
Mardi Gras Variant
Mariner
Mary
Mayflower, 1950s
Meadow Beauty

Meadowlea, 1950s
Medley
Memory Lane
Memphis
Meylinda
Mickey
Ming Blossom, 1950s
Ming Tree (No. 4387), 1950s
Mod Tulip
Moss Rose (No. 4486), 1950s
Mountain Aster
Mountain Bells
Mountain Cherry, 1951
Mountain Ivy, 1951
Mountain Nosegay
Mountain Sweetbriar, 1950s
Muriel
Nadine
Nautical
Night Flower, 1952
Nocturne
Norma
Normandy, 1950s
North Star Cherry
Obion
Orchard Glory
Oriental Poppy
Orion
Painted Daisy
Pandora
Paper Roses
Partridge Berry, 1950s
Pastel Poppy
Patchwork Posy
Patricia, 1950s
Pauline
Pembrooke
Penny Serenade
Peony
Peony Bouquet
Periwinkle

Petunia
Picardy
Piedmont Plaid
Pilgrims, 1950s
Pinecone, 1950s
Pink Dogwood, 1950s
Pink Petticoat
Pinkie, 1950s
Pippin, 1950s
Plantation Ivy, 1950s
Plum
Plum Duff
Plume
Poinsettia, 1950
Polka Dot
Pom Pom
Potpourri
Primrose Path
Priscilla
Pristine
Queen Anne's Lace, 1950s
Quilted Fruit, 1950s
Quilted Ivy, 1950s
Rainelle
Razzle Dazzle, 1950s
Red Apple
Red Bank
Red Barn, 1950s
Red Cone Flower
Red Rooster
Red Tulip
Red Willow
Rhapsody
Ribbon Plaid, 1950s
Ridge Rose
Ring-O-Roses, 1948
Roan Mountain Rose
Roanoke
Rock Castle, 1950s
Rock Garden, 1950s
Rock Rose
Rockport Rooster

Rooster (or Game Cock), 1950s
Rooster Motto
Rosalinde
Rose Hill
Rose Red
Rosette
Rosey, 1950s
Roundelay (No. 4499)
Ruby
Rugosa
Rustic Plaid, 1950s
Rutledge
Sampler, 1948
Saratoga, 1952
Sarepta
Shadow Fruit, 1950s
Sherry
Shoo Fly
Showgirl
Signal Flags, 1948
Silhouette, 1950s
Skyline Songbirds, 1950s
Smoky Mountain Laurel
Snappy
Soddy-Daisy, 1950s
Sonata, 1950s
Songbirds
Southern Camellia, 1948
Southern Dogwood, 1950s
Sowing Seed
Spiderweb, 1950s
Spindrift
Spray, 1950s
Spring Glory
Spring Hill Tulip
Square Dance
Squares, 1950s
Stanhome Ivy, 1954
Stardancer
Still Life
Strathmoor
Strawberry Patch

Strawberry Sundae, 1950s
Streamers, 1950s
Sun Drops
Sunbright
Sundance
Sundowner
Sunfire
Sunflower, 1947
Sungold
Sunny
Sunrise, 1950s
Sunshine
Susan, 1950s
Susannah
Sweet Clover
Sweet Pea
Sweet Rocket, 1950s
Symphony
Tanglewood
Tazewell Tulips
Tempo, 1948
Texas Rose
Thanksgiving Turkey, 1950s
Think Pink
Thistle, 1954
Tic Tack, 1948
Tickled Pink
Tiger Lily
Tropical, 1920–1957
Tulip Trio
Tuliptime
Tuna Salad, 1950s
Turkey with Acorns, 1950s

Unicoi
Valley Violet
Vegetable Patch, 1950s
Veggie, 1950s
Verona
Veronica
Victoria
Vintage
Violet Spray, 1950s
Waltz Time
Waterlily
Weathervane (No. 4277), 1950s
Wheat, 1950s
Whirligig, 1950s
Wild Cherry No. 1, 1950s
Wild Cherry No. 2, 1950s
Wild Cherry No. 3, 1950s
Wild Irish Rose
Wild Rose
Wild Strawberry
Wildfire
Wildwood
Windflower, 1940s
Windjammer
Winesap, 1950s
Winnie, 1950s
Wishing Well, 1950s
Wren
Wrinkled Rose
Yellow Poppy
Yorktown
Zinnia

Stangl Pottery, Flemington and Trenton, New Jersey, 1930–1978

REFERENCE BOOKS

Duke, Harvey. *Stangl Pottery.* Radnor, Pennsylvania: Wallace-Homestead, 1993.

Rehl, Norma. *Collectors Handbook of Stangl Pottery.* Privately printed, 1979 (P.O. Box 556, Milford, NJ 08848).

———. *Stangl Pottery, Part II.* Privately printed, 1982 (P.O. Box 556, Milford, NJ 08848).

PATTERNS

ABC, mid-1940s–1974
Adrian, 1972–1974
Amber Glo, 1954–1962
Americana, 1930s
Antiqua, 1972–1974
Apple Delight, 1965–1974
Aztec, 1967–1968
Bachelor's Button, 1965
Bella Rosa, 1960–1962
Bit Series, mid-1940s–1974
Bittersweet
Blossom Ring, 1967–1970
Blue Bell, 1942
Blue Carousel, mid-1940s–1974
Blue Daisy, 1963–1974
Blue Elf, mid-1940s–1974
Blue Tulip
Blueberry, 1940
Bo Peep, mid-1940s–1974
Bonita
Brown Satin
Bunny Lunch, mid-1940s–1974
Carnival, 1954–1957
Cat and the Fiddle, mid-1940s–1974
Cherry, 1940
Chicory, 1961
Circus Clown, mid-1940s–1974
Colonial, 1926
Colonial Dogwood
Colonial Rose, 1970–1974
Colonial Silver, 1970
Concord, 1957
Cookie Twins, mid-1940s–1971
Cosmos
Country Garden, 1956–1974
Country Life, 1956–1967
Cranberry
Crocus
Dahlia, 1970–1974
Daisy, 1936–1942

Deco-Delight
Delmar, 1972–1974
Diana, 1972–1974
Dogwood, 1965
Ducky Dinners, mid-1940s–1974
Fairlawn, 1959–1962
Festival, 1961–1967
Field Daisy, 1941–1942
First Love, 1968–1973
Five Little Pigs, mid-1940s–1974
Flora, 1941
Floral, 1941–1942
Floral Plaid, 1940–1942
Florentine, 1958
Florette, 1961–1962
Frosted Fruit, 1957
Fruit, 1942–1974
Fruit & Flowers, 1957–1974
Galaxy, 1963–1970
Garden Flower, 1947–1957
Garland, 1957–1967
Ginger Boy, mid-1940s–1974
Ginger Cat, mid-1940s–1974
Ginger Girl, mid-1940s–1974
Golden Blossom, 1964–1974
Golden Grape, 1963–1972
Golden Harvest, 1953–1973
Grape, 1973–1974
Green Grapes
Harvest
Heritage
Holly, 1967–1972
Humpty Dumpty, mid-1940s–1974
Indian Campfire, mid-1940s–1974
Inspiration, 1967–1968
Jack in the Box, mid-1940s–1974
Jonquil
Kitten Capers, mid-1940s–1974
Kumquat
Laurel, 1942

Laurita
Lime, 1950
Little Boy Blue, mid-1940s–1974
Little Quackers, mid-1940s–1974
Lyric, 1954–1957
Magnolia, 1952–1962
Maple Whirl, 1965–1967
Mary Quite, mid-1940s–1974
Mealtime Special, mid-1940s–1974
Mediterranean, 1965–1974
Monterey, 1967–1968; 1970
Morning Blue, 1970
Mother Hubbard, mid-1940s–1974
Mountain Laurel, 1947–1957
Newport, 1940–1942
Norma
Old Orchard, 1941–1942
Olivia
Orchard Song, 1962–1974
Our Barnyard Friends
Paisley, 1963–1967
Peter Rabbit
Petite Flowers, 1970–1974
Pie Crust, 1969
Pink Carousel, mid-1940s–1974
Pink Cosmos, 1966
Pink Dogwood
Pink Fairy, mid-1940s–1974
Pink Lily, 1953–1957
Playful Pups, mid-1940s–1974
Plum, 1940
Pony Tail, mid-1940s–1974
Posies, 1973
Prelude, 1949–1957

Provincial, 1957–1967
Ranger
Ranger Boy, mid-1940s–1974
Red Ivy, 1957
Rialto
Ringles, 1973–1974
Rooster, 1970–1974
Roxanne, 1972–1974
Rustic, 1965–1974
Rustic Garden, 1972–1974
Sculptured Fruit, 1966–1974
Sesame, 1972–1974
Sierra, 1967/1968–1970
Spun Gold, 1965–1967
Star Flower, 1952–1957
Stardust, 1967
Sunshine
Susan, 1972–1974
Terra Rose, 1941–1942
Thistle, 1951–1967
Tiger Lily, 1957–1962
Town & Country, 1970s
Trinidad, 1972–1974
Tulip, 1942–1973
Water Lily, 1949–1957
White Dogwood, 1965–1974
White Grape, 1967
Wild Rose, 1955–1973
Wildwood
Windfall, 1955–1957
Wizard of Oz, mid-1940s–1974
Woman in the Shoe, mid-1940s–1974
Wood Rose, 1973–1974
Yellow Flower, 1970

Sterling China Co., East Liverpool, Ohio, 1917–present

REFERENCE BOOKS

Sterling Vitrified China. Catalog. East Liverpool, Ohio: Sterling China Company, 1991.

PATTERNS

Russel Wright, 1948   Sterling, 1947

Steubenville Pottery Company, Steubenville, Ohio, 1879–c.1960

PATTERNS

Adam	Rhea
American Modern, 1939–1959	Rose Bud
Aztec	Shalimar
Aztec on Desert Sand	Spring
Jean	Susan
Lenore	Tyrol
Monticello	Violet
Pate-Sur-Pate	Woodfield
Remembrance	

Sunrise, see Sears, Roebuck and Company

Syracuse China Corporation, Syracuse, New York, 1871–present

PATTERNS

Edmonton
Rose Leaf
Traveler, 1937–1969
Vogue

Taylor, Smith and Taylor, Chester, West Virginia, and East Liverpool, Ohio, 1901 (sold to Anchor Hocking Corporation in 1972; production ended in 1981)

REFERENCE BOOKS

Meehan, Kathy and Bill. *Collector's Guide to Lu-Ray Pastels.* Paducah, Kentucky: Collector Books, 1995.

PATTERNS

Alia Jane, 1933–1934	Coffee Time, 1950s
Autumn Harvest	Conversation, 1951
Beverly, 1940	Coral-Craft, 1939
Blue Crocus, 1940	Daisy
Boutonnier, 1958–1965	Design 69
Bridal Flower	Dianthus, 1958–1965
Center Bouquet, 1930–1940	Dogwood, 1942
Chinese Temple, 1937	Dutch Tulip, 1940

Dwarf Pine, 1950
Emma Susan, 1933–1934
Ever Yours, 1958–1965
Fairway, 1934–1940s
Floral Bouquet, early 1930s
Garland, 1933–1942
Green Dots, early 1930s
Happy Talk, 1958–1965
Heathertone, 1930–1940
King O' Dell, 1950s
Laurel, 1930s
Leaf
Lu-Ray, after 1938
Mexican Fantasy, 1940
Morningside, late 1920s
Moulin Rouge, 1958–1965
Mums
Pebbleford, 1958–1965
Peppermint Roc, 1960–1972

Petit Point
Petit Point Bouquet, late 1920s
Platinum Blue, 1960s
Red Wheat, 1938
Reveille, 1958–1965
Rooster, 1950–1960
Rose Lattice, 1930–1940
Shasta Daisy, 1960s
Sirocco, 1960s
Sweet Pea
Taverne
Touch of Brown
Tulips
Twilight Time, 1958–1965
Versatile, 1950
Vine Wreath, 1933–1934
Vistosa, 1938
Wood Flower, 1960s

Universal Potteries, Inc., Cambridge, Ohio, 1934–1956

PATTERNS

Autumn Fancy
Ballerina, 1947–1956
Ballerina Mist, 1950s
Bird in the Heart
Bittersweet, 1942–1949
Calico Fruit, 1940s
Cat-Tail, 1934–1956
Fountain, 1950
Fruit & Flowers
Hazelnut
Hollyhock
Iris

Largo
Mermaid, 1950
Moss Rose, 1953–1955
Painted Desert, 1950
Passy, 1950
Rambler Rose
Roxanna
Thistle
Tulip
Windmill
Woodvine

Vernon Kilns, Los Angeles and Vernon, California, 1912–1958 (name and molds purchased by Metlox Potteries)

REFERENCE BOOKS

Nelson, Maxine. *Collectible Vernon Kilns: An Identification & Value Guide.* Paducah, Kentucky: Collector Books, 1994.

———. *Versatile Vernon Kilns.* Privately printed, 1978 (P.O. Box 1686, Huntington Beach, CA 92647).

———. *Versatile Vernon Kilns Book II.* Paducah, Kentucky: Collector Books, 1983.

PATTERNS

Abundance, 1939
After Glow, 1935–1937
Anytime, 1955–1958
Aquarium, 1938
Arcadia, 1942; 1950–1955
Autumn Ballet, 1940
Banana Tree, 1937
Banded Flower, 1935–1937
Barkwood, 1953–1958
Beige, 1935–1937
Bel Air, 1940; 1955
Bellflower, 1939
Beverly, 1942
Bird Pottery, early 1930s
Bird's Eye
Blend No. 4, 1938
Blend No. 10, 1938
Blossom Time, 1942
Blossoms, 1937
Blue Bow, 1938
Blue Feather, 1938
Blue Star (Constellation), 1938
Blueberry Hill, 1957–1958
Bouquet, 1938
Briar Rose, 1944
Brown Eyed Susan, 1938–1958
Calico, 1949–1955
California Originals, 1947; 1954
California Series, 1930s
California Shadows, 1953; 1955
Carmel, 1942–1950
Casa California, 1938
Casual California, 1947–1956
Chatelaine, 1953
Chinling, 1950
Chintz, 1942; 1950
Choice, 1939

Coastline, 1937
Colleen, 1939
Coral Reef, 1940
Coronado, 1935–1939 (grocery promotion)
Cosmos, 1942
Cottage Window, 1937
Country Cousin, 1957–1958
Country Side, 1950
Dainty, 1935–1947
Delight, 1940
Desert Bloom, 1944; 1955
Desert Mallow
Dewdrop Fairies, 1940
Dis 'N Dot, 1957–1958
Disney, 1940–1941
Dolores, 1942–1947
Dreamtime, 1950
Duo-Tone, 1938
Early California, 1935–1947
Early Days, 1944; 1950–1955
Ecstasy, 1940
Enchantment, 1940
Evening Star, 1935–1937
Fairyland, 1940
Fantasia, 1940
Five Fingers, 1938
Fleur de Lis
Flora, 1938
Floral Series, 1935–1937
Floret, 1939
Flower Ballet, 1940
Four Winds, 1950
Frolic, 1955
Frontier Days, 1950; 1954
Fruitdale, 1942–1947
Garden Plates, 1938

Gayety, 1948; 1954
Gingham, 1949–1958
Glamour, 1938
Golden Maple, 1935–1937
Good Earth
Grace, 1939
Harvest, 1938
Hawaii, 1942
Hawaiian Coral, 1952; 1956
Hawaiian Flowers, 1938
Heavenly Days, 1956–1958
Heyday, 1954–1958
Hibiscus, 1944; 1954
Hilo, 1938
Homespun, 1949–1958
Honolulu, 1938
Imperial, 1955–1956
Joy, 1940
Lei Lani, 1938–1942; 1947–1955
Linda, 1940
Little Mission, 1937
Lollipop Tree, 1957–1958
Lotus, 1950
Marine, 1937
Mariposa Tulip
May and Vieve Hamilton
May Flower, 1942–1955
Meadow Bloom, 1947
Melinda, 1942
Mexicana, 1950–1955
Michigan Coastline, 1937
Milkweed Dance, 1940
Moby Dick, 1939
Modern California, 1937–1947
Mojave, 1955
Montecito, 1935
Monterey, 1942; 1950–1954
Montezuma-Aztec, 1937
Morning Glory
Multi Flori California, 1935–1937
Native American, 1935–1937

Native California, 1942–1947
North Wind, 1948
Nutcracker, 1940
Olinala (Olena)-Aztec, 1937
Orchard, 1937; 1939
Organdie, 1940s & 1950s
Our America, 1939
Palm Brocade, 1950
Pan American Lei, 1950
Pear Turnpike
Pedro & Conchita, 1937
Peppers, 1937
Phacelia
Philodendron, 1942; 1950–1954
Polychrome A, 1935–1937
Pomegranate, 1935–1937
R.F.D., 1951–1953; 1954
Raffia, 1950
Raisin
Rio Chico, 1938
Rio Verda, 1938
Rio Vista, 1938
Rosa, 1938
Rose-A-Day, 1958
Rosedale, 1950
Salamina, 1939
Santa Anita, 1942
Santa Barbara, 1939
Santa Clara, 1939
Santa Maria, 1939
Santa Paula, 1939
Seven Seas, 1954
Shadow Leaf, 1954–1955
Shantung, 1953
Sherwood, 1955–1958
Sierra Madre, 1938
Southern Rose, 1942
Spice Islands, 1950
Style, 1939
Sun Garden, 1953
Tahiti A, B, C

Tam O'Shanter, 1939
Taste, 1939
Tickled Pink, 1955–1958
Trade Winds, 1954–1956
Trailing Rose, 1939
Trellis, 1935–1937
Tweed, 1950–1955
Two-Some, 1938
Two-Tone, 1938
Ultra California, 1937–1942
Vera, 1938

Vernon 1860, 1944; 1955
Vernon Rose, 1944; 1950–1954
Victoria, 1939
Vintage, 1950
Walt Disney, 1941
Wheat, 1942
Winchester '73, 1950
Year 'Round, 1957–1958
Young in Heart, 1958
Zodiac, 1937

Vernonware, division of Metlox Potteries, Manhattan Beach, California, 1958–1989; bought and produced some Vernon Kilns patterns

REFERENCE BOOKS
Gibbs, Carl, Jr. *Collector's Encyclopedia of Metlox Potteries.* Paducah, Kentucky: Collector Books, 1996.

PATTERNS

Accents, 1961
American Heritage, 1980
American Heritage-Gourmet Set, early
  1980s
Antique Blue, 1975
Autumn Berry, 1978
Autumn Leaves, 1960
Big Sur, 1978
Blue Fascination, 1967
Blue Zinnias, 1963
Brookside, 1976
Butterscotch, 1960
Capistrano, 1978
Caprice, 1967
Castile, 1964
Catalina, 1978
Cinnamon, 1973
Cinnamon Green, 1976
Classic Antique, 1963
Classic Blue, 1977
Classic Flower, 1964
Classic Roma, 1964

Classic Wheat, 1977
Cognac, 1978
Colonial Garden, 1967
Fancy Free, late 1950s
Flower Basket, 1976
Fruit Basket, 1961
Gigi, 1978
Golden Amber, 1968
Golden Garden, 1967
Happy Days, 1978
Hermosa-Dos, 1978
Hermosa-Mucho, 1978
Hermosa-Tres, 1978
Hermosa-Uno, 1978
Italian Delight, 1979
LaMancha Gold, 1968
LaMancha Green, 1968
LaMancha White, 1971
Laura, early 1980s
Lemon Tree, 1975
Lime Tree, 1975
Margarita, 1969

Marigold, 1980
Marissa, 1980
Meadow, 1980
Mesa, 1976
Monterey, 1977
Morning Glory, 1980
Mount Whitney, 1978
Old Cathay, 1976
Painted Desert, 1977
Patrician White, 1959
Petalburst, 1968
Pink Lady, 1960
Quail Ridge, 1979
Rattan, 1979
San Fernando, 1966
Sculptured Berry, 1973
Sierra Flower, 1962
Sorrento, 1980
Spring Garland, 1979

Springtime, 1961
Sun 'N Sand, 1962
Tisket-a-Tasket, late 1950s
Town & Country, 1961
Tradition White, 1967
True Blue, 1959
Vernon Antiqua, 1966
Vernon Bouquet, 1974
Vernon Calypso, 1971
Vernon Della Robbia, 1965
Vernon Florence, 1969
Vernon Gaiety, 1970
Vernon Nasturtium, 1972
Vernon Pacific Blue, 1971
Vernon Pueblo, 1972
Vernon Rose, 1965
Vernon Tulips, 1971
Vineyard, 1960
White Rose, 1977

Waterford Wedgwood Group, Burslem, England, 1759–present. See Franciscan Ceramics Inc.; Johnson Brothers, Ltd.

Watt Pottery Company, Crooksville, Ohio, 1922–1965

REFERENCE BOOKS

Morris, Sue and Dave. *Watt Pottery: An Identification and Value Guide.* Paducah, Kentucky: Collector Books, 1993.

Thompson, Dennis, and W. Bryce Watt. *Watt Pottery: A Collector's Reference with Price Guide.* Atglen, Pennsylvania: Schiffer Publishing Ltd., 1994.

PATTERNS

Apple, 1952–1960s
Autumn Foliage, 1959–1965
Cherry, mid-1950s
Cut-Leaf Pansy, 1950s
Daisy, 1949–1953
Dogwood, 1949–1953
Dutch Tulip, 1956
Eagle, 1950–1960
Esmond, 1950–1960

Floral
Moonflower, 1949–1953
Morning Glory, late 1950s
Old Pansy, 1950s
Orchard Ware, 1949–1959
Pansy (also called Cross Hatch), 1950
Raised Pansy (also called Wild Rose), 1950s
Rooster, 1955–1958

Royal Danish, 1965
Silhouette, early 1950s
Starflower, 1950s
Tear Drop, mid-1950s

Tulip, mid-1950s
Valencia, 1937–1940
White Daisy, 1950–1960

Enoch Wedgwood, Ltd., Hanley and Stoke, England (now part of Waterford Wedgwood Group)

PATTERNS
Liberty Blue, 1977

General Reference Books

Chipman, Jack. *Collector's Encyclopedia of California Pottery.* Paducah, Kentucky: Collector Books, 1992.

Cunningham, Jo. *Collector's Encyclopedia of American Dinnerware.* Paducah, Kentucky: Collector Books, 1982.

———. *The Best of Collectible Dinnerware.* Atglen, Pennsylvania: Schiffer Publishing Ltd., 1995.

Derwich, Jenny, and Mary Latos. *Dictionary Guide to United States Pottery & Porcelain (19th and 20th Century).* Privately printed, 1984 (P.O. Box 674, Franklin, MI 48025).

Duke, Harvey. *Official Price Guide to Pottery and Porcelain.* 8th edition. New York: House of Collectibles, 1995.

Eva Zeisel: Designer for Industry. Chicago: University of Chicago Press, 1984.

From Kiln to Kitchen: American Ceramic Design in Tableware. Springfield, Illinois: Illinois State Museum, 1980.

Gates, William C., Jr., and Dana E. Ormerod. "The East Liverpool, Ohio, Pottery District: Identification of Manufacturers and Marks." *Historical Archaeology* 16 (1982). Washington, D.C.: The Society for Historical Archaeology.

Hayes, Barbara, and Jean Bauer. *California Pottery Rainbow.* Privately printed, 1975 (1629 W. Washington Blvd., Venice, CA 90291).

Kerr, Ann. *Collector's Encyclopedia of Russel Wright Designs.* 2nd edition. Paducah, Kentucky: Collector Books, 1998.

———. *Russel Wright and His Dinnerware.* Privately printed, 1981 (P.O. Box 437, Sidney, OH 45365).

———. *Russel Wright Dinnerware: Designs for the American Table.* Paducah, Kentucky: Collector Books, 1985.

———. *Steubenville Saga.* Privately printed, 1979 (P.O. Box 437, Sidney, OH 45365).

Klein, Benjamin. *Collector's Illustrated Price Guide to Russel Wright Dinnerware.* Smithtown, New York: Exposition Press, 1981.

Kovel, Ralph and Terry. *Kovels' Antiques & Collectibles Price List.* 30th edition. New York: Crown Publishers, 1998.

———. *Kovels' Guide to Selling, Buying, and Fixing Your Antiques and Collectibles.* New York: Crown Publishers.

———. *Kovels' Know Your Collectibles.* New York: Crown Publishers, 1981, updated 1992.

———. *Kovels' New Dictionary of Marks—Pottery & Porcelain: 1850 to the Present.* New York: Crown Publishers, 1986.

Lehner, Lois. *Complete Book of American Kitchen and Dinner Wares.* Radnor, Pennsylvania: Wallace-Homestead Book Co., 1980.

————. *Lehner's Encyclopedia of U.S. Marks on Pottery, Porcelain & Clay.* Paducah, Kentucky: Collector Books, 1988.

Newbound, Betty. *Gunshot Guide to Values of American Made China & Pottery.* Privately printed, 1981 (4567 Chadsworth, Union Lake, MI 48085).

————. *Gunshot Guide to Values of American Made China & Pottery, Book 2.* Privately printed, 1984 (4567 Chadsworth, Union Lake, MI 48085).

Piña, Leslie. *Pottery: Modern Wares 1920–1960.* Atglen, Pennsylvania: Schiffer Publishing Ltd., 1994.

Pottery 1880–1960. Encino, California: Orlando Gallery, 1973.

KOVELS' LIBRARY

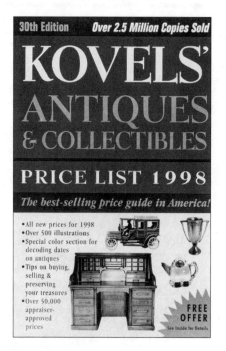

Kovels' Antiques and Collectibles Price List
30th Edition

Kovels' Antiques & Collectibles Price List is the premier
source of prices for both amateur and serious collectors. This
year's 30th edition features a 16-page color insert packed
with information about decoding dates on antiques. The price
list includes more than 50,000 reliable, all-new prices gath-
ered from shops, markets, sales, and auctions nationwide;
hundreds of factory marks and logos; plus hints on buying,
selling, and preserving antiques and collectibles. *Kovels'
Antiques & Collectibles Price List* includes information on
classic 18th- and 19th-century antiques as well as the hot
20th-century favorites. And the computer-generated, cross-
referenced index is the most complete of its kind available.

0-609-80142-2
896 pages / $14.95 paperback

Kovels' Quick Tips
799 Helpful Hints on How to
Care for Your Collectibles

Wearing their hats as the Heloise of the antiques world, the Kovels give you quick and handy tips on how to care for all the treasures in your home, from your favorite jewelry, heirloom silver, and childhood toys to your Coca-Cola bottle collection, kitchen collectibles, books, and family photographs. Organized by subject matter and charmingly illustrated, this book includes 799 tips collected by the Kovels over the past twenty years.

0-517-88381-3
176 pages / $12.00 paperback

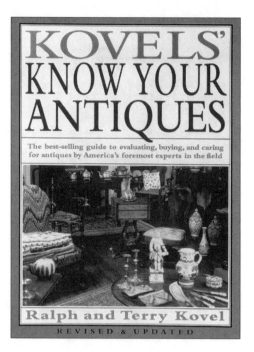

Kovels' Know Your Antiques
Revised & Updated Edition

The best guide in print today for beginning collectors. Learn
how to recognize, evaluate, and purchase virtually any type of
antique—large or small—like an expert. There is detailed
advice about caring for your antiques, identifying fakes, and
finding bargains. This best-seller is used by collectors and
college classes alike.

0-517-57806-9

368 pages / $16.00 paperback

Kovels' Dictionary of Marks
Pottery & Porcelain (1650–1850)

A classic in the field, *Kovels' Dictionary of Marks* is a comprehensive guide to more than 5,000 American and European pottery and porcelain marks. It shows at a glance the geographical location of the factory, family name or manufacturer's name, type of ware, color of mark, and the date the mark was used.

0-517-70137-5
288 pages / $17.00 hardcover

Kovels' Know Your Collectibles
Updated Edition

The guide to what's selling in shops and at shows today. The collectibles category covers items made since 1890, including the coveted Depression glass, Tiffany lamps, Mission furniture, and advertising items. Marks, catalog reprints, and photographs make every category clear. An in-depth study of jewelry includes names, dates, and artists information.

0-517-58840-4
416 pages / $16.00 paperback

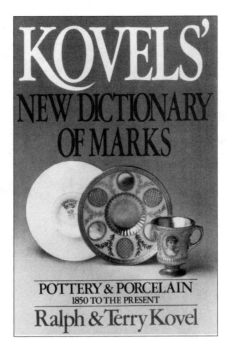

Kovels' New Dictionary of Marks
Pottery & Porcelain (1850–Present)

Kovels' New Dictionary of Marks provides the quickest and easiest way to identify more than 3,500 American, European, and Oriental marks from 1850 to the present. The perfect companion to the Kovels' original best-seller *Kovels' Dictionary of Marks—Pottery & Porcelain,* this is the most comprehensive reference manual for the nineteenth- and twentieth-century marks.

0-517-55914-5

304 pages / $19.00 hardcover

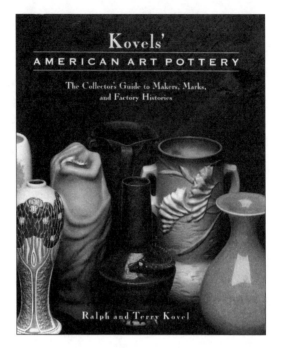

Kovels' American Art Pottery
The Collector's Guide to Makers, Marks,
and Factory Histories

Kovels' American Art Pottery contains alphabetical listings and information on 104 potteries and 95 tile factories. More than 700 fabulous color and black-and-white photographs show details of design, lists of makers with the identifying marks, factory marks with dating information, and hundreds of clues to help the beginner or serious collector identify all types of art pottery.

0-517-58012-8

336 pages / $60.00 hardcover

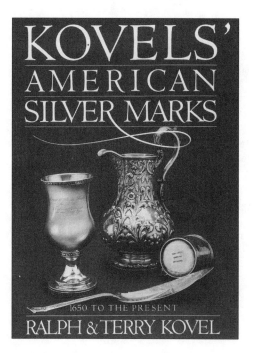

Kovels' American Silver Marks
(1650–Present)

Kovels' American Silver Marks is a simple-to-use guide to identifying marks and monograms that appear on silver. Collectors and professional dealers can quickly determine the maker of a piece of silver. Each listing includes working dates, location, mark (if known), and bibliographic references to more than 200 books and articles. More than 10,000 silversmiths are listed in alphabetical order, with a cross-indexing system for monograms and pictorial marks.

0-517-56882-9

432 pages / $40.00 hardcover

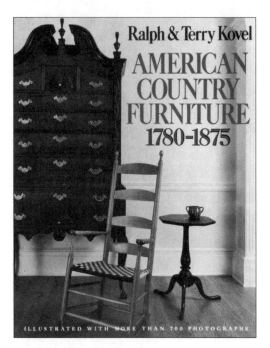

American Country Furniture
1780–1875

More than 700 photographs identify styles, construction, woods, finishes, hardware, and other details. Here is all the information you need to be an expert on American country furniture. There are special sections on Pennsylvania, Shaker furniture, spool furniture, and furniture construction, plus an illustrated glossary of accessories and terms.

0-517-54668-X
256 pages / $16.95 paperback

Kovels' Bottles Price List
10th Edition

Kovels' Bottles Price List is the complete guide to collecting bottles of all types. More than 10,000 current pieces are included in this, the most complete bottle book available. More than 200 illustrations in full color and black and white aid in identification of bottles. Included are old and new bottles, bitters, perfumes, figurals, flasks, Avons, Beams, and a host of others. Notes on styles of manufacturers, lists of bottles magazines and clubs, recommended reading, and a bibliography for the serious collector make *Kovels' Bottles Price List* the best listing of current bottle prices available.

0-517-88435-6
240 pages / $16.00 paperback

The Label Made Me Buy It:

From Aunt Jemima to Zonkers—the Best-Dressed
Boxes, Bottles & Cans from the Past

Filled with over 300 beautiful and often humorous color
labels from the past 150 years, this new Kovels' book takes
readers on a visual journey through the history of labels and
early advertising. Drawing on their collection of more than
10,000 labels, the Kovels reveal the histories of companies,
printers, and label designs. Labels are grouped by image such
as Famous Men & Women, Dogs & Cats, Sports, and
Patriotic Symbols. Learn how to decode the mysteries of
patent numbers and legal wording. A book for collectors of
labels, lovers of graphic art, and students of history.

(AVAILABLE IN NOVEMBER 1998)

0-609-60168-7

224 pages / $40.00 hardcover

K O V E L S

SEND ORDERS & INQUIRIES TO: **Crown Publishers, Inc.**
c/o Random House, 400 Hahn Road
Westminster, MD 21157

ATT: ORDER DEPT.

SALES & TITLE INFORMATION
1-800-733-3000
FOR ORDER ENTRY
FAX# 1-800-659-2436
INTERNET http://www.randomhouse.com

NAME_____

ADDRESS _____

CITY & STATE _____ZIP _____

PLEASE SEND ME THE FOLLOWING BOOKS:

ITEM NO.	QTY.	TITLE		PRICE	TOTAL
0-609-80142-2	_____	Kovels' Antiques & Collectibles Price List, 30th Edition *New!*	PAPER	$14.95	_____
0-517-58012-8	_____	Kovels' American Art Pottery	HARDCOVER	$60.00	_____
0-517-54668-X	_____	American Country Furniture 1780 –1875	PAPER	$16.95	_____
0-517-70137-5	_____	Kovels' Dictionary of Marks— Pottery & Porcelain	HARDCOVER	$17.00	_____
0-517-55914-5	_____	Kovels' New Dictionary of Marks (1850-present)	HARDCOVER	$19.00	_____
0-517-56882-9	_____	Kovels' American Silver Marks	HARDCOVER	$40.00	_____
0-517-88435-6	_____	Kovels' Bottles Price List, 10th Edition	PAPER	$16.00	_____
0-609-80310-7	_____	Kovels' Depression Glass & Dinnerware Price List, 6th Edition	PAPER	$16.00	_____
0-517-57806-9	_____	Kovels' Know Your Antiques, Revised & Updated	PAPER	$16.00	_____
0-517-58840-4	_____	Kovels' Know Your Collectibles, Updated	PAPER	$16.00	_____
0-517-88381-3	_____	Kovels' Quick Tips: 799 Helpful Hints on How to Care for Your Collectibles	PAPER	$12.00	_____

_____ TOTAL ITEMS   TOTAL RETAIL VALUE_____

CHECK OR MONEY ORDER ENCLOSED
MADE PAYABLE TO CROWN PUBLISHERS, INC.
or telephone 1-800-733-3000
(No cash or stamps, please)
Charge: ☐ Master Card   ☐ Visa   ☐ American Express
Account Number (include all digits) Expires MO._____YR._____

_____

Signature _____
                              Thank you for your order.

Shipping & Handling Charge
$2.00 for one book;
50¢ for each additional book.
Please add applicable sales tax.   _____

TOTAL AMOUNT DUE _____

PRICES SUBJECT TO CHANGE
WITHOUT NOTICE. If a more recent
edition of a price list has been published at
the same price, it will be sent instead of the
old edition.

We Want to Send You a Gift.

Because you love antiques, we know you will be interested in our monthly newsletter, *Kovels on Antiques and Collectibles*, a nationally distributed, fully illustrated publication now in its 24th year.

- Current prices, collecting trends, landmark auction results for all types of antiques and collectables
- Tax, estate, security, and other pertinent news for collectors
- Fakes and foibles of the market place
- All in 12 information-packed pages each month, plus a free yearly index

For a free sample copy of the newsletter, just fill in your name and address on this order form and mail to: **Kovels on Antiques and Collectables**
P.O. Box 420349
Palm Coast, Florida 32142-9655

[ ] **YES!** Please send me a FREE sample of *Kovels On Antiques and Collectibles*.

Name _____ 67KKPL

Address _____

City _____ State _____ Zip _____

NOW IN COLOR